PROPERTY OF
BLUE RIDGE COMMUNITY COLLEGE
LIBRARY

BLUE RIDGE COMMUNITY COLLEGE LIBRARY

1000022606

NA
1121
.V4
A813

Arslan, Edoardo
Gothic architecture in
Venice

NA 1121 .V4 A813
Gothic architecture in Venice.
C.1 brcc,main

3 7213 000 329 280

# Gothic Architecture in Venice

Gothic Architecture in Venice

# Edoardo Arslan

# Gothic Architecture in Venice

## Translated by Anne Engel

**Phaidon**

NA
1121
.V4
A813

LIBRARY
BLUE RIDGE COMMUNITY COLLEGE
P. O. BO    O
WEYERS CAVE, VIRGINIA 24486

Phaidon Press Limited, 5 Cromwell Place, London SW7

Published in the United States of America by Phaidon Publishers, Inc.
and distributed by Praeger Publishers, Inc.
111 Fourth Avenue, New York, N.Y. 10003

First published 1971
Originally published as *Venezia Gotica*
© 1970 by Electa Editrice. Industrie Grafiche Editoriali S.p.A. – Venezia
Translation © 1972 by Phaidon Press Limited

ISBN 0 7148 1410 5
Library of Congress Catalog Card Number: 76-138244
All rights reserved

No part of this publication may be reproduced, stored in a
retrieval system or transmitted in any form or by any means,
electronic, mechanical, photocopying, recording or otherwise,
without the prior permission of the Copyright owner

Printed in Italy by Fantonigrafica®, Venezia

*To Renata*

# CONTENTS

This book is concerned only with the Gothic secular architecture of Venice, leaving out the sacred. These two aspects of Venetian architecture, in the centuries here considered, cannot, in fact, be integrated as they could be in other Italian regions from Lombardy to the South.

Venetian churches are closely related to the buildings which, on the Venetian mainland, even in secular structures, were marked by the 'Lombard' style from the thirteenth to the fifteenth centuries. Venetian secular Gothic, however, with its specific characteristic—the inflected arch—stands quite apart and develops coherently from the thirteenth century to the beginning of the sixteenth, spreading also on the mainland along the great arc which, until the end of the Republic, traces the frontiers of the Venetian state, from Bergamo to the Veneto, to Istria and to Dalmatia.

This work derives its unity from considerations assembled here for the first time with as ample a documentation as could be required on the birth and diffusion of a very particular trend in secular architecture.

I must confess that one weighty reason, more than any other, made me hesitate before undertaking this task: Venice is a city without compare in the world, and not only because of its architectural expression, formed through the centuries. It forms a very complex environment, with innumerable aspects—not only representational—which acts strongly on the visitor's soul; an entirely new, indeed unique environment, which tends to imprint itself on his reactions, to alter his usual standards of judgment, inducing his mind to fall under a kind of spell, favouring even the rise of histrionic tendencies which, if they may favour the creation of a work of art, should nevertheless be resolutely suppressed if a critical judgment is to be formed.

The first causes of this must be sought in the special, indeed unique position of this city in time and space; detached and isolated in the lagoon, with the singularity of its landscape, of its institutions, of its customs and so on, it has since many centuries established a dialectic relationship with the world. On this situation was founded one of the most remarkable of the adventures of the human spirit, characterized by a multiplicity and delicacy entirely its own.

It is easy to understand, at this point, why writing about the architecture of Venice, indeed about one of the most fascinating and mysterious periods of that art, may prove difficult for whomever cannot entirely avoid the influence of the atmosphere that came into being in this corner of the earth, so laden with suggestions from near and far; an atmosphere which may cause even the most careful enquiry to run into risks.

The poetic and human freedom which the Venetian artists enjoyed under the sternness of the oligarchic state certainly broadened their imaginative possibilities; and it is precisely by considering this freedom that it is possible to understand fully the mark it left on musical works of the highest order, on a large poetic output, on the theatre and on the fiction of the West, on all those—foreigners or Italians—who found in that city a common motivation. But it is precisely this which fosters and justifies in lagunar art its characteristic instability or independence, even though it draws its sustenance not only from the East but also from the West.

The axis in time of the highest representational manifestations always appears in Venice more or less displaced in comparison with what occurs on the mainland. This phenomenon, as we shall see, is even more conspicuous in Gothic secular architecture; many forms, and not necessarily minor ones, follow at a distance of more than a century.

Now, if it is true that the history of Venetian painting is one of the most difficult and dangerous to consider (and the events of the last decades have demonstrated this, to the point of making us witness a systematic disfigurement, on a critical level, of the true features of the great masters: Giovanni Bellini, Giorgione, Titian, Tintoretto, Veronese, Tiepolo, the Guardis), it is easy to imagine how an attempt at a critical ordering of secular Gothic architecture may prove even more problematic; and this is thus the second point which makes this caution right and proper.

Venetian material is, in fact, really very ample and very seldom of poor quality. It covers a span of three centuries, from about 1220 to about 1520. Its critical ordering, moreover, should have been preceded by extensive researches in the archives; and these, in the last seventy years or so, have been carried out only for a very few buildings.

Beside Ruskin's brilliant studies, more than a century old but still indispensable, we must mention here the researches of Paoletti (the fundamental work of 1893) and some isolated essays on the Ca' d'Oro, the Doge's Palace and the Soranzo-van Axel Palace. I was afforded invaluable assistance in the very intricate Venetian topography by the List (ELENCO) of Monumental Buildings compiled in 1905 by the Municipality of Venice.

It is, however, quite clear to everyone that, even if the enquiry were limited to Venice alone, all this would still be very little when set against the enormous congeries of buildings, large and small, whole or fragmentary, which constitute, in the eyes of the whole world, the most genuine 'facies' of the city; a spectacle which, for centuries, has impressed both the cultured and the uncultured visitor and has come to form part of a vital inheritance which in varying degrees leaves something inside each of us, and which, for the rest of his life, even the most unequipped visitor does not forget.

Strange therefore that this fabulous store of architectural beauty, conceived in exceptional historic, social and landscape conditions in the heart of old Europe, has not yet found at least the beginning of a critical elaboration, which alone could explain its birth, its various motivations and inflexions and its long and complex course; thus making more subtly attractive the nature of the separate and infinite parts.

As will be better said later on, the Romano-Byzantine style seems to be an obligatory point of departure, which allows one to cover the course of the variations and evolutions of building activity through the thirteenth century and precedes and conditions the Gothic. The first half of the fourteenth century, though difficult to organize in a system, ends by shaping itself into a theme for a useful critical lecture, even if not always clear and indisputable. The great novelty here is the appearance of the inflected trefoiled arch which will supplant the Gothic two-centred arch of French origin.

But the second half of the fourteenth century shows itself, immediately afterwards, as very difficult to investigate. Building fervour, in a city overflowing with wealth and advancing towards the summit of its glory, carries with it ever more numerous teams of workers, offers abundant and immense work to stonecutters and masons, local and foreign, favours the rise of an infinity of buildings, in which new stylistic practices fuse with the old, repeating their forms, often to the letter. There appears in fact, as quite characteristic of Venice, an extraordinary conservative spirit which impedes a critical enquiry since it never slackens but remains vigorous and deceptive, providing most often too few (or almost no) *points d'appui* for advancing or retarding a building by twenty or thirty years in time. Mouldings, capitals, inflexions of the arches, small decorative details, even the proportions (if one can speak without risk of proportional modules in Venice), everything returns, even if with changed distributions, and thus explains that disconcerting diversity of opinion which, for the last century and a half, it will be possible to follow in these pages in respect of everything written on the subject.

One should refer in this connection to the notes which accompany the chapters, the bibliography, art historians (who may be counted on the fingers of one hand), guides more or less successful or sensitive (from the beginning of the nineteenth century to our day) and other occasional judgments on the timing of a given building, none of which reveal any noticeable effort to bind together the vast material in a coherent discourse.

This variety of opinion cannot be explained except in the light of the quality of the object examined, which, incredibly, maintains itself at a constantly high level, without displaying those signs of decadence which ought unfailingly to appear with the passing of the decades. It is not surprising therefore (and we shall endeavour to document this) that the second half of the fourteenth century—which contains that absolutely exceptional work, the Doge's Palace—and the first half of the fifteenth century (until about 1440) should indeed represent a very difficult test in the history of Italian art for whoever tries to establish successions in time, to provoke comparisons or, even worse, to risk attributions.

In Venice, builders do not hesitate, if this is demanded by practical requirements, to shorten or lengthen a building without scruple. It is true that, at this point, one could quote the case of the Medici-Riccardi Palace in Florence; but occurrences of this kind do not have, in the more monumental urban centres of the peninsula, the frequency observable in Venice. For example, the depth of a building, as we shall show later, is not subject to any aesthetic or proportional exigencies. But there is yet another point: Venetian builders do not hesitate (indeed, they make a practice of it) to relegate to parts of the building considered socially less noble certain elements of style obsolete for more than a century (which in another region would have been banned), such as the typical fourteenth-century capital. However, they also have the supreme merit of harmonizing these archaic-like elements with those *à la page* (which they reserve for the more noble areas), with results which at times throw into confusion the most careful investigations. In spite of this impediment, this architecture manages to attain on one side the supreme freedom of a visionary and inconsistent world and, on the other, the expression of a coherent (and today, one hopes) untouchable beauty.

Venice also seems to have another strange capacity: that of absorbing, of subduing and of adopting foreign grafts into its urban frame provided they reach, obviously, a tolerable level of taste. These forms of tolerance, which are also found elsewhere (one thinks, naturally, of Paris) explain sufficiently those aspects of the conservatism inherent in the lagunar spirit towards the most archaic elements of the local Gothic. The most famous example is offered by the Doge's Palace, whose elements can be related, in many essential parts, to the French taste of the preceding century, which a great unknown architect put together in a synthesis without equal, a miracle of illogical coherence and of beauty wholly new and original.

After the turning-point between the end of the fourteenth and the beginning of the fifteenth century (which we have not attempted to explain clearly with an acceptable chain of facts, but have explored with continuous reservations), we finally reach the Ca' d'Oro. This is a famous example of the floriated Gothic, but this does not exclude the possibility that these 'floriated' forms may have appeared before that date, already at the end of the fourteenth century.

The imposing complex of great palaces with quatrefoil tracery finally offers sufficiently reliable datings around the middle of the fifteenth century; parallel to them, however, develop in a hundred aspects those forms of the more mature floriated Gothic which enjoyed a vigorous life until about 1480. However, at the same time, other phenomena of retardation at high level, which could not really be imagined anywhere except on the lagoon, abounded.

One of the most difficult problems in these same decades is constituted by the contamination with elements of the Renaissance which, on the lagoon, were to appear earlier than one would have thought–as I have attempted to indicate, case by case, with all possible reservations. It is clear, however, that at least until the arrival of Pietro Lombardo, such a study of Renaissance infiltrations in Venice could not be undertaken here with the required thoroughness. But who has ever attempted a critical ordering of Renaissance manifestations discernible in Venetian architecture from about 1420 to about 1470?

The 'cohabitation' of Gothic forms with Lombardic from 1470 onwards finally takes us to about 1520. The beautiful Gothic villas of Ragusa are attributable to the second or third decades of the sixteenth century.

It is clear from what has been said that if there is a group of monuments, major or minor, which today eludes any 'method' (as art historians mean it), this is Venetian secular Gothic. And this seems even stranger when one considers that the group of remaining buildings is very large, and when one reflects on the fact that, in such cases, the research is usually greatly facilitated by the possibility of an infinity of comparisons. However, as we have said, those structural indications, those subtle guiding threads which make recalls and groupings possible are missing—particularly in the most difficult and intricate periods of this very long stretch of time. The recalcitrant style manifests itself in each building with variations, now small, now considerable, from what appears in other buildings thought, in the light of logic, to be near in time. It also appears with deceptive affinities in the harmonious structuring of the various parts, to such an extent that one is easily tempted to attribute all these manifestations to the same master-workmen. The moment then comes when one has to recognize in these buildings, with surprise, things rather distant in time from each other. The Renaissance may stand by the side of the Gothic, with disconcerting contrasts, but who would say, for instance, that the church of Santa Maria dei Miracoli by Pietro Lombardo, and the nearby palace of the Soranzo (later van Axel) are, dates on hand, contemporaneous works?

If one tries then to find out where certain deceptions lie (besides those imponderables which criticism will never succeed in weighing because they elude all calculation), one has every reason, particularly in Venice, to be disheartened by the miserable level to which are restricted investigations into the archives; and one notices how little would be needed to-morrow to demolish the demonstrations asserted by vain and presumptuous pseudo-critics.

Equally, these deceptions may indeed arise from other circumstances: from the additions made to the building, from the changes made through the centuries for purely utilitarian reasons, but particularly from certain photographic interpretations, as for instance, when the incidence of light involved in a particular photographic reproduction has the power to change, from dawn to dusk, the appearance of a building, causing confusion between 'plasticity' and 'colour', 'luminosity' and 'chiaroscuro' (which are all words which with hundreds of others ought to be rigorously defined). And it happens then that projections with a real plastic effect are flattened, or that plastically illusory ones are obtained as a result of a photographic lens being opened, for instance, at sundown.

The chromatic component, moreover, represents another element which may affect the stability of criticism. The nature of the chromatic element in Venice is not only determined by the incrustations, by the use of coloured marble, new or re-used, by the limestones of the mainland, by the contrast of the terracotta (often already covered with frescoes and thus not intended to be seen) and Istrian stone. Where bricks are used, these sometimes represent a chromatic element and the exposed part is then rubbed with boiled linseed oil (Paoletti, 1893, I, pp. 30–31) in the same way as Istrian stone was treated with oil whitewash—as stated by Giacomo Boni. It derives also from the atmospheric changes which are never so diverse, at each hour of the day, as in Venice.

If it is quite true that Venetian builders adapt their vision (one should think of the loggias, the marble traceries) to the mobile effects of the waters and of the incomparable light, it is no less true that, as we said above, this cannot constitute a basic, decisive, objective element for a critical judgment of a building. Purely chromatic considerations, based on the meteorological vicissitudes of the moment, have certainly their merit but it is evident that in the end they do not lead to the history of art; they tend instead, fatally, to merge with the interpretations of Francesco Guardi, or of Kokoschka (one does not want to include the *Cathedrals* of Monet); these works of pictorial art obviously do not make the slightest contribution to the achievement of critical construction, to be included into the reasoned and calibrated economy of a history of architecture.

It should not displease therefore if, in tackling such a fluid, and as yet, critically, largely elusive subject, I have endeavoured to avoid snares and to approach this architecture with great caution. I have sought to draw from maximum adherence to the real factual data in the description of the object, carefully avoiding whatever could obscure and, sometimes, even distort that intimate, pristine representational meaning. I have above all avoided giving an appearance of visual concreteness to that which is, sometimes, merely critical suggestion, accepting as existing descriptive elements which are not really found in the work itself, and which (it is painful to confess) in some cases I have absolutely not succeeded in seeing.

The difficulties of clarification are moreover aggravated by a terminology in fashion today and by a complex of new grammatical and syntactic elements noticeable in the current diction of much art criticism which, if interesting to our linguists as signs of the transformation of the language, have undoubtedly brought with them incomprehensions, discomforts and obscurities. We meet this phenomenon in texts dictated by scholars of repute, as well as in large and small works of minor critical 'commitment'; in the *dépliants* of contemporary art exhibitions, and wherever people write about ancient and modern art. In more extreme cases, there is a senseless, almost pathological search for the new and the different, originating without doubt in a real inability to translate into plain, balanced writing certain specific representational values; whereas, from Giotto to Pollock, I believe that everything can be said and explained with extreme clarity, sobriety and efficiency, even if at the cost of effort.

There is no terminology belonging to science, to literary criticism, to musicology, to the theatre, to psychoanalysis, to the cinema, to any human activity whatever, which has not been exploited by art criticism. True, it is sometimes a case of generic extension of a term, and it is then up to the intelligent reader to understand it; thus, no one will ever repudiate 'harmony' and 'melody', which in the hands of the musicologist have none the less a very precise technical meaning. However, 'timbre' and 'timbric' have a quite precise meaning like the other two quoted above, but the use made of them in the criticism of representational art totally ignores this meaning because it is not at all suited to what one is talking about.

These fashions date very rapidly (like some sectors of the representational arts themselves) and in twenty years they will be ridiculed or forgotten. In the best case, they will be treated as 'documents' of a time too quickly gone by. The reader must and will therefore forgive a critical line in these pages, which to some may seem too cautious (coming near to aridity), leaving ample margin for additions and clarifications, for subsequent corrections and shifting of opinions, not precluding, in short, different critical positions in the future. This has resulted in an ordering which I should like to call provisional, where the bare juxtaposition of buildings, their aligning themselves in accordance with itineraries which often are only proposals, may perhaps to some extent guarantee the search for a way leading to a less unsure philological 'apparatus'.

*Romano–Byzantine Prelude*

A study of Venetian Gothic secular architecture cannot leave out of consideration the architectural forms which immediately preceded it and from which, by imperceptible steps, it descends. One does not exaggerate in the least by asserting that this 'passage' has never been clarified, witness the datings current for the well-known 'Veneto–Byzantine' buildings, which in serious publications on the history of architecture are still classified today, with a vague formula, as works of the twelfth to thirteenth centuries[1]. Such a dating, embracing a period of over two hundred years, appears inadmissible today; not only because of the progress in relevant studies but also because of the continued existence of so many monuments relevant to this important problem.

No study exists, however, at present of Venetian Romanesque architecture, which includes both the sacred and secular monuments east of Verona, that is to say a territory of which Venice is certainly a very important centre but in which it is clearly not possible to isolate the city with its estuary and leave aside the Venetian hinterland, Istria and Dalmatia. If it is true that elements of a Byzantine derivation are particularly conspicuous in Venice, it is just as true that the architecture of the lagoon is also open to other influences which bind it to the whole ample area of the Po, to Verona itself and to Lombardy.

The round-headed arch on pillars, which in the thirteenth century is so interestingly manifest in Venice, had been diffused for centuries in the Mediterranean area, from Greece to Italy and to the Iberian peninsula. In fact, the Venetian manifestations are merely the last and most striking. To quote only some Italian examples: the Ansperto Chapel in S. Maria presso S. Satiro in Milan[2], of the ninth century, the stilted arches of the campanile of Pomposa (1063), those of S. Salvatore in Ravenna (*Secretariat of the Exarchs*) of the eleventh century, and of the porch of the Salerno Duomo; those of the eleventh-twelfth centuries of S. Fosca in Torcello[3] and of the Contarinian church of S. Marco (the arcades of the naves, of the end of the eleventh century); those in the interior of S. Donato in Murano of the twelfth century; of the campanile of S. Samuele in Venice of the end of the twelfth century[4], and other examples, not Venetian, anterior to the twelfth century.

But as it is first of all important to establish the period of the 'Veneto–Byzantine' palaces and houses on which the earliest 'Gothic' will graft itself, we shall note at once that critics appear increasingly inclined to displace them towards the thirteenth century, to which, in our opinion, virtually all those in existence today belong. The writers, the authors of guidebooks, even authoritative ones, of the nineteenth century went back, as is well known, sometimes even beyond the eleventh century in the dating of these palaces which, on the other hand, already in 1847 Selvatico was inclined to attribute to the thirteenth century[5]. Ruskin placed them between the eleventh and the thirteenth centuries[6]. Toesca[7], forty years ago, was inclined to attribute them to the thirteenth while Fiocco[8], more recently, considers them all of the twelfth century (including Ca' da Mosto); for Bettini[9] 'no palace in Venice today goes back beyond the twelfth century'; for Demus[10] 'no great building activity seems to have taken place there (i. e. in Venice) in the twelfth century'; the same author[11] attributes all the existing buildings to the thirteenth century; and some have even accepted, rather lazily (and yet in a context of high interest), a dating of the eleventh–twelfth centuries[12].

The only building of the twelfth century in Venice for which, though it has itself disappeared, we have reliable historical and representational documentation is the Procuratie erected by the Doge Sebastiano Ziani (1172–8), clearly visible in Gentile Bellini's painting of the *Procession of the Relics in St. Mark's Square*. The arcade, with round–headed arches, is supported by columns with truncated cube capitals, while the rhythm of the gallery above is derived from slender, elongated columns also, as far as can be made out, with truncated cube capitals, but more slender. There is no trace of a stilted arch in the Byzantine style which Gentile, in his (almost Canaletto-like) fidelity to architectural reality would certainly not have neglected to observe and record[13].

It is evident that this is a building erected by an architect from the mainland, where, in fact, nothing Byzantine is to be found. The date is the second half of the twelfth century, and these forms are undoubtedly of Veronese origin. The truncated cube (or parallelepiped) capital with annulet (shaft ring)—quite different from the Lombard type—has a long and firm tradition in Veronese Romanesque architecture, where it is almost exclusively wrought in the local limestone, white and red. As from the twelfth century, it is found everywhere: in churches, in cloisters, on tombs, in S. Maria Antica, in the Trinità, in the SS. Apostoli, in the capitular cloister of the Calavena Abbey. It persists, in secular buildings, until the fourteenth century (the Casa di Romeo).

As it is so often to be found in Venice (frequently executed in red Veronese limestone), there seems to be substance in the belief that associations of Veronese stonecutters were established on the Lagoon and that to these stonemasons-builders are due some of the buildings of the twelfth and thirteenth centuries which show, in the mouldings and the capitals, a total absence of Byzantine-like characters, though they retain at times, in the cut of the windows, the stilted arch of Byzantine origin. It is indeed probable that these Veronese (or Lombard) stonecutters were active from the end of the twelfth century through the thirteenth.

Cattaneo, as we know, had already allotted a very large share in the Contarinian Basilica to Lombard interventions, allowing to the work of Mazulo an excessively large field of action[14]. Coming down in time[15], he noted in the interior of St. Mark's 'the simple cornice in red Veronese marble which runs under the present-day plutei, fully characteristic, in its profile, of the thirteenth century'.

The attribution of cornices with reversed leaves to the ninth century seems doubtful, but it can still be found today and is a supine acceptance of one of Cattaneo's opinions. Cattaneo, it is known, attributes to the ninth century the 'cornices of large and rough leaves of barbarian acanthus' which can be seen in the chapels of SS. Pietro e Clemente in St. Mark's[16], and associates with them (and thus considers of the ninth century) those visible on the house in rio delle Beccarie, on Ca' da Mosto, on Palazzo Bembo, on Palazzetto Dandolo (al Carbon), on the lateral door of the Carmini and on the Bragadin–Favretto House[17]. However, he considers the similar cornices which were put in hand in St. Mark's Basilica on the removal of the matronea (parts of the church reserved for women), with 'leaves of Romanesque

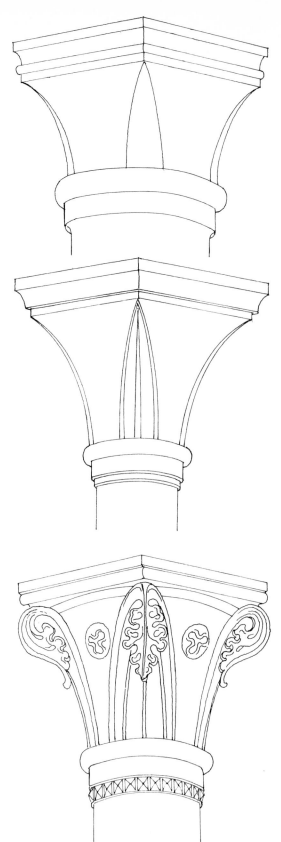

character'[18], to be of the middle of the twelfth century.

All these cornices would seem to be Romanesque, of the twelfth and thirteenth centuries, and sometimes, as we shall see farther on, contemporaneous with the thirteenth-century buildings themselves. In St. Mark's, they appear in four different variants: with dentils and flat acanthus leaves under the banisters with plutei; with dense, reversed leaves where the matroneum used to be; with reversed leaves at wide intervals over the chapels of SS. Pietro e Clemente (as may be seen also in Palazzo Bembo at the Rialto); similar cornices to the latter, but with leaves closer to each other, may be seen on the falling lines of the vaults.

But it may well be that these variants are attributable to different workers, not to different times. An accurate definition, if it is ever to be achieved, is very important because it involves the dating, the exact critical appraisal and the history of sculptural decoration in the High Middle Ages in Venice (and not only in Venice). This would help us escape from the present confusion of ideas on the subject and achieve a distinction between the High and the Later Middle Ages.

In Venice, Romanesque truncated cube capitals, like those already mentioned, often cut in Veronese limestone, are very common (and they impressed Ruskin) and imply the existence of very active masons' yards; leaving aside the round-headed arches which certainly mark the most ancient building phase of Venetian secular architecture—and here one must mention the beautiful walled porch in the corte del Fontego at S. Margherita[19], the arches in the courtyard of the Old Theatre[20] and a thirteenth-century porch in calle del Rimedio near Palazzo Soranzo[21]—we must give due importance to those arcades or *sottoporteghi* which represent a striking characteristic of Venetian town architecture in that, while exploiting to the utmost the area usable for building which is limited by the water, none the less allow a 'pedestrian' passage. They are constructed of beams supported by buttresses, i. e. by double wooden brackets[22] held up by pilasters or columns, mostly in Veronese red, with truncated tube capitals. Examples are innumerable and, in general, the profiles of the brackets indicate the epoch. Those with a right-angled section are the most ancient, those with a curvilinear section are later in date and those with the 'owl beak' profile are mostly of the fifteenth century. For the first, two notable examples will suffice: the buttresses of the cloister of S. Gregorio, of about 1340, and that very remarkable construction, the 'Granary' of Chioggia, which bears the date 1321, a long building erected on sixty-four columns by a certain Matteo Caime, entirely arcaded on the ground floor, supporting a first floor largely disfigured by the restoration of 1864[23].

For the second type, it will be enough to recall the sottoportego de la Furatola[24]. The owl-beak type, which reflects the sinuosities of international Gothic is the most widespread[25]. Thirteenth-century capitals of the Padan type are also to be found in palaces which will be discussed subsequently (Ca' Farsetti, Ca' da Mosto, Ca' Soranzo, etc.), in churches (S. Marco, Carmini, S. Giovanni in Bragora); on the two columns of the Piazzetta, whose capitals are very probably of the thirteenth century, as Ruskin thought, but whose bases must be considered of 1172[26].

Ruskin's still very useful table is reproduced here, to which we shall return also for other types. Numbers 1 and 2 are two types with truncated cubes. We find them again in Palazzo Farsetti. The buildings commonly called Veneto-Byzantine, which from now on we shall call Romano-Byzantine (a designation which appears more exact) are of the thirteenth century. It is important to mention them because it is from the style they represent that the very first Gothic forms are derived. A further good example is Palazzo Farsetti (Dandolo), although much restored, which Toesca places at the beginning of the thirteenth century[27]. Equally, the report that Enrico Dandolo sent the marbles for the decoration of the palace after the conquest of Constantinople (1204) is not to be ignored[28].

Very significant for this century is the use of tall and slender coupled colonnettes on the *piano nobile*, even if the first appear in buildings of the end of the twelfth century[29]. Their origin is, in fact, Lombard, or to be more exact, Veronese; and it is enough to recall those of the wheel of Brioloto on a façade[30] of the end of the twelfth century, and those, later by a century, of the S. Zeno cloister[31]. Examples abound throughout the thirteenth century: from the Zen chapel in St. Mark's to the façade of S. Anastasia in Zara[32], from the façade of Udine cathedral[33] to the pulpits of the Traù and Spalato cathedrals[34], and on to the cathedral of Ferrara, where the presence of these coupled colonnettes in the (walled-up) matronea and along the two sides of the temple represents an imposing example of the wide use made of them[35]. We conclude, once more on the Lagoon, with the considerable remains of a Romanesque building in the garden of Da Mula in Murano, a coherent group which can only be considered of the thirteenth century[36].

Palazzo Loredan must have been erected, in fact, in the same period, as is shown not only by the columns and capitals of the *piano nobile*, which have a clearly Byzantine–like character, but equally by certain elements of the ground floor which turn out to be nearly identical in the two buildings, as for instance the profile of the cornices at the level of the abaci, the pilaster dividing the lateral windows, with the same elongated colonnettes. Here also, therefore, the ambiguous assignment to the twelfth-thirteenth centuries must be replaced by a definite attribution to the thirteenth[37].

The most famous—and most disfigured— of these buildings, the Fondaco dei Turchi (called thus since 1621), reveals in its legible parts (the lower parts of the 'torri'), a complete analogy with the Farsetti and Loredan palazzi: namely the small 'Romanesque' capitals and colonnettes and the profiles of the horizontal elements (string-courses and mouldings at the impost of the arches). Zanotto's dating to the tenth century[38], that of Selvatico[39], supported by Beylie[40], to the eleventh—while Ruskin had already been in favour of a dating to the eleventh-twelfth centuries[41]—as well as that to the twelfth adopted by Schnaase[42], Molmenti[43], Swoboda[44], Fiocco[45] and Mariacher[46] having been abandoned, the attribution to the thirteenth century has many supporters— from Sagredo–Berchet[47] to Ricci[48], to Toesca[49], to Miozzi[50], to Demus[51], to Forlati[52], to Muraro[53], to Ackerman[54] (who discerns a distant precursor of the fifteenth-century villa) to Bassi[55], to Maretto[56]. This appears the most probable since, in full agreement with certain stylistic observations, Tassini[57], relying on the genealogist Barbaro, makes Giacomo Palmieri of Pesaro, who came to Venice about 1225, its founder. Lorenzetti, on the other hand, retains the vague ascription to the twelfth-thirteenth centuries[58]. A date about 1225 accords well with the remarks made so far, and permits us to arrive at a more appropriate localization in time of the minor buildings as well, after the three major ones. I refer here in particular to Palazzo Donà Dolcetti[59] at the Traghetto della Madonnetta (S. Polo 1429) and to Palazzo Barzizza[60] which, near each other on the Grand Canal and facing the large Loredan and Farsetti complexes, must be considered to be of the same period. The rhythmic modulation of the beautiful rows of window in Palazzo Donà Dolcetti (no. 1429) vividly recalls the Palazzo Farsetti prototype. Casa Donà is even advanced in time by some, the beautiful loggia on the top floor being supported by coupled colonnettes identical, except in length, to those of Palazzo Loredan. Ca' Barzizza too is assigned by Toesca[61] to the beginning of the thirteenth century. Here the arch on a pillar is less slender, but the abaci have the same profile as in Palazzo Loredan and, on the right side, the usual coupled colonnettes appear also[62].

The dating of the splendid remains in red Veronese limestone and Istrian stone giving on to rio S. Pantalon seems more questionable. A large water portal, round-headed and flanked by arches of a much smaller radius but with very high pillars (the slenderest seen so far) is supported by the usual coupled colonnettes.

*Evolution of the capitals in Venetian buildings (after Ruskin)*

Gabelentz[63] considered it of the twelfth century. Marzemin[64] earlier than the ninth century, Lorenzetti[65] and Toesca[66] placed it at the end of the twelfth century; Molmenti[67] in the thirteenth; Fiocco declares it 'certainly the most ancient house' of Venice[68]; Bettini[69] puts it in the thirteenth, Forlati[70] in the twelfth century, Trincanato without hesitation in the thirteenth[71]. A more precise definition could be obtained here from the presence of the double colonnettes, customary in the thirteenth century in Venice and elsewhere, and also from a careful examination of the sculptures. Accepting as certain that the well-known portal in Corte Seconda del Milion and the one in Corte Bottera (Castello 6279) belong to the twelfth century (and, surely, to Lombard stonemasons), the passage to a freer and therefore more advanced style is made more palpable by the projection of the fauna beyond the limits of the fields created by the scrolls, as well as by the presence of already Gothic profiles with torus. The portal on rio di S. Pantalon must therefore be associated with that on rio di San Tomà[72], that of Ca' Barzizza[73] with the arcades of Ca' da Mosto and with that of Palazzo Contarini Porta di Ferro[74] which are, in my opinion, among the most refined products of that type of sculpture at the beginning of the thirteenth century[75]. But, above all, the great arcade in question is very similar to the already mentioned thirteenth-century arch of the Da Mula Palace in Murano[76].

More perceptive critics[77] have recognized other buildings, now no longer in existence, such as Casa Giustiniani and Ca' Grande dei Barozzi, both at S. Moisè, as belonging to the thirteenth century. The first especially, of which there remains a clear engraving by Pividor[78], accords well with extant buildings through the presence of coupled colonnettes as well as arcades on the ground floor which, by their sturdy build, recall the only one remaining at Ca' Barzizza[79]. This architecture must have been fairly prevalent in Venice. In fact, other traces of windows and rows of windows with stilted semicircular but smooth arches, often without those dentil decorations seen in the Realtine palaces remain, and the evident kinship with certain forms in St. Mark's Basilica becomes apparent. The stilted round-headed arch first appears in the Contarinian basilica itself, in the interior, with splendid examples on the western front of St. Mark's, which received its present facing between 1225 and 1250. Equally, the arch of S. Alipio, towards the Piazzetta dei Leoncini, which blends with the side of the loggia of Palazzo Loredan, the second portal and the second great arch of the left front, in all of which the arch is also on pillars[80], are relevant here.

It is interesting to consider these simpler architectural forms with the arch on pillars because the successive phases of this style (which, in fact, constitutes the transition towards the first Gothic manifestations) are abundantly displayed in a series of modest but highly representative buildings. It is almost always a question of fragmentary remains, hesitantly attributed to between the twelfth and the thirteenth centuries, like the well–known two–light window in salizzada S. Lio, to which we shall subsequently return; the entrance arch of corte Briani in calle della Corona at Castello, made of brick[81]; the door, also in terracotta with brick arch, in corte del Bianchi at S. Aponal (S. Polo 1508); a three–light window on the right of Palazzo Civran at S. Giovanni Crisostomo on the Grand Canal[82]; the beautiful water-gate in Veronese limestone of Palazzo Gritti Loredan (this last certainly of the thirteenth century[83]); and the remains of a beautiful arch in terracotta with rich voussoirs in calle delle Oche (S. Croce 1035) of the thirteenth/fourteenth centuries.

A significant example is the five–light window with stilted semicircular arches carried by 'Romanesque' truncated cube capitals in ramo del Tamossi (S. Polo 1513). That this rare example of Romano–Byzantine architecture in Venice belongs to the thirteenth century would appear to be confirmed by the three–light window above it, which is an example of the period immediately following (but it is not excluded that the two works may be contemporaneous[84]).

A three–light window (with thirteenth–century truncated cube capitals) and a single–light window of the same type as those with stilted round arches in ramo del Tamossi may be seen in Palazzo Cappello–Malipiero at S. Samuele (salizzada di Ca' Malipiero).

The structuring of the Venetian house takes shape already in the thirteenth century in forms which, with variations brought about by new town–planning requirements, will remain valid for centuries.

The 'distributive-structural' types which mark the Venetian house (dictated by town–planning and economic considerations) are those in compact blocks, in L, in C (with variants in U, in double L). While, however, in the Romano-Byzantine epoch the building makes use of very deep but modestly wide rectangular areas, from the second half of the thirteenth century onwards the structures become more flexible and adaptable and give rise to the plans mentioned above[85]. In view of their frequent reoccurrence, we shall mention them only when they assume a distinct and decisive value.

The type in C (where the courtyard penetrates into the heart of the house) is so frequent that it seems difficult to draw from it any chronological or stylistic data. It will be, as maintained by Maretto, in the second half of the fourteenth and in the fifteenth century 'in a thousand architectural representations... the main protagonist of the whole building and town-planning history of Venice'. The volume of trade by water leads to the creation of a great hall flanked by smaller rooms on the ground floor, intended for storehouses and offices, and it traverses the whole building from the canal generally to a courtyard, where there is always a well and an uncovered staircase leading to the upper stories. The courtyard may often be found adjoining the axis of this great hall traversing the ground floor. Sometimes, in more complex organisms, there are two courtyards. The diversity of systems, from the thirteenth to the fifteenth centuries, has been well illustrated by Maretto[86]. There are nearly always two entrances: a water-gate which, in the Gothic period (and contrary to what one sees in Romanesque palaces) is, generally, modest; and a second portal, reached on foot, which leads into the courtyard and has a more ornate and monumental character. Buildings were not lacking, however, to which access was only by water[87]. The kitchen also gives on to the courtyard[88]. The *piano nobile* reproduces the distributive scheme of the ground floor and is characterized by a great hall (the *portego* coinciding with the hall on the ground floor and flanked, on both sides, by living-rooms). It becomes apparent at this point that such a plan could arise only in the very peculiar environmental conditions of Venice, where, moreover, there was no reason to turn the house, as on the mainland, into a building equipped for defence.

The buildings of the first half of the thirteenth century, in the Romano-Byzantine style, only partly legible on the plan (because the rear has been, in all of them, considerably altered[89]) make nevertheless quite clear the transition from a plan based initially on a 'traversing' hall developing towards the front into a great longitudinal room parallel with the great loggia (Palazzo Loredan and Palazzo Donà-Dolcetti, no. 1429) and a plan in which this last room appears bounded on the sides by two minor rooms, not aligned with the hall, corresponding to the division of the façade into three parts (Ca' Farsetti, Ca' Businello, Ca' Barzizza), finally to reach the hall along which are aligned the minor rooms (Palazzo Donà no. 1426) in accordance with a principle which will become typical of Venetian Gothic[90]. The loggias were, it appears, open, not closed. It would be rash, however, to rely on this 'evolution' in order to fix the points in time of a chronological and stylistic succession. What remains is, obviously, only a part of what was built; it is not to be excluded that structures which appear to be, and are, more archaic may be coeval with others which are more progressive. The history of Venetian medieval architecture, as we shall see later, offers many other examples of retardation, also on the level of style and taste and even if the quality

remains constantly high. Criticism should always be cautious in dealing with them. During the Gothic period there were indeed many examples of buildings without a traversing hall[91].

It is therefore apparent that the Venetian house has no particular problems concerning load-bearing structures, given the lack of vaults and the limited thickness of the walls supporting the floors; and it is equally evident that the absence of such problems of statics was decisive also in establishing the dimensions of the building. Particularly in depth, these would not appear to be bound to any specific proportional modules, and the consequences, also on an aesthetic level, are such as to differentiate it profoundly from any building on the mainland. The Venetian urban aggregate, being conditioned by the intense use of the land available, makes Venice, as has been justly observed, unique in the world.

'Every citizen, without the shadow of a regulatory plan, with the object of gaining access to the waterway, brought about a progressive disappearance of the free areas on which, owing to the increase in ground values, he built houses no longer of two but of at least three floors. Thus arose in Venice, by the side of the large and autonomous palaces, a multitude of buildings which are blocks of flats or series of small houses, devoid of a 'courtyard' (*corte*), intended for the cohabitation of several family units and in which the ground floors were reserved for shops'[92].

In this way the Venice we know at present grew up: not just a multitude of buildings on large or small islands but a complex of blocks in which houses, canals and streets are inextricably linked together, yet remain independent of each other. If this urban aggregate, which to the unthinking or superficial observer may perhaps look like a decorative complex devoid of meaning, or a labyrinth, constitutes today an ordered and well-functioning system of communication and habitation, this is the merit of the town-planning of the fourteenth and fifteenth centuries, and also of the rationalization and technical sagacity of building art as practiced in the Venice of the fourteenth century, a feat not appreciated as much as it deserves, without compare in the Italian and European Middle Ages and one which remains until the eighteenth century a model for the town-planning of the great European cities, as for instance, Paris[93]. The front of the Venetian house appears the only external part of the building fully marked by a representational dignity, to the entire detriment of the sides, which are never worked out as a continuation of the front but, on the contrary, are awarded a merely utilitarian treatment, in which, although details (windows, doors, cornices) have some merit, a formal synthesis does not exist. No proportional and rhythmic law appears either realized or even contemplated by the architect; whereas the inner courtyard, however arranged, is committed, on the whole, to a taste which, instinctively and without calculations of perspective or rational prejudices, enhances in the juxtaposition and in the contrast the external staircase, the ground porch, the multi-light window, the well-parapet, etc.; a beauty born from imaginative decoration, from polychrome masses, from the most fascinating and most unreal expressions of a refined wealth. 'Ancient mixed building technique (in bricks and stone) was radically rationalized... Marble window frames, marble supports and string courses were provided for and worked out in the required measure; the chimneys, often obtruding on several sides and applied to the exterior, were carefully isolated from the roof and from the wooden structures and carried outside the building by high smoke-stacks'[94].

One should consider the free manner in which the marble terminal cornices, on the front and on the sides, follow the deformation of the walls caused by the smoke-stacks, ending in an entirely irregular contour. But, as is well-known, a capricious fancy was allowed in the stack–tops[95]. A functional quality, in other words, resolving itself in colour yet renouncing any prefabricated geometric, proportional plan. The proof of it is found in that eminently 'pictorial' freedom which also informs the façades of Venetian houses, in the sense that the architects enlarge (or reduce), if they can, the dimensions of these façades well beyond the

limits which would have been respected by an architect of the fourteenth or fifteenth centuries in Florence. The fanciful grace of the Gothic style peculiar to these façades encouraged a licence which, in Florence and Siena, would have been as far as possible avoided. (Consider the asymmetrical layout of surfaces, of certain façades unusually long or lengthened with total lack of restraint, even, in some cases, doubled when the volume of the building increased.)

It is not that there is any lack (in other cities of the continent and well into the Renaissance) of buildings with unusually enlarged façades. But it seems clear—and every Gothic house in Venice demonstrates this—that the façades are, aesthetically, mere screens and not external projections of an organism derived from the application of specific rhythmic laws peculiar to each architect. Nothing is farther therefore (in the Venice of the fifteenth century) from the precepts of the great theoreticians (even where their rigour is attenuated) than Venetian Gothic. In the Doge's Palace, already in the fourteenth century, and in the Ca' d'Oro, it offers the most disconcerting elements of an irrationalism which is at exactly the opposite pole from the Albertian *concinnitas*, to the extent that these Venetian secular buildings were judged, until the Age of Enlightenment, barbarous and 'Germanic' (*tedesche*)—an epithet from which nothing connected with Gothic architecture in general, ours (Italian) or transalpine was exempted. This was a derogatory judgment from which the structure of a Gothic church could at least in part save itself, but a page of architecture like the one presented by the Ca' d'Oro could not. If attentively analyzed, the Ca' d'Oro offers perhaps the most manifest example of an unprecedented disdain for any symmetrical norm whatever. The ordering of each constructive or, rather, compositional element is in open and strident contrast to the one next to it.

If it is undoubtedly evident that a reality as fanciful as that of the works of art which they were freely creating could never correspond to their dictates, theoreticians (who were also architects) employed the precepts of codified knowledge in order to make them the instruments of a very free imagination. In Venice, this freedom imposed itself with an even greater absence of prejudice. Similarly, the paintings and sculptures in which a perspective mode of viewing has been rigorously respected in accordance with the rules applied by Brunelleschi, codified by Alberti and resumed by Mantegna are not at all common. Perspective soon became a very new instrument to be used with the utmost freedom, entirely or in part, never an element determining in an absolute manner the value of a work of art—from Paolo Uccello to the last baroque artists[96].

We have dwelt somewhat at length on these observations in an attempt to underline, once and for all, a formal premise which informs the whole of Venetian art (and therefore secular Gothic architecture). In no other Italian centre of art and artistic theory were the laws of proportion and perspective in current practice as little respected as in Venice, especially in Gothic secular architecture which, in the Venetian State, lives its own life entirely.

It has been justly observed that in Venice the façade of the building stands on its own and 'has no organic connection' with 'its own body'[97]. It thus happens that at various times, in the twelfth century and the sixteenth, structures are possible in Venice which, practically, develop in space an infinitely repeated motif, as the Procuratie of Ziani (afterwards repeated by Coducci) and the Library begun by the Tuscan Sansovino, to whom the aesthetic norm which presides over architecture in Venice, entirely different from the one in use on the mainland, became immediately clear. An architecture, therefore, in part utilitarian, if we leave out the façade (but for this last, obviously, a different point of view must be required). The *utilitas*, in fact, in the best made and most admired façades, is not gained to the detriment of the *venustas* if one bears in mind that this last arises from a balance of colour which by itself establishes the values of solid and hollow spaces, as in contemporary Venetian painting,

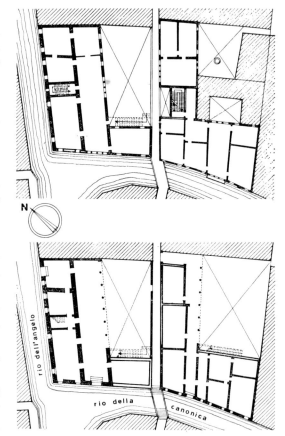

more than from an equilibrium of areas and masses. Not infrequently even today, one deceives oneself that one is interpreting critically what is in fact due only to the patina of time, the spell of the water, of the air, of the hour, and not to the intentions of the builder—who may have intended to spread plaster where we, today, ingenuously admire the different chromatic notes of the terracotta.

It must be admitted, however, that if these façades are aesthetically indifferent to what stands behind them, their intimate connection with the lagunar landscape is an element which greatly surpasses the 'town-planning' value of a building erected on the mainland. Finally, as Ackerman noted: 'Venice was the only medieval Italian city which could afford in its civil architecture an elegant and open style; and this contributed to the development of the Venetian taste for a more intimate union between the architectural and the natural environments, as a consequence of the opening of the building more towards the exterior than towards the interior'[98].

From these considerations arises the great importance of the façade in Venice, neither more nor less than as a painting to be interpreted in two dimensions, a material of primary importance for the history of art. We should not, however, reject the assistance which may come from the study of the town-planning character of the Venetian house and of its varying aspects through the centuries (the rational exploitation of the ground, the distributive character of the covered and open rooms, the social or economic import of the changes succeeding each other through the centuries). We shall be chiefly interested in these pages in the study of forms, in their succession in time, as is obvious when dealing with the history of art, drawing when necessary from studies of a town-planning character the elements needed to clarify some particular problem. It is fortunate that, to help our studies, excellent contributions on Venetian town-planning by Renata E. Trincanato, Saverio Muratori and Paolo Maretto have appeared in the last few years[99]. These do not merely represent a generous help for the students of the history of art but also provide valuable items of information to those who defend today the beauty of this unique and incomparable city.

As is well known (and as we saw above) the façade of the Romano-Byzantine palace is characterized by arcades and by very ample rows of windows piercing the whole wall.

In the Fondaco dei Turchi (Palazzo Pesaro) and in Palazzi Loredan and Farsetti, these openings are so numerous that the architect feels the need to impose a rhythm, marked on the ground floor by the extension of the entrance porch (which in the Fondaco dei Turchi is the largest in existence in medieval Venetian architecture after the much later one of the Doge's Palace) and in the upper storey by variations in the style of the capitals (Palazzo Loredan), by a couple of columns (Palazzo Farsetti) and by a pilaster (Fondaco dei Turchi).

The last-named building clearly indicates that also in the two preceding ones there were probably two 'towers' on the wings[100]. In one of the minor palaces of the Realtine zone also, namely in Casa Donà Dolcetti at the Madonnetta (no. 1429) the row of windows covers the whole façade from one end to the other.

In an important essay, Karl M. Swoboda[101] has clarified the non-Byzantine origin of these large rows of windows by reference to Early Christian architecture, quoting as an example Diocletian's palace at Spalato (Split) as well as, in respect of the lateral towers, the Roman villas with a portico in the centre, flanked by projecting lateral blocks. According to Swoboda, the Venetian façade with portico of the thirteenth century has no connection (as others have believed) with the contemporary Byzantine architecture.

The villas with porch and projecting lateral blocks (*Eckrisaliten*) represent instead a new structural rhythm which had its beginnings in the second century and, in substance, represent a spatial interpretation, a projection[102]. The façade of the Fondaco dei Turchi, according to Swoboda, reveals itself as a derivation of the late–antique style of the fifth and sixth centuries[103]. Swoboda[104] remarks that that type of palace must have had other famous proto-types (Diocletian's palace in Antioch), recognizing in the Fondaco dei Turchi and in the Palaz-zo Loredan the clear recollection of those projecting blocks visible also in African mosaics not earlier than the fourth century. The Spalato palace is a valuable precedent for the Vene-tian palaces in that the *basis villae* (already projecting in other examples) appears aligned with the whole façade[105].

Developing these concepts, Bettini shows precisely how the porch between towers ap-pears in Roman territory on country estates. The principle is then found again in the villas of the Middle Empire, in harmony with the new 'illusionist' principles, from the second century onwards. The palace in Spalato must therefore be placed in the 'passage phase from the middle to the late Roman period—for which reason the last development, which is at the origin of the Venetian palaces, has not yet been achieved[106] ... the phase in which the porch was placed in front of the mass of the building, as an independent constructive element is over ... the visual unity of the façade—its transformation into an absolute surface of only chromatic value—is not yet completely attained ... because there still remain strong residues of plasticity'[107]. The same author is, at this point, of the opinion that 'an absolute visual unity, of chromatic value only' was perhaps already attained in 'the façade of the imperial palace of Milan' and 'even more in that of the palace of Ravenna'[108].

The inquiry, at any rate, is far from being concluded, and this chiefly for one reason: the 'Romanesque' architecture of the territories which had belonged to the Exarchate, Venice and the lands which artistically (even if not politically) depend on it, from the Venetian main-land to the Friuli, to Istria, to Dalmatia, a vast arc in which everything is bound together, is as yet not at all clarified; indeed, the very diverse opinions of scholars have even increased the disorientation. We lack a comprehensive study, to which only a dense network of com-parisons between the very numerous monuments can give a resolving clarity. However fully one may accept the decisive influence of the Spalato villa on Venetian building, one must still add that the investigations of the Roman villas are far from being concluded[109].

Less convincing is Fiocco's thesis[110] which, though accepting Swoboda's ideas, insists above all on the contacts with Ravenna and with the Exarchate[111]. If it is true that the roof parapet of the Fondaco dei Turchi and that of the now vanished Ca' Grande dei Barozzi in S. Moisé[112] reproduce the well-known elements of the Drogdone House in Ravenna, a limi-tation of Swoboda's suggestions seems preferable to a too decisive orientation towards Ravenna and the Exarchate, at least until the characters of that architecture are completely clarified. Swoboda's precise pointing to the Spalato palace seems therefore more than sufficient for our purposes and has fully satisfied Demus also. According to that scholar[113], the structure with galleries could have arisen only in a city which fully dominated the sea and in which order and peace prevailed. The return to paleochristian forms can therefore be considered as the expression of the idea of *Renovatio* of the Christian Empire, in order to justify its conquests in the East. Finally, we would add that one should not forget that the splendour of these buildings may be explained also by the fact that Venice was, in the thir-teenth century, the major mercantile power in the Mediterranean.

The vigorous interventions of the Lombard representational culture which we recognize everywhere in Venice explain why the house with galleries extending over the whole façade (or with multi–light windows) was not the only structural scheme in existence. In this city, where the clear atmosphere transfigures the colours and the polychrome reflections of the waters, different from one moment to the other, condition an architecture which in turn contributes to a continuous instability of vision, one finds also structures of Padan character, though with some adaptations to the local environment.

Trincanato has clearly described a thirteenth-century structure in salizzada S. Lio (Castello

5691–5705) in which are evident the remains of two blocks in line, developed in height and joined by an arch in the centre which gave perhaps access to an inner courtyard, now no longer visible[114]. There remain, of the older part, traces of a shop, the connecting arch and, in the left block, a two–light window, round–headed, on pillars of clean proportions[115].

A similar complex of buildings, in the same salizzada S. Lio (Castello 5662–72) was described by the same authoress. The connecting arch is pointed here and the remaining two–light window in the building on the right already has a pointed extrados, justifying perhaps a slightly later dating[116]. The waterside porch of the small Palazzo Priuli–Bon at S. Stae has revealed (at the sides of the later central portal) two openings with two–light windows, with arch on pillars, of quite similar proportions to those of the already mentioned two–light window in salizzada S. Lio[117].

The considerations set out in the preceding pages on the Romano–Byzantine architecture of thirteenth–century Venetian palaces do not presume to deal fully with a matter which does not appear to concern the substance of this book—dedicated to Gothic architecture—but are, it seems to us, indispensable to clarify the blossoming of the first Gothic in Venice. This will immediately become quite clear when we point out, precisely in a Romano-Byzantine façade (that of Palazzo Businello) a sudden shrinking of the gallery[118] which had elsewhere traversed the buildings we have examined from one end to the other; the tripartite arrangement more or less indicated in them here appears radically transformed. Two six–light windows open in line with the porch with three arches on the ground floor, between two wings of solid wall, each pierced by six single windows. Thus is born, in a still pre–Gothic climate, that division in three parts which, with various rhythms, will form for nearly three centuries the basis of innumerable façades of Venetian secular Gothic.

Similarly, a splendid five–light window, decorated with carved roundels and surmounted by a string–course cornice marking, perhaps, the limit in height of the more ancient building, is at the centre of another Donà Palace, called della Madonnetta (S. Polo 1426) and it seems without doubt that the remainder of the façade, completely rebuilt, must have followed, in ancient times, a pattern akin to that of Ca' Businello[119].

The tendency completely to pierce a building (the Doge's Palace and some very rare buildings represent quite particular episodes) which was justly recognized as an inheritance from late antiquity comes to an end at this point. That 'portico–style' which identifies the Venetian architecture of the thirteenth century, expression of a sense of political security, in which Demus[120] discerns the rise of a Renaissance style (with better reason, this style is to be recognized in the Florentine architecture of the eleventh century), is replaced by a new conception which, although maintaining unmistakable characteristics peculiar to Venice, undoubtedly has its point of departure in buildings of the Po valley. I have no doubt that there were in Venice examples of asymmetrical façades of type 1C, as we shall see in the next chapter (now vanished), which were expressions of that illusionism on which Nickhoff based his well-known interpretation of Romanesque art, understood as a breaking of previous patterns with a 'progressive and ever more emphasized discrediting of the values of perspective spatial effect and plastic form'[121].

Venice represents in the later Middle Ages and in the Gothic the most resounding confirmation of this inversion of the representational vision, as we shall see later on.

Examples of clearly Padan Romanesque architecture with round arches not on pillars are not lacking in Venice. These are isolated instances (two– or three–light windows), perhaps fragments of vanished buildings, in terracotta with the archivolt (*ghiera*) marked by a cornice, or double archivolt with receding steps and with truncated cube capitals of the simplest type. They may be thought of the thirteenth, even the fourteenth century.

We have already alluded to the undoubted participation of Lombard stonecutters (and

25

certainly also master-masons) in the capitals (which clearly reproduce Veronese forms), in the cornices and in the mouldings which are certainly not Byzantine but purely Padan (we should recall Palazzo Loredan).

We should not be surprised therefore if, faced by these six–light windows (as, also, by the three–light windows of a Romanesque house in calle del Pistor (Cann. 4552a) at SS. Apostoli, our thoughts run at once to the galleries on the façades and the balconies inside the thirteenth–century churches, to the town halls, to the cloisters, baptisteries and belfries; because it is evident that when the direct late antique motivation disappeared, it was replaced, in the tripartition and, more, in the establishment of the taste for multi–light windows in the centre, by a clear echo of the innumerable suggestions of the Italian mainland, even if we want to limit ourselves to the first half of the thirteenth century. It is a whole façade in calle del Pistor, with two three–light windows in the centre and four single windows on each side on the façade, capitals of a thirteenth-century type and terracotta cornice ornamented with chevrons and dentils which would not be out of place in a city of the Venetian or Emilian mainland. Other examples of this Padan style are to be found in Venice, always in baked earth[122].

*The arch on pillars with cusped extrados (twelfth century)*

The 'orders' established more than a century ago by Ruskin to distinguish the successive phases of Venetian secular Gothic have not, even today, lost much of their validity; it should be said nevertheless that his criticism, though always to be respected for its perspicacity and for its philological scruples, would certainly have dated much more if in these hundred years there had been more studies on this period, one of the most beautiful in the history of art. But it is precisely because the history of art, in its infinite inexhaustible aspects, has offered so many attractive themes that this fascinating sector has been since then almost entirely neglected. Leaving aside contributions of a merely philological nature and some articles on the Doge's Palace or on some individual palace, nothing more, in fact, has been written on the problems of this architectural style which covers two and a half centuries and has given Venice its urban and artistic character with the presence of innumerable monuments and of instances of 'minor' architecture; that face, in short, which for some centuries has been a source of fascination, of amazement and of inspiration, even for those little drawn towards the representational arts. If one then considers that this architectural phase not only lasted in Venice for more than two centuries, but that it had notable repercussions, with variations of style, in the territories and cities dominated by Venice, from Verona to Istria, to Dalmatia and even to Ragusa, one can well speak of a considerable critical void, even if some mention worthy of note was made in the nineteenth century by students of the history of architecture like Kugler, Mothes and Schnaase.

This goes back to a century ago, or a little less. But these are mentions which, barely skimming the question in the course of dealing with much wider matters, have left this ground more or less untouched.

Ruskin[123], then, made a second and a third order follow the first (the one he calls 'Byzantine' and we call Romano-Byzantine).

There is no reason why, at a distance of more than a century, one should give up the use of these convenient terms, even if there will arise chronological variants and new problems of style, brought about by the quantity of major and minor monuments here examined. Because substantially, though with variations and displacements and superpositions and 'co-existences' of the various 'orders', and with more precise definitions which will sometimes alter its extent and meaning, Ruskin's sequence is correct, in the sense that it indicates a progressive enrichment of motives which corresponds, in the abstract, to a logical evolution of the forms. We see no reason therefore to give up in this treatment the use of a terminology (aiming to define the propounding of variants in time and also in space) which has shown itself, until today, to be the clearest.

Ruskin's 'second order' marks the appearance of the inflected arch on the extrados of the Romano-Byzantine window; the 'third' the extension of the inflected arch also to the underside of the arch.

With some liberality and without insisting on a too rigorous chronological succession, Ruskin places the spreading of these two forms in the thirteenth and the beginning of the fourteenth century.

It is evident that in view of the enormous spread of these forms in Venice, as we said in connection with the 'first' order, it would be absurd to insist on minute chronological distinctions. The requirement, valid for so many other sectors of the history of art, to exercise greater prudence as the remains are scarcer, be they paintings or the remains of an architectural period, must apply also in our case when the monuments are moderately numerous, and increasingly numerous as we go forward in time. Because Venice has been a conservative city, particularly in the course of these centuries, the course of development differed from that of other centres of the Peninsula, where the 'retardation' impoverished the quality (and we do not speak of the artistically 'depressed' regions, those far from the great centres of cultural irradiation). In Venice, because of a mysterious phenomenon, archaic elements survived, sometimes indolently but always worthily adapted (and, where necessary, subordinated) without loss of quality, without appearing too 'surpassed' and, on the critical plane, unworthy of attention.

A typical example of this singular aspect of Venetian architectural civilization, and one we wish to quote here, is represented by the use of the typical fourteenth–century capital, with a rosette on the four sides, until the late fifteenth century; and, it should be noted, with good reason, because in the great building complexes of the later Gothic it is often applied to the columns which divide the multi–light windows of the top floors, more modest, in obvious contrast with the rich capitals with thick leaves which adorn the great rows of windows of the *piani nobili*.

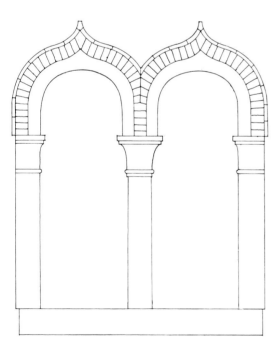

There is naturally a limit to the elasticity granted to the boundaries of the various periods in which the 'orders' are placed, because it seems obvious that, for the most part, in the classification of the values going from the simplest to the most complex, the first always precedes the second, and it is advisable to add that in doubtful cases the best method is that which makes use of all the available elements in order to arrive at a more precise placing in time and at a more appropriate critical definition of a building, or part of it.

A typical building of the second order, and one which is often mentioned together with Romano–Byzantine buildings, is Ca' da Mosto. The façade of Ca' da Mosto is certainly very close to those of the Romano–Byzantine palaces studied above; and, like them, it did not rise, perhaps, beyond the two remaining floors. Marked by time but untouched by restorations, it has, more than the others, a charm entirely its own, not only because of the patina of time, but also because of the magnificence of the panels which enrich the *piano nobile*, which are very dense but nevertheless do not disturb the unfolding rhythm of the seven–light window (one of the arches is walled-up) between the two accents marked at the ends by the two single windows. The principle realized in the façades of Ca' Businello and the little Palazzo Donà (no. 1427) is here refined to the point of reaching a stability and harmony of proportion unseen until then, even in its relations to the water-side porch, reduced from five to three lights and reconstructed with carved arcades which, effectively, seem more ancient[124] than the upper floor, remade as taste demanded, with smooth, high, clearly visible pillars. The capital to the right of the major arch seems later than the other two, truncated and of a thirteenth–century character.

The work 'at once simple, graceful, and strong, the most extensive and perfect' of this type was considered by Ruskin to belong to the first half of the thirteenth century[125], and equally by Tassini[126]. Lorenzetti[127] attributes it to the thirteenth century; Toesca[128], alluding to the first floor capitals ('they seem original') speaks of the late thirteenth century, of which he is put in mind also by the inflected cornices; Salmi[129] also seems clearly to allude to the thirteenth century, noting the 'pointed archivolt in the Mussulman manner'; Trincanato is for the twelfth–thirteenth centuries[130], Fiocco for the twelfth[131], Bettini[132] considers it 'probably the most ancient' of the Romano–Byzantine palaces on the Grand Canal and attributes it to the thirteenth century; Demus[133] is for the thirteenth, Scattolin[134] for the twelfth to thirteenth century.

In reality, the thirteenth-century elements clearly prevail in this façade, even if the arcades on the ground floor adapted to a reconstruction of the thirteenth century must be considered older than those of the upper parts. The affinity to the palaces with semicircular stilted arches is very evident; nor, as in Palazzo Loredan, are the coupled colonnettes at the sides lacking. Peculiar to the traversing hall, as Maretto noted, is its widening towards the balcony, as in the oldest Romano-Byzantine examples. The terminal cornice is similar to those of the thirteenth century already mentioned in Palazzo Contarini at S. Giustina, in the lunette of Palazzo Malipiero at S. Samuele[135], in Palazzo Da Mula in Murano, with plaited and slack scrolls (the cornice with reversed leaves under the balcony must be of the thirteenth century[136]).

What is most striking about this façade is the novel manner in which the extrados of the arches of the row of windows is treated, so that by means of an element inserted like a wedge in the round arch there appears a cusp with inflected arch. Even if this imposing complex was erected at the same time as some of the Romano-Byzantine palaces (we have arrived at a limiting date around 1250 and are inclined to believe Ca' da Mosto to be of this time) our palace still represents a step forward from the group gathered round the Rialto, and it is impossible, at this point, not to pose the problem of the appearance of this element in Venice around the middle of the thirteenth century.

Gothic art had already been in existence for some time on the Venetian mainland, but the ogival arch which had made its appearance in its simplest form in the cities of the Veneto cannot be taken into account here, considering that the inflected Gothic arch is at this time entirely non-existent this (Italian) side of the Alps, and that in France it became established only towards 1375, while in England it appeared only at the end of the thirteenth century.

The 'cusped' arch, as it was called, is in fact of oriental, not western, origin because even from a simply functional point of view, it cannot derive from the simple Gothic arch but is nothing else than a subtle variation of the Romano–Byzantine arch which we have taken as a starting point.

Not without reason, Kugler[137] spoke of stilted arches 'with the point treated in the oriental manner', followed by Beylié[138] who, speaking of 'ogives de style copte ou arabe' (with reference to Ca' da Mosto) is certainly inappropriate in his expression but is moving in the right direction. And in any case the presence of the Islamic element in Venice was an undisputed fact also for the more or less qualified scholars of the last century, from Fontana[139] to Selvatico[140] (who goes as far as India) and for all those who concerned themselves with Venetian architecture.

Cusps with inflected arch are indeed found in the East, even several centuries before the thirteenth; but without touching on the Indian temples of the first or second centuries, the examples of Ajanta of the sixth to seventh centuries[141], or the later manifestations in the

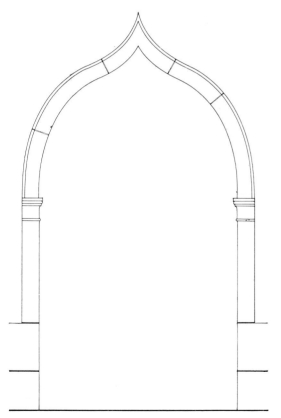

minor Islamic arts, it is sufficient to keep in mind certain examples in existence in Venice itself, such as the arcades of the Tesoro (Treasury) gates, of the Fiori and of S. Giovanni, always considered of an 'Arab style' by Ruskin[142], by Selvatico[143], by Cattaneo[144] (who thought them of the twelfth century) and by Lorenzetti[145].

More precisely, Demus believes the Tesoro gate to be of 1225–50, pointing out its 'Saracen'[146] form, and he considers the Fiori gate to be of a somewhat later date, i. e. about 1250[147], and places last the tympanum of the S. Giovanni gate[148] (1250–1300). The references are for him the Fatimid, and particularly Ayyubid art forms. The Venetians, adds Demus, could have discovered these forms in Syria and in Egypt (as he believes is confirmed by the screens used above the S. Alipio gate)[149]. But these very singular works cannot be disjoined from certain portal crownings of the façade towards the Piazza, the inflected arch of which can certainly not have originated in the West (also, as we saw, because the dates are incompatible). Consider the first doorway on the right which Demus dates to about 1230[150], where even the intrados is an inflected arch, the panel above the door of S. Alipio (considered later than 1250)[151], the red marble windows of the central cupola (which follow the Ca' da Mosto type), also of the thirteenth century[152], and finally the panel with two peacocks in St. Mark's, studied by Demus, with the pointed arch of the third order, which is also of the thirteenth century[153].

In this connection one should re-examine that very beautiful pulpit of the Duomo of Grado, which has a cupola baldacchino carried by arches similar to the Islamic-like ones considered here, supported by Romanesque truncated cube capitals, which can very well be placed therefore in the fourteenth (approximately)[154] or, as Tigler[155] now proposes, between the thirteenth and the fourteenth centuries. The front of St. Mark's received its present facing from 1225 onwards[156], work was still proceeding about 1267[157], but it is certain that it must have been completed by that year, also because the various arches offer examples of round-headed tracings on pillars, a proof of what we were saying above, namely that though pointing to different moments succeeding each other in time, these orders have left us architectural examples which were perhaps, on occasion, contemporary.

However, the appearance of these inflected arches in Venice before the middle of the thirteenth century, while excluding any influence of western Gothic, confirms the hypothesis of Demus, according to whom we are here reminded of Fatimid, and especially Ayyubid forms which the Venetians could have seen in the Near East; and that, moreover, this 'Saracen' style had really influenced Venetian architecture, particularly secular, from the thirteenth century onwards until the fifteenth, mixing with the Gothic[158]. Even the double dentilling which often borders the arches and sculptures of these times is, for Demus, of Islamic derivation[159].

Seen in this context, the *piano nobile* of Palazzo Da Mosto seems to be justly considered a structure erected around the middle of the thirteenth century, a period to which other buildings can also be referred. They are not many but, in quality, they form a remarkable complex. If in Palazzo Da Mosto the façade is enhanced in value by the dense sequence of reliefs on the seven–light window and by the dentil cornices along the intrados and extrados, in these other buildings the archivolt moulding is smooth and only edged by a slightly rounded profile, which will be found the same wherever these forms appear.

One of the most notable and less incomplete examples is the so–called Casa del Salvadego in Bocca di Piazza, considered to be of the end of the thirteenth century[160], but perhaps a little earlier, with the four–light window not quite in line at the top with the lateral windows, loose in rhythm on the *piano nobile* but sufficiently framed above by the loggia, which recalls that of the Palazzo Donà–Dolcetti at the Madonnetta. The four–light window (with the thirteenth–century capital) is in fact only a two–light window flanked by two single windows, perhaps originally provided with balconies. Casa del Salvadego is one of the noblest examples of the Venetian palace, as it evolved after the abandonment of the solemn and symmetrical façades with loggias of the Romano-Byzantine palace. The façade of the Venetian-Gothic house, from the thirteenth to the fifteenth century, is certainly among the most 'free' one can find in the late Italian Middle Ages; its freedom, its resilience (and we shall see how many examples can be produced) none the less never reach the point (even where there are no string-courses) of destroying the unity—essentially picturesque and not only plastic—suggested by all its elements, horizontal and vertical, which were certainly bound together where today the naked brick is visible by frescoes which have now disappeared[161].

The Salvadego house recalls another building in rio delle Beccarie where in the five–light window the balconies (modernized) alternate with the windows with sills. It is notable for being perhaps the first example which has come down to us of a lateral displacement of the axis of the building, until now, as we should remember, always placed in the centre, a theme resumed by later Gothic. It is difficult to believe this house to be later than 1300, because of the presence of the thirteenth–century capitals, as well as the shape of the water-gate where the insertion of the cusp is very clear, as at Ca' da Mosto: a contamination of the Gothic arch of western derivation with the oriental suggestion which determines the physiognomy of the third order[162].

A third complex where Ruskin found his second order, a 'fully established type', is the internal façade of Palazzo dell'Angelo (Soranzo)[163]: two four–light windows nearly intact (in the upper one a restoration has levelled the sills, which were otherwise lowered, in the same measure as at the Casa Salvadego in the first and fourth openings) and, on the ground floor, a rather large porch with architrave in respect to which the axis of the four–light windows must have appeared displaced to the left, as in the house in rio delle Beccarie; on the extreme right at a lower level than that of the lower four–light window, a small round–headed, two–light window; to the left of the four-light windows there may have been two single windows, to balance the two on the right; the capitals of the porch and of the four–light windows are Romanesque truncated cubes. More full of gaps than restored, the whole has a certain austerity not unlike that of the Casa del Salvadego, sustained by a steadier and more tranquil rhythm. The dating should not go outside the second half of the thirteenth century, a conclusion reached also recently by Maretto[164], who identifies on the horizontal plane an L–shaped construction, in that the great hall is parallel to the front and the building continues westward with a single wing perpendicular to the front[165].

A fairly well–known building is Ca' Falier at SS. Apostoli (dear to the romantic illustrators). A recent accurate investigation[166] has shown that of the original façade there subsist the two four–light windows one above the other (that of the *piano nobile* was at least a five–light window, but the two rows of windows are not, however, on the same axis) and the pilasters of the porch, the arches of which have been rebuilt. The affinity of the rhythmic relation between the two multi-light windows and the two four–light windows of Casa Soranzo is very apparent; and here also one must assume that the buttressed roof was jutting out immediately above the higher four–light window. The alternating reliefs on the lower multi–light window recall Ca' da Mosto. The capitals are of similar type to those on the columns of Marco and Todaro in the Piazzetta, a truncated cube with long angle leaves on the corners and stars or rosettes on the faces. One cannot exclude the possibility that the capitals of Ca' Falier as well as those of the columns may even belong to the end of the twelfth century, when one thinks that the columns were erected in 1172–8. Ca' Falier, once thought to be of the beginning of the thirteenth century, then generically assigned to that century and, finally, by Toesca to the fourteenth[167], must be considered of the second half of the thirteenth. The supports of the porch (which is not certain to have been open) are ancient, but the arches

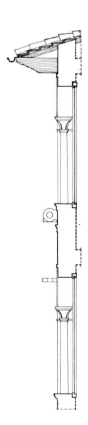

are of a later date and it is not possible to recognize anything other than a structure not unlike, perhaps in ancient times, the façade of Ca' Soranzo, even if on a different plan, with normal traversing hall.

A neat four–light window surmounted by carved crosses alternating with paterae (which also surmount the crosses) is what remains, together with the strong projection of the roof, of the ancient house of the Zane at S. Maria Mater Domini (S. Croce 2174). The columns stand on a stone base which perhaps marks the height of small plutei, the capitals have an abacus with dentils. An Andrea Zane was living in 1297 in the S. Maria Mater Domini quarter and in 1310 the Zane family were branded for having taken part in the plot of the Tiepolo and the Querini[168]. There should be no doubt about the attribution to the thirteenth century (second half)[169].

Palazzo Viaro–Zane is also very interesting for its L–shaped structure and for the absence of a traversing hall, as shown by Maretti in buildings of the same or nearly the same period (in campo S. Margherita, in calle Larga dei Proverbi and in other houses included by him among the 'late Byzantine'), another proof of the inconstancy, or better, elasticity of certain planimetric data from the outset in Venice[170].

There are many remains of this type of architecture in Venice. Not all, of course, are as fine as those we have just discussed. Two four–light windows, one above the other, may be seen at the S. Andrea bridge (Cann. 4130), perhaps somewhat altered. The columns are short and on high pedestals. The capitals are no longer truncated cubes, but have angular volutes and the rosette, of a type, however, in advance of the usual fourteenth–century model and which may therefore be considered of the end of the thirteenth.

The capital adorned with rosettes on four faces, of which we shall speak again later, is typically Venetian and is very widespread in the city as well as in the Venetian mainland (it does not appear, to my knowledge, in Lombardy), even in the Marches (in Fano, in Palazzo Malatesta and in the porch of S. Francesco), in the Abruzzi (in the Duomo of Città S. Angelo) and, I believe, elsewhere also. It appears in these two four–light windows in its most ancient version, which Ruskin had already placed in the thirteenth century, namely with simple angular volutes (see no. 10 and 13 of Table II of vol. 3 of *Stones of Venice*; whereas the fourteenth–century version, with volutes with reversed leaves, is represented by no. 3). Another notable fragment of this architecture is constituted by a good part of the façade on the rio delle Ostreghe at S. Maria Zobenigo, namely the water gate (of the 'cusped' archaic type), the four–light window (with capitals with leaf patterns, perhaps of the thirteenth century) and higher up, in line, a dwarf two–light window.

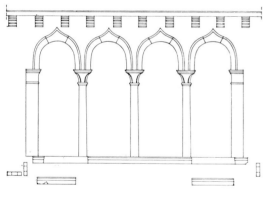

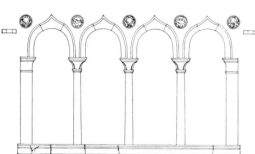

A first floor in calle Larga dei Proverbi (Cann. 4582) must also be of the thirteenth century, where, as in the house in rio delle Beccarie, the four–light window is displaced to the right, while on the left there are three single–light windows[171]. The capitals are truncated cubes[172]. But as we have seen with the remarkable example of Ca' da Mosto, the smooth arch profiles with torus listel do not exclude those of the same epoch with Byzantine dentil decoration (*fregio a scacchi*). The beautiful four–light window of calle Bosello (Castello 3682) is an example of this, with columns on high cylindrical supports (also an archaic feature) and truncated cube capitals. A three–light smooth window with capitals of the same type in rio delle Beccarie[173] surmounts a simple, very pointed portal with smooth arch profile and torus listel in western Gothic style. Water-gates of this type are very common in Venice and were particularly popular in the fourteenth century; it cannot be excluded that this one may be a little earlier in time. Another three–light window in ramo del Tamossi, near the corte Salviati (S. Polo 1513), stands above the five–light window of the first order[174] which has been already considered.

The four–light window (with two columns and a pilaster) at the entrance to calle del

Paradiso on rio di S. Maria Formosa, part of a group of buildings typical of minor Venetian architecture, may also be attributed to the thirteenth century and is a continuation at the same level of a window and of another three–light window giving on the calle del Paradiso, in which, however, also the underside of the arch is inflected and the extrados has the usual Byzantine dentil ornament. Calle del Paradiso precisely divides two parallel long and low buildings between salizzada S. Lio and the rio di S. Maria Formosa. The ground floor is occupied by shops and the upper storey of the two buildings is used for dwellings and leans on the side of the calle on a row of hewn stones (*cani*) which jut out and secure it a certain width.

An arch connects the two blocks at their ends on the salizzada S. Lio, while a second Gothic arch, with very elegant tracery of the beginning of the fifteenth century, unites the two ends on the rio which, so Trincanato thinks, had originally 'a turreted aspect' akin to that of the two small Romanesque palaces in salizzada S. Lio, of which we spoke initially[175].

One can clearly find a typical example of 'retardation' in the façade of Palazzo Vitturi at S. Maria Formosa: the three–light window, and the single windows which flank it on the floor below the *nobile* are of the second order, but the proportions are substantially altered if compared, for instance, with the refined elegance of the four–light window of Palazzo Viaro–Zane, in respect of which they certainly appear to be later in time, perhaps of the last years of the thirteenth century.

Single windows, or groups of windows, appear everywhere in Venice. A beautiful surviving two–light window of good proportions is in the sottoportego della Pasina towards calle Sbianchesini[176]. There is no lack of other remains[177], scattered[178]. The original purity of the thirteenth–century examples is increasingly lost in the later forms which should not go beyond 1400. A curious example is provided by the two Palazzi Benzi Zecchini on the fondamenta della Madonna dell'Orto (Cannaregio 3458–9) which must be considered, in the nobler parts, certainly not older than the fourteenth century. In the second of them, there is even a dwarf three–light window on the mezzanine floor, with fourteenth–century capitals with rosettes. A stripping of the two façades could throw light on possible successive changes, and on the authenticity of those archaic elements.

There is no trace left of this second order, or even of the third on the Venetian mainland nor, as far as we know, on islands of the estuary. It may be that this is to be attributed to the fact that in the thirteenth century Venice was still entirely turned towards the sea, and it is undeniable that political domination undoubtedly favoured the spreading of Venetian secular Gothic on the mainland as was to happen in the fifteenth century. The only really archaic example of which there is a record is that of the house in via Malcanton in Trieste, demolished in 1938, with a three–light window, certainly of the thirteenth century[179]. Another example of the reappearance of this second order on the other shore of the Adriatic is known to be in Ragusa, where however it must be placed at least a century later and assumes a graceful rhythm. The four–light window of the Zamanja house, where the arches contrast with the long and strong columns, is articulated with a compact rhythm (the coats of arms are of the Gozze family)—a precious rarity, where the delay of more than a century does not affect the quality. Artistic forms, however, as is well known, do not know frontiers. In this case, moreover, if it is true that the forms of which we speak are not found on the Venetian mainland, it is nevertheless a fact that we find this 'second order' in Ferrara on the southern side of the cathedral[180].

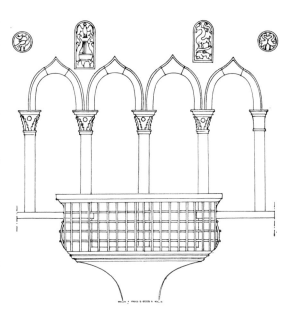

We have already alluded to the very large use made here of the typical motif of the coupled colonnettes. These are found not only dividing the three–light windows of purely Padan–Romanesque style which in a long series form this gallery, but also as supports of a second gallery with small arches typical of the Venetian 'second order', disposed so as to form twelve four–light windows, two five–light windows and one three–light window. All were surmounted at one time by triangular tympanums which relaxed the monotonous appearance of this interminable series of small arches. If the lower gallery on this side is considered of the second half of the twelfth century, the upper gallery, of a different material and with the multi–light windows not in line with the three–light windows underneath, may be considered as dating towards the middle of the thirteenth century.

### *The arch on pillars with cusped extrados and intrados (thirteenth century)*

The difficulty in establishing a progression in time between the first and second order, on the basis of the surviving monuments, has been mentioned. Equally there are cases of 'co-existence' (as we have actually seen in the houses of calle del Paradiso and in Palazzo Vitturi). It seems evident, however, that these forms, though partly coexisting with the previous ones, are yet somewhat more advanced in time, and that they represent a clearer, more explicit departure from the original Romano–Byzantine style, since the round–headed arch disappears permanently.

It is, however, indispensable to try to fix, first of all, points of departure of some validity. To begin with, it should be made quite clear that this 'third order' of Venetian medieval architecture cannot yet be called Gothic and this is confirmed by the remains of two buildings which show explicit accents of the Muslim style. In them the moulded profile of the archivolt is definitely larger than what we have so far seen, and the 'cusps' bordered by Byzantine dentil ornaments (*fregio a scacchi*) have become pointed, rigid, nearly cone–like, so as to recall more than ever the 'Saracen' tympanums in St. Mark's, particularly those of the Porta dei Fiori.

The essential difference between the 'Islamic' inflected arch and the western one in Venice lies above all in the fact that the latter is produced by means of curves and countercurves traced by using the compass from four centres, while the former is only a transformation of the round–headed arch and ends in an inflected cusp.

Among the brightest and most charming examples of Venetian medieval architecture are those offered by Palazzo Lion in corte del Remer (Cann. 5701–11) and by Palazzo Priuli–Bon at S. Stae (S. Croce 1979), both on the Grand Canal. In the first, the beautiful gate with horseshoe arch, although Romanesque of the thirteenth century and entirely similar, as we saw, to others already mentioned, reveals a clear Islamic accent and there can be no doubt that it is contemporaneous with the two two-light windows which flank it, and are connected with it by a moulded fascia[181]. Of very similar style is the row of windows of Palazzo Priuli–Bon where the rhythm of the windows (restored) follows that of Palazzo Vitturi and of the ground floor of which, more ancient, we have already spoken. The five–light window, among the most elegant of those overlooking the Grand Canal, has been, I believe, renewed in the fifteenth century, since the little balcony on the lion heads must be assigned to this later period. That the two buildings do not date beyond the middle of the thirteenth century at most seems proved by the still fully Romanesque arch of the corte del Remer on one side, and by the capitals of Palazzo Priuli–Bon, which are entirely similar to those of Palazzo Falier at SS. Apostoli, these and those echoing the two huge ones placed on the Piazzetta columns[182].

Still on the Grand Canal, the four–light window of the little Palazzo Bragadin (later Favretto) is related to that of Palazzo Priuli–Bon in the neat marble framing which was to become a customary refinement in the more magnificent façades of the fourteenth and fifteenth centuries. The two surviving windows on the sides if, as it seems, contemporaneous (in these also, as in Palazzo Priuli–Bon, the cusp hardly emerges from the marble frame) must have accompanied the two restored ones towards the centre. In this case the non–aligned vertices of the openings must have displayed an archaic arrangement like that of the Casa del Salvadego, which would be confirmed by the 'Byzantine' cornice (almost certainly thirteenth–century) which acts as a string course and is related to that of Ca' da Mosto. We are therefore in the thirteenth century, perhaps in the middle[183]. Later, but still within the thirteenth century, are found other forms, which are however related to those dealt with previously.

Although altered by additions, Palazzo Vitturi in campo S. Maria Formosa (Cast. 5246) is representative of this period. Freer and less antique than Ca' da Mosto, it does not possess its dense rhythm. The axes of the openings appear more relaxed, as in Casa del Salvadego and Palazzo Priuli–Bon and, as in Casa del Salvadego, the vertices of the arches are not in line. Nevertheless, a feeling of balance and richness is imparted by the *piano nobile*. The arches of the four–light window are surrounded by a Byzantine dentil ornament and finely modulated on the intrados of the moulded archivolt (*ghiera*—thinner than at Palazzo Priuli–Bon), supporting, suspended almost in equilibrium on their points, the four paterae with the cross in the middle and achieving a harmonic relation not unlike that sensed in the Casa del Salvadego. It seems superfluous to point out how these paterae, crosses and panels, constantly detached from any architectural element, loose, almost floating on the red walls (when not intended for a pictorial decoration) represent an element of the first order in the constitution of the eminently chromatic and, as far as possible, antiplastic character of this architecture, which is averse to any 'rational' law and escapes any assessment at an intellectual level. The columns, on high cylindrical bases, have three Byzantine–like capitals. It would therefore appear that Palazzo Vitturi, also because of the particular style of the sculptures and capitals, should be considered of the second half of the thirteenth century[184].

The arches of the multi–light window of Palazzo Vitturi are related, in outline, to those of the beautiful two–light window of Palazzo Zorzi–Bon in calle Bon (Cast. 4907), surmounted by a second two–light window with architrave. It is difficult to assess how much has been restored in this little façade (in which the upper two–light window would be unique of its kind); the two lateral capitals of the lower two–light window were, perhaps, restored and the balustrade added already in the fifteenth century[185].

Of the façade on rio S. Severo we shall speak later. The antique character of this and other parts of the complex in which it appears incorporated does not at all exclude the dating we have proposed for this two–light window, even if it then appears older than the façade. Even more decidedly heralding the Gothic, and thus to be attributed unhesitatingly to the end of the thirteenth century (if not actually in the first years of the fourteenth), Palazzo Moro in campo S. Bartolomeo (S. Marco 5282) attests to the persistence of the third order, no longer used to express the dense and elegant structures of Palazzi Vitturi and Priuli–Bon but called upon to enliven an entirely different environment[186].

The six–light window is its centre, which the plutei (perhaps already in existence in some preceding structure) clearly reinforce, linking the surfaces together with the cornice which, joined to the six-light window, runs along the whole façade. The aspect is no longer 'Byzantine' but of a later character. The wings, however, no longer obey the ancient rhythm, because the distribution of the axes does not follow a rigorous aesthetic principle but is adapted rather to practical requirements, as will often happen in Venetian façades. It is clear that on the second mezzanine as well as on the uppermost floor, openings must have existed of which we ignore the nature. The cornice with braided fillets on moulded brackets is perhaps one of the last still remaining of a long series, if it is really contemporaneous with the *piano nobile*.

This is the type of terminal cornice in Istrian stone, supported by short brackets. It will remain typical of the Venetian Gothic façade, which, repudiating the great projections used on the mainland, and reducing this element to a thin strip of colour, adapts it to the general chromatic principle of surface[187].

The capitals are particularly interesting. The one with rosette appears in its most primitive form, as well as the one with large, full leaves, reversed, of Romanesque Padan origin— two on the corners and one, lower down, in the centre— (a very similar type is at Ca' da Mosto: it was imported into Venice perhaps by Veronese stonecutters and it is found, for instance, in the cloister of S. Zeno in Verona). There are also very simple types, with angular volutes (late Romanesque).

Among the more singular manifestations of this particular style is the beautiful six–light window of Palazzo Sagredo at S. Sofia (Cannaregio 4199), as much for the dash of the pillar as for the rich moulding of the arch itself, which has a hardly stressed cusp so that, from a distance, one seems to see round–headed arches. Ruskin[188] spoke of the beginning of the thirteenth century, but it appears more likely to be towards the end of the century. Those capitals with large angular leaves, to which we have just alluded, but characterized by caulicoles over the leaves (common in Venice in the second half of the thirteenth century and the beginning of the fourteenth) appear here next to those with rosettes, definitely replacing the various Byzantine–like capitals and those with truncated cubes.

The most striking example of these capitals with caulicoles is represented in Venice, on the Grand Canal, by the ground floor arcade of Palazzo Michiel dalle Colonne, erected by Sardi in the second half of the seventeenth century[189], where the Ticinese architect re–used without scruples what must have been an arcade of the thirteenth or fourteenth century, altering its original rhythm.

Another example may be seen in a four–light window of the fourth order on rio S. Marina (visible from the corte delle Muneghe).

Returning to the six–light window of Palazzo Sagredo, it flanks three windows of the third order of a traditional type, of different height which demonstrate an archaic structure.

This contemporaneous proliferation of forms which are *à la page* at the time and of forms affecting archaisms, evidence of different workers more or less attached to elements of style sometimes already surpassed, is very frequent in Venetian Gothic architecture.

The spread of the simpler type of third order, with smooth archivolt bordered by a torus fillet, is remarkable in more modest houses which, in various states of preservation, can be found almost everywhere and may perhaps be attributed to the same decades in which those of the second order were erected.

The palace, not far from the Rialto, of Marco and Pietro Querini must have had a remarkable aspect, at least in view of its size. These two, together with Bajamonte Tiepolo, organized the well-known plot of 1310, when Pietro Gradenigo was Doge. When this faction was defeated, the Ca' Mazor, or Ca' Grande, as the dwelling of the Querini was called, was two–thirds demolished and confiscated. The remains of the ancient palace, called Stallon, where in 1339 the public slaughter–house of the Rialto was lodged (later transformed into a prison on the upper floor and a poultry market on the ground floor) were, in 1907, used to erect, in false Gothic, a building to accommodate the fish market[190].

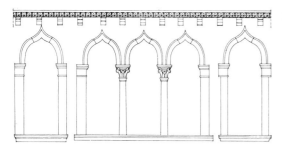

These remains are easily identified. Even if it is not possible to reconstruct from them the form of the ancient building, they are nevertheless of the greatest importance since it is possible to argue that they were in 1310 as we see them now, and that they are attributable to the second half of the thirteenth century, before the famous plot[191]. It is possible to recognize on the façade towards the Grand Canal a three–light window and two large sharp–pointed arches on the ground floor, on the side towards rio delle Beccarie two two–light windows and a single one, on the side towards campo delle Beccarie a three–light window and a single one, with other arches on the ground floor. The capitals are of the type with rosette, already widespread before the fourteenth century. A notable feature is the presence of the large arches on the ground floor, obviously Gothic and ogival, with Byzantine dentil border and moulded hollow, a profile of the end of the thirteenth century[192].

Two remarkable thirteenth–century façades of more modest houses, one with arch without fillet in salizzada S. Stae (S. Croce 1920), the other with a torus fillet in rio Terrà del Barba Frutarol (Cannaregio 4726)[193] are evidence, also in the 'minor' architecture, of the discreet nobility of this style, even without a particularly rigorous layout. The first has Romanesque bell capitals and a portal which is also Romanesque with semicircular terracotta lunette[194]. An aggregate posing an interesting problem of 'coexistence' is that of a house in calle dei Mercanti (S. Croce 1828–9) in which the two four–light windows, one above the other, displaced to the right, seem contemporaneous, with rosette capitals and the balcony on the extreme right. However, while the lower one is of the third order, the upper one has trefoil arches (of the fourth order). We are certainly at the beginning of the fourteenth century[195].

Among minor works of architecture, the most notable examples of these small aggregates are the two houses in campo S. Margherita at nos. 2961 and 2945 of Dorsoduro. The first has a three–light window displaced to the left, with a small balcony in the middle and a roof jutting out on buttresses (as in Palazzo Soranzo) while on the right there must have been two other windows, of a type similar to the one we saw in salizzada S. Stae. The pillars are high and narrow, the capitals with superimposed caulicoles, the ground floor with shops. The second house has a two–light window in the middle, supported by a pilaster between two windows. The upper cornice is much higher than that of the adjacent house (the low roof 'frowning' slightly over the oculi of the openings is a Romanesque characteristic). The arches are of a larger type and affect Gothic features.

It seems evident that the house on the right (no. 2961) must be more archaic (if not actually anterior), more of a thirteenth–century character[196], while the one on the left (no. 2945) is decidedly fourteenth century[197]. And it is not possible to bring together two better examples to make clear the course of the second order between the thirteenth and the fourteenth centuries.

A different type is displayed by a house in ruga Giuffa (Cast. 4898) on the second floor of which two paired two–light windows with, on their right, two single windows, stand in line from left to right; given the presence of truncated cube capitals, the whole may be considered of the thirteenth century[198].

A beautiful four–light window, born with the wall in which it opens, over a coeval arcade with architrave, may be seen in the courtyard of Casa Donà in campo S. Polo (S. Polo 2177). It is remarkable because ornamented by capitals of a type already mentioned, with large volutes surmounted by caulicoles (the large capitals of the ground floor are also of this type)[199].

Another beautiful four–light window of a still archaic mould, with capitals like the preceding one on a high square plinth[200], may be seen at the ponte della Corona (Cast. 4743).

Numerous examples, scattered fragments, are traceable in Venice, and they attest to the wide spread of this clearly individualized type[201]. A rare example in terracotta with double archivolt profile and obtruding row of voussoirs may be seen in calle Pasqualigo in Cannaregio. An extraordinarily similar motive is visible in the terracotta frieze of the transept in S. Zanipolo[202].

Certainly this aspect of Venetian architecture could have begun in the middle of the thirteenth century and then continued into the first decades of the fourteenth. And as the freer, more relaxed, less severe forms are found in the first decades of the fourteenth century, it is possible to propose a dating for those windows of the Doge's Palace which adorn the top

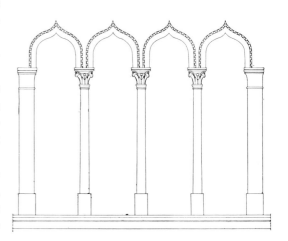

floor of the side facing the rio di Palazzo. Palazzo Ziani, completed in the second half of the twelfth century, must have undergone modifications if in a document of 1253[203] there is question of master–workers working *ad opus faciendum et repezandum palatium domini ducis* (and we may suppose that to this period belongs the eastern side of the Sala del Piovego, adorned by late Romanesque arcadings).

In 1292[204] there is mention of *facere Salam de supra canale*, probably the Sala del Maggior Consiglio which a document of 1255[205] lets us suppose was located on the ground floor, and which was enlarged in 1296[206].

There is probably a reference to this in a document of 14 July 1301 in which it is said that as the Sala del Maggior Consiglio is no longer adequate, it has been decided to enlarge it[207]. Sanudo says that in 1305 the Sala Grande[208] was being built. Finally, the date of completion of that room—1309—is transmitted to us by Sansovino and by the Sivos and Magno chronicles, together with that of 1301 attesting the beginning of the work under Pietro Gradenigo[209]. The same Sivos chronicle states that meetings were held there until 1423[210].

We have no precise clues today regarding the position of that room[211]. According to Sansovino it was beside the *Torresella*, namely that corner tower whose existence has for long been accepted and which is clearly visible in the well–known engraving by Reenwich[212]. It is not improbable that the vanished room, built in the first decade of the fourteenth century, was close to the tower if we consider the two windows–one with two lights and one with three lights of the third order–remaining on the top floor of the front on rio di Palazzo, undoubtedly a little earlier than the two large windows below them, the date of which is related to the building of the new Sala del Maggior Consiglio, towards the quay, which was ordered in 1340.

These openings (partly remade, but faithful to the original) display more elaborate profiles than those common to windows of this type which we have already considered. A dating to 1300–20 as put forward by Ruskin[213] is suggested also by the presence of a very archaic type of capital, and by the three horizontal ornaments (also in late Romanesque style) located one immediately under the above–mentioned windows, a second at half the height of the gallery on the quay side, the third in continuation of the marble cornice of the arcade, which is still clearly visible, and effectively corresponds to floors still remaining with some small differences in level on this eastern side corresponding to the corner tower, all residual traces of which towards the quay have now disappeared, but not the internal horizontal structures, certainly later than those of the old Ziani palace[214].

We have dwelt at length upon these valuable testimonies of the thirteenth century because they arose parallel to the spreading of Gothic church architecture in Venice and the Veneto which, incidentally, has not yet been studied by anyone in this particular set of circumstances. Fortunately, such an examination, even reduced to the minimum, is made superfluous by the observation that the Gothic arch of western origin had been widespread already for some time in the whole of Italy when the cusped arch of oriental origin appeared in Venice.

As far as Venice is concerned, a single example will suffice, and that is the presence, already at the beginning of the thirteenth century, of two pointed arches, clearly Gothic, on the door of the northern front of St. Mark's, which then disappeared in the middle of the thirteenth century under the marble incrustation[215]. It was inevitable that a kind of contamination between the cusped arch of oriental origin and the inflected Gothic of western origin should gradually take place.

It is very interesting to follow in Venice this process which was to prepare Venetian representational culture for the reception of entirely new forms.

The two single windows and the two–light window of Palazzo Bosso in S. Tomà (S. Polo 2862) where we find, perhaps for the first time, the small paterae placed very close to the extrados of arches of a laboured design, with archivolts too slender for the forced stretching of the arch, have an almost Gothic accent. The example is significant even if it is possible to displace prudently the date *ad libitum* within the fourteenth century. The Gothic elements here are the torus fillet along the edge of the intrados and the capital with rosettes. The upper cornice, already Gothic, very similar to that of Palazzo Moro at S. Bartolomeo, is perhaps coeval with the *piano nobile*[216]. The windows of Palazzo Bosso, in their ambiguity, display well the fundamental difference between the 'cusped' Islamic arch and the Gothic arch of western origin.

The pointed Islamic arch, in which the intrados also follows the course of the extrados, creates in Venice the conditions for the adoption of the inflected arch of western origin, which, as we shall see, will assert itself from the beginning of the fourteenth century.

That this decisive turning point occurred at the beginning of the fourteenth century had been already correctly affirmed more than a hundred years ago[217], and is confirmed today, because qualified scholars antedate that passage by a century[218], evidently thinking of the simple two–centred arch present—but we would say, not very widespread—in Venice in the thirteenth century. The alternative however (as evidenced by the imposing mass of examples in secular architecture, which almost ignores the non–inflected arch) is between the cusped arch of Islamic appearance and the inflected one of western origin. Shrewder and more far–seeing than all the others, Ruskin had already subtly distinguished the two forms—related but very different—concluding that at the end of the thirteenth century the window was ready for the formulation of the fifth order[219].

The third order, to use Ruskin's diction, spread also beyond the estuary. We see it in Padova, extolled in the two most beautiful belfries of the Santo erected in the second half of the thirteenth century[220], in Capodistria[221], in the two peculiar four–light windows, one above the other, of rather rough execution but powerful effect in the so–called Bembo Castle in valle d'Istria (perhaps of the advanced fourteenth century)[222], at Traù (Trogir) [223], at Spalato (Split)[224], and at Ragusa[225] (Dubrovnik). But in Dalmatia we are certainly dealing with retarded forms.

**1.** I quote the recent *Studi per una operante storia urbana di Venezia* by S. Muratori and P. Maretto, Rome, 1959–60.

**2.** G. Chierici *La chiesa di S. Satiro a Milano*, Milan 1942, figs 5 and 8. On the arch on pillars, see Ruskin, *The Stones of Venice* - fourth edition, 1886, II, p. 249.

**3.** *S. Bettini in Torcello*, Venice 1940, p. 47.

**4.** G. Lorenzetti, 1956, p. 491.

**5.** Selvatico, 1847, p. 73 et seq. and p. 81.

**6.** Ruskin, 1886, II, p. 188 et seq.

**7.** Toesca, 1927, p. 675, note 98: 'the arches with round-headed cornices may be referred to the beginning of the thirteenth century'.

**8.** Fiocco, 1949, p. 42.

**9.** Bettini, 1953, p. 45.

**10.** Demus, 1960, p. 116.

**11.** Demus, 1960, p. 102; Hubala, 1966, passim.

**12.** Maretto, 1959, Plate I (concerning the *palazzata* at S. Silvestro).

**13.** See Forlati, 1958, p. 667.

**14.** Cattaneo, 1890, p. 184.

**15.** Cattaneo, 1890, p. 188.

**16.** Cattaneo, 1890, p. 161.

**17.** Cattaneo, 1890, p. 128. Another cornice of this type may be found on Palazzo Minotto on the Grand Canal (Lorenzetti, 1956, p. 615). We consider late also the one in corte della Grana (Castello 2510) which connects with an element similar to the well-known one on the Drogdone House in Ravenna, with a scroll ornament (cf. Salmi, 1936, p. 51).

**18.** Cattaneo, 1890, p. 161. His opinion is still supported today (after Marzemin, 1937, pp. 333–4, who thought of the ninth-tenth centuries) by some art historians.

**19.** Elenco, 1905, p. 167, no. 340 (Dorsoduro 3422); Trincanato, 1948, pp. 255 et seq.; Maretto, 1960, p. 33 (to thirteenth century).

**20.** Elenco, 1905, p. 166, no. 137 (S. Polo 1767;) Maretto, 1960, pp. 7 and 35.

**21.** Maretto, 1960, p. 34, (Castello 4418).

**22.** *I sottoporteghi*, Paoletti, 1920, p. 92. See also Trincanato, 1948, p. 90.

**23.** *Chioggia, Granary*. The data are supplied by Tiozzo, 1926, p. 41. Previous literature makes it later by a year (Zanotto, 1847, p. 514; Selvatico, 1852, p. 278; Zanotto, 1856, p. 656; Hare, 1884, p. 167; Lorenzetti, 1956, p. 821). The building is now a fish market.

**24.** Elenco, 1905, p. 117, no. 151 (S. Polo 1946–9): to the fifteenth century. On eight square pilasters.

**25.** *I sottoporteghi*. In rio Terrà ai Frari (Hotel Alex), on square pilasters; in two porches side by side in corte del Taiapiera (S. Polo 1555); in the well-known house at Biri; in corte delle Ancore (Elenco, 1905, p. 6, no. 58; to the fourteenth century; S. Marco 899); in corte Paruta on rio di S. Pantalon (Elenco, 1905, p. 169, no. 370; Dorsoduro 3725; to the thirteenth century); on rio Menuo *(sottoportego de le colone;* S. Marco 1958–62); in calle Erizzo (Castello 4002); a long house in calle della Madonna (Cann. 4422–5, with buttresses and stone plates; the *sottoportego* of Ca' Dolfin at S. Polo; the one on rio di S. Felice (Cann. 3710–12) with round-headed and pointed arches, with capitals certainly of the thirteenth century, *il sottoportego Frizier a Castello*, etc.
Very often these passages are part of buildings of monumental character: thus in Palazzo Costantini (Dorsoduro 70); in Palazzo Benedetti (Cann. 4172–3) perhaps the most beautiful example of the merging of the various architectural elements; a building on fond. Manin in Murano; and so many other examples which we need not quote now. An example, unique of its kind, I believe, is represented by the corte delle Carampane, with three loggias one above the other (Tassini, 1863, 1915 ed., p. 145; the so-called 'of Ca' Rampani'; Elenco, 1905, p. 116, no. 146: S. Polo 1895c). To the fifteenth century belongs also the one, with rather rough capitals with thick leaves, in almost Renaissance style, in corte delle Muneghe (or delli Amadi) at the Miracoli: one of the most secret and isolated places at the time of Venice (Mothes, 1859, pp. 210–11: to 1300–40; Tassini, 1879, p. 85; Elenco, 1905, p. 202, no. 634; Cann. 6076–86; Lorenzetti, 1956, p. 329). Mention must also be made of the Foscari loggia in the Doge's Palace, by Bartolomeo Bon: the most sumptuous example of the kind.
A late example (very much restored) gives on the corte di palazzo Gheltoff-Alberà (S. Marco 3366; corte Corner 3378); see Elenco, 1905 p. 17, no. 262; Chiminelli, 1912, p. 231; Lorenzetti, 1956, p. 490. The whole building, with the uncovered staircase, is attributed to the fifteenth century.

**26.** *The columns in the Piazzetta*. Tradition attributes to Niccolò Barattiero the erection of the two columns at the time of Ziani (1172–8); but the two great capitals manifestly recall those of Palazzo Falier at SS. Apostoli, which we consider of the second half of the thirteenth century (which, naturally, does not at all exclude that the Ca' Falier capitals may be old ones re-used). The 1329 date offered by Zucchini (1785, II, pp. 312–13) is certainly due to a mistake. To the excellent article on Barattiero contributed by Elena Bassi to the *Dizionario Biografico degli Italiani*, VI, 1964, p. 7, should be added: Zanotto, I, 1853, p. 26; Bettini, in *Arte Veneta*, 1961, p. 275 (there is no doubt that the sculptor of the bases is a Lombard of the second half of the twelfth century).

**27.** P. Toesca, 1927, p. 628.

**28.** Tassini, 1879, pp. 7 et seq. (the information is transmitted by the Magno chronicle). See also: Zanotto, 1847, p. 420; Selvatico, 1852, p. 233 (to the twelfth century); Zanotto, 1856, p. 597 (to the eleventh century; he remarks that 'the atrium columns have as bases reversed Corinthian capitals taken from buildings of late Roman times'); Bettini, 1953, fig. 43a (to the thirteenth century); Miozzi, 1957, I, pp. 446–7 (to the twelfth century); Forlati, 1958, p. 668.

**29.** Schnaase had already noticed (1876, VII, p. 216) the presence in these buildings of coupled columns and capitals with buds in the typical nordic form of the twelfth century.

**30.** E. Arslan, *L'architettura romanica veronese*, Verona 1939, Plate III.

**31.** Op. cit., Plate 131.

**32.** Cecchelli, *Zara*, Rome 1932, pp. 20 et seq. (reconstructed after 1202 and consecrated in 1285); Brunelli, 1913, pp. 411 et seq.; Tamaro, 1919, p. 351.

**33.** The pairs of colonnettes of the blind gallery are certainly the remains of the structure begun in 1225 and utilized by that master mason Pietro Paolo who in 1368 was engaged on the reconstruction of the Duomo.

**34.** Toesca, op cit., p. 840 (two pulpits are confirmed to belong to the thirteenth century).

**35.** See good illustrations of this little known and studied part in: *La cattedrale di Ferrara*, Ferrara 1955, (Plates XIV, L and LII accompanying an essay by A. Giglioli).

**36.** *Murano, Palazzo da Mula*, Zanetti, 1866, p. 91; Lorenzetti, 1956, pp. 789–90 (to the twelfth-thirteenth centuries).

**37.** *Palazzo Loredan*. See, among the many references: Zanotto, 1847, p. 420; 1856, p. 597 (to the eleventh century); Selvatico, 1852, p. 233 (to the twelfth century); Schnaase, 1876, VII, pp. 217–18; Bettini, 1953, fig. 43*b* (to the thirteenth century); Forlati, 1958, p. 668 (to the twelfth-thirteenth centuries).

**38.** *Fondaco dei Turchi*, 1847 pp. 418 et seq., Zanotto, 1856, p. 608. The attribution to the tenth century was adopted by Raschdorff, 1903, Plate I.

**39.** P. Selvatico, 1847, pp. 75–6; Idem, 1852, p. 236.

**40.** De Beylié, 1902, pp. 157–8.

**41.** Ruskin, 1886, II, p. 249.

**42.** Schnaase, 1876, VII, pp. 217 et seq.

**43.** Molmenti, 1925, p. 273.

**44.** K. M. Swoboda, 1924, p. 195.

**45.** Fiocco, 1949, p. 42. He places also the Loredan and Farsetti Palaces in the twelfth century.

**46.** Mariacher, 1954, p. 46.

**47.** Sagredo–Berchet, 1860.

**48.** C. Ricci, *L'Arte nell'Italia settentrionale*, Bergamo 1910.

**49.** Toesca, 1927, p. 629.

**50.** Miozzi, 1957, I, p. 451.

**51.** Demus, 1960, p. 102.

**52.** Forlati, 1958, pp. 667–8.

**53.** Muraro, 1957, p. 29.

**54.** Ackerman, 1963, p. 13.

**55.** Bassi, 1962, I, p. 32.

**56.** Maretto, 1960, p. 32.

**57.** Tassini, 1879, pp. 36 and 45; See also: Gruyer, 1887, p. 390 (who, at pp. 397–8, offers evidence concerning the state before 1870).

**58.** Lorenzetti, 1956, p. 638.

**59.** *Palazzo Donà Dolcetti*, G. Mariacher, 1954, p. 48 (the dating concerns the capitals). See also: Bettini, 1953, fig. 64*b* (to the thirteenth century); Miozzi, 1957, I, p. 426.

**60.** *Ca' Barzizza*, see the study by Torres, 1937, p. 13.

**61.** Toesca, 1927, p. 675, note 98; Bettini, 1953, fig. 46*a* (to the thirteenth century).

**62.** An excellent reading of this building is made possible by Giorgio Scattolin's essay: *Le case - Fondaco sul Canal Grande*, Venice, 1961, pp. 47 et seq.

**63.** H. von der Gabelentz, 1903, p. 117.

**64.** *Casa in rio S. Pantalon*, Marzemin, 1912, p. 328.

**65.** Lorenzetti, 1956, p. 560.

**66.** Toesca, 1927, p. 628.

**67.** Molmenti, I, pp. 227–8.

**68.** Fiocco, 1930, p. 65.

**69.** Bettini, 1953, fig. 42.

**70.** Forlati, 1958, pp. 667–8.

**71.** Trincanato, 1948, pp. 251 et seq. See also: Miozzi, 1957, I, p. 428.

**72.** Already for Ruskin (1886, III, 350) and then for Gabelentz (1903, p. 117), it is of the twelfth century; for Molmenti (1926, I, p. 278) of the thirteenth.

**73.** In spite of the archaic-looking characters, I do not consider the portal of Ca' Barzizza of another period than the other thirteenth-century remains of the building: the abaci are thirteenth-century, like those of the multi-light window of the first floor, where we also find the same torus profiles.
The simple round-headed arch is widely used in Venice in the thirteenth century, in the Padan way, next to the stilted arch. The most famous example is in the north wing of the St. Mark's portico, later covered with marble incrustations but which, on an extensive testing, revealed itself organized with three-light windows, two-light windows and arcading of the early thirteenth century (now hidden), in terracotta of clear Padan inspiration (Demus, 1960, pp. 76 et seq.).

**74.** Attributed to the thirteenth century by Tassini, 1879, p. 176 and by Lorenzetti, 1956, p. 373.

**75.** To which may be added the beautiful basin in the Budapest Museum, attributed by Balogh to the beginning of the thirteenth century (J. Balogh, *Studi sulla collezione di Sculture* in 'Acta Historiae Artium', XII, 1966, p. 233).

**76.** *Palazzo da Mula a Murano*. Forlati, 1926–7, p. 50 (on the restoration).

**77.** *Casa Giustiniani and Ca' Grande dei Barozzi*. Demus, 1960, p. 102; Fundamental on these two buildings no longer in existence is the article published in 1933 by Giulio Lorenzetti in the *Miscellanea Supino*, in which a date around 1164 is advanced. See also Forlati, 1958, p. 667.

**78.** Selvatico, 1847, pp. 74–5; Idem, 1852, pp. 74–5.

**79.** *Casa Giustiniani and Ca' Grande dei Barozzi*. Contrary to the current opinions which, as usual, make the dating oscillate between the eleventh and the thirteenth centuries, Demus (1960, p. 102) is for an attribution to the thirteenth.

**80.** Demus, 1960, pp. 100 and 141. Already Ruskin in his time was reminded, concerning the palaces, of the proportions of certain arches of the façade of St. Mark's Basilica. (Ruskin, 1886, II, 126).

**81.** Elenco, 1905, p. 50. no. 342 (Castello 4498).

**82.** Fontana, 1845, Plate 64; Elenco, 1905, p. 99, no. 572 (Cann. 5741).

**83.** Molmenti, 1925, p. 278 (to the twelfth?).

**84.** Ruskin, 1886, II, p. 254.

**85.** Elenco, 1905, p. 115, no. 116. This building aspect has been well clarified by Maretto (1960, pp. 2–10).

**86.** Maretto, 1960, pp. 16–17.

**87.** Molmenti, 1925, I, p. 292.

**88.** Molmenti, op. cit. p. 292.

**89.** According to Maretto (1960, p. 6) the rear front of the *portego* in these houses was presumably defined by a great vault or by an arcade, as in 'Ca' del Papa' at S. Silvestro (no. 1116), now completely altered.

**90.** For further details, see the excellent treatments by Trincanato (1948, pp. 51 et seq.) and Maretto (1960, pp. 5, 16, 18, 29 and 32); and the valuable Plate I with the plans of the *palazzata* in S. Silvestro clearly visible also in the view by De Barbari. Also the establishment at the beginning, as we have said, of the 'block' type (Palazzo Loredan), in parallel with the more articulate structures which will be dear to the Gothic, is made clear there. On the *portego* in T see also: Mariacher, 1951, p. 155.

**91.** Maretto, 1960, pp. 7 and 8.

**92.** *Shops. (Botteghe).* Ancient shops, with one or more openings for selling and an entrance door, are common in Venice from the thirteenth century onwards. In calle della Passione, at Frari, 2987 (of the fourteenth century); in fond. Briati, Dorsoduro 2372; in Casselleria, at S. Maria Formosa; in calle dei Botteri, S. Polo 1553; in calle del Campaniel, at S. Polo 1757 and 1763; in salizzada S. Lio (Castello 5071–6); in calle della Madonna (S. Marco 3613), with a wooden cable ornament; and many others. See on this subject: Trincanato, 1948, pp. 88 and 148–50.

**93.** Hubala, 1966, pp. 610–11.

**94.** Idem, p. 611.

**95.** See: Trincanato, 1948, pp. 90 et seq.

**96.** See in this connection, A. Paronchi (*Studi su la dolce prospettiva*, Milan 1964, pp. 468 et seq.). That it should have gone much too far in its studies on these artists-scientists of the early Tuscan fifteenth century, to the point of offending the intelligence of the poetic sense of their work and of speaking, no less, at times, than of 'semi-artists' is saddening for a criticism whose task is to distinguish and above all to create art history (the 'semi-artist' would be Paolo Uccello). Similarly, it is certainly legitimate to study the technical processes known to the builders of the Gothic cathedrals, but here also it is not proper to confuse the history of technology (or engineering) with the history of art: buildings which are disintegrating (or have even collapsed) because of the incompetence of the builders are, and remain, without reservations, worthy of a historical-artistic treatment.

**97.** Bettini, 1953, p. 35.

**98.** Ackerman, 1963, p. 16.

**99.** R. E. Trincanato, *Venezia minore*, Milan 1948; S. Muratori, *Studi per una operante storia urbana* di Venezia, Rome 1960; P. Maretto, L'edilizia gotica veneziana, Rome 1960.

**100.** *Houses with two towers.* The houses with two towers were presumably of the Romanesque period (eleventh-thirteenth centuries). A house 'of the two towers' at S. Pantalon was given in 1439 to Francesco Sforza (on the site where Palazzo Foscari was erected later) (Tassini, 1879, p. 167); Palazzo Molin on riva degli Schiavoni (Castello 4112) mentioned by Petrarch who lived there (1362, *geminas angulares turres*) was called 'of the two towers' (Zanetti, *Dell'origine di alcune arti ecc.*, Venice 1758, p. 60; Tassini, 1863, 1915 ed., pp. 246 and 667; Tassini, 1879, p. 130; Elenco, 1905. p. 48, no. 304; Mariacher, 1954, p. 44; Bassi, 1962, I, p. 32); a house with two towers (which gave its name to the rio delle due torri) did exist, it seems, in 1105 at S. Maria Mater Domini (Dezan, 1821, Plate 22; Tassini, 1863, ed. 1915, pp. 254-6; Mariacher, 1951, p. 1: it was the original palace of the Pesaro at S. Stae); it is believed (Ongaro, 1935, p. 9; Bassi, 1962, I, p. 32) that the *palatium comunis* erected by Ziani by the Quay also had two towers, and the structure of at least one of them has been discerned quite some time ago at the corner between the façade on the Quay and the rio di Palazzo. The original Palazzo dei Rettori in Ragusa was also of the type with two towers (Freeman, 1881, p. 245; Karaman, 1952, p. 52).

**101.** K. M. Swoboda, 1924.

**102.** Idem, 1924, p. 77 et seq. and p. 133.

**103.** Idem, p. 195.

**104.** Swoboda, *Palazzi antichi e medioevali*, in 'Bolletino del Centro di Studi per la storia dell'architettura', no. 11, Rome 1957, p. 3 et seq. See also R. Paribeni, *Le dimore dei potentiores nel Basso Impero* in 'Römische Mitteilungen' LV 1940, p. 132 et seq.; Ackerman, 1963, pp. 14 and 15 (with extensive bibliography).

**105.** Swoboda, 1957, pp. 142 and 148. He is less persuasive when he sees in the western façade of Amida (for Guyer of 600-50) a link in this chain.

**106.** Bettini, 1953, pp. 36-7.

**107.** Bettini, 1953, p. 37; Idem in *Arte Veneta*, 1961, p. 269.

**108.** Bettini, op. cit. p. 38.

**109.** See also on the subject: E. B. Thomas, *Römische Villen in Pannonien*, Budapest 1964, p. 363. Bettini mentions the villas which existed along the Adriatic littoral, from Ravenna to Pola, of which, however, very little is known (1953, p. 36). In the villa of Mogorilo, illustrated by Dyggve (*Drei Paläste* etc., in 'Festschrift Swoboda', Vienna 1959, p. 83 et seq.), of the fourth century, the façade was turned towards the inner courtyard.
Only a wider and better documented case study could throw light on the diversity of types, which we so far ignore.

**110.** G. Fiocco, 1930, pp. 65-6; Idem, 1949, p. 39 et seq., Bettini, 1953, p. 35 et seq.; Idem in *Arte Veneta* 1961, p. 269.

**111.** Ackerman (1963, p. 16) adheres to the 'exarchal' thesis and sees in the palace of Galeata near Forlì another proof of Ravennate influence.

**112.** Lorenzetti, 1933, p. 27.

**113.** Demus, 1960, p. 102.

**114.** Trincanato, 1948, p. 127 et seq.; Lorenzetti, 1956, p. 356, (to the thirteenth century).

**115.** Fiocco, 1930, p. 76.

**116.** The wooden corbels which support the beams covering, besides the great arch, the calle delle Vele have a typically angular profile sharply contrasting with the curved ones which begin, I believe, in the second half of the fourteenth century, and this is certainly one of the most ancient examples of the kind.

**117.** *Palazzo Priuli-Bon: water-side entrance.* The capitals have an unusual Corinthian character of their own and the arches have very simple mouldings with a terracotta voussoir archivolt. As far as I know, only Lorenzetti (1956, p. 634) mentions it, assigning it to the thirteenth century.

**118.** *Palazzo Businello.* A recent restoration has demonstrated the structural homogeneity of this façade; believing that the loggia had been mutilated, Ruskin wrote (1886, II, p. 120) that only the great central arches remained. Toesca puts the building in the early years of the fourteenth century (1927, p. 675, Mezzanino note); Bettini, 1953, fig. 47a (to the thirteenth century).

**119.** *Casa Donà* at S. Polo 1426 (*Della Madonnetta*). Selvatico, 1852, p. 232 (to the twelfth century); Ruskin, 1886, II, pp. 120 and 389; III, p. 285; Zanotto, 1856, p. 594 (to the twelfth century); Bettini, 1953, fig. 47b (to the thirteenth century); Miozzi, 1957, I, p. 425 (of the fourteenth with some more ancient elements).

**120.** Demus, 1960, pp. 101-2.

**121.** S. Bettini, *L'arte alla fine del mondo antico*, Padua 1948, p. 16.

**122.** A two-light window in calle Marcona (Dorsoduro 3886), a three-light window in corte Gregorina (Elenco, 1905, p. 6, no. 60) (S. Marco 994a), another three-light window in campo dei Santi Filippo e Giacomo (Castello 4523), a two-light window in corte Ca' Coppo (S. Marco 4351) at S. Luca; another in corte del Teatro (Elenco, 1905, p. 23, no. 387, S. Marco 4624, attributed to the twelfth century; Lorenzetti, 1956, p. 355); The round arch of the entrance to corte del Bianchi (S. Polo 1508) with voussoir archivolt (without pillars); equally the two-light windows opening in the already mentioned Romanesque structure behind Palazzo Da Mula in Murano. These are examples which can be identically found on the Venetian mainland and along the Adriatic coast (See the two-light window, certainly of the thirteenth century, reproduced by Salmi, 1936, p. 22).

**123.** Ruskin, II, p. 249; II, p. 245 (Plate XV).

**124.** A very accurate survey, with good photographs, by G. Scattolin (1961, p. 17 et seq.) allows a perfect reading of this façade.

**125.** Ruskin, II, p. 253; III, p. 277.

**126.** Tassini, 1863, p. 380; Idem, 1870, p. 7 et seq.; Idem, 1879, p. 33.

**127.** Lorenzetti, 1956, p. 631.

**128.** Toesca, 1927, p. 675.

**129.** Salmi, 1936, p. 51.

**130.** Trincanato, 1948, pp. 70-1.

**131.** Fiocco, 1949, p. 42.

**132.** Bettini, 1953, p. 39 and fig. 41.

**133.** Demus, 1960, p. 102.

**134.** Scattolin, 1961, p. 18. See also, for a complete bibliography: Zanotto, 1847, pp. 421-2; Selvatico, 1852, p. 235 (gives a drawing of the windows); Zanotto, 1856, p. 101 (Palazzo Zorzi); Marzemin, 1912, p. 333 ('the upper floors' to the fourteenth century); Molmenti, 1925. p. 273, (with reservations to the ninth century); Forlati, 1958, p. 668 (to the thirteenth); Miozzi, 1957, I, p. 429; Maretto, 1960, pp. 6, 18 and 31; Muraro, 1953, p. 30 (to the thirteenth century).

**135.** Dated to about 1000 by Cattaneo (1877, p. 146).

**136.** We say *should* because of the uncertainty which, after Cattaneo's ascription (1889, ed. of 1891, p. 275) to the ninth century, this decorative element causes. I would point out in this connection, without going deeply into the matter, that an element akin to the Ca' da Mosto cornice is found in the decoration of the arches of the western front of St. Mark's, with the almost identical motif of large reversed leaves; and there is no doubt that these are of 1230-50 (Demus, 1960, p. 141).

**137.** Kugler, 1858-9, II, p. 45.

**138.** De Beylié, 1902, p. 157.

**139.** Fontana, 1845, p. 283.

**140.** Selvatico, 1856, p. 216.

**141.** Rivoira, 1914, pp. 116 and 154.

**142.** Ruskin, II, p. 250.

**143.** Selvatico, 1847, pp. 95-6.

**144.** Cattaneo, 1881, p. 203.

**145.** Lorenzetti, 1956, p. 171.

**146.** Demus, 1960, p. 144.

**147.** Demus, 1960, p. 144.

**148.** Demus, 1960, pp. 146-7.

**149.** Demus, 1960, pp. 104-5.

**150.** Demus, 1960, p. 141.

**151.** Demus, 1960, p. 141.

**152.** Cattaneo, 1881, p. 188; Demus, 1960, p. 123, note 169.

**153.** Demus, 1960, pp. 147-8.

**154.** Planiscig, 1915, p. 15.

**155.** Hubala-Tigler, 1966, p. 221.

**156.** Demus, 1960, p. 100.

**157.** Demus, 1960, p. 103.

**158.** Demus, 1960, pp. 104-5; the mainland Gothic appears at the beginning of the thirteenth century, precisely in St. Mark's, in the two arches above the door of the northern façade; then disappears under the marble incrustation (Demus, fig. 6); and those arches were of the same time as the late Romanesque elements revealed by that same façade, of which we have already spoken.

**159.** Demus, 1960, pp. 147-8, fig. 24.

**160.** *Casa del Salvadego.* For Lorenzetti (1956, p. 458) of the end of the thirteenth century; for Fiocco (1930, p. 78) of the fourteenth century. Cf. Marzemin, 1912, p. 331 (to the thirteenth century) Miozzi, 1957, I, p. 431. On the restorations which, in 1926, brought to light the original parts of the loggia, see: Forlati, 1926–7, pp. 50, 58; and Torres, 1937, p. 13.

**161.** Maretto, (1960, p. 21) denies to Venice 'the façade... as a continuous wall, representing it as a composition of enclosing and binding elements' (the openings framed) and sees, in the end, 'the wall between them... as a buffer and a welding'. We are inclined to see in the colour areas offered by the brick walls the virtues of a patina certainly not foreseen by the builder. Brick alternating with tuff, on the Romanesque of Verona, is, however, an intended colour with chromatic function; but brick is more skilfully used in Verona than in Venice, as an element to be kept in view.

**162.** *Casa in rio delle Beccarie.* Nothing has been written about this façade; the other Gothic façade, at the back, gives on calle dei Botteri at no. 1565.

**163.** *Ca' Soranzo, o dell' Angelo.* Ruskin, 1886, II, pp. 253–4; Tassini, 1873, pp. 328–9; Idem, 1879, p. 68.

**164.** Maretto, 1960, pp. 16 and 34 (end of the thirteenth century).

**165.** *Calle del Rimedio,* Cann. 4419. Elenco, 1905, pp. 49, no. 326; Marzemin, 1912, p. 331 (end of the thirteenth); Forlati, 1926–7, p. 60 (on the restoration); Toesca, 1950, p. 150 (puts the whole in the fourteenth century on the strength of the well-known angel relief on the outside); Lorenzetti, 1956, p. 362 (end of the thirteenth and beginning of the fourteenth century); Miozzi, 1957, I, p. 432.

**166.** *Ca' Falier ai SS. Apostoli.* Scattolin, 1961, p. 33 et seq.

**167.** Zanotto, 1847, p. 421 (to the eleventh century); Selvatico, 1847, p. 97. Idem, 1852, p. 143 (to the thirteenth century); Ruskin, 1886, II, pp. 253–4; Plate XV; III, p. 277, Plate II, fig. 7 (first half of the thirteenth century); Mothes, 1859, pp. 151–2; 1220–50; Elenco, 1905, p. 98, no. 562; Molmenti, 1925. I, p. 277 (to the twelfth/thirteenth centuries); Lorenzetti, 1956, p. 393 (to the thirteenth); Fiocco, 1930, p. 77; Trincanato, 1948, p. 72 (to the thirteenth century); Toesca, 1950, p. 150 (to the fourteenth century); Maretto, 1960, pp. 19, 31.

**168.** *Palazzo Zane at S. Maria M.D.* Tassini, 1863, 1915 ed., p. 437; Idem, 1879, pp. 289–90.

**169.** Elenco, 1905, p. 141, no. 204; Lorenzetti, 1956, p. 467; Muratori, 1960, p. 81; Maretto, 1960, p. 19.

**170.** Maretto, 1960, pp. 74–8.

**171.** Elenco, 1905, p. 90, no. 433: to the thirteenth century.

**172.** *Calle Larga dei Proverbi.* Elenco, 1905, p. 90, no. 433 (to the thirteenth)

**173.** *Three-light window in rio delle Beccarie.* This is the house giving on calle dei Botteri at no. 1537 (Elenco, 1905, p. 115, no. 119: to the fifteenth century) which we shall mention shortly.

**174.** Ruskin, 1886, II, p. 254.

**175.** *Houses in calle del Paradiso.* See: Tassini, 1863, 1915 ed., pp. 517–8; Lorenzetti, 1956; p. 356; Trincanato, 1948, p. 136 et seq.; Muratori, 1960, p. 13 ('a single plan, of the end of the fourteenth century'); Maretto, 1960, pp. 60–1 (a complex of 'late Byzantine' origin). The two buildings

certainly go back to the end of the thirteenth century. The stone which can be read towards the salizzada San Lio: 1407 DIE ULT. DE ZUGNO FO COMENZADO QUESTE CAXE SOTO MISSIER DON ANDREA DE POMPOXA GASTALDO PIER ZANE DE CONTERIS (1407 last day of June were begun these houses under Messer Andrea de Pomposa, Steward Pier Zane de Conteris) cannot mean the two ends towards rio di S. Maria Formosa, but work begun somewhere else. It may well be that in this year 1407, the Pomposan monks may have put in hand the carving of the arch towards the canal with the double image of the Virgin. The coats of arms of the Foscari and the Mocenigo were certainly added later, when the whole complex became the property of the two families, as Tassini justly thinks (1879, p. 94).
Lorenzetti (1956, p. 356) also thinks of the beginning of the fifteenth century, differing in this from the conflicting opinions of eminent scholars, and we consider him to be right.

**176.** Elenco, 1905, p. 111, no. 75; Lorenzetti, 1956, p. 603.

**177.** A window in campiello della Chiesa at S. Marina (Castello 6055–6) (Elenco, 1905, pp. 59 and 515).

**178.** Here are some examples: salizzada Zusto, S. Croce 1362a, two windows, together with fourth and fifth order elements of a later date (Elenco, 1905, p. 136, no. 127); calle del Cristo at S. Angelo, S. Marco 3576 (three windows); campo S. Zan Degolà, S. Croce 1714 (two windows); fond. Alberti at S. Barnaba, Dorsoduro 3130–1 (two windows); fond. Madonna dell'Orto, S. Marco 3458 (four windows); salizzada del Pistor at SS. Apostoli, Cann. 4555, a three-light window and two windows in line on rio della Fava; two four-light windows one above the other at the ponte di S. Andrea (Cann. 4130) displaced to the left, of noble proportions (Elenco, 1905, p. 87, no. 372, 4131a); rio Terrà at Frari, S. Polo 2610 (one window). The type is mostly the one with the smooth archivolt bordered on the outside by a torus profile. I do not know how faithful is the restoration of a Casa Monico in campo S. Lio (*Un restauro ecc.*, 1929–30). A rather late example (or the result of a reconstruction) is the lower three-light window of Palazzo Benzi Zenchini (Cann. 3459).

**179.** See a reproduction in: Ferrari-Antoniazzo, 1955, p. 26.

**180.** See: A. Giglioli, *La Cattedrale di Ferrara,* Ferrara, 1935, pp. 209–10; Plates LIV, LVI, LVIII, LXIV, LXV, LXVI and LXXII. The capitals, partly with truncated cubes, are also thirteenth century. I am indebted to my son Ermanno for pointing out to me this purely Venetian element on the side of the Ferrarese cathedral.

**181.** *Palazzo Lion.* Selvatico, 1852, p. 235 (to the thirteenth century); Zanotto, 1856, p. 601 (to the twelfth century); Ruskin, 1886, I, p. 248; II, pp. 25 and 255; Tassini, 1893, 1915 ed., p. 608; Elenco, 1905, p. 98, no. 568 (Cann. 5701; corte del Remer); Idem, p. 98, no. 567 (on rio di San Giovanni Crisostomo a window and a three-light window); Lorenzetti, 1956, p. 392 (to the thirteenth century); Toesca, 1927, p. 675, no. 98 (to the thirteenth century); Bettini, 1953, fig. 5b (considers Coptic the basket capital re-used here); Maretto, 1960, p. 32 (typical example of a more ancient

house with the front pulled back from the Grand Canal).

**182.** *Palazzo Priuli-Bon.* Ruskin, 1886, p. 255; Lorenzetto, 1956, p. 634 (says it has been radically remodelled; to the fifteenth century); Miozzi, 1957, I, p. 427; Maretto, 1960, p. 32 (considers the upper framing, probably fifteenth-century'). The capitals appear to be really thirteenth-century.

**183.** *Casa Bragadin-Favretto.* Quadri, 1834, Plate 12; Elenco, 1905, p. 142, no. 218 (S. Croce, calle della Rosa 2232); the string-course cornice is attributed to the ninth century; Lorenzetti, 1956, p. 632 (to the fourteenth century; the string-course cornice to the eleventh century).

**184.** *Palazzo Vitturi.* Tassini, 1879, p. 246 (Ludovico della Torre, Patriarch of Aquileia, stayed there in 1359); Marini, 1905, p. 82 (to the fourteenth century); Elenco, 1905, p. 55, no. 427 (to the thirteenth century); Marzemin, 1912, p. 331; Lorenzetti, 1956, p. 381; Bettini, 1953, fig. 57b (to the fourteenth century); Mariacher, 1954, p. 48 (to the thirteenth century); Miozzi, 1957, I, pp. 436 and 457, note 55; Maretto, 1960, p. 19 and Plate XXXI (plan).

**185.** *Palazzo Zorzi-Bon.* We refer to the rear side of Palazzo Zorzi-Bon at S. Severo (Ruskin, 1886, II, p. 256), mentions this small façade among the 'most superb examples of that order' [the third!] in Venice; see also Zanotto, 1856, p. 210; Tassini, 1863, 1915 ed., p. 40; Idem, 1879, p. 251; Elenco, 1905, p. 52, nos. 386–7; Lorenzetti, 1956, p. 363 (to the thirteenth century).

**186.** *Palazzo Moro.* Ruskin, 1886, II, p. 256 (to the thirteenth century); Elenco, 1905, p. 26, no. 449 (to the thirteenth century); Lorenzetti, 1956, p. 390 (to the fourteenth century); Toesca, 1950, p. 150 (to the fourteenth century); Maretto, 1960, p. 19; Hubala, 1966, p. 743 (to the fourteenth century).

**187.** See also Trincanato, 1948, p. 83.

**188.** *Palazzo Sagredo at S. Sofia.* Ruskin, 1886, II, p. 257, II, pp. 343–4. See also: Fontana, 1845, Plate 22; Zanotto, 1856, p. 603 (to the thirteenth century); Musatti, 1905, p. 211 (to the thirteenth century); Marini, 1905, p. 85 (the first floor windows not later than the thirteenth century); Elenco, 1905, p. 87, no. 383 (to the thirteenth century); Lorenzetti, 1956, p. 633 (to the thirteenth century); Miozzi, 1957, I, p. 434; Maretto, 1960, p. 32.

**189.** *Palazzo Michiel dalle Colonne.* Lorenzetti, 1956, p. 418

**190.** *Palazzo Querini.* Selvatico, 1852, p. 193 (to the thirteenth century); Zanotto, 1856, p. 602 (to the thirteenth century); Tassini, 1863, 1915 ed., pp. 68 and 532, note 1; Miozzi, 1957, I, p. 457. Not far from the houses of the Querini (at nos. 203–4) were the houses of the Ziani, in campo C. Battisti, of the fourteenth century (Elenco, 1905, p. 107, no. 7; Hubala, 1966, p. 747).

**191.** See Tassini, 1863, ed. 1915, p. 575.

**192.** *Palazzo Querini Secondo.* Ruskin, 1886, II, pp. 225–6: 'the most perfect examples' of the third order; a statement which, today, should perhaps be attenuated; he did not think them later than about 1250. Molmenti (1905, I, pp. 69 and 277) thought them of the twelfth and thirteenth centuries; Elenco (1905, p. 108, no. 16) puts them in the fourteenth; Lorenzetti (1956, p. 464) in the thirteenth; Bettini (1953, fig. 57a) in the fourteenth century. See also Torres, 1937, p. 14 (with the plans).

**193.** *House in rio Terrà Barba Frutarol.* Elenco, 1905, p. 92, no. 459.

**194.** *House in salizzada S. Stae,* 1920. Lorenzetti, 1956, p. 470 (end of the thirteenth century); Maretto, 1960, p. 7 (he finds there a plan in L, already established in the archaic period, without traversing hall).

**195.** *House in calle dei Mercanti,* 1828-9. Elenco, 1905, p. 138, no. 170.

**196.** *House in campo S. Margherita, Dorsoduro 2961.* Elenco, 1905, p. 165, no. 301 (to the fourteenth century); Trincanato, 1948, p. 256 et seq. (to the fourteenth century).

**197.** *House in campo S. Margherita, Dorsoduro 2945.* Elenco, 1905, p. 165, no. 300 (to the fourteenth century); Trincanato, 1948, p. 256 et seq. (to the fourteenth century); Lorenzetti (1956, p. 556) mentions the two houses and ascribes them to the fourteenth-fifteenth centuries).

**198.** *House in Ruga Giuffa 4898* Elenco, 1905, p. 52, no. 385 (to the fourteenth century).

**199.** *Casa Donà in campo S. Polo.* Maretto, 1960, p. 46 and Plates XIII and XIII bis (we note that the four-light window is not an addition because it was formed together with the wall on which leans the Gothic staircase, evidently later in time).

**200.** *Ponte della Corona,* 4743. Elenco, 1905, p. 52, no. 371 (to the thirteenth century).

**201.** Of the type decorated with dentils, I mention here only a four-light window in ruga Giuffa (Cast. 4745) with rosette capitals (columns and a pilaster). Cf.: Elenco, 1905, p. 52, no. 372 (Lion coats of arms are mentioned). The portal lunette nearby would take us, however, to the middle of the fourteenth century. But here is a list of architectural fragments of this order with smooth archivolt and a torus listel: a four-light window in campo S. Maria Zobenigo (S. Marco 2466) with three Romanesque capitals on shafts of ancient marble, perhaps already of the fourteenth century (for Maretto, 1960, p. 7, of the second half of the fourteenth century); another (S. Marco 2806), certainly more archaic, with capitals with caulicoles, in campo S. Stefano (Elenco 1905, p. 14, no. 205); a third in campo S. Angelo (S. Marco 3567-8) (Elenco, 1905, p. 12, no. 173); another four-light window on the façade on rio della Pergola at ponte del Cristo (S. Croce 2047a: Palazzo Zanetti); a three-light window at ponte dell'Agnello (S. Croce 2278-9) with rosette capitals, of an antique type, perhaps of the early fourteenth century (Elenco, 1905, p. 142, no. 225: to the end of the fourteenth century); a three-light window in calle delle Oche (S. Croce 1036) of which we shall speak again later; a three-light window in campo S. Moisè (S. Marco 1463/4) with truncated cube capitals (Elenco, 1905, p. 7, no. 92); a three-light window on the façade beyond the *sottoportego del Torniben* (S. Marco 2624) with capitals with superposed caulicoles and octagonal bases (and also two windows on the façade in calle Zaguri); a three-light window of noble proportions with capitals with superposed caulicoles, above a great entrance arch, round-headed and with a smooth archivolt with listel, on fond. Moro (Cann. 2447) remains of a complex later altered, perhaps still of the thirteenth century (Elenco, 1905, p. 78, no. 212),

a three-light window (transferred?) in the court-yard of Hotel Gabrielli on riva degli Schiavoni; the remnants of various types in calle dei Botteri (S. Polo 1540) where again there is the problem of the coexistence of archaic (third order) and late (fifth order) forms. It is that same house with façade on rio delle Beccarie which we have examined; Elenco, 1905, p. 115, no. 119.) The two-light window in calle del Forno (S. Marco 2678) supported by a pilaster in the middle and with more richly shaped archivolt (Elenco, 1905, p. 13, no. 192); a two-light window in calle della Testa with thirteenth-century capital (Elenco, 1905, p. 67, no. 6: Cann. 6217); a two-light window in campo S. Angelo; a two-light window in corte Morosina with torus profile (belonging to the building, more ancient, on corte del Milion); a two-light window in calle dei Saoneri (S. Polo 2721), the graceless execution of which shows a delay of at least a century; two single windows (Elenco, 1905, p. 11, no. 150) in campo del Traghetto at S. Maria Zobenigo (S. Marco 2465), a window in corte del Teatro at S. Luca (S. Marco 4623); a window in calle del Tamossi at S. Aponal (S. Polo 1512); in calle Bon (Castello 4902), in campiello di Ca' Albrizzi; in calle di Ca' Moro Lin (S. Marco 3243), at the Carampane (S. Polo 1510a); on rio del Fontego a Castello, in calle Friziera (Castello 1887), (Elenco, 1905, p. 35, no. 88) in rio dell' Osmarin (surmounted by a very unusual Gothic cornice).
In rio dell'Ogio (Giudecca 452) but in such condition that it cannot be judged with certainty (Elenco, 1905, p. 174, no. 27), in campo S. Barnaba (Dorsoduro 2770) with smooth archivolt (Elenco, 1905, p. 164, no. 287); in calle del Scaleter (three windows); in calle de la Toleta (Dorsoduro 1238) where a window of our type accompanies another, trefoiled, of a rather rough type, with similar moulding; in calle Martinengo delle Palle (Castello 5965), (a window with Byzantine dentil ornament); in fond. Gherardini at the Carmini (Dorsoduro 2825-6). (See further notes); the four-light window in line with another of the fourth type in calle dei Mercanti, which makes one think of the elasticity of certain chronologies in Venice (Elenco, 1905, p. 138, no. 170; S. Croce 1828-9).
Nor should we forget two strange complexes: a façade in calle Drio la Sagrestia (Castello 4498), in which we see two four-light windows, one above the other, with the two openings in the middle with round arches while the two at the ends are of the third type, perhaps a reinforcement of a later period, with single windows of the fourth and fifth type; and a façade in calle dell' Ogio (Castello 3044) in which similar strange mixtures are again found. It should be added that in these two complexes, which may rightly be qualified as 'minor' architecture, the archivolts are all of the smooth type with a torus profile on the extrados.

**202.** Lorenzetti, 1956, p. 337.

**203.** Lorenzi, 1868, p. 1, doc. I.

**204.** Lorenzi, 1868, p. 5, doc. 15.

**205.** Lorenzi, 1868, p. 1, doc. 2.

**206.** Lorenzi, 1868, p. 5, doc. 16.

**207.** Lorenzi, 1868, p. 7, doc. 21.

**208.** Sanudo, Vite, in RIS, XXII, col. 582. The same Sanudo elsewhere (Diarii, XXV, p. 120) gives the date of *c.* 1310).

**209.** Sansovino, 1663, p. 324.

**210.** Information on this first hall is provided also by Cadorin (1837, p. 9), Cicognara (1883, I, p. 68), Ruskin, (1886, II, p. 291), Zanotto (1853, pp. 41 and 47, no. 13; p. 48, no. 18) who states that it had been demolished in 1523.

**211.** See concerning the uncertainty of the location of this hall: Bassi, 1962, I, pp. 37-8.

**212.** Cadorin (1837, pp. 9-10), on the strength of a statement of Barbo who attributed to Calendario the tower in question, thought that as (according to Sansovino) the tower and the hall were contiguous, the latter was also Calendario's work. But if the hall was finished between 1301 and 1309, it is highly improbable that Calendario, who died, no longer a young man, in 1355, was involved.

**213.** Ruskin, 1886, II, pp. 257, 281 et seq. and 290; III, p. 214 (these windows correspond 'exactly in mouldings and manner of workmanship to those of the chapter-house of the Frari'; dates them to the early fourteenth century; considers however—mistakenly in our opinion—the ornament to be of the time of Ziani). See also Bassi-Trincanato, 1960, p. 11.
The chapter-house of the Carmini also has two three-light windows, now partly walled-up, with simple inflected arches, certainly fourteenth century; of western character. (Lorenzetti, 1956, p. 553, to the fifteenth century).

**214.** Cf. Arslan, 1966, pp. 64-5 (the late-Romanesque ornaments are without doubt later than the thirteenth-century ones, already mentioned, of the well-known Venetian 'Romanesque' portals). Zanotto, (1853, p. 61) had noted the 'Romanesque' string-course continuing the marble cornice of the arcade on the quay-side; and had deduced that there had been a loggia also on rio di Palazzo, corresponding to the one on the Piazzetta—where Calendario was hanged between the two red columns in 1355—on the façade of the ancient Palazzo della Ragione.

**215.** Demus, 1960, p. 76 and fig. 6.

**216.** *Palazzo Bosso at S. Tomà.* Elenco, 1905, p. 122, no. 241; Lorenzetti, 1956, p. 572 (to the fifteenth century!) Trincanato, 1948, p. 71 (to the thirteenth century).

**217.** Mothes, 1859, pp. 143 and 204.

**218.** Molmenti, 1925, I, p. 281. For Bettini the Gothic predominates from 'the end of the thirteenth to the middle of the fifteenth' (1953, p. 50). According to Demus (1960, p. 101) the ogival arch arrived in Venice at the end of the twelfth and the beginning of the thirteenth century.

**219.** Ruskin, 1886, II, p. 255.

**220.** *Padova, campanili of the Santo.* G. Gasparotto, *Guide della Basilica di S. Antonio in Padova,* in "Il Santo", II, 1962, p. 229 et seq.

**221.** A window on the façade of Palazzo Pretorio, certainly belonging to the most ancient part.

**222.** Tamaro, 1893, p. 471; Ferrari-Antoniazzo. 1955, pp. 77-8. Karaman, 1963, pp. 54 and 115,

**223.** Of graceful fifteenth-century form.

**224.** In the (walled-up) three-light window next to the Temple of Jupiter.

**225.** In the Zudioska ul.

ROMANO-BYZANTINE PRELUDE

*1. Gentile Bellini: 'Procession in St. Mark's Square', Detail. Venice, Gallerie dell'Accademia.*
*2. St. Mark's Square. The Procuratie Vecchie.*

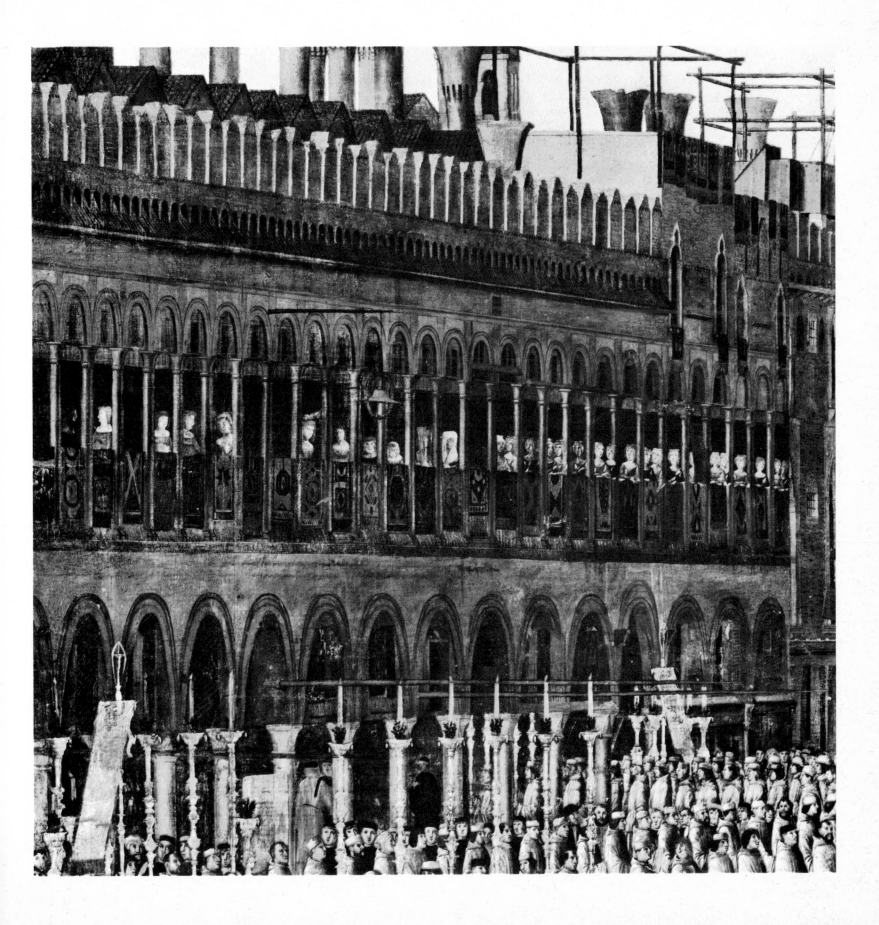

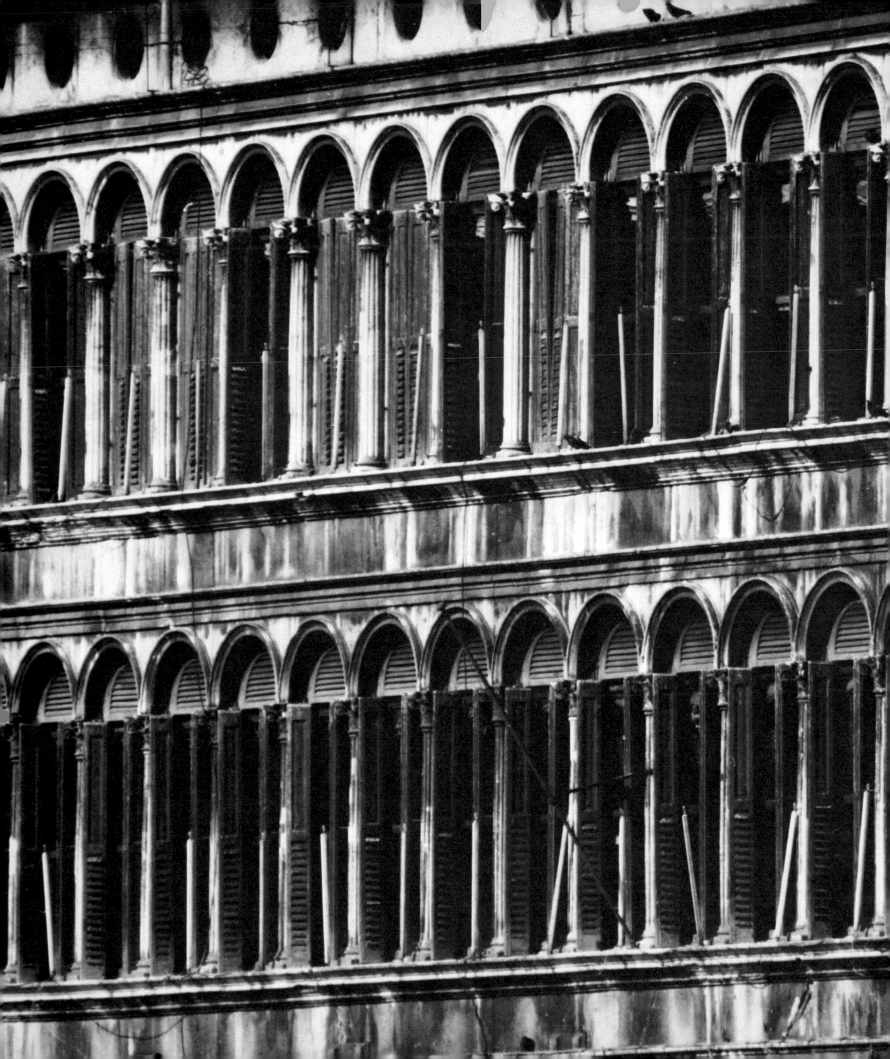

3. *Frieze of Sottoportego del Tamossi in Fondamenta Banco Salviati.*
4. *Three-light window of a house of S. Stae.*

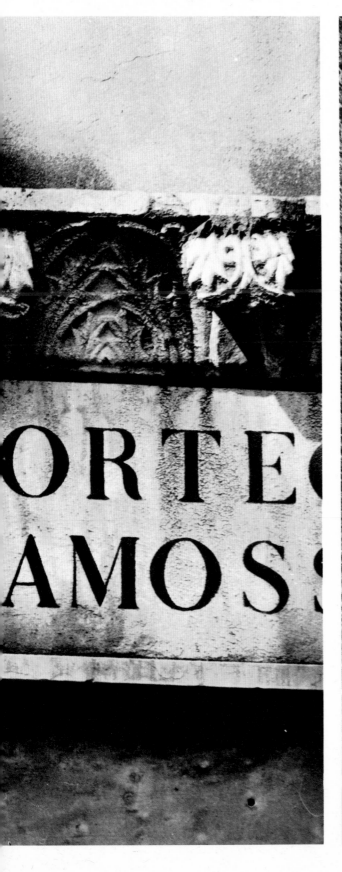

*5. Fondaco dei Turchi.*

*6, 7. Ca' Loredan. Façade on the canal and detail.*

8. *Palazzo Donà della Madonnetta.*

9. *Palazzo Bernardo, Palazzo Donà della Madonnetta and Palazzo Donà.*
10. *Palazzo Donà della Madonnetta. Detail of the gallery.*

9. *Palazzo Bernardo, Palazzo Donà della Madonnetta and Palazzo Donà.*
10. *Palazzo Donà della Madonnetta. Detail of the gallery.*

12. *Palazzo Donà. Detail of the second order five-light window.*

13. Palazzo Businello.

*14. Palazzo Da Mosto on the Grand Canal. Detail of the arch with cusped extrados.*

15. *Palazzo Da Mosto. Façade.*
16. *Palazzo Da Mosto. Location on the Grand Canal.*
17. *Palazzo Da Mosto. Detail of the multi-light window.*

21. *Four-light windows at Ponte S. Andrea in Cannaregio.*
22. *Two-light window of a Romano-Gothic building at S. Lio.*

*23. Ragusa (Dalmatia). Casa Zamanja. Four-light window.*
*24, 25. Duomo of Ferrara. Details of the sides.*

29. *Palazzo Vitturi in Campo S. Maria Formosa. Four-light window.*
30. *Palazzo Vitturi in Campo S. Maria Formosa.*

31. *Palazzo Moro in Campo S. Bartolomeo.*
32. *Palazzo Moro in Campo S. Bartolomeo.*
*Two-light window.*
33, 34. *Palazzo Moro in Campo S. Bartolomeo.*
*Details of the multi-light window.*

37. *Carmini cloister. Three-light window of the Chapter-house.*
38. *Frari cloister. Three-light window of the Chapter-house.*

*39. Doge's Palace. Two-light window on rio di Palazzo.*
*40. Doge's Palace. Three-light window of the façade on rio di Palazzo.*
*41. Doge's Palace. Frieze on the façade on rio di Palazzo.*

42. *Traù (Dalmatia). Two-light window of a Palazzo.*
43. *Valle d'Istria. Main façade of Bembo Castle.*

*Contacts with English Gothic*

As we saw, the two–cusped arch of oriental origin was gradually modified, early in the fourteenth century, by contact with the inflected Gothic arch of western character.

It is quite probable that the simple western ogival arch—the two–centred broken arch—which had been widely spread for some time throughout Italy and had appeared also in Venetian religious architecture at the beginning of the thirteenth century (as in the north front of St. Mark's), had not yet been adopted by Venetian secular architecture in the first decades of the fourteenth century. The same applies to the simple trefoiled arch, not inflected, which had also been current for some time throughout Italy and was present in Venice in the first half of the fourteenth century. We find it in Venice, dated with certainty in the secondary apses of the Frari, 'already erected and covered' in 1336[1]. It may seem more surprising that not only the simple inflected arch, but also the inflected trefoiled arch, should appear at the same time beside the simple trefoiled arch, and to such an extent as to make us think that the more complex form predominated in the Lagoon over the simpler one from the beginning, both in quantity and quality. It was Ruskin's belief[2] that the inflected trefoiled arch had been introduced to Venice from the mainland, more precisely from Verona. But the Veronese Gothic houses in 'Venetian' style are all, as is attested also by the dates, of a late period and represent a spreading of Venetian features after the conquest, a phenomenon similar to that which occurred in Vicenza, Padova, Treviso and other centres of the Veneto.

We are faced here, in fact, with the very peculiar problem of the two different orientations in Venetian architecture, religious and civil. The pointed arch, simple and trefoil, originated from the mainland and was, in fact, a derivative of the Western Gothic which was predominant in France. The inflected arch, on the other hand, simple or trefoil, was almost non–existent at the beginning of the fourteenth century, not only in Italy but in the whole of the European continent. It was most probably at the fount of the English Gothic, which directly inspired the Venetian builders. The inflected arch of purely western style appeared fairly rapidly in Venice at the beginning of the fourteenth century and it is entirely out of the question that it should have come from the Po valley, where it is extremely rare, and even less from France. These forms were, in fact, infrequent in France at that time, but they none the less acquired there the name of 'Gothic Flamboyant'. Already Viollet–le–Duc[3] had noted that the inflected arch, the principle of the 'countercurve', appeared in France around 1375 in the windows of the north chapels of Amiens cathedral. In support of this, Enlart[4] spoke (in 1904) of the *flamboyant* as a 'product of the English occupation', pointing out that the forms of this style existed in England at the beginning of the fourteenth century. He confirmed his opinions in a subsequent article[5]. In turn, Bond[6] confirmed that the inflected arch, root of the *flamboyant*, actually appeared in England at the end of the thirteenth century, and initiated an imposing series of works of art marked by that style, which laid the foundation for the subsequent developments in French architecture.

A. St. Paul[7] rejected the theses of Enlart and Bond and insisted on French priority, with examples which convinced neither Enlart[8], who took an active part in this discussion, nor Bond[9], who emphasized the 'inactivity' (*stasis*) which characterized French architecture between 1330 and 1440, compared with the very rapid evolution of British architecture towards entirely new forms penetrating all structures (Bond quotes numerous examples[10], particularly of flowing tracery)—nor Lasteyrie[11]. The latter though admitting, when faced with the evidence, that a considerable time–lag existed (little less than a century) between the French *flamboyant* and the decorated or curvilinear style of the English, yet excluded a direct derivation from the English style and maintained the independence of French art: 'The English and the French were led by the logic of things to similar solutions.'[12]

One could quote here the example of the years which run (from the thirties to the fifties) between the first manifestations of the Tuscan Renaissance and those appearing north of the Appennines, or of the half century which runs from the Italian art of the third decade of the sixteenth century, and that freed from the Gothic of the transalpine countries. But no–one would think of denying for that reason the decisive contribution of Italian art to those countries. Lasteyrie[13] insists on the striking number of French tombs with inflected arch from the beginning of the fourteenth century onwards, and concludes[14] that *l'accolade* was not imported into France from beyond the Channel, but that its appearance is the fruit, in France, of a long incubation beginning in the thirteenth century. It seems to us that one cannot exclude in this context the activities of English stonecutters on the Continent, as, indeed, is definitely proved by documents[15]. Lasteyrie also denies that in the richest and most sinuous mouldings England precedes France, where they were allegedly common already at the end of the thirteenth century.

In all this, however, that author's admission[16] that the English curvilinear style was born before it was fully constituted in France, and that so many of its constitutive elements (arches in *accolade*, typical fillings of the windows, *soufflets, mouchettes*) do not appear before the reign of Charles VI (1380–1422)[17] is essential. Elsewhere[18], the same author indicates the origin of the inflected arch in the triforium of Amiens (second half of the thirteenth century), at the point where the trefoiled oculi are grafted onto the underlying pointed arches; he agrees, however, that *il est difficile de croire que le dessin flamboyant fut jamais sorti d'un pareil embryon*. These 'embryos' (derived, in substance, from the arch which inserts itself above between two curves, and tends therefore to inflect itself) are found not only in France around 1330 (S. Urbain at Troyes, the choir of Nevers cathedral, begun in 1308)[19], but also in Germany (in the Stiftskirche of Fritzlar, of about 1300[20], and in the octagonal cusp of Freiburg cathedral of 1320–50)[21]. But they precede by almost half a century in continental Europe the first true inflected arches, not as an expression of the geometric, rational, French Gothic, but as an entirely autonomous and imaginative manifestation. Nor are other sporadic derivations of the English curvilinear style lacking in buildings datable between 1325 and 1350 in northern France, the Low Countries or Portugal[22].

Now, if it is true that the inflected arch, the *accolade*, is found in funerary monuments of the beginning of the fourteenth century in France, like the tombs of Jean († 1304) and Blanche († 1310) de Laon at Royaumont[23] or the tomb of Bernard de Camiat († 1337)[24] and also, sporadically, in some churches, it still remains valid, for Enlart as for Lasteyrie, that the inflected arch appears in very rare cases[25] in France at the end of the thirteenth century and the beginning of the fourteenth, but that it asserts itself for the first time on French soil as an explicit and serious manifestation of style about 1375 in the chapel of Cardinal Lagrange in Amiens cathedral and on the front of Rouen cathedral[26]. On the fact that the *flamboyant* style (the flowing tracery) passed about 1370 into France and ended by dominating the whole continent, the critics appear, today, in full agreement.

According to Pevsner 'the architecture of England between 1250 and 1350 was, although the English do not know it, the most forward, the most important, and the most inspired in Europe'[27]. This observation obviously refers to the particular qualitative level of European Gothic, excluding what, for instance, was being done in those hundred years in Italy. Nor are other authors less explicit: 'After 1300 the use of contrasted concave and convex lines' constitutes a new source of inspiration, establishing decorative schemes which anticipate by more than fifty years the French *flamboyant* style[28].

The history of English Gothic architecture since the end of the thirteenth century has been by now authoritatively treated. Its great importance, however, as Pevsner has pointed out, is not yet fully appreciated. I think it appropriate to mention here again the quality of these forms, given their importance in comparison with Venetian architecture. The trefoiled inflected arch which has been mentioned did not originate in England, at the end of the thirteenth century, from those forms which a century before had characterized the Canterbury choir or Lincoln cathedral, recognizable by the high and narrow pointed arch. The inflected arch is, on the other hand, derived without doubt through precedents of French inspiration, amongst which may be counted the masterpiece which is the Abbey church of Westminster, erected between 1245 and 1269[29], the forms of which, inspired by the classical French Gothic (Reims) lead everywhere to the adoption of the trefoiled arch. The wall is organized at Westminster in a French spirit; and it has been justly observed how, in this phase of classical Gothic (at Reims in about 1212; and thirty years later, at Westminster), it is no longer the wall which appears hollowed out by planes sloping down in depth, but the window which is devised instead to be inserted in the wall[30]. The new principle finds applications in monuments like the cathedrals of Bridlington (1275–1300)[31], of Lincoln (Angel Choir), of Exeter (1280–91) and of Wells, the rows of windows of which undoubtedly show the precedence of the French style.

The signs of French influence are very frequent: nothing is more *champenois* than the openings (windows and doors) of the staircase leading to the chapter–house of Wells, where the wall is divided into superimposed spaces, or the naturalistic foliage of the capitals in the chapter–house of Southwell, of about 1300[32]. But as English architecture maintains from its beginnings an unmistakable aspect of its own[33], so also the subsequent connections with French taste do not exclude the persistence of that originality.

Nevertheless, it is very important to point out that Enlart noticed in England (from the thirteenth century onwards) a greater complication of the profiles than in France[34], with the penetration of the mouldings into the pillars abolishing the capitals[35]. It is well known how, already about 1298, a real revolution in structure took place, with astounding spatial solutions in St. Mary Redcliffe in Bristol[36] and in the Lady Chapel of Wells, of about 1300, buildings in which was realized an interpenetration of various spaces (which will become typical of the late Gothic style)[37]. Now, if it is true that these structural facts do not concern us, because Venetian secular Gothic does not know any of these problems, it is equally true that there had been during these years a change in the decorative *facies* of English Gothic. This appears closely connected with a total transformation of the structural principles of the building. The inflected trefoil arch (ogee arch) is born precisely in these last years of the thirteenth century, so decisive in the transformation of the English Gothic. The passage is clearly discernible in two well–known monuments: the Angel Choir at Lincoln and the chapter–house at Wells. In the Angel Choir the wall carries above the triforium large trefoiled four–light windows supported by columns on which stand, in line with the first and the third column, two trefoil oculi. On these double two–light windows (because, in fact, these are two two–light windows crowned by a pointed arch) there is a large multi–foil oculus, on whose vertex stands the great pointed arch embracing the whole four–light window.

It is easy to find French architectural precedents for this structure; at St. Jean–des–Vignes[38], at St. Denis[39], in the cloister of Rouen cathedral[40] (first half of the fourteenth century), and in England itself (windows of the Salisbury cloister, of 1220–60)[41].

The Angel Choir is dated around 1260. Stone[42], on the basis of the sculpture, puts it in 1270–80. This early dating will not only appear more convincing to the Italian scholar, who will see in the two–light windows of the triforium an effective parallel to the almost coeval forms realized by Nicola Pisano, but will be even more convincing if we consider the rows of windows of the Wells chapter–house.

Enlart[43] and Clasen[44] have already drawn attention to the importance of the multi–light windows of this famous work. The dating is between 1286 and 1319, when the work was already completed, but the inclination today is to place it in the first years of the fourteenth century[45]. Nor will this placing appear too early if one thinks that these windows, in which the inflected arch now appears, recall those of Lincoln. The rows of windows at Wells (and the earlier ones at Lincoln) are therefore of the greatest importance if one considers that they may represent the prototypes of the Venetian ones, and that the inflected trefoil arch appears in Venice, initiating a journey of two centuries, about twenty years later, remaining ignored—when it is not directly an English import—on the whole of the European continent until about 1370. This arch is obviously one of the roots of the style commonly known as *flamboyant*.

The appearance of the ogee arch is also documented in England from 1291–4 in Eleanor's Cross, at Hardingstone near Northampton[46], in 1292 in St. Stephen's at Westminster[47], in the monument of the Earl of Lancaster, who died in 1296, at Westminster[48], in the screen enclosing the choir at Canterbury, due to Henry of Eastry (1285–1331) and in the tomb of this last–named († 1331—also in Canterbury), in the tomb of J. Peckham (1279–92) and in other monuments. By about 1315 it is in general use[49], and about the same time the arch with the countercurve appears in Venice (not excluding, however, the fact that it was precisely the arch with countercurve of Islamic type which prepared, on the Lagoon, the arrival of the English trefoiled one). And we may well ask ourselves at this point whether the ogee arch which appears in England at the end of the thirteenth century should not be seen as a derivation of that arch with countercurve found in Muslim art already in the eleventh century in Spain and in the Maghreb.

English Gothic architecture, renovated throughout in its structural and decorative elements, predominates beyond the Channel until the middle of the fourteenth century. Lasteyrie rightly speaks of 'innumerable' cases of flamboyant Gothic in England in the fourteenth century[50], and Webb of the extraordinary number of early fourteenth–century buildings in the counties of the west and middle west[51]. Between about 1320 and 1350, there are marvellous works like the rood–screen of the Exeter choir; Prior Crauden's Chapel at Ely; the wonderful presbytery of Wells; the Lady Chapel of Lichfield; the tomb of Edward II at Gloucester; the very rich rood–screen of Southwell; the Lady Chapel and the great octagon at Ely; St. Mary Redcliffe in Bristol; the very beautiful windows of the Tewkesbury choir; Merton College at Oxford.

These are only a few and incomplete instances from among a long series of monuments which reveal even to the most unequipped observer who has crossed the Channel and has

still in his mind's eye the geometrical, 'rational' French Gothic of the thirteenth and fourteenth centuries an entirely new world. A world of forms to which we must return when speaking of Venice, because other elements also generated by the inexhaustible decorative wealth of the curvilinear style must have interested the Lombard and Venetian master-masons and stonecutters. These include traceries above the great rows of windows which, rigidly geometric in France, are treated with the utmost freedom in England (the reticulated alveolar traceries from 1320 in Lichfield, Exeter, Wells, Selby, Hull, etc.) and inflected, multi-foiled arches. The ogive with baldaquin, the nodding arch, the most splendid examples of which are seen in the Lady Chapel of Ely and which, according to Bond, appear immediately after 1300 are found also in Hereford, Exeter, Lichfield, Lincoln, Winchester, Bristol, Salisbury, a very singular element which must have been noted by the Venetians, as seems proved by the niche containing the statue of S. Biagio in Ragusa, in the wall of the tower to the right of the Pila gate. Even if it is a fifteenth-century work, it still attests that this motif reached Ragusa, probably through Venice, or directly from England.

It may be said that at this time 'were laid, broad and deep, the foundations of all our later Gothic. At this period too the art of architectural composition reached (in England) a level that never afterwards was surpassed'[52]. One should not therefore be astonished if these forms awakened an interest in the masons and stonecutters of the Continent and if the English masters were sought after and induced to cross the Channel. In 1321-2, an English master-mason, Hugh Wilfred, built a chapel at Notre–Dame–des–Doms in Avignon[53], of which, however, nothing remains. To a Wilfred or a Johannes Anglicus (active between 1336 and 1351) is due the tomb of John XXII in Avignon cathedral, and in the considerable remains may be recognized the influence of the English architecture of the beginning of the fourteenth century[54]; in 1332-41 Raynardus dez Fonoyll, *anglicus lapicida* erects the southern wing of the cloister of Santes Creus, in Spain, begun in 1303[55]. The edifice is quoted as the first manifestation of the flamboyant style in the Iberian peninsula, but is recognized by the Spanish scholars themselves as an imported work, absolutely exceptional and outside its time.

Where, however, these forms of flamboyant Gothic are not directly imported by English artists, they arrive on the Continent with considerable delay, and, until 1370, their appearance is rare and intermittent.


### The inflected trefoiled arch in the first half of the fourteenth century

The inflected arch appears in Venice very early in the fourteenth century. The roads which took it there, however, do not seem to cross the mainland. We quote two examples; each for its own particular significance is important.

A two–light window of the Castle of Angera, datable to the first half of the fourteenth century[56], presents two cinquefoiled arches terminating in an inflected arch; the inflected arch and the cinquefoiled form make one think of the English Gothic of the first half of the fourteenth century. The example is an isolated one in Lombardy at this time, and it seems clear that this is not the road leading to Venice. Another example, very rare, is visible as the cornice crowning a relief of Sesto al Reghena, with the Annunciation, in which has been recognized the 'work of Guido da Como'; it consists of three inflected trefoil arches. Here a connection with Venice is, to my mind, very probable, but in the sense that this is the work (rare on the Venetian mainland) of stonecutters originating from the Lagoon. We are in about 1300, according to Toesca[57], in the first half of the century according to Zovatto[58]. It may perhaps be possible to find more examples of this kind here and there in the territories of the Upper Adriatic, but they cannot be indicative of an *iter* which, across the mainland, leads to Venice. In Milan, it is only in 1390-1[59] that work was being done on the inflected trefoil arches of the upper part of the Duomo apses and there are not many dates, in Venice, to document the appearance of the inflected arch, be it trefoiled or simple, with one lobe.

Other dates concern various aspects of the secular architecture of Venice. A rectangular portal is the one formerly in S. Nicolò della Lattuga, founded in 1332 by Nicolò Lion, now the entrance doorway to the State Archives at the Frari. From the time of Doge Giovanni Soranzo (1312–28) to whom we owe the Baptistery of St. Mark's[60] comes certainly the relief with the *Baptism of Christ* built into its wall[61] (the inflected trefoiled arch we see there is therefore the first of which we have notice today). Another inflected trefoiled arch is on the ground level tomb, now vanished, dated 1338, of the Abbess Margherita Trevisan, once in S. Marta[62]. The two three-light windows which opened on the western front of St. Mark's, supported by small twisted columns and surmounted by two quatrefoil oculi, are mentioned here, together with the two, similar but somewhat simpler, which opened on the northern and southern fronts. Demus, the only one who to my knowledge has concerned himself with them, considered them of about 1309[63] but now inclines towards a later date, in the time of Bartolomeo Gradenigo (1339–42). This second date agrees well enough, it seems, with the characters peculiar to that time, as is quite visible in the manifest hypertrophy of the central lobe. The execution, the feeling for proportions are there, but less refined than in other products of master-workmen engaged on lay buildings.

Two important monuments of around 1340 are the Abbey of S. Gregorio and the two large windows of the Doge's Palace on the quay towards the Ponte della Paglia. The only fourteenth-century parts remaining of the Abbey are the cloister and the façade on the Grand Canal, erected by Abbot Fridiano († 1342)[64]. The two large windows with tracery on the façade towards the quay of the Doge's Palace belong to the new Sala del Maggior Consiglio, begun in 1340 and completed by 1365, when Guariento painted the *Paradise* fresco there.

There are, therefore, until the middle of the century few but important references. We have, unfortunately, no date relating to a complete dwelling-house which would further facilitate the tracing of the course of this style. But even from an examination of the few elements mentioned above many considerations arise which define that critically delicate period, the first half of the fourteenth century.

First of all, a necessary observation is that these arches (in which Ruskin recognized his fourth order) are noticeably different from those which will follow in the fourteenth century and throughout the fifteenth century. In the arches of Sesto al Reghena and in that of the *Baptism of Christ*, which vividly resemble each other, the tracing is irregular, while the fillet marking the extrados is accompanied in both cases by a dense perforated foliage which is not repeated later. The arch of the Trevisan tomb, which fully adopts the Gothic style in its sinuous, elegant profile, appears however somewhat crushed, namely the upper inflected lobe is lower than usual because of the hesitation with which the two lateral lobes are traced. A very different character, also abnormal, is shown by the trefoiled windows of the façade of the S. Gregorio cloister, which lean right against the door. Framed according to the fashion already established in Venice in a marble-encrusted rectangle surrounded by a Byzantine dentil ornament, they have the profiles deeply hollowed and marked, also on the jambs, by a cyma and two spirals with rich capitals with thick leaves. However, the upper trefoil is particularly developed, and heart-shaped, in comparison with the lateral lobes. The same tracing is noticeable in one of the large windows of the Doge's Palace which we have mentioned. The meaning of these 'anomalies' encountered in monuments which are certainly of the beginning of the fourteenth century is quite clear. We are dealing with an adaptation process of the stonecutters to the new formulae which had arrived from the west and were to erase all Byzantine recollection. The water-gate of S. Gregorio is also unusual, being the work of the same stonecutters who deepened the cymae and spirals, adding on a vast fascia

a motif of rosettes between small coffers (which we find again on the façade of the Doge's Palace).

Thus follow from one end to the other of the small, sumptuous decorative complex a very great variety of mouldings which, refusing any pause which might point to a constructive substratum, increase the fleeting reflection of the water. The Holy Father under the two sloping roofs between the spiral columns similar to those of the Trevisan tomb and the large windows of the Doge's Palace (a motif certainly of Campionese origin) confirm again the ascription to the beginning of the fourteenth century of this complex, in which among such density of decoration, the wide obscure space of the door creates a zone of ample repose. In the square cloister of S. Gregorio which Ruskin had already declared 'exactly contemporary with the finest work of the Ducal Palace, circa 1350', defining it as the loveliest 'cortile' in Venice[65], the ceiling of the ambulatory is supported on the outside by columns erected on a low wall, which sustain wooden architraves in which modillions have been carved. Marzemin[66] had already noted exactly how 'the shape of the few original modillions is that typically in use in the fourteenth century'. They have profiles with sharp angles and not with the sinuous penetrations in 'owl beak' to which the international Gothic style was to lead. Another example, with similar modillions, is offered by a house with galleries in calle Cavanella (Castello 4484) which is justly attributed[67] to the fourteenth century. Returning to S. Gregorio, we notice capitals of several kinds, in part with superimposed caulicoles, in part of the type with thick leaves.

Apart from its value as a stylistic *point d'appui*, the S. Gregorio cloister is less worthy than its fame (excluding the façade). Neither in the rhythm of the columns, nor in the quality of the materials employed does it in fact realize any particular architectural 'idea', one which is not dictated by practical requirements[68]. The unknown stonemason of the façade on the Grand Canal right at the dawn of what we may call, more appropriately, Venetian Gothic, has realized on the other hand an extreme example of how the Gothic could be interpreted in a city immersed in the constantly changing fascination of water and atmosphere, which modified fundamental values of structure and formal balance. These later on would have brought some order, of lines, of masses and of pauses also to this architecture which otherwise would have dissolved in an orgy of colour.

A similar and really spectacular case is provided by the Doge's Palace, which began to assume its present aspect in the middle of the fourteenth century. We shall speak of this later on. The four large windows with tracery, two on the quay and two on the rio di Palazzo, represent, however, a separate event, visibly inserted in an organic plan undoubtedly due to one of the major architects of the Italian fourteenth century. They show today what all the others must have been like in the two façades on the quay and the Piazzetta, as well as on the small northern façade, before the fire of 1577, when Antonio da Ponte removed all the tracery from the remaining windows[69]. An idea of how the façades of the palace would have appeared before 1577 is given first of all by the well-known painting of Gentile Bellini, *Procession in St. Mark's Square*, more approximately by the well-known *View of Venice* of Jacopo de' Barbari of the year 1500, by a view of the Piazzetta façade in a codex of the end of the fifteenth century at Chantilly[70], and by the partial view of the palace in the background of Carpaccio's St. Mark's lion of 1516, as well as by the well-known engraving by Reenwich of 1486. From all these graphic testimonies, it may be deduced that the vanished traceries probably repeated the type of the one on the quay nearest to the eastern corner.

As for the period—leaving aside the loggia and the arcade—there is no doubt that the large windows of the stretch on the rio di Palazzo, on the southern façade and on the stretch of the western façade containing the six arches of the ground floor, should be dated between 1340 and 1365, and that the others on the Piazzetta and on the small northern stretch were put in hand between 1424 and 1438, repeating to the letter the fourteenth–century models. The window with two lights visible in Bellini's painting reproduces, in fact, the one which on the rio encloses two small quatrefoils within the major pointed arch. What are, finally, the most specific characteristics of the four large eastern windows is not an easily solvable problem. It is perhaps worth considering these works because, even if they qualify as typical of the high fourteenth century, they are yet exceptional.

The first to mention the four large windows was Ruskin, who justly recognized them as 'of the finest early fourteenth–century work'[71]. Since then the problem has not been posed again by anyone in true and real terms. It is perhaps opportune to note how these magnificent windows fit the period about 1340–60. First of all, the capitals of the two three–light windows are an exception in Venice, because they are due to particularly capable stonecutters, but they do not go beyond the fourteenth century. Those of the left three–light window, with swollen foliage and lion heads, unlike those with thick leaves in use towards the middle of the fifteenth century, are unusually rich for Venice, as will be seen from a study of the course and the types of the Venetian capital from the thirteenth to the middle of the fifteenth century.

The capital naturally assumes in Venice (and on the mainland) a great variety of forms in the fourteenth century, due to a great variety of workmen, among whom are foremost Venetians and Lombards. Two types, however, in buildings reasonably considered of the fourteenth century prevail numerically over all others. They represent two formulations, which are on the whole very simple. The first type has the bell surrounded by a single turn of large, smooth leaves folding towards the outside, on which caulicoles are curled under the abacus, two or four on each face; as one can see, for instance, in Palazzo Ariani; in the courtyard of Casa Donà (S. Polo 2177) in campo S. Stefano; on the ground floor of Palazzo Michiel delle Colonne; in the courtyard of the Abbey of S. Gregorio (about 1340); in three houses, one in calle della Bissa (S. Marco 5512), the second on the fondamenta Moro (Cann. 2447), the third on rio di S. Canciano; in Palazzo Agnusdio; in the Reggia Carrarese of Padova, etc. It is a type born, perhaps, in the thirteenth century[72].

Another type, however, was to dominate the second half of the fourteenth century, not only in Venice but also in the whole Venetian mainland. It is found, as we saw, in the Marches and the Abruzzi. It is the one with usually a somewhat elongated bell, covered at the corners by a leaf which folds, curling, on itself, and with a rosette in the centre. It was employed even beyond the middle of the fifteenth century (those, for instance, of the boat of S. Andrea della Zirada in Venice may be accepted as of 1475). It appears regularly also in the large Gothic secular buildings of virtually the whole of the fifteenth century, supporting the multi–light windows of the top floors, while the *piani nobili* are characterized by capitals with thick leaves.

The capitals of the three–light window of the Doge's Palace point, on the other hand, to an unusual apparition in the middle of the fourteenth century, which will find an explanation only if we remember those rich examples diffused throughout the fourteenth century in an entirely different area by Campionese master–masons. Whoever compares the capitals worked out by these stonecutters with specifically Venetian ones notices a radical difference. From the Longhi tomb in S. Maria Maggiore in Bergamo[73] to the northern portal of that same church (by Giovanni da Campione, in 1353)[74], to the arch of Cansignorio[75], to so many other 'Campionese' works, this type of capital is always very rich, with an exuberance of foliage, different from the Tuscan as well as from the Venetian. The spiral columns of the upper aedicule of the arch of S. Pietro Martire in S. Eustorgio in Milan repeat, almost to the letter, those of the two three–light windows in the Doge's Palace.

To conclude: The Campionese introduced also in Venice towards the middle of the fourteenth century the taste for these new, rich features in architectural decoration, in contrast to the local tradition. They are, however, tied here to architectural structures which are due, almost certainly, to a Venetian planner. We should, however, add that if these features are typical of the Campionese, it is also evident that this as yet ill–defined association of stonecutters are ready to 'execute' here and elsewhere with their established expertise many other conceptions of architectural decoration.

We reach here the heart of one of the most complicated problems of the architectural decoration of the second half of the fourteenth century. If, in Milan, Giovanni di Balduccio asks for the collaboration of the Campionese on such an important undertaking as the arch of St. Peter Martyr, and they appear in Venice at work on the Government palace, their presence is equally certain in other parts of the peninsula and raises a multitude of questions; particularly in those territories which, like Tuscany, were distinguished by a high degree of representational culture. But it is not here that we shall answer them. Instead, we shall only examine more closely the tracery of the large windows of the Doge's Palace.

They undoubtedly represent, compared with what was being done elsewhere, a distinctly Venetian style. We must note first of all that the trefoiled arches are cut out in such a way that they appear as if traced by a fillet of marble against the void behind them, and this is an archaic feature in Venice, typical of fourteenth–century buildings. Characteristic examples are provided by church architecture. We have seen the three–light windows in St. Mark's and we shall mention here also the great rose window on the southern front, which is considered of the fourteenth century, if only for the elongated heart shape of the central lobe of the outside trefoils, for the semicircular tracing of the trefoils of the 'internal' rose and for the style of the capitals[76]. The distinctly heart-shaped design of the upper trefoil, with uninflected arch, of the large window of the Doge's Palace is indeed also archaic. In reality, the motif of the trefoiled arch cut out against the void becomes increasingly rare as we advance farther into the fifteenth century.

In the tracery of the great window, we pass from the interlacing of the arches which generate the ogives (a very common pattern since the Romanesque period in the Po valley and to be found, for instance, in the great wheel–windows of church fronts) to a more complicated play which is found also in other buildings of the middle of the fourteenth century. A similar example is found exactly at this time in the two three–light windows on the façade of the Duomo of Monza, of 1340–70[77], and in the two three–light windows facing the Square of the Court House (Broletto) of Bergamo, that is to say, those on the sides of the large central window.

A comparison between the two in Monza and the two in Venice is instructive: in the first, the gradual scansion of the wall is of distant Lombard Romanesque origin and the upper tracery of clear transalpine derivation; in the second we notice a repeating of the two tracery motifs with greater chiaroscuro subtlety and the gradual introduction of clearly Venetian motifs (inflected arches), while the border is only a thin cornice and the three–light windows, their depth reduced to a minimum, represent visually only a continuation of the wall. The workmen, in both cases, were certainly Campionese, active around the middle of the century, showing, however, a notable capacity to acclimatize themselves to the local taste. In fact, these Campionese are, very often, merely executants. It may well happen that some critic will succeed in identifying some stylistic element peculiar to them (like those I have myself noted) but in the sum total of their vast and widespread activities, in the Po valley and elsewhere during the fourteenth century, there is no easily recognizable, uniform style. It is easy to notice how these gifts as executants, as interpreters of other peoples' ideas, are common to all the artists originating from around the Lombard lakes, stucco–workers, stonecutters, master–masons, found all over Europe; but, precisely because of this, most of them are devoid of any style peculiar to themselves. However (as in their spreading, as stucco–workers beyond the Alps in the eighteenth century, of Rococo taste) they were very active transmitters of ideas, at times extraordinarily new and fertile.

The effect achieved in Venice in the two large windows of the Doge's Palace is distinctly chromatic and is supported by a shrewd choice of materials; the spiral columns of the great windows on the quay side are in Carrara marble, the capitals in Veronese limestone. The remainder is in Istrian stone. But there is yet more. The Campionese worked out, in Venice and in Lombardy, motifs which had reached their apogee in the first half of the fourteenth century in England. The great rows of windows of Tewkesbury (about 1325)[78], of the Octagon[79] and of the Lady Chapel at Ely[80], and of Prior Crauden's Chapel (also at Ely; the tracery of the large window in the Doge's Palace is similar to this)[81] had a large following in Europe, by paths which are all still to be ascertained, and may easily remind one of the mouldings of the great window on the west side of the southern front of the Doge's Palace; whereas, as we said before, and this is admitted even by French critics, France arrived at these *flamboyant* forms only towards the end of the fourteenth century. The often quoted traceries of the Lagrange Chapel in Amiens Cathedral (of 1373–5) are only the beginning of a large use of a style henceforth decisively diverging from the classical, rational French Gothic. To confine ourselves to Italy, this style arrives in Venice in the first half of the century and in Siena, for instance, about 1340 in the great windows with ample traceries of the *Obergaden* in the Duomo and of the 'Duomo Nuovo'.

Nor should they be confused with the related manifestations of the Arabic interlaced arch, visible, for instance, in the porch of the Amalfi Duomo (at the beginning of the thirteenth century); a taste to which even the English masters of the 'decorated' style certainly paid attention[82]. It may not always have been the Campionese who spread and interpreted this style of English origin, but in Venice, at least, this is fairly certain.

In the three–light window on the right, and the two–light window next to it on rio di Palazzo, the inflected trefoiled arches which, as we saw, are not at all a novelty in Venice in the middle of the fourteenth century, form a typically Venetian element (the two–light windows in the upper part of the inner courtyard wall resemble, in their particular style and the presence of the torus element, the two–light window on rio di Palazzo but, owing to the suspected restorations, one cannot be sure).

The considerations to which we have been led by the great windows in the Doge's Palace and the four three–light windows in St. Mark's bring us to the problem of a greater awareness on the part of the stonecutters and builders working in Venice just before the middle of the fourteenth century than one would assume from the examples of Sesto al Reghena and the little front of S. Gregorio, even if it is true that in the latter the lesser rigour applied in building and design improves rather than diminishes the colour effect. We must face the problem not only of the derivation of the inflected trefoiled arch, but also of the means whereby these results were achieved at the beginning of the fourteenth century; indeed, even if sea trade and, generally, political and commercial relations contributed to it, yet it seems interesting to mention those Campionese master–masons who left clear traces in the execution of the great windows of the Doge's Palace.

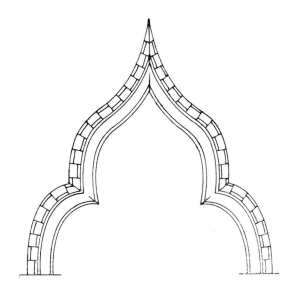

Many other buildings of the beginning of the fourteenth century still exist in Venice. For none do we have entirely reliable dates or evidence. No studies have been made, however, in this connection, except for purposes of town–planning. These are valuable when accompanied by other data of stylistic character, but by themselves they are not very trustworthy because the predilection for a certain kind of ground plan may last well over fifty years.

We must say at once, however, that even the stylistic data must be interpreted with a certain flexibility. We would suggest an approximation of not less than twenty years where the quality is higher, and fifty years where the style is common or indifferent; and we should be content with such a result in a sector of the history of art in which it is even today difficult to distinguish between fourteenth century, fifteenth century and the first decades of the sixteenth. It is always important not to force the evolution of the forms into rigid chronological schemes—often prefabricated—but to establish a reasonable succession which would accord with reasonably flexible chronological criteria. This is particularly necessary in a city like Venice, where medieval architecture repeats and preserves its forms much more than in other important artistic centres of the peninsula. With the appearance of the trefoiled inflected arch in Venice at the beginning of the fourteenth century begins a long period which—even considering its variants and enrichments—will vanish entirely in the first decades of the sixteenth.

The absence of compelling structural reasons gives this form of opening a freedom of expression which has established itself everywhere, in the large buildings as well as the small. It is a truly dominant element which ends by rooting itself in the memory like a symbolic sign, emblematic, haunting, living its own poetic life outside any architectural context, widespread—also on the mainland—and incredibly tenacious.

But let us look at possible data on Venetian building activity at the beginning of the fourteenth century.

One of the very few houses assigned by all to the fourteenth century is the Corner Foscolo at S. Margherita (Dorsoduro 2931) and that on the basis of two payment notes of 1381 and 1390 (published by Paoletti)[83] to Pier Paolo Celega, drawn up in such general terms[84] that it would be rash to relate them to the whole building as we see it today. Of the front, the left side is particularly remarkable (the right wing with the two windows looks like a later addition, but may be the work of another hand); the door, of Romanesque foundation and with a squared lunette (in French taste) is certainly of the fourteenth century, as the emblem in the centre with the three angels attests; the large window above it and the four–light window have the heart–shaped upper foils which we saw appearing a little before the middle of the century; the arches have the by now usual Byzantine dentil border, but the moulding is simpler than at Sesto al Reghena or S. Gregorio. Here a cyma and a fillet announce a purely Gothic Style of western origin, which will be later infinitely repeated; the capitals have superposed caulicoles; the roof juts on buttresses. As we see, these are all archaic features which cannot point to anything but the fourteenth century, probably the first half. The details of value (in particular, the door) do not form a whole having a particular significance (obscured, perhaps, by possible additions and changes) except that of colour (common to so many Venetian houses). The inner courtyard has an exterior staircase completely remade with banisters carried by colonnettes at wide intervals and supported by diminishing, very pointed arches (the original ones from the fourteenth century); the parapet round the well with two–handled vases and rosettes is of the fourteenth century; a porch (walled) with architrave and certainly with fourteenth–century capitals (but of an entirely unusual cut) ran parallel to the front, bending in a right–angle, but it does not clarify the planimetry[85].

There are not many examples of such forms in Venice. On the fondamenta Pesaro (S. Croce 2078) there is a four–light window framed in a Byzantine dentil ornament which shows the same greatly developed upper lobe, while the interesting capitals, with foliage adhering to the bell, may be assumed of the fourteenth century. As for the frame (which, as we saw, was probably already in use in the 'Romanesque' period), it provides another confirmation of the early appearance of such features, which are usually thought to be later in time. The contrast between the robust supports and the slender, archaic grace of the arches creates a notable effect[86].

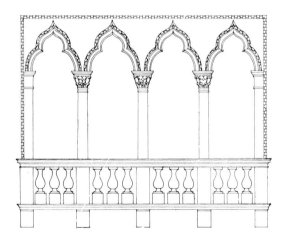

An opposite effect, however, is achieved by the four–light window on the fondamenta del Banco Salviati (S. Polo 1499c, 1500) to which corresponds, on calle Tamossi, a three–light window where the short, slender columns, with fourteenth–century capitals with rosettes, carry trefoils which are almost forcibly expanded[87]. However, the fourteenth–century character of these abnormal forms seems definitely confirmed by what can be seen of Palazzo Ottoboni (fond. S. Severo, Cast. 5136); the remains of a walled–up four–light window, with capitals with superposed caulicoli and a clearly fourteenth–century sculpture on the architrave of the door, certainly contemporaneous[88].

There is a beautiful trefoiled three–light window of this type in corte de Ca' Mosto, almost certainly of the fourteenth century. A last example, the small Palazzo Foscari near the Station bridge (S. Croce 729)—namely, the larger building on the right—displays archaic features in the irregular heights of the Gothic cusps, in the very pronounced upper foils, and in the capitals[89], an example of the way in which the Gothic façade was taking shape, on a pattern already elaborated in a preceding epoch, in the middle of the fourteenth century. Naturally, these are not the only manifestations of fourteenth–century secular Gothic, so scarcely provided with reliable dates in Venice. The style is recognizable, for instance, where one sees crushed trefoils, with a pressed down upper foil (as it appears precisely in England, round the middle of the fourteenth century, in Perpendicular Gothic, e. g. at Gloucester); besides, of course, where the rhythms of the façades do not yet appear settled (in spite of 'Romanesque' precedents), and are not yet stabilized in fully balanced harmonies. Also here, naturally, it is sometimes difficult to distinguish between forms certainly born in the fourteenth century and those lazily taken up again in later periods. In such cases (as in those previously mentioned), other concomitant elements should help, if possible, to arrive at a less approximate dating. Let us give some examples: two façades in campo dell'Anatomia and the nearby campiello delle Strope.

In the first (S. Croce 1055–6), a four–light window and three single windows are the surviving elements of an altered organism; the pressed–down trefoils rest, in the four–light window, on fourteenth–century capitals with rosettes (one with truncated cube), and the archaic structure is confirmed by the stocky colonnettes on high bases[90]; in the second (S. Croce 1057), the whole of the first floor is still preserved, a four–light window with arches similar to those of the previous one, two capitals with rosettes and one with truncated cube, and four single windows, two each side, over which the Gothic cornice hangs low.

This small group, however modest, indicates a fashion presumably widespread in the first half of the fourteenth century, and justifies the extension of the inquiry to more significant structures. Such is the Casa Barbaro in S. Maria Mater Domini (S. Croce 2177) where the four–light window with fourteenth–century capitals is, as in the previous houses, sheltering under the cornice, and the high plinths return[91] and the small house in fondamenta S. Anna (Cast. 1132–33) where there still remains the upper cornice and the four–light window with short columns and high plinths, sheltering under the cornice, with fourteenth–century capitals and somewhat depressed trefoiled arches[92]. Also the small Palazzo Dandolo on riva del Carbon is relevant here. The two four–light windows, one above the other, pierce the small front, and the cornice stands immediately above the upper one. Capitals with closely adhering foliage stand above the stocky columns and the pilasters. Byzantine dentil ornaments frame the two rows of windows. Under the Gothic cornice, high up, runs a frieze with rosettes, similar to the one decorating the door of S. Gregorio. It is difficult to say whether this is the whole of the original front of the small building. The crowding of architectural elements, the variety of the supports, the crushed trefoiled arches, bring out a feeling of embarrassment, denoting the work of a master–mason rather than that of an architect[93]. Late Romanesque capitals also carry the arches of the four–light windows in the centre of

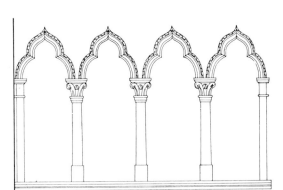

*Four-light window in Fondamenta del Banco Salviati at S. Polo*

Palazzo Giustiniano in crosera di S. Pantalon (Dorsoduro 3820–21). The façade of a whole floor is preserved, repeating the symmetrical arrangement already used in the Romanesque period; capitals with rosette; the level of the window sills marked by a plain dog–tooth frieze; lunette of the (vanished) portal in terracotta, like the one in campo S. Margherita, with a coat of arms in the centre in a quatrefoil patera (which we saw also in Palazzo Barbaro at S. Maria Mater Domini); cornice pressing upon the multi–light window[94]. There was perhaps on the first floor of this building another four–light window, as can be inferred from a similar building, Casa Perducci on the Grand Canal, with a similar symmetrical arrangement but with only two two–light windows in the centre (calle dell'Aseo, Cann. 5772). In the upper one of the windows are repeated the flattened arches and the short column with archaic capital on a high plinth (and in this connection we may recall that the Perducci came from Lucca in the fourteenth century and by 1361 were already Venetian citizens)[95].

The left side of Palazzo Cendon in S. Giobbe (Cann. 534) would also be brought into this series, were it not that it carries a coat of arms with the clear date of 1437. We consider, though, that these flattened arches, flanked by others, simple, hog–backed (ogee) with short columns on high pedestals and capitals with rosettes, are all elements which fit the fourteenth century; and the suspicion may then arise that the right side (no. 435a), which is certainly later in time, had brought about a general reorganization, a single cornice being made to run along both buildings, and that the shield was placed then[96].

While we consider other aspects of secular Gothic still far from that more rational organization which it will asume (at least in the tracing of the arch) in a more mature epoch, and which make one think, therefore, of archaic forms in course of development, we should not neglect those arches in which the upper foil appears reduced in size and sometimes strangled. The examples are not numerous but worthy of consideration. We find both organized wholes and fragments. Among the latter are four windows in campo Drio al Cimitero, at Angelo Raffaele (Ca' Trevisan; Dorsoduro 170–5) where a simple torus profile surrounds the flat archivolt[97], a two–light window at Rielo, also at Angelo Raffaele (Dorsoduro 1871), with Romanesque capital and a colonnette on a high pedestal[98], and, in a cruder form, in calle della Toleta (Dorsoduro 1238). To quote more striking examples: the façade on campo S. Marina of Palazzo Bollani Dolfin (Cast. 6073): a surviving floor in which a three–light window borne by pilasters is closely flanked by two single windows (excluding the wings; the façade on the rio is later in time)[99]; or the façade of Palazzo Molin in Marzaria S. Zulian (S. Marco 783): a set of four floors, perhaps restored, but which certainly reflects a primitive order, with non–aligned windows and capitals with large archaic leaves[100]. Some of the openings of this type are defined, as we saw, by a very simple profile, with the smooth faces at right angles and the archivolt bordered by a torus, exactly as in Romanesque buildings. Similar profiles are found occasionally in Venice and, naturally, their archaic character is not sufficient to place in the fourteenth century the windows which display them. These are simple forms, perhaps dictated by economic considerations, and ones which fifteenth–century stonecutters could lazily copy. Two organic wholes of this kind are found in rio Terrà dei Franceschi (Cann. 4595–6 and 4597–8)[101]; two three–light windows, one above the other, in rio Terrà Barba Frutarol (Cann. 4720)[102]. Two windows of the fourth order in calle delle Oche (S. Croce 1036), accompanying an archaic three–light window of the third type, all with the same profile, must certainly be of the fourteenth century.

Of lesser importance, but to be mentioned as pertaining to the beginning of the fourteenth century, is another fragment with the same characteristics in corte Cavallo (Cann. 3486): a two–light window and two single windows on the first floor, remarkable for the truncated cube capital on a high plinth; a beautiful four–light window flanked by two single windows on each side in calle dei Fabbri (S. Marco 4680) with rosette capitals[103]; a three–light window

and a single window in calle dell'Aseo[104] (Cann. 1896) where the moulding is surrounded by a Byzantine dentil ornament, and other fragments[105].

Finally, a very peculiar case concerning this typical manner of profiling is presented by a house in rio Madonnetta. It is on two floors, with semicircular doorway and a three–light window with Romanesque capitals, the windows of which, however, are semicircular. It may be that there are cases, in the Gothic period, of the employment of the round Romanesque arch or we may be dealing with a façade of a later period.

If among the unusual, abnormal forms which, at the beginning of the fourteenth century, characterize the inflected trefoiled arch, we must first mention those which display deformations due to an unsure interpretation of transalpine prototypes, we should not, for that, neglect other examples which display signs of archaism. They must be attributed to the first half of the fourteenth century.

Strange as this may appear, it is nevertheless surprising that to the irregular layout of a façade not subject to a symmetrical or, at any rate, 'architectural' (in the sense this word could have on the Italian mainland and, particularly, in Tuscany) order should correspond, insistently, in the house in salizzada S. Stae (S. Croce 1988) indubitable signs of archaism. It is difficult to reconstitute the original aspect of the façade, of which there remains the Gothic upper cornice and a five–light window on the second floor, partly supported by fourteenth–century type capitals (without rosettes, with a short column on a high plinth). The window on the extreme right appears connected to it by a pilaster and is provided with its own balcony, while a window of smaller type than the others flanks it immediately on the right. On the first floor, the surviving three–light window was evidently part of a similar organic whole (whose length is marked by the cornice of the sill) on low columns with capitals with caulicoli. These are, undoubtedly, the most fascinating cases. And this is the richest, even if incomplete example presented to us so far of the Venetian Gothic façade, such as it will later form itself, with greater regularity, in the late fourteenth and in the fifteenth centuries. We consider it to be of the first half of the fourteenth century[106].

More a Palazzo than a house in the sober distribution, at long intervals, of the surviving ancient parts, it shows the beginning of a rhythm which we shall meet again later and which is to be noticed, with clearer and more regular variations, in Palazzo Venier on rio dell'Arco (in the Castello quarter), the front of which is, except on the top floor, almost intact. There are, however, irregularities which manifest themselves particularly in the left wing (irregular alignment of the windows), as well as in the part illustrated by the photograph, with the different heights and levels of the windows, the short columns of the second floor (and those, too long, of the first), the purely fourteenth–century type capitals, and the high plinths. These are all elements which, even in their irrationality (which is so much part of the spirit of the city itself) and in the absence, one could swear, of pre–established rules of proportion, come together in a remarkable harmony. And it is easy to imagine how the different heights of the impost stones of the arches, here almost mischievously close to each other[107], would scandalize, say, a French builder.

Finally, we shall mention the cases in which truncated cube capitals of the most archaic Romanesque type (like the one illustrated by Ruskin, no. 1 of Table II)[108] are combined with the fourth order, as, for instance, the remarkable façade on calle Drio la Sagrestia (Cast. 4501) where we see, on different axes, a two–light window, a four–light window and a three–light window, in which some pilasters are inserted also; a two–light window and two single windows in piscina del Forner (Dorsoduro 858)[109]; the pleasing façade of a house on rio di S. Canciano, with two three–light windows in line displaced to the extreme right and capitals with caulicoli in one and rosettes in the other[110].

We should not be surprised if we were to obtain one day documentary proof that, in Venetian secular architecture, the inflected trefoiled arch preceded the simple, uninflected trefoiled arch with four centres of western origin.

Today, we can only say that both appeared at least at the same time. And we shall first discuss the latter. In this respect, the already mentioned Palazzo Bosso in S. Tomà (S. Polo 2802) is very interesting. Its windows were added, interrupting its frieze, to an old Romanesque house to which the water–gate also belongs. The arches are timidly drawn, but they already depart from the late Romano–Byzantine models characterized by Islamic inflexions. The placing of the small paterae which almost touch the extrados appears equally undecided. We have seen already that these forms may be assigned to the early fourteenth century.

A more definitely western trend is visible in Palazzo Zorzi–Bon on rio S. Severo. This structure raises substantial problems for the student of Venetian secular Gothic. It is the first large Gothic palace (an uncommonly imposing one) which we meet and our attention is at once concentrated on the great central five–light window and on the four–light window above it. This is one of those cases where colour is one of the essential components. In the window suite, columns of red limestone alternate with others of grey between the white of the mouldings and of the capitals. Of these last, the two central ones, with large, reversed leaves, recall the most ancient capitals on the Ponte della Paglia side of the Doge's Palace gallery, which must be assigned to the middle of the fourteenth century. The other two and the three of the four–light window above do not resemble others known in Venice to be of the fourteenth century, but they can even less be compared to those, decorated with thick leaves, common from the second half of the fourteenth century onwards. The organization of this great central theme appears, therefore, unique and its elements, among which the hog–back (ogee) is foremost, take us to about the middle of the fourteenth century.

The façade shows an impressive development; it expands and breaks the rhythms which should animate the axes marked by the windows of the wings (because it is evident that only practical reasons suggest a different width for the interaxial surfaces) according to a principle which will become specific to a somewhat later Venetian building practice (recalled also by the right corner, where alternate quoins mark with a striking colour note the clear limit of the wall mass, as will happen in the middle of the fifteenth century). The windows are neatly framed by the Byzantine dentil ornament. Such a methodical application, however, had not appeared so far, but was to become frequent at a later date. Should we, then, recognize in this façade one of the first examples—in the middle, let us remember, of the fourteenth century—of a formula which will assert itself particularly in the advanced fifteenth century? Or should we think of successive enlargements inspired by a rigorous imitation of the particular style peculiar to the central axis? If the corner with quoins appears, by the nature of its masonry, perhaps remade, the remainder of the masonry is uniform from one end of the façade to the other. We should also recognize two archaic features in the placing of the paterae on the vertices of the arches and in the presence of the two plain Gothic doors on the rio[111]. The plan of the building and of the adjacent structure giving on the ruga Giuffa favours on the whole an archaic dating, at least of the central nucleus. This would explain why the calle dell'Arco reaches to the centre of the palace (and we have already studied the late Romanesque two–light window lighting from that side the L–shaped room on the *piano nobile*) and almost takes over, in the centre of this complex of dwellings which displays also on the ruga Giuffa archaic features, that part of the traversing hall already born with the Romano–Byzantine structures[112]. However, I suspend judgment on a building deserving deeper study[113].

Of a different quality, but significant and akin to the previous one (even if suspected of having been substantially restored), Palazzo Grandiben–Negri by Ponte Erizzo (Cast. 4003) is of a considerable height, intended to accommodate large rooms. The ground floor, with a door still recalling the Romanesque, round–headed and very simple, is important, as is the *piano nobile* with the five–light window flanked by the usual windows in pairs. Here also there are paterae standing above the vertices of the ogee arches (not trefoiled); the capitals are of the fourteenth–century type, with rosettes. On the top floor, the window of five small lights with segmental arches and the lateral windows pose, for the first time here, the problem of these mezzanines whose apertures we are inclined to consider the original ones. It displays a practical 'utilitarian' character, unconcerned with any particular refinements[114].

One of the characteristics of Palazzi Zorzi–Bon and Grandiben–Negri is the large area left by the pointed arch above itself within the frame formed by the Byzantine dentil ornament, which is scarcely filled by a patera above its vertex. Later this surface will be somewhat reduced and the upper part of the ornament will touch the apex of the flower finials placed on the point of the arches, while the paterae will be ranged by the sides of the finial, in line with the columns (this last a peculiarity which finds precedents in the Romanesque epoch, during which, however, the habit of placing the paterae on the vertices of the arches was also frequent).

These specific features therefore provide a further clue to the identification of other buildings of the fourteenth century, even if we continue beyond the middle of the century. Of the two Palazzi Soranzo in campo S. Polo, the one which is visibly older (the left one, at no. 2170) prompts Lorenzetti to some remarks which extend beyond the critical generalities to which this subject has been confined for a century.

'Interesting example of a Gothic house of the beginning of the fifteenth century, with structural and decorative elements which suggest fourteenth–century forms and motifs of the Veneto–Byzantine style, as more particularly shown by the ornate architraves of the two doorways...'.

In reality, the two doorways have such a conspicuously archaic character that they could be taken as belonging to the height of the fourteenth century. The animals facing each other still have a Romanesque air, but they are clearly placed on the axes of the four lateral windows which flank the two four–light windows in perfect symmetry, and these two sets of windows must be considered contemporary with the two doorways, with elements in which we recognize specific indications of the fourteenth–century Venetian building style; namely, on the *piano nobile* the ogee arch (not trefoiled) is surmounted by a vast, smooth, framed area in which the paterae have not yet found a regular arrangement and the capitals have not been provided with the thick leaves prevalent in the fourteenth century (already noted by Ruskin); on the second floor are capitals of the same type and trefoiled arches, but with a pronounced upper foil and the projections between the lobes with tracery.

The oldest of the Soranzo structures therefore marks an important stage towards the constitution of the canonical type forming the basis of so many buildings of the late fourteenth and of the fifteenth centuries. The main axis of this façade is displaced to the right, but this does not diminish the charm of a by now established rhythm, by virtue of which the left wing detaches itself from the compact group on the right contained between the axes marked by the two doors, yet remains bound to it by measured and sober intervals[115]. Nor can the interior of Palazzo Soranzo and of the palazzo next to it, as well as of the whole block between campo S. Polo, rio della Madonnetta and calle Cavalli which constitutes 'a block of building units entirely self–sufficient yet strongly interrelated' avoid recalling the rhythms of Palazzo Barbaro at S. Vidal. The courtyards are thus integrated with each other according to an obviously pre–established plan[116].

On the lines suggested by the Soranzo building, the older parts of Palazzo Priuli at S. Severo can also find a reasonable ordering. The building displays at least two styles, as is implicitly admitted by the observation that the corner window towards rio dell'Osmarin is of a later date than the rest. This corner window must have represented a novelty in Venice, as we shall see also later. In 1431–4 Marino Contarini asked the stone–mason Nicolò Romanello that the three balconies of his house (the Ca' d'Oro) *di esser a muodo de quello de la casa fo di ser Chostantin de prioliji quelo e suso al chanton inverso sam Zacharia*[117]... (should be in the manner of that at the corner towards S. Zacharia in Costantino de Priuli's house). We do not know to about what year the window of Palazzo Priuli could be attributed, but it is certain that the rio dell'Osmarin front of the building and, by analogy, the one in the calle dei Preti and campo S. Severo are older by some decades and therefore contemporary. The corner window, towards the bridge, with a simple inflected arch, seems older than the other. But it is equally evident, on close analysis, that the climate is the same as that of Palazzo Soranzo at S. Polo and, perhaps going back a little, of the Grandiben–Negri and Zorzi–Bon structures. The high framed fascia above the lights of the four/six–light window on the rio and the multi–light window on the campo, the archaic capitals, the simple ogee arches on the rio and trefoiled with tracery on the campo, the low balustrades between the columns—everything hangs together to the point of confirming that these elements belong to the end of the fourteenth century, perhaps even to an earlier time. The coats of arms are placed in two paterae. The balconies are clearly additions. If, then, we add to these elements the pilasters supporting the arches of the multi–light towards the campo (multi–light incoherently connected to another isolated window inside the usual frame made by a Byzantine dentil ornament—this also an archaic indication) and the peculiar structure of the portal surmounted by a balcony under it, we have additional reasons to place this singular structure back towards the middle of the fourteenth century. Of fundamental importance is the large walled–up window above the doorway, concerning which Paoletti observed that this 'singular opening must originally have been decorated by a tracery and, at the sides of the arch, by lions, of which traces still subsist'[118].

These are observations of great import if one considers that the proportions of this opening are very similar to those of the large windows of the Doge's Palace, which, as we saw, are attributed to around the middle of the fourteenth century. At this point many other parts of this large block become significant. The four–light on the mezzanine of the first floor over the rio (of type 4) with a taller window closely flanking it; the top floor which over the canal certainly had a multi–light standing above the six–light, flanked by single windows, while on the campo there is a four–light closely connected with the usual taller window, but not in line with the *piano nobile*; the cornice, certainly belonging to the older structure, which is placed above the top floor, almost touching the vertices of the arches (in a style similar to that found in those houses—in campo dell'Anatomia, etc.—which we have attributed to the beginning of the fourteenth century).

An incoherent whole, certainly regulated more by practical needs than by aesthetic considerations, but which nevertheless realizes in invaluable fragments some peculiar assertions of taste; and this is the first time that we encounter a motif which will often return in the fifteenth century, that of the tripartite six–light, almost a triptych, articulated in an entirely new way[119].

Of prime importance, in Palazzo Priuli, is the steep external staircase, still entirely preserved though in a bad state, which in every part confirms that the structure belongs to the late fourteenth century, from the simple faces of the steps, provided with torus cornices (as in Palazzo Magno–Bembo), to the cylinders instead of colonnettes, to the handrail ornamented with foliage, to the small arches in the balustrade of the top landing (similar to those of

Palazzo Contarini Porta di Ferro), to the worn–out sculptures surmounting the balustrade, clearly of the fourteenth century (and similar to those of the above–mentioned Palazzo Contarini), to the splendid well parapet. This beautiful staircase of three flights, accommodated in a narrow space, blocked on the western side by two Gothic fifteenth–century arches supported by a ringed column, is of capital importance for an understanding of this building and of the late fourteenth–century architecture of Venice. The simple inflected arch, such as we have seen it so far, enters the patrimony of Venetian secular architecture, even if it is to be employed somewhat sporadically in comparison with the extraordinarily widespread use of the trefoiled inflected arch.

*Particular of the water-gate of Palazzo Agnusdio*

A doubtful case is that presented by the courtyard façade of Palazzo Corner della Frescada (Dorsoduro 3911). The four–light on the courtyard, supported by fourteenth–century type capitals, makes one doubt whether it is contemporaneous with the façade or an ancient element utilized in the new building (the balcony is certainly of the end of the fifteenth century). Palazzo della Torre, probably adapted and insignificant (Cann. 1304; in rio Terrà S. Leonardo)[120], is equally perplexing. And we need hardly add that windows of this type appear, also in important examples, in full fifteenth century (second floor of Palazzo Bembo in Rialto; Palazzo Pisani–Moretta)[121].

From the examples so far quoted, which developed coherently through a period of two to five (at most) decades, a valuable and intact fragment (due certainly to a stone–mason who was also an architect) detaches itself, namely, the five–light window of Palazzo Agnusdio at ponte del Forner (S. Croce 2060), whose façade it is by now impossible, with the remaining elements (the five–light, the beautiful gate on the bridge, the water–gate surmounted by the round plate with the Agnus Dei and the cornice) to restore to its primitive aspect.

It is difficult to find precise correspondences between the figures adorning this five–light window and fourteenth–century Venetian sculpture, but it is easy to notice the characteristics of an art which is not very far from the middle of the century[122]. The Byzantine dentil ornament confines clearly into a narrow space the six reliefs of the Annunciation and of the Gospel symbols, the latter displaying open and symmetrical wings which contrast with the subtly modulated inflected arches. The two arches at the ends leaning on pilasters are a little wider and a little taller than the three central ones. The capitals are robust and archaic, with plain dog–tooth ornaments (*punte di diamante*)[123]. The general effect is of a live and compact plasticity, because of which—contrary to the case of the other multi–lights we have seen—this particular feature of the façade must be singled out as the work of a stonecutter. And it is not possible here, logically, to leave out of consideration the rich portal towards the bridge which recalls Andriolo (the documented figures on the Vicentine portal) particularly clearly and explicitly in the three angels enclosed in the archivolt moulding with scrolls in Romanesque style (of the early thirteenth century), obviously adapted to the Gothic arch[124].

We must now mention the very scant evidence remaining of another form, that of the simple trefoiled arch with two centres, widespread all over the Italian mainland but confined in Venice, in the fourteenth century, to religious architecture, while the simple arch with two centres is found even in the thirteenth century (in St. Mark's). It may be that examples of this type, which points directly to the west, were more numerous at one time but it would appear that the inflected trefoiled arch was the one preferred.

A Venetian building, unique of its kind, the Palazzo Ariani (Dorsoduro 2376) confirms our suppositions aptly, and is one of the very few which the exceedingly scant bibliography on secular Gothic in Venice is concordant in assigning to the fourteenth century[125]. The six–light window of Palazzo Ariani is unique and cannot be fitted into any architectural sequence, even less so than the very singular five-light window of Palazzo Agnusdio. If the distribution of the supports (three columns with capitals with well developed and decidedly archaic caulicoli, and two pilasters) and of the balustrades[126] is in the Venetian tradition, the remainder is entirely different, particularly the arch and, above all, the filling of the high fascia above the windows framed by the usual dentil ornament and resolved into a double row of quatrefoils, in addition to the trefoil oculi placed between the arches, defined by a torus moulding which appears essential also for the definition of the arches (a determining element in one Venetian building only—the Doge's Palace).

All these non–Venetian elements evidently refer us to the transalpine Gothic, French more than English. The torus profile, as a linear definition of mass in surface, is typical of a very important current in the French architecture of the thirteenth century. It was centred in Champagne, in the *école rémoise*, and is visible on the northern side of Notre Dame de Paris, in the 'red door' and in the chapels of the ambulatory which flank it (by Pierre de Montreuil, pupil of Jean de Chelles, who in about 1250 was building the northern area of the transept and in 1258 was working on the southern transept). This soft roundness of the profiles is more in evidence in the Parisian cathedral in that it differs *toto coelo* from the dry, angular profiles of metallic thinness by Jean de Chelles.

The activities of Pierre de Montreuil himself ended with his death in 1267, but his work was then continued by Pierre de Chelles, certainly a relative of Jean, in the chapels round the choir (1296–1320), where the style of Jean de Chelles reappears.

This is not the place to describe precisely the diffusion of these particular aspects of the French architecture of the second half of the thirteenth century. Clearly, Pierre de Montreuil's influence extends to the external aspect of the building elements which had been present for some time in the bearing structures of French Gothic (it is enough to consider the profiles of the many–styled pilasters and of the vaulting ribs) and even in the 'decorative' part of certain exteriors (e. g. the façade at Amiens) conferring, however, on these new surfaces a softer and more human aspect which lends itself, with the elimination of too sudden passages, to a subtler, more colourful play of chiaroscuro. This was typical of the Reims school ( let us recall the longitudinal façades of St. Denis and Strasbourg and St. Sulpice de Favières), while a continuation of the style of Jean de Chelles is visible in the lower part of the façade of Strasbourg cathedral.

One could, with more justification, dwell upon the connections with Italian art, where those 'lexical' elements were well received. Nicola Pisano, in the pulpit of Siena, was not insensitive to these trends and this is decisively confirmed by the base of the column (with the liberal arts), where the inner torus, curiously flattened, placed above the octagonal base and protruding over it, is almost identical to those executed by Pierre de Montreuil in the Sainte–Chapelle and at St. Denis[127].

The other motif of this set of windows, that of the reticulated tracery, is equally significant. Tracery of this type was very widespread in England throughout the fourteenth century and is found also in France[128] and then, still in the fourteenth century, in Spain (Burgos, S. Maria del Castro Urdiales, Tortosa, etc.) owing to English and perhaps also Muslim influence. The Venetian version is purely geometrical, far removed from the fantastic exuberance of fourteenth–century English Gothic, and therefore nearer to French art. The somewhat timid execution could suggest an Italian stonecutter around the middle of the fourteenth century (as the parapet sculptures confirm). Moreover, the two windows on the right do not seem inserted by breaking into the wall. If so, they are (with a torus profile on the outside) among the first examples of the trefoiled inflected arch. The left corner of the façade is supported (a fairly rare occurrence) by a wooden architrave which turns through a right–angle and produces an arcade borne by tall columns. An exterior staircase climbs in two flights to the first floor around a small courtyard at the side of the building. The pointed arches which support it reproduce exactly the simple forms of the water–gates which we have already noted (on pilasters with cube imposts, without capitals). As for the torus profiles, in Venice itself we may recall here also the windows of the minor apses of the Frari, dated to about 1361.

Burckhardt's judgment[129] that this façade is good 'for the painters in water–colours' is certainly exaggerated but expresses, crudely, the aesthetic deficiencies of the building compared with works carried out with a more refined sensitivity. This work, perhaps the only one of a stonemason–architect fallen suddenly in the lagunar environment and certainly unadjusted to the trends in taste dominant at the time and also devoid of a personality strong enough to impose itself in a different and superior manner (as is the case with the architect of the Doge's Palace), has nevertheless its place in fourteenth–century Venetian architecture, in the fabric of which this kind of episode is not infrequent. This was also the case in the fifteenth century with the Ca' d'Oro. The simple trefoiled arch is equally found in the only Gothic window still remaining in Palazzo Soranzo Pisani in rio Terrà Primo del Parrucchetta (S. Polo 2279), in line with a door, of which there remains a notable bas–relief accepted as of the fourteenth century.

From it can be deduced also the age of the window (and of the building, the upper cornice of which still remains), above which stands, in line, a quatrefoil, each foil, in turn, trefoiled, of direct French origin[130]. And one recalls immediately a quite similar feature visible in the large second–order windows of the main apse of SS. Giovanni e Paolo, a work certainly carried out around the middle of the fourteenth century[131]. If we add to this the torus profile which, as in Palazzo Ariani, outlines the window and the oculus above it, we must conclude that the few remains cannot go beyond the year 1400 at most[132].

We reproduce here an engraving by Fontana of an imposing, even if inconsistent (and now marred by the addition of another storey) building on the Grand Canal, namely Palazzo Gritti–Pisani at S. Maria Zobenigo (S. Marco 2466), the *piano nobile* of which displays simple trefoiled arches, while the second floor carries ogee arches with flower finials (dated by Lorenzetti to the beginning of the fifteenth century, but it is advisable, for the moment, to suspend judgment)[133].

The simple trefoiled arch appears only once in a structure of some importance in the fifteenth century. The *piano nobile* of Palazzo Manolesso–Ferro (Ramo Secondo di Ca' Minotto, S. Marco 2322) has, in a distribution of great rhythmic regularity, the usual four–light with two windows on each side, where, however, the vertex of the arches connects directly with the horizontal cornice which, also on the sides, closely frames the openings according to a principle which, still in the fourteenth century, we see realized in transalpine Gothic[134]. The Renaissance frieze immediately above it, the late Gothic capitals, and the balustrade with spindle colonnettes (of fifteenth–century type) should leave no doubt that here we have a late and unique example of this trend, perhaps already of the second half of the fifteenth century[135].

**1.** A. Sartori, 1956, p. 8.

**2.** Ruskin 1886, II, p. 258.

**3.** Viollet-le-Duc, 1854, I, p. 9; IV, p. 279.

**4.** C. Enlart, *Manuel d'Archéologie*, 1904, Vol. II, pp. 12 and 588.

**5.** C. Enlart, 1906, p. 38 et seq.

**6.** Bold, 1905, p. 270.

**7.** Anthyme Saint-Paul, in *Bulletin Monumental*, 1906, p 493; and do 1908-9.

**8.** C. Enlart, 'Origine anglaise du style flamboyant. Réponse à M. Anthyme Saint-Paul' in *Bulletin Monumental*, 1910, p. 125 et seq.

**9.** Bond, 1913, II, p. 616.

**10.** Bond, op. cit. p. 611 et seq.

**11.** Lasteyrie, 1926-7, II, p. 46 et seq. and p. 66.

**12.** Op. cit. p. 63.

**13.** Op. cit., II, p. 53 et seq.

**14.** Op. cit. p. 56.

**15.** Op. cit., II, p. 63 et seq.

**16.** Op. cit., II, p. 66.

**17.** Op. cit., 1926-7, II, pp. 21-2.

**18.** Op. cit., II, p. 52, fig. 590.

**19.** Behling, 1944, p. 25. In connection with this beginning of the 'countercurve' present in 'certain ancient French forms', Focillon's position is somewhat singular (*Vita delle forme*, Milan, 1945, p. 172). He says that French art 'does not release it, but on the contrary confines it, dissimulates it, as a beginning to the stability of architecture', and then admits that 'beginning with the second half of the thirteenth century, stylistic development in England verges on the Baroque (sic), abounds in curves and countercurves, confesses and defines a new phase in architecture, which, however, it must soon renounce. 'Because —continues Focillon—English Gothic remains for long faithful to the concept of masses, of Norman Art, while in the tracing of curves it rapidly anticipates, thus being at the same time a precocious and a conservative art'(p.173). Forgetting, in one of those 'syntheses' which only too often make one lose contact with concrete historical fact, that one of the glories of English architecture is precisely the revolution, right from the beginning of the fourteenth century, of the internal space concept.

**20.** Behling, 1944, fig. 26.

**21.** Behling, 1944, fig. 44. On the clear precedence of the English forms over the German, see the same authoress, p. 37.

**22.** Bond, 1905, pp. 131-2.

**23.** *Bulletin Monumental*, 1908, pp. 261 and 263.

**24.** *Bulletin Monumental*, 1894, p. 428.

**25.** C. Enlart, 1933, p. 588.

**26.** C. Enlart, 1906, p. 42.

**27.** N. Pevsner, *An Outline of European Architecture*, London, 1960, p. 167.

**28.** See: Hürlimann, 1948 or 1950, p. 30; *Enciclopedia dell'Arte*, VI, p. 354.

**29.** Bond, 1905, p. 118.

**30.** Webb, 1956, p. 112.

**31.** Bond, 1905, p. 122.

**32.** Webb, 1956, pp. 52-3.

**33.** We should remember Viollet-le-Duc's open admission of the entirely English character of Lincoln cathedral, with the consequent exclusion of any reference to French art, quoted by Bond, 1905, pp. 112-13.

**34.** C. Enlart, 1906, p. 76. This fact has been confirmed, obviously, by all the English historians.

**35.** C. Enlart, 1906, p. 74; as confirmed also by Hürlimann, 1950, no. 38.

**36.** N. Pevsner, *The Buildings of England, North Somerset and Bristol*, London 1958, pp. 374-5.

**37.** Webb, 1956, figs. 121, 125*a*. Webb does not think we are dealing with regional facts but with an impulse coming from London: as would be shown by the admirable tomb of Edward II in Gloucester cathedral.

**38.** Viollet-le-Duc, III, p. 447.

**39.** Viollet-le-Duc, III, p. 451.

**40.** Hürlimann, 1948, figs. 66, 67.

**41.** Webb, 1956, Plate 115.

**42.** Stone, 1955, Plate 102 (to 1270-80).

**43.** C. Enlart, 1906, p. 54 et seq.

**44.** Clasen, 1930 p. 224.

**45.** Webb, 1956, p. 155; Pevsner, *North Somerset and Bristol*, London 1958, pp. 289-90.

**46.** Bond, 1905, pp. 122 and 270; Stone, 1955, p. 129.

**47.** Stone, 1955, p. 129.

**48.** See: Pevsner, *Buildings of England*, London 1962; Vol. I, 2nd edition, p. 300.

**49.** Bond, 1905, p. 270.

**50.** Lasteyrie, 1926-7, II, p. 34.

**51.** Webb, 1956, p. 137.

**52.** Bond, 1905, p. 127.

**53.** E. Castelnuovo, *Un pittore italiano alla Corte di Avignone*, Turin, 1962, p. 17.

**54.** Idem.

**55.** L. Torres Balbas, *Arquitectura gotica*. Madrid 1952, p. 263. This author remarks that the *flamboyant* style appears in Catalonia only at the end of the fourteenth - beginning of the fifteenth century (p. 263).

**56.** Romanini, 1964, p. 199.

**57.** Toesca, 1950, p. 400.

**58.** L. Zovatto, *Guida di Portogruaro* etc., Portogruaro 1962, p. 79.

**59.** See: 'Annali della Fabbrica del Duomo di Milano...', Milan 1883, Appendice I, pp. 45 and 134 (payment *pro assidibus 3 consignatis mag. Johanni de Firimborg causa fatiendi astellas pro cornice exteriori fabricae*). I owe this information to my student, Dr. Antonio Cadei.

**60.** Demus, 1960, p. 207.

**61.** Cod. Gradenigo-Dolfin, no. 228/II, Plate 40 (Grevembroch somehow connects it with the name and the tomb of Soranzo); Gabelentz, 1903, p. 213 (to the beginning of the fourteenth century); Planiscig, 1916, p. 46; Lorenzetti, 1956, p. 206 (thirteenth-fourteenth centuries); Toesca, 1950, p. 403 (late Byzantine type).

**62.** Cod. Gradenigo-Dolfin, no. 228/III, Plate 6 (Venice, Museo Correr).

**63.** Demus, 1960, pp. 112, 113, 140 and 207. In a letter sent to me on 4 July 1962, Demus definitely inclines towards the second date

**64.** Marzemin, 1912, p. 107.

**65.** Ruskin, 1886, III, pp. 300-1.

**66.** Marzemin, 1912, p. 108.

**67.** Trincanato, 1948, pp. 146-7.

**68.** *Abbazia di S. Gregorio.* See, in addition to Ruskin and to Marzemin's work: Gabelentz, 1903, p. 230 et seq.; Lorenzetti, 1956, p. 531 et seq. (to 1342); Toesca, 1950, p. 411 (puts the external statue of the saint in about 1350). The church was reconstructed in the fifteenth century. As Marzemin and Lorenzetti rightly observe, the marble fragments of parapets on the low wall of the cloister are a later adaptation.

**69.** On Da Ponte's repair work after the fires of 1574 and 1577 see: Temanza, 1778, p. 500 et seq.; Bettio, 1837, 2v.; Cicognara, 1838, pp. 58-9; Zanotto, 1853, I, pp. 121, 128, 143, 145 et seq.; Paoletti, 1893, I, pp. 8-9. The large windows were remade after 1577.

**70.** The title of the Codex is: *Description ou Traicté du gouvernement et régyme de la cité et seigneurie de Venise* (see: Meurgey, 1930, p. 176, Plate 117). In this view, except for the western façade of the Doge's Palace, certainly not exactly rendered but not entirely unfaithful, all the remainder (the Square, the Basilica, the houses with façades of northern type, with tympana in steps) is completely imaginary; obviously the miniaturist had a precise graphic reproduction under his eyes of only the Palace façade.
In fact, all the constituent elements of the western façade appear there (even if the number of arches is different). It is, however, rather curious that in place of the Porta della Carta there appears another gate, rectangular and surmounted by a statue, standing, of Justice, with sword and scales. The codex had been written for Admiral Louis Malet de Graville, who died in 1516. I owe this important information to my student, Prof. Fernanda de Maffei.

**71.** Ruskin, 1886, III, p. 214.

**72.** I find a similar example of Fatimid art, with the same characteristics, in Tunis (G. Marçais, *L'architecture musulmane d'Occident*, Paris 1954, fig. 60).

**73.** C. Baroni, *Scultura gotica lombarda*, Milan 1944, fig. 26.

**74.** Baroni, op. cit., fig. 63.

**75.** Baroni, op. cit., fig. 246.

**76.** From indications derived from the architecture of some parts of the southern transept of St. Mark's, Demus (1960, p. 207) has deduced the date of 1419-39. But as he himself writes to me (13 October 1964), 'there is no direct and documented date for the large window'. Its shape and mouldings are very like those of the great window of SS. Giovanni e Paolo (in the right transept) which are, for me, certainly of the fourteenth century.

**77.** Romanini, 1964, I, p. 337.

**78.** See them illustrated in: Brian Purefoy, *The Pictorial History of Tewkesbury Abbey*, London, n. d., pp. 12 and 13 (in the series *Pride of Britain*); and in the old, very useful, Bond, 1905, p. 165.

**79.** Bond, op. cit., p. 45.

**80.** The admirable Lady Chapel of Ely (1321-49) constitutes indeed that 'specific and absolutely independent variety of the English Gothic which in the fifteenth century will strongly influence the late French, German and Spanish Gothic' (M. Hürlimann, *Englische Kathedralen*, Zürich, 1948, p. 20). For reproductions see also: C. P. Hankey, *The Pictorial History of Ely Cathedral*, in the series *Pride of Britain*, p. 14 (the octagon) and p. 23 (the Lady Chapel).

**81.** An excellent survey of Prior Crauden's Chapel is provided by Bond, 1905, p. 130.

**82.** See in this connection, G. Castelfranco's article in *Bollettino d'Arte*, January 1933, p. 314 et seq.

**83.** Paoletti, 1893, p. 5, note 5.

**84.** Trincanato, 1948, p. 258 et seq.

**85.** *Casa Corner Foscolo.* Trincanato has studied this house, obtaining from its interior indications of more ancient structures, in this as well as in the contiguous building on the left (op. cit.). See also: Mothes, 1859, pp. 202-3 (to the end of the thirteenth century); Elenco, 1905, p. 165, no. 298; Molmenti, 1925, I, p. 288 (to the end of the fourteenth century and to P. P. Celega); Chiminelli, 1912, p. 226 (to P. P. Celega); Lorenzetti, 1956, p. 556 (erected by the Celega); Torres, 1937, p. 37 (to the Celega); Toesca, 1950, p. 150 (to the fourteenth century). Maretto (1960, Plate X) has identified from town-planning data a complex of buildings of the first half of the fourteenth century in that part of the S. Agostino quarter which goes towards the rio di S. Polo. The indication is plausible even if unsupported by striking representational evidence; and is mentioned here as being of some importance (see, particularly, at no. 2313 of ramo Astori; with few remains).

**86.** *House in fondamenta Pesaro at S. Croce.* Elenco, 1905, p. 140, no. 193. Note the irregularity (almost always a sign of archaism) of the two windows isolated on the left of a type, apparently, more mature and different at lower level.

**87.** *Fond. Banco Salviati*, S. Polo 1499c, 1500. Elenco, 1905, p. 114, no. 111.

**88.** *Palazzo Ottoboni.* Elenco, 1905, p. 54, no. 411.

**89.** *Palazzetto Foscari, S. Croce.* Quadri, 1834, p. 15; Ruskin, 1886, II, p. 257, Plate XVI (with some exaggeration he calls it one of the purest examples of the fourth order; and places it at the end of the thirteenth century); Tassini, 1863, 1915 ed., pp. 677 and 681; Idem, 1879, p. 105; Elenco, 1905, p. 133, no. 80; Lorenzetti, 1956, p. 640; completely restored in 1959.
The heart-shaped motif of the upper lobe appears, now and then, also later (e. g. on the second floor of the house at ponte delle Maravegie, which we shall mention again later) in full fifteenth century, and in the façade of Palazzo Bembo Boldù.

**90.** *House in campo dell'Anatomia.* Elenco, 1905, p. 136, no. 125. A beautiful three-light window on tall cylindrical bases with squat colonnettes and fourteenth-century capitals is to be found in ramo Corte de Ca' Barbo (S. Croce 20); I should say fourteenth century.

**91.** *Casa Barbaro at S. Maria Mater Dei.* Elenco, 1905, p. 141, no. 205 (to the middle of the fifteenth century); Chiminelli, 1912, p. 228; Lorenzetti, 1956, p. 467 (to the fourteenth century); Muratori, 1959, p. 81 (plans). The left wing, higher, is certainly later.

**92.** *Fond. S. Anna* 1132-33. Elenco, 1905, p. 34, no. 60 (with the mark of the Gesuati). Another four-light window, with quite similar framing, it too surviving with the cornice, is to be found on fond. della Croce at the Giudecca (nos. 68-71) and is remarkable because it is in fact a two-light window attached, on the sides, to two taller windows by means of two pilasters (Elenco, 1905, p. 173, no. 9). Rebuilt?

**93.** *Palazzetto Dandolo, Riva del Carbon.* This small building had impressed Ruskin (1886, III, p. 284) as 'one of the most interesting and ancient Gothic palaces' and assigned it to about 1300; Zanotto, 1856, p. 599 (to the eleventh century); Tassini, 1879, p. 98; Lorenzetti, 1956, pp. 458 and 627 (to the fourteenth century).

**94.** *Palazzo Giustinian in crosera S. Pantalon.* Elenco, 1905, p. 169, no. 373 (to the fifteenth century).

**95.** *Casa Perducci sul Canal Grande.* Tassini, 1879, p. 262; Elenco, 1905, p. 99, no. 578 (points out the coats of arms of the end of the fifteenth century); Lorenzetti, 1956, p. 631.
Other examples of trefoiled windows with depressed arch may be given in campiello del Piovan (Castello 3790-1): a three-light window with fourteenth-century rosette capitals (Elenco, 1905, p. 47, no. 295; dated to the beginning of the fifteenth century); a three-light window on pilasters is found in campiello della Chiesa at S. Luca (S. Marco 4039) (Elenco, 1905, p. 21, no. 345); two windows in salizzada del Fontego dei Turchi (S. Croce 1726-7); seven windows (with jambs and architraves remade) at the Zattere (Dorsoduro 791-4); a window (still retaining its ancient grille) in ramo di Ca' Bernardo (S. Polo 2179a); a window in Palazzo Vendrame (S. Polo 1121; cf. Elenco, 1905, p. 111, no. 75); six windows on a second floor in rio dei Miracoli (at ponte del Teatro) have the cusp somewhat crushed. And, of course, these last indications do not at all guarantee, without uncertainty, the assignment of these fragments to the fourteenth century.

**96.** *Palazzo Cendon at S. Giobbe.* This is a supposition which we approach very cautiously.
See: Tassini, 1863, 1915 ed., p. 178 (with useful information); Elenco, 1905, p. 70, nos. 60, 61 (to the beginning of the sixteenth century, misled by Tassini); Lorenzetti, 1956, p. 444 (puts the two houses in the fourteenth century). A two-light window with pressed-down ogee arches of archaic profile is found in calle dei Saoneri (S. Polo 2721).

**97.** Vucetich, 1896, p. 6 (to the thirteenth century!); Elenco, 1905, p. 159, no. 196.

**98.** Elenco, 1905, p. 160, no. 214.

**99.** *Palazzo Bollani Dolfin.* Elenco, 1905, p. 160,

no. 214. For the façade on the campo: Elenco, 1905, p. 59, no. 518; Lorenzetti, 1956, p. 327 (to the fifteenth century).

**100.** *Palazzo Molin at S. Zulian*, S. Marco 784. Tassini, 1879, p. 254; Elenco, 1905, p. 5, no. 49 (to the fifteenth century); Douglas, 1925, p. 84. The Molin shield is Renaissance. It is not clear whether what may be seen on the top floor are the remains of a loggia. In spite of some archaic elements, the building must be considered of late date.

**101.** *Houses in rio Terrà dei Franceschi*. We are considering two houses: one on two floors with two rows of single windows (5 and 5) (Elenco, 1905, p. 91, no. 439); the other on three floors with three pairs of single windows. The regular distribution does not recall an archaic example.

**102.** *Rio Terrà Barba Frutarol*. Elenco, 1905, p. 92, no. 457. This also perhaps not archaic. Other examples: in calle del Campaniel (S. Polo 1760); in calle delle Colonne (S. Marco 4484*a*); in corte Corner at S. Canciano; in rio dell'Arco (Castello 3517); in calle della Madonna at SS. Apostoli (Cann. 4410-11) (Elenco, 1905, p. 89, no. 402); in calle del Magazen (S. Polo 2485; cf. Maretto, 1959, p. 65).

**103.** *Calle dei Fabbri*, 4680. Elenco, 1905, p. 23, no. 393.

**104.** *Calle dell'Aseo*, 1896. Elenco, 1905, p. 74, no. 150.

**105.** A first floor in piscina Venier (Trincanato, 1948, p. 272: Dorsoduro 834; to the fifteenth century). In calle della Bissa (S. Marco 5512) a three-light window with caulicole capitals (and, on the ground floor, a walled-up porch—Elenco, 1905, p. 27, no. 469); in calle Drio al Magazen (Castello 4772) a four-light window with rosette capitals; at ponte del Teatro at S. Luca two three-light windows, one above the other, with rosette capitals, two windows on each side, Gothic cornice and very pointed simple door on the canal; two-light windows and one single in calle Veriera two at S. Zanipolo (no. 6295-6 on which see Maretto's useful observations (1960, p. 64); the façade of the complex is in calle della Madonna at nos. 6302-3; see further); a three-light and three single windows on rio dei Scoacamini at S. Marco (no. 4689), with Byzantine dentil ornament on the extrados, at ponte delle Pignatte; a four-light window in rio Terrà Secondo (S. Polo 2240), with two pilasters inserted, in Palazzo Pisani, referred to elsewhere (Elenco, 1905, p. 118, no. 180); four windows (of type 4 and 5) in Riello (Sestiere Castello); in calle del Campaniel (S. Polo 1763), with a shop on the ground floor (Elenco, 1905, p. 116, no. 134: note four Michiel shields of the fifteenth century); a single-light window in calle dei Frati (Dorsoduro 941*a* – Elenco, 1905, p. 154, no. 112); a three-light window, with thirteenth-century type capitals, in calle del Pistor (Cann. 3911*a* – Elenco, 1905, p. 82, no. 352: to the fifteenth century); two windows on rio della Guerra at S. Zulian.
A particular character of 'lesser' architecture is found (always within the stylistic meaning of the quoted examples) in the series of dwarf two-light windows in salizzada S. Lio (Castello 5472) alternating with single windows, with truncated cube archaic capitals (Elenco, 1905, p. 56, no. 448; Trincanato, 1948 pp. 148, et seq.: to the fifteenth century). Other examples of two-light windows in series may be seen in calle dei Barcaroli (S. Marco 1796-9: eight

two-light windows in two rows of four, with strange capitals; remade?) and on the Zattere (Dorsoduro 1508) with a suspicion, however, of some restoration; but these are probably late examples.
Other examples of the fourth type (archaic or archaic looking) worth mentioning are: a beautiful three-light window with smaller upper lobes in salizzada S. Francesco (Castello 3198-9); two windows of very simple structure, perhaps really archaic, on a very ancient wall with string-course in campiello Selvatico (Cann. 5659); two three-light windows in calle Vitturi (S. Marco 2914); two three-light windows and one single, presumably archaic, in calle della Morte left of Palazzo Gritti Badoer; a four-light window in an internal courtyard of calle del Cafetier (S. Marco 1997) with a Romanesque truncated cube capital and remains of an ancient staircase (the arches, perhaps inflected, have disappeared); a three-light window in corte di Ca' Barbo (S. Croce); a house in campo Do Pozzi (Castello 2612) where one should note the height of the openings and the large torus in the angular profile of the trefoils (of the fourteenth century?). Difficult to interpret (perhaps because of restorations) is the first floor (four-light window and two windows per side) of Palazzo Contarini-Notarbartolo-Principi di Sciarra on rio di S. Marina (next to Palazzo Marcello Papadopoli del Longhena). The entrance is from calle Marcello or Pindemonte (Castello 6109). Perhaps of the fourteenth century, two three-light windows in rio Terrà del Biri Picolo (Cann. 5396) with walled-up arches, single framing, capitals with caulicoles (Elenco, 1905, pp. 96, 529: Palazzo Loredan in rio S. Vidal (Lorenzetti, 1956, p. 497); the remains (two windows, cornice and chimney flue on the façade) of a house in calle della Testa (Cann. 6361 - Elenco, 1905, pp. 9, 67); other remains in fond. Venier (Cann. 396 and 399); a tall and graceful four-light window in calle del Tragheto at S. Barnaba (Dorsoduro 2786; there is, by its side, a two-light window of the fifth order with rather archaic capital), worth studying; a three-light window on fond. Rezzonico (Dorsoduro 3140 - Elenco, 1905, p. 166, no. 315: to the fifteenth century); the two floors of fourth order single windows underlined by a very long string-course cornice in calle del Ridotto (S. Marco 1355-6): of the fifteenth century; a small house, certainly of the fifteenth century, in piscina S. Martino (Castello 2599 - Elenco, 1905, p. 40, no. 163); various openings in the façade in Lista di Spagna 173-4 (Cannaregio; calle del Forno) (Elenco, 1905, p. 68, no. 31); a first floor in calle dei Avvocati (S. Marco 3836) with an altered (or vanished?) three-light window in the middle and two single windows on each side; Gothic cornice (Elenco, 1905, p. 18, no. 298); a group of houses in calle dei Preti (Castello 1980-2 and 2018-26), of the fifteenth century. (Trincanato, 1948, p. 156 et seq.). - As we saw the fifteenth century has been suggested here and there, but it is difficult, if not actually impossible, to lay down a limit: the fourth order will spread until the second half of the fifteenth century in Venice and on the mainland. Future enquiries will bring greater precision and more detail. One likes to imagine that the house of Cristoforo Moro, thought to be that of Othello, once at campo dei Carmini 2615, a building 'demolished a few years ago' and considered of the fourteenth century (Selvatico, 1852, p. 222), believed by Brown and Ruskin (1886, III, p. 309) to have belonged

to Desdemona's husband, was of the types described above. Vucetich (1896, p. 11) places in the fourteenth century the so-called *Camatta* at S. Marta (Dorsoduro 2021) with the Franceschi coat of arms of the fifteenth century; the Gothic arches, he says, had been removed; but he records also 'the very elegant design, spoiled by ill-considered innovations'.
An imaginative application of the fourth order, with two-light windows (the only one of the kind remaining, I believe) is found in the graceful campanile of S. Fosca in Venice, of the beginning of the fifteenth century; one of the points in Venice where the religious and the lay Gothic meet.

**106.** *House in salizzada S. Stae*. Elenco, 1905, p. 139, no. 179.

**107.** *Palazzo Venier on rio dell'Arco*. Elenco, 1905, p. 39, no. 156 (the façade is assigned to the fifteenth century!).

**108.** Ruskin, 1886, Vol. III.

**109.** *Piscina del Forner*, Dorsoduro 858. Elenco, 1905, p. 152, no. 90.

**110.** Adjacent to calle Larga G. Gallina.

**111.** Water-gates of this type are very common in Venice. The oldest are certainly of the fourteenth century; but they were faithfully reproduced also later.

**112.** See: Maretto, 1960, p. 59 (with other interesting observations).

**113.** *Palazzo Priuli Bon*. V. M. Coronelli, *Singolarità di Venetia*, Vol. II, Palazzi, Plate 64; Ruskin, 1886, II, pp. 264-5; Mothes, 1859, pp. 147-8 (it is called Palazzo Priuli-Zorzi); Tassini, 1863, p. 40 (the Zorzi coat of arms is twice repeated there); Idem, 1879, p. 251; Lorenzetti, 1956, p. 363 (to the fifteenth century).

**114.** *Palazzo Grandiben-Negri*. Ruskin, 1886, II, p. 262, Plate XVII (mistakenly calls it Palazzo Erizzo; which is really the one nearby at no. 4002 and is Renaissance; he sees in it the fifth order in its *early purity*); Tassini, 1879, p. 151 (on the door, in calle Erizzo, there is the coat of arms of the Grandiben, the founder of which family was a Marchiò who lived in the fifteenth century); Elenco, 1905, p. 48, [no. 301; Lorenzetti, 1956, p. 314.

**115.** *Palazzo Soranzo at S. Polo*. Visentini, 1742, III/4 (one of the two doors appears rectangular, the other round-headed!); Zanotto, 1847, p. 428 (to the fifteenth century; information on the internal destructions); Fontana, 1845, p. 26; Ruskin, 1886, III, pp. 310-11 (Ruskin also reproduces a capital); Paoletti, 1893, I, p. 29 (in the 'plates' of the windows he sees 'an ornamenter used to another school than the Italian'); Elenco, 1905, p. 118, no. 173; Musatti, 1905, p. 370 (to the fourteenth century); Marini, 1905, p. 82 (places both palaces in the fourteenth century); Lorenzetti, 1956, p. 568 (to the early fifteenth century).

**116.** As well demonstrated by Maretto (1960, Plates XIII and XIII bis).

**117.** Paoletti, 1893, I, p. 25.

**118.** Paoletti, op. cit. p. 25, no. 6.

**119.** *Palazzo Priuli at S. Severo*. Clearly visible in the *View* by Jacopo de Barbari; Fontana, 1845, Plate 17; Zanotto, 1847, pp. 421 and 426 (remarks on its beauty); Selvatico, 1852, p. 98 (to the fourteenth century); Zanotto, 1856, p. 209

('magnificent door, which in a way reminds one of the style of the Bon'; to 1350–1400); Ruskin, 1886, II, p. 266 (mentions the traceried lobes in the windows as signs of an advanced epoch, contrary to what we have been trying to prove); Id. III, p. 311 (*a most important and beautiful early Gothic palace*); Mothes, 1859, pp. 203 and 206 (places it between the second half of the thirteenth century and the beginning of the fourteenth); Venise, 1861, p. 126 (to the second half of the fourteenth century); Tassini, 1863, 1915 ed., p. 671 (says it was founded by Giovanni Priuli, who died in 1456; Giovanni was the son of the Costantino mentioned in the document quoted above (of 1431–4) which was published by Paoletti; the palace appears in it as already built; the source from which Tassini derives his information should therefore be checked); Paoletti, 1893, I, p. 25; Idem 1920, p. 108; Marini, 1905, p. 84 (to the fifteenth century); Lorenzetti, 1956, pp. 318 and 363 (to the fifteenth century); Toesca, 1950, p. 150 (moves it from the fourteenth to the fifteenth century). The walled-up remains of a two-light window with architrave on rio di S. Severo are interesting: an infrequent motif in Venetian Gothic.

**120.** *Palazzo Della Torre*. Lorenzetti, 1956, p. 440 (to the fifteenth century).

**121.** Examples of windows of this type may be seen in rio della Frescada (Elenco, 1905, p. 170, no. 384).
There are two whole floors in rio Terrà San Leonardo (Cann. 1304), with the three-light window carried by archaic colonnettes with truncated cubes; the arches are walled-up (Elenco, 1905, p. 72, no. 101; to the fifteenth century); another example—but of type 6 and with walled-up arches—is on rio dell'Angelo (Castello 5310; calle di Casselleria); but it should be studied more attentively (Elenco, 1905, p. 55, no. 439); there are three windows on calle della Chiesa (at Castello 4499), with others of the fourth type, an interesting set with various interpolations. There are two dwarf windows of this type (with other elements of the fourth type) in calle della Vissiga (S. Croce 794–6 - Elenco, 1905, p. 134, no. 87).

**122.** *Palazzo Agnusdio*. I consider, with reservations, a pupil of Andriolo de Sanctis (about whom see E. Arslan, *Vicenza, Le Chiese*, Rome, 1956, p. 120 et seq.). On Palazzo Agnusdio (ponte del Forner, S. Croce 2060): Selvatico, 1852, p. 194 (to the fourteenth century); Ruskin, 1886, II, p. 265; Elenco, 1905, p. 140, no. 187 (to the end of the fourteenth century); Lorenzetti, 1956, p. 469 (of the fourteenth and fifteenth centuries).

**123.** *Plain dog-tooth ornaments* (*Fregi a punte di diamante*). This motif is of clearly transalpine origin; it is common in England (the *dog-teeth*

from the twelfth (Canterbury) to the thirteenth century (Lincoln). See: Bond, 1905, p. 74; *Bulletin Monumental*, 1907, p. 534.

**124.** The simple ogee (*schiena d'asino*) arch will not entirely die out either: we shall see it again, in the fifteenth century, in the five beautiful windows of the scuola di S. Giovanni Evangelista, in the campiello of that name, on the (second) *piano nobile* of Palazzo Barbaro at S. Vidal (also of the fifteenth century); in the remarkably developed façade of a palace with four-light window on rio dei Scudi, with three doors with round arch which I consider contemporary with the remainder.
Of the advanced fourteenth century or the fifteenth? The capitals have rosettes. One of the many cases to be left in suspense.

**125.** *Palazzo Ariani Cicogna*. Zanotto, 1847, p. 435; Selvatico, 1847, p. 117 (to the fourteenth century); Selvatico, 1852, p. 220 (to the fourteenth century); Zanotto, 1856, p. 425 (Palazzo Minotto: 'first years' of the fourteenth century); Mothes, 1859, p. 227 (after 1370; in a bad state of disrepair); Ruskin, 1886, II, p. 265; Tassini, 1863, 1915 ed., p. 108 (to the middle of the fourteenth century); Idem, 1870, p. 17 et seq. (to the first half of the fourteenth century); Idem, 1879, p. 121; Paoletti, 1893, I, p. 27; Vucelich, 1896, p. 7 (to the first half of the fourteenth century); Raschdorff, 1903, XIII (to 1400–30); Marini, 1905, p. 82 (to the fourteenth century); Elenco, 1905, p. 161, no. 245; Chiminelli, 1912, p. 229; Paoletti, 1920, p. 108 (to the second half of the fourteenth century); Venturi, 1924, pp. 309 and 315 (to the fifteenth century); Molmenti, 1925, I, p. 286 (to the fifteenth century), p. 288 (of the end of the fourteenth century); Lorenzetti, 1956, p. 544 (of the second half of the fourteenth century); Torres, 1937, p. 19; Toesca, 1950, p. 150 (to the fourteenth century); Miozzi, 1957, I, pp. 449–50.

**126.** These parapets between columns, a kind of plutei, of modest height, are certainly an archaic element (we find them even in the fifteenth century) in Palazzo Barbaro at S. Maria Mater Dei, da Mula at S. Lio, Giustiniani Faccanon, Marcello on fond. Mirotto, Moro (certainly of the fourteenth century) at S. Bartolomeo.

**127.** It is rare for this motif, purely French, to be reproduced with such fidelity; we see it for instance, deformed, on the bases of the piers of the Orvieto Duomo (*Enciclopedia Italiana*, Milan, 1930, Vol. VI, p. 276).

**128.** E. g. at Carentan, in the Manche department (a region more exposed to English influence).

**129.** Burckhardt, 1855, 1925 ed., p. 150 (strangely said to be good for 'the water-colour painters',

but in itself of no importance (*gering*).

**130.** You can see it at Meaux, in the thirteenth century (Lasteyrie, 1926–7, II, p. 264) and at Howden in the advanced thirteenth century (Bond, 1905, p. 72). Mariacher (1951–2, p. 232) attributes the sculpture to the fourteenth century.

**131.** Thode, 1895, p. 87.

**132.** *Palazzo Soranzo Pisani*. Elenco, 1905, p. 119, no. 186 (to the fifteenth century). Lorenzetti, 1956, p. 602 (to the beginning of the fifteenth century); Maretto, 1960, Plate X (discerns a plan in U, presumably of the early fifteenth century).

**133.** *Palazzo Gritti-Pisani*. Visible in J. de Barbari's *View*. For Sansovino (1563, p. 139) it is 'in the German manner and of durable and solid form'; in Quadri (1834, p. 35) one notes, again, the Gothic windows of the upper mezzanine, which repeat those below; Zanotto, 1856, p. 581 (to the fourteenth century; 'altered... in the subsequent restorations, so that little remains that is ancient'); Fontana, 1845, Plate 66; Zanotto, 1847, p. 431 (to the fourteenth century; he notices 'many alterations'); Elenco, 1905, p. 11, no. 151; Lorenzetti, 1956, p. 613 (beginning of the fifteenth century). It is now the Palace Hotel. The edges of Istrian stone with tall corner colonnettes recall examples of the middle fifteenth century and awaken the suspicion of an enlargement of the central core. The two two-light windows with architraves on the ground floor recall those, probably of the fifteenth century, in the Palazzi Soranzo at S. Polo (see above).

**134.** See: *Congrès Archéologique*, 1921, p. 9 (at Limoges), *Congrès du 1923*, p. 170 (at Saint-Antoine en Viennois); in the cathedrals of Vitoria and Toledo in Spain; in that of Winchester (all examples, among many, of the thirteenth and fourteenth centuries).

**135.** *Palazzo Manolesso Ferro*. Visible in J. de Barbari's *View*. Fontana, 1845, Plate 74 (it is, substantially, that of today); Selvatico, 1852, p. 229 (to the fourteenth century); Zanotto, 1856, p. 581 (to the fourteenth century); the ground floor altered in the seventeenth century; Ruskin, 1886, III, p. 290 (*very hard and bad*); Mothes, 1859, I, p. 229 (says it was modernized; and points out those peculiar forms); Musatti, 1905, p. 143 ('several restorations'); Elenco, 1905, p. 10, no. 138; Chiminelli, 1912, p. 247 (had an uncovered staircase); Lorenzetti, 1956, p. 613 (to the fifteenth century).
There is a four-light window over the courtyard, with inflected trefoil arches with paterae, two columns and a pilaster, certainly contemporary with the part mentioned on the Grand Canal; and other single and two-light windows, perhaps adapted.

44. *Wells Cathedral. Detail of a four-light window.*

THE TREFOILED INFLECTED ARCH IN THE
FIRST HALF OF THE FOURTEENTH
CENTURY

*45. St. Mark's. Detail of a three-light window
of the façade.*
*46. Church of SS. Giovanni e Paolo. Large
Gothic window.*

*47. Three-light window in Salizzada delle Gatte.*
*48. Door of the S. Gregorio Abbey.*

49. St. Mark's Square in a miniature in a codex of the late fifteenth century. Chantilly. Musée Condé.
50. Gentile Bellini: 'Procession in St. Mark's Square'. Detail. Venice, Gallerie dell'Accademia.

51. *Campanile of S. Fosca.*
52. *Palazzo Donà in Campo S. Polo. Capital and architrave in the courtyard.*
53. *Palazzo Michiel dalle Colonne (now Donà dalle Rose). Detail on the Grand Canal.*

54. *St. Mark's. Large window of the southern side.*
55. *Doge's Palace. Detail of the façade towards the quay.*
56, 57. *Doge's Palace. End three-light windows on the quay side.*

54

58. *Doge's Palace. Façade on rio di Palazzo. Detail of window.*
59. *Doge's Palace. Façade on rio di Palazzo. Two-light window.*
60. *Walled-up three-light window in Fondamenta S. Severo.*

61. *Palazzo Foscari. Multi-light window.*
62. *Palazzo Dandolo on the Grand Canal.*
*Detail of the façade.*

63. *Windows on rio dell'Arco.*
64. *Palazzo on rio dell'Arco from Ponte Storto.*

*65. Palazzo Zorzi on Fondamenta S. Severo.*
*66, 67. Palazzo Zorzi on Fondamenta S. Severo. Details of the five-light window.*

68. *Palazzo Grandiben-Negri, Castello, Ponte Erizzo.*
69. *Palazzo Bosso at S. Tomà. Detail of frieze.*
70. *Palazzo Bosso at S. Tomà. Portal.*
71. *Palazzo Bosso at S. Tomà.*
72. *Palazzo Soranzo at S. Polo.*

73. *Palazzo Soranzo at S. Polo. Detail of the main façade.*
74. *Palazzo Soranzo at S. Polo. Detail of the multi-light window of the façade.*
75, 76. *Palazzo Soranzo at S. Polo. Foreshortened perspective of the façade.*

77. *Palazzo Priuli in rio dell'Osmarin. Four-light windows.*

78. *Palazzo Priuli in rio dell'Osmarin. Fore-shortened perspective of the façade.*

79. *Palazzo Cicogna, formerly Arian. Detail of the decorative motif of the quatrefoils.*

*80-82. Palazzo Cicogna, formerly Arian. Details of the six-light window.*

84. *Palazzo Agnusdio. Detail of the five-light window.*

85. *Single-light window in rio Terrà Secondo at S. Agostino. (Palazzo Soranzo-Pisani).*

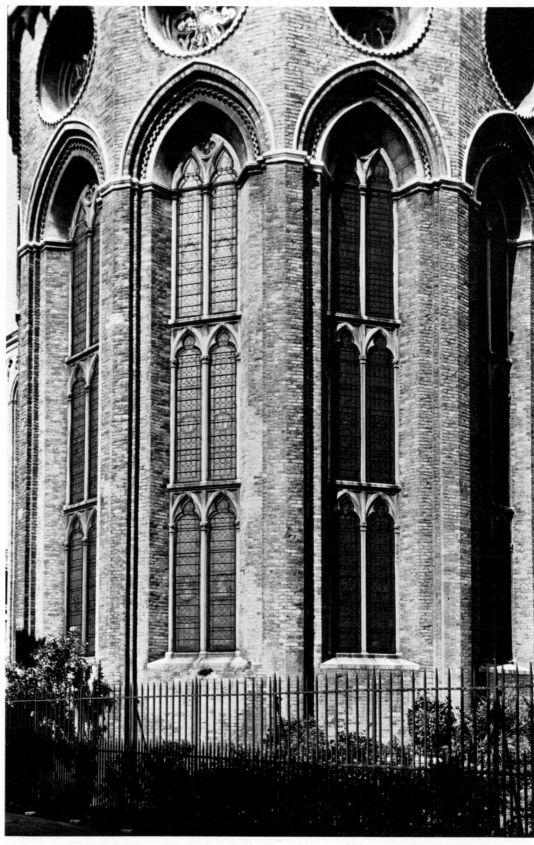

*88. Palazzo Gritti. Façade.*
*89. Palazzo Manolesso-Ferro. Façade on the Grand Canal.*

# Chapter III

# TOWARDS THE FLORIATED GOTHIC

*The Doge's Palace (the fourteenth-century structure)*

The palace built by the Venetians for the seat of the government and of the judicial authority was probably begun in 1340 on the site of buildings erected by the Doge Sebastiano Ziani (1172–8), of which we have no concrete record, and which sheltered—separately, it seems—the political and judicial authorities; it seems highly probable that the appearance of this palace (or palaces, giving on the quay and on the Piazzetta) was very similar to that of the structures erected in the thirteenth century, with two corner towers, a porch and a loggia[1].

We have already mentioned that somewhat earlier part of the structure which gives on rio di Palazzo and is contained between the fourteenth-century façade and the wing erected by Rizzo. But we can take as the object of this study only the palace renovated towards the middle of the fourteenth century (and continued for some decades) which corresponds to the present building facing the quay. It is certainly the most admirable and brilliant creation of Venetian secular Gothic, conceived by a single creative mind even if, as we saw, we must accept in respect of the large windows the intervention of teams of 'specialized', probably Campionese, stonecutters.

It is as well to say at once that the rooms, large and small, into which the building was divided in the fourteenth century have since undergone such extensive transformations as no longer to provide any critically relevant elements for our enquiry. To the fourteenth-century façade on the quay, which is obviously of the same period as the narrow part which goes round to the rio di Palazzo and which continues on the Piazzetta up to the figure of Venice in line with the seventh pilaster of the arcade, must be added the similar façade which since 1424 goes on to Porta della Carta. This was followed by the galleries which on the western and southern sides of the courtyard were continued beyond the middle of the fifteenth century. This is the domain which interests us, but our examination will be limited here to the fourteenth-century part. (The beginning of the subsisting fourteenth-century building cannot be placed before 1340: documents of the 17 and 18 December speak for the first time, in fact, of the new Sala del Maggior Consiglio (Hall of the Grand Council) which was to make up the internal structure, obviously a decisive factor also for the exterior[2]. The well-known document of 28 December 1340 is of fundamental importance. On that date it was in fact decided to rebuild *ex novo* the Sala del Maggior Consiglio, to the size and extent of the one still subsisting, up to the part which gives on to the Piazzetta[3], starting from the eastern wall on which was painted in 1365 Guariento's *Paradise*. As Zanotto has proved[4], the sums quoted in the 1340 document must refer only to the second floor of the palace.

The course of the work on this hall can easily be followed. There is a resolution of 10 March 1342: *quod dictum opus Sale continuetur ultra Quarantiam veterem usque supra plateam*[5]. The 23 June 1343 work was proceeding actively, because the Dominicans ask *quod omnes schaie* (sic) *lapidum vivorum que parantur pro opere palacii… dentur eis* for the church, begun ten years before, of SS. Giovanni e Paolo[6] and, in fact, on 30 December 1344 the side of the hall *de versus canale* was finished[7]. A staircase connecting the ground and first floors, of which no trace remains[8], was ordered between 1340 and 1344. On 5 July 1348, it was resolved that the hall *tota coperiatur*, and orders were given to clear away all that was found *circa dictum Palacium, tam lapides quam lignamina*. On 10 July, however, all work ceased and all expenditure was suspended[9]. The plague reached Venice and paralysed all activities. Resumption of work was ordered only on 24 February 1350, because *non videtur honorabile dimittere tantum et tam magnificum opus inexpletum*[10]. According to Zanotto[11], it is very likely that the prosecution of the work was hindered from 1355 to 1357 and also by the plague from 1359 to 1361, and was speeded up again on 15 December 1362 so that the hall *non vadat in tantam desolationem* and should be brought *ad terminum* and it was insisted that *dicta sala nova compleri debeat*[12].

The huge room was finished in 1365, Lorenzo Celsi being Doge[13]. His successor Marco Cornaro, elected on 21 July 1365, gave Guariento the commission to paint the *Paradise* fresco on the eastern wall[14]. In 1366 it was decided to remove the portrait of Marin Faliero[15]. The hall, with the large traceried windows, placed at a higher level than the two on the east side for better lighting[16], was therefore completed.

At this point the question of the appearance of the lower part of the building while the Sala del Maggior Consiglio was being built arises. Ruskin[17] and Zanotto[18] were of the opinion that the loggia and portico on the quay were by then already completed as we see them to-day, and this opinion was shared by Paoletti[19], on the grounds of the very considerable cost of the work (estimated by Zanotto, through a computational error, at much less than it actually was). Paoletti is even more precise, stating that 'the external foundations of the old portico were totally replaced by others corresponding to the new columns'. It is sufficient, however, to observe that problems of this kind should not have been insoluble for the engineers of that time (recalling the works undertaken by Aristotele Fioravanti), if we consider the building of the ground floor portico on the southern and western sides of the courtyard of the Doge's Palace, carried out at the beginning of the seventeenth century by Manopola while retaining the two galleries above (completed in 1468[20]).

Another opinion, opposing that of Ruskin, is formulated by Cicognara[21], who does distinguish the part supposedly executed by Calendario (namely the southern façade) from that on the Piazzetta added in 1423. He ends by believing that the style of the latter ultimately influenced the older part, restored in 1423, making it uniform with the new. Cicognara also considers the white and red marble incrustations to be of 1423[22]. One should merely add that such confusion was only brought about by a disconcerting observation, namely the fact that one of the two façades was a copy of the other and that the façade on the Piazzetta was made according to precise instructions which obliged the executants to copy exactly the features of the older façade.

Cicognara's opinion none the less has gained a foothold and he found a follower in Selvatico, according to whom the whole exterior of the Doge's Palace should be considered later than 1424. Selvatico believed, in fact, that he had found confirmation of this in a passage of the *Zancaruola* chronicle which, speaking of the decision to demolish the old Palace of Justice of Ziani, said that it was intended to *refare le fazade del palazo vechio* (remake the façades of the old palace)[23]. And he attributes to Bartolomeo Bon and to Pantaleone 'the major part and perhaps the whole of the two façades'[24].

*The Doge's Palace from a drawing in an anonymous fifteenth-century chronicle in St. Mark's Library.*

This thesis found, however, an opponent in Zanotto[25], who pointed out in particular the diversity of the capitals. And Selvatico himself seems subsequently to have realized the obstacle offered to his opinion by the presence of the central balcony towards the quay, unambiguously dated to 1404[26]. Against the opinions of Cicognara and Selvatico are also those of Amico Ricci[27], Kugler[28], Dall'Acqua[29], and Schnaase[30].

This thesis was, however, found acceptable by Adolfo Venturi, who attributed to the Lombards and to the first decades of the fifteenth century the spread of the 'floriated Gothic' (according to a definition which there is absolutely no reason to accept in such simplistic terms if one inquires into what preceded, in Venice, the arrival of Raverti). Thus, referring to the Doge's Palace, Venturi writes that 'having completed the front towards the Piazzetta, they went on to continue it in the larger façade towards the quay', seeing in this building a 'palace reconstructed (in 1422) in accordance with the forms of the Lombard floriated Gothic'[31]. For Bettini, who follows Venturi's guide line, 'the present form of the whole external façade is not, in all probability, anterior to the first decades of the fifteenth century[32], and is due to a particular cooperation of Venetian master workers gathered round the workshop of the Dalle Masegne inherited by the Bons, Lombards led by Raverti, Tuscans guided by Lamberti'. These are statements on which could be based a discussion of the portico capitals but which cannot affect the large windows of the middle of the fourteenth century and even less the architecture, which is the fruit of a single mind[33].

The idea that the quayside façade of the Doge's Palace was due to a single great architect did not fail to gain early support, as a consequence of the greater understanding favoured by the Romantic spirit. Ruskin[34] asserted it strongly, and undoubtedly went much beyond those who merely disagreed with Selvatico's thesis. Paoletti[35] insisted on the separation between the fourteenth and fifteenth-century parts; in favour of an attribution to the fourteenth century argued Della Rovere[36], Pauli[37], Molmenti[38]—who proclaimed it 'by a single and great master', Folnesics[39], Ongaro[40], Lorenzetti[41], Toesca[42], Pignatti[43]. Toesca would appear to be nearer the mark than the others in denying that the façade on the quay is of 1365, because the capitals and the sculptures of the loggia and portico, as well as the roundel with Venice, are of the last quarter of the fourteenth century. He concludes therefore that the internal structures were preserved while the lower external part was being restored[44]. The same scholar considers 1404 the year in which the work on the quayside ended[45].

Besides the fact that, as we shall seek to prove, many capitals of the southern loggia (and also some of the portico underneath) may be considered of about the middle of the fourteenth century, the conclusions reached by Toesca, who combines a lucid vision of the architecture with penetrating investigations of the portico capitals and the major sculptures (attributed to the last quarter of the fourteenth century), definitively confirm a dating of this façade between 1340 and 1404 (which is the date of the large central window).

I share Toesca's opinion and consider that the portico and loggia of the old Palazzo Ziani (because the façade towards the quay must have had such a character) in all probability supported the Grand Council Hall; and no doubt, for this purpose, the supports of the portico were reinforced. The upper wall of this façade is therefore of the middle of the fourteenth century. It is bound so closely with the loggia and the portico that one must deduce, as will be demonstrated, the presence of a single mind, faithful, at any rate, to a single plan even if carried out over a certain length of time.

Some light may be thrown on this question by an examination of the capitals of the portico and of the loggia of the 'fourteenth-century' side, on which work was certainly being done at least since 1344[46].

The long row of capitals of the loggia, from the Ponte della Paglia to Porta della Carta, attests to the presence of teams of stonecutters working to a high standard. There are no

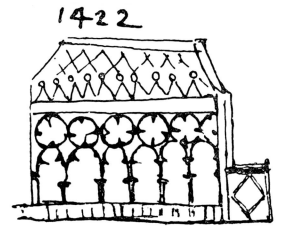

1422

capitals of the type 'with rosette' nor of that with 'superposed caulicoli', nor of any other simple or current type. We find, instead, the constant use of capitals with thick leaves.

It is worth mentioning, in its main points, the development of these forms.

The capital with thick leaves is found in Venice from about 1340. One of its first appearances is to be found in the capitals of the cloisters of S. Gregorio, a work attributable to about 1340. There, we find standing next to each other, capitals of the most common fourteenth-century type and others with a double row of large leaves reproducing a still Romanesque arrangement but one in which in place of the large water-leaves, smooth and of substantial thickness, there are large cabbage leaves gathered in globular masses, though clearly defined so as to display their particular vegetable nature, and well separated from each other. On occasion, a head peeps out from the centre under the abacus. It is a type not very different from those we have seen in the large windows of the Doge's Palace.

Another primitive type (which can be dated) of capital with thick leaves is the one crowning the columns erected in the Sala del Piovego in order to support the Grand Council Hall in the course of construction, of which there is mention in the document of 1340. Here we see very clearly the passage from antique-like forms dominated by the acanthus to others where the cabbage leaf prevails.

Palazzo Zorzi–Bon which may be accepted as erected towards the middle of the fourteenth century (and of which we have already spoken) also has capitals, in the magnificent multi-light window, in which the beautiful fleshy cabbage leaves appear next to the aristocratic, finely serrated, acanthus leaves.

These are the simplest forms, marked by a certain rigorous symmetry expressed by the stalks, or by the vertical nervures which support (or around which spreads) the leaf.

It must be admitted that examples are not numerous in the second half of the fourteenth century, even if one takes into account church architecture. Venetian builders remain, in fact, faithful, even in structures of great importance, to the fourteenth-century types of capitals, and to that with rosettes.

Capitals with thick leaves adorn the niches erected as ornaments on the façades of St. Mark's. The one on the corner of S. Alipio is of 1385, as is the one opposite, on the corner towards the campanile, with the Annunciation. The two niches fronting S. Basso[47] are of 1415, so that Cattaneo concluded that 'the intermediate pinnacles of the main façade and those of the lateral façades came after' (1385)[48]. Capitals with thick leaves may be seen also in the two tabernacles built in the wall on the sides of the main altar in St. Mark's, which are of 1388[49].

These are, on the whole, rather rigid forms, without the imaginative freedom or exuberant swelling of the capitals with thick leaves which appear around 1400 and continue in the well-known examples of the buildings erected in the first half of the fifteenth century. If Venturi erred in transferring to the first half of the fifteenth century the diffusion, due to the Lombards, of the floriated Gothic, he on the other hand correctly perceived this passage—though without pinpointing it in time—when he wrote that 'having caused the Milanese Gothic to lose the geometrical stamp of the foliage, the spherical form round which were cut the cabbage leaves, the Venetian masters will make the leaves spread, quickened by a more fecund sap, fat, full, swelling'[50].

If we now look at the capitals of the southern loggia of the Doge's Palace, we must admit that they fit in with the examples of which we have spoken, and that they can be placed in the second half of the fourteenth century and may even be considered of about the middle of the century.

Starting from the Ponte della Paglia we meet chiefly two types of capitals: one clearly more archaic, one less. Of the more archaic types (to mention the more conclusive examples)

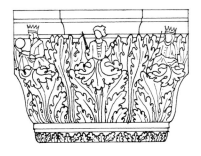

are the first, eighth, tenth, twenty–fourth and twenty–ninth capitals; after turning the corner of the southern façade to the point of connection with the 'new' façade, we have the twenty–eighth, twenty–ninth, thirty–third, thirty–sixth and thirty–seventh capitals, starting the count from the Porta della Carta.

The principles which inspire the composition are similar to those of the works already listed. We see the thickened acanthus leaf or, already, the cabbage leaf, in the clearly vertical sequence of large leaves, no longer globular as in S. Gregorio but erect and with the upper edge folded over. On the central axis of the bell there is a head seen full face, or a figure.

A novelty in comparison with the preceding capitals is represented by small volutes (almost caulicoli) which fold under the corners of the abacus.

In the less archaic type, the caulicoli on the upper side disappear and are replaced by thick, outwardly curled leaves. It may be said that the capital with thick leaves, which is absolutely characteristic of Venetian floriated Gothic, lasting almost a century, is born here; with the difference, however, that in this second type of capital, along the southern loggia, the vertical arrangement of the stalks remains (see for examples of this trend the capitals 5, 9, 11, 15, 16, 23, 24, 27, 31, 32, 33, 34, starting from Ponte della Paglia, and 24, 25, 31, 32, 35 starting from Porta della Carta).

Even a brief comparison between these capitals of the southern wing of the Doge's Palace and those one sees in buildings later than 1404 convinces one that the first antedate the second, that they belong to the fourteenth century (as far as the more clearly archaic capitals with caulicoli–volutes are concerned, even to about the middle of the century). We find indeed already in the capitals of the Ca' d'Oro windows (around the third decade of the fifteenth century) totally different characters. There the thick leaf stirred by the wind—inspired by old Byzantine examples—entirely upsets those principles of 'verticality' which we have so far encountered, in an explosion of almost unbridled naturalism. A similar fanciful irregularity, and a greater elegance, with very clear influences of an international style (large openings over deep cavities) are noticeable in the capitals of Ca' Foscari (later than 1450); an exuberant and riotous richness, of similar origin, is visible in Palazzo Dandolo (Danieli) of about the same period; a similar curling-up of thick and swelling leaves in Palazzo Donà–Giovanelli.

We are looking, therefore, at buildings of the mature floriated Gothic, where the divergence from the capitals of the Doge's Palace loggia is very marked. And we must add that this 'evolution' which extends over the whole first half of the fifteenth century does not affect the capitals of the western side of the fifteenth century part of the loggia, where a team of the Bons is at work. There are clear signs of a very new taste, in which the massive foliage, marked by the shadow patches of deep cavities, surround the whole bell with wavy and exuberant volutes and expand under the abacus (this is a characteristic feature which clearly distinguishes them from those of the fourteenth–century part)—indeed greatly overflowing its limits.

A more adequate critical definition of this architecture cannot be reached without an examination of the famous, important and elegant capitals of the portico and of the sculptures with great figures on the corners towards the quay organically related to them, even if due to another hand.

These large capitals are of two entirely different types, except for the octagonal abaci which are the same for all, and recall those of the great Venetian churches begun early in the fourteenth century (Frari, SS. Giovanni e Paolo), similar buildings on the Venetian mainland and the French and English examples of the thirteenth and fourteenth centuries[51].

A prevalent type has thick leaves, densely crowded, which envelop the whole bell and frame single figures or small scenes on each side, thus making up small cycles of allegories or of everyday events in man's life, according to a well–defined pictorial plan[52]. A lesser number of capitals, however, have a simpler character, with large leaves, isolated and multi–lobed, folded outwards underneath each corner of the abacus with, between the leaves, room for representations of animals or of heads, of men or beasts, of notable size. These display, in comparison with the previous ones, a much more archaic and harsh tone.

The first type has particularly attracted the attention of art historians. Venturi, who concerned himself with them in 1908 and 1924, was the first to attempt a stylistic definition. He was seeking here too confirmation of his theory[53] of the Lombard influx which would have determined, at the beginning of the fifteenth century, the shape of the whole structure, recognizing first of all in the great *Venice* relief a sculptor acquainted with jewellery works, revealing a Lombard character and attributing it to the same hand which made the capital dedicated to *Love* (i.e. the thirteenth from Porta della Carta) which must surely belong to an older structure and is located under the *Venice* relief. To the same hand he attributes the *Noah* group and that of the *Progenitors*, insisting on the 'Lombardo–Nordic workmanship'.

In 1924 Venturi thought he recognized in this sculptor a master akin to Michelino da Besozzo (and he dated him accordingly to the first years of the fifteenth century).

A more subtle investigation of these capitals of the southern wing was made by Toesca, who assigned them to about 1375–1400 and discerned two masters. He defines, more acutely, the one singled out by Venturi for his 'Gothic workmanship, less plastic but more pictorial, which he went on developing from the capital of the *Creation* and others on the more ancient parts of the Doge's Palace to the relief with *Venice*'. He attributes to him and his assistants the *Love* capital and the great sculptures of the *Original Sin*, *Noah drunk* and the *Two Archangels*, places the *Venice* relief among his last works and lists a number of kindred sculptures in Venice and the estuary[54].

Toesca sees in this sculptor an artist educated on the Lagoon, rather than a Lombard. Toesca's thesis has been recently restated by Pope–Hennessy, who places the two biblical groups at around 1390 and the *Venice* at around 1420, associates to them the Zodiac capital (i. e. of the Creation, or the Planets) and quotes the name of Giovanni Bon, maintaining that this master had been acquainted with Austrian and Southern German works[55].

Toesca discerns another master, with a greater plastic gift, in the *Childhood* capital (at the corner on Ponte della Paglia), in the capital of the *Four Saints* and in that of the *Trades* (the second and the fourth on the Piazzetta starting from the corner on the quay). On thorough examination, Toesca's observations appear sufficiently clarifying, be it for the Byzantine–like elements of style which qualify the first master (note the creation of man, represented on the *Creation* capital, very unlikely to be the work of a Lombard), be it for the period (last quarter of the fourteenth century) in which these sculptures are placed, and for this purpose the manner, still clearly of the fourteenth century, visible in the *Creation* capital (*Venus*, *Mercury* and the *Moon* recalling Giovanni da Milano). The Veneto–Byzantine component is indeed very strong in this master, particularly in the large sculptures, as shown by its success in attenuating these accents of the 'gracious' Gothic which would have been far more evident had these sculptures been made fifteen years or so later (leaving aside Raverti and the Ca' d'Oro sculptors around the thirties). It is thus apparent in the absorbed, almost sorrowful *Progenitors*, in the pathetic *Noah and his Sons*, and equally in the fixed stare and the uniform, compact heads of hair of the Archangels Michael and Raphael[56] and the superb *Venice*, skilfully centred in one of the quatrefoil oculi[57].

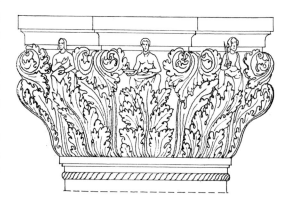

It seems, on the whole, that the example offered by the capitals and sculptures which can be referred to two distinct hands serves most of all to place all the capitals of this type which exist in the southern wing, at a time not before about 1375[58], even if one cannot exclude the participation of some Lombard stonecutter in their execution[59].

*The Doge's Palace. Capitals of the ground floor loggia towards the Piazzetta (from Zanotto)*

The form of these capitals moreover corresponds, stylistically, to that of the 'evolution' of the capital with thick leaves in Venice around 1400, at times with stalks clearly revealing a vertical movement (as in those already examined in the Loggia), at other times with swollen foliage and with elaborate perforated cavities enveloping the whole bell in an interplay of masses which tend to obscure the vertical elements of the structure. We quote, as examples of the less elaborate type, the one with the *Emperors* (the fifth from the Ponte della Paglia) and of the more elaborate and later the capital with little angels (fourth from Ponte della Paglia).

The other, more archaic, type of capital of the portico has never been seriously considered. These capitals are few in number but very significant and they carry the mark of a team of workers with their own very particular characteristics; i.e. the second from the Ponte della Paglia, with pelicans eating fish; the third, with human heads strongly jutting out; the sixth, with heads of young women; the eleventh, again with pelicans; the thirteenth, with lion heads; the sixteenth, with heads of men and women; the twentieth (on the Piazzetta) with animal heads. To these we should add the twenty–seventh, with baskets full of fruit, but this belongs to the fifteenth–century wing and must, in all probability, be considered a copy of a fourteenth–century original[60].

Works of austere conception, they cannot possibly be attributed to the same hands as the other more diversified and exuberant group previously discussed; only the abacus is the same in the two groups. Instead of a cyma, we have here a torus–shaped element followed by a listel, which interrupts the large leaves with a strongly accented plastic character, spherical on top of very large flat vegetable elements, with ample vertical bands. The arrangement is sober, demonstrating a spirit gifted with a power for synthesis and capable of expressing itself with limited means, and this is confirmed by the human and animal heads, the large birds and the baskets full of fruit.

The human heads in particular reveal a very singular character, lacking precedent in fourteenth–century Italian sculpture. Whoever observes the head of a young woman, with the arches of the eyes curving neatly above the slightly swollen eyelids, the shape of the eye, her thoughtful glance, the sensual lips hinting at a smile, or the heads of hair or the beard made up into curly rings, or the bitter curve of the old woman's mouth and the two furrows aslant her cheeks, or the soft folds of the clothes forming arches under the chin, cannot help recalling a human nature which is not at all that seen by Giotto, not even the passionate one of Giovanni Pisano, but the one found in the statues—mild, serene, made blissful by a mystical or subtly sensual smile, which we see on the French cathedrals of the first half of the thirteenth century: the Virgin and Elisabeth, the High Priest, the Synagogue of Reims[61], and so on.

This observation raises a question which extends to various other manifestations of Venetian Gothic architecture which take up motifs elaborated decades before by the French and English west, and sometimes more than a century before. From this it appears impossible to consider these capitals, like the others, as of the end of the fourteenth century; they must be placed instead in the middle of the century.

Their presence poses, in more complex but at the same time more acceptable terms, the whole uneasy problem of the magnificent and unitary southern façade of the Doge's Palace. Work on this began, as both the documents and the style concur in attesting, a little before the middle of the century, with the construction—unavoidable for the Venetians—of the Grand Council Hall, while the portico and loggia followed and were completed within the century, if in 1404 the Dalle Masegne finished the central balcony.

It would seem that the contradictions suggested by the elements of this façade which—as always happens in such cases—pushes the critics in various directions, may be reconciled within these limits. The unitary conception of this façade confirms that it was the fruit of a single mind, because every member of the structure unites in perfect harmony with the others, without any of those differences in workmanship, those changes in style which old buildings usually clearly display; and this unity is such that it influenced even the opinion of those who attributed the whole complex to the fifteenth century.

The great coherence of this façade induces one instead to believe that the two floors of the portico and the loggia were built after the upper part, but always following a plan drawn up in the middle of the fourteenth century. The capitals of the loggia giving on the quay fit well indeed with a placing in the middle of the fourteenth century (the stonecutters' workshops were certainly already active in 1340) and subsequent years: and as for those of the portico, together with the large sculptures, they were integrated into the building planned some time before, together with the older capitals which should be of the middle of the fourteenth century.

It is interesting to notice how the imposing wall mass above the loggia, suggested perhaps as Cicognara already guessed, by the cubic constructions peculiar to Islamic art, ties with the lower part even if the large windows (and with them the quatrefoil oculi above) are not in line with the rhythmic scansion of the arcades below, as was often the case in thirteenth and fourteenth–century buildings.

The cornices, the horizontal string courses, and the clear vertical divisions, create a framework within which the vast areas have only a purely chromatic significance (and the lozenge decoration, in Veronese pink limestone and in Istrian stone, of Islamic inspiration, contribute to the effect of negating any expression of architectural constructivism), and in these the large openings of the windows and of the quatrefoil oculi, the former unconnected by string courses, are arranged with a freedom from any rigorous symmetry which, while contributing to the pure colour effect, is not perceived by the observer as a disturbing element.

Even the placing of the two windows on the east side at a different level from the others, which would certainly have disturbed a mainland architect (not only Tuscan but also Paduan) does not break the harmony; and to this local blurring of the architectural sense must have certainly greatly contributed all the large windows when the traceries still existed. One symmetrical principle, however (even if approximate rather than rigorous) is always preserved, namely the one which puts three large windows on each side of the large central window (which is lower, richer and has a balcony).

The cornice atop the loggia, defined by a few neat voluminous horizontal elements, expressed with new vigour, effects the passage to the complex, articulated geometrical structure below it, where the symmetry is this time rigorously respected: one begins to sense here the greatness of the architect, and the novelty of a formal procedure which has no equal in any other Venetian building.

The cornice on the loggia corresponds in fact to that very singular element which is the column placed at the corner, bounding the four walls, with a spiral shaft vertically divided by three elements in the shape of capitals; which are nothing other than a repetition of the cornice, characterized by a ring of strong plain dog teeth.

These 'columns' are a 'stabilizing' element of the walls of the upper part. The four segments into which they are divided repeat, to some extent, the measures in height of the parts of the portico and loggia; the last segment is furthermore characterized by three colonnettes which mark the passage to the pinnacle on the corner, which leans out slightly, while in the roof parapet two merlons correspond—even if not with absolute rigour—to each arch of the portico.

A line of merlons is placed on the uppermost cornice, admirably crowning the mass underneath, gathering its unusual compactness together. The examples of such lines of merlons which one can find in the Muslim world are very numerous. One of the best known and most beautiful is the gate of the Omayyad castle of Qasr al–Hayr–al–Gharbi, reconstructed in the Damascus Museum[62]. The derivation from those examples is certain, and the fusion with other disparate examples derived from the West carried out by the Venetian builders is admirable.

Within these limits, firmly marked and of solid rhythm, the somewhat free play of the openings undoubtedly acquires its own stability, while the decoration of lozenges scaled on the diagonals—a chromatic element which would certainly tend to unbalance the firm framework of horizontal and vertical elements—is contained, leaving to the colour, up to the limit, its freedom to spread over all the available area.

The cornice over the gallery gradually effects the passage to the lower part; it surmounts in fact an ornament of rosettes immediately under which there is a large torus profile which forms the framework of the loggia as well as the portico up to the impost line of the great capitals. This torus profile is an element of great simplicity which agrees perfectly with that of the cornice and it leads one to think that the older capitals of the portico (with the heads, etc.), marked by a similarly robust simplicity of workmanship and by a large torus profile, may have been designed by the architect of the palace. As we have spoken also in connection with those capitals of works of the middle of the fourteenth century, this may be a confirmation of the attribution of this southern façade to 1350 or thereabouts, even if the actual execution was completed towards the end of the century.

This torus is of purely French origin; it takes up here again, at a distance of more than a century, one of the constituent elements of thirteenth–century French architecture between the Champagne and the Ile–de–France; it admirably surrounds, with delicate strength, all the openings, namely the quatrefoil oculi, the inflected arches of the loggia, the great *Venice* relief and the archangels in the corner niches.

Broadly modelled, the portico storey too is crowned by a cornice which repeats the same elements and rhythm of the upper one, displaying a torus instead of the plain dog–tooth ornament and a more tranquil profile in tune with the rounded shapes of the columns, of the banister colonnettes and of the torus which returns, in greater size, as the horizontal crowning of the arches (of which the same element constitutes the moulding). Nor should one forget the rosette ornament which, in smaller size, also decorates this cornice. We have insisted on this torus element because in its course it really marks the components of the building with a design which visibly binds the structures and the openings, and offers itself in surface to the incidence of light which gives it the maximum relief. It constitutes, naturally, also the element which seals on the outside the simple firm profiles, entirely similar to those of the horizontal cornices already noted in the arches and in the quatrefoil oculi of the loggia. In the portico it receives, again, a plain dog–tooth ornament. There is enough here to demonstrate the extraordinary artistic coherence of the fourteenth–century building, over which must have presided an architect of very remarkable intellect.

From the above considerations it is clear that the building reflects a conception reached towards the middle of the fourteenth century. The treatment of the great loggia, where we meet the trefoiled inflected arch placed on columns of limited height with rich capitals and, for the first time in Venice, the quatrefoil oculus in line with the column, is therefore most important.

The idea is of clear French origin and probably with no precedent in Venice. Ruskin thought he recognized in the large windows of the main apse of the Frari church the 'real root' of the Doge's Palace; and added that 'the originality of thought in the architect of the Doge's Palace consists in his having adapted those traceries in a more highly developed and finished form, to civil uses'[63]. But this precedence did not really happen, because it is now proved that the main apse of the Frari began to acquire its present aspect in 1407 and was completed in 1420[64].

Its large windows contain some elements recalling the forms of the Doge's Palace: in particular the profiles, the use of the torus and the lion heads in the blind triangles between the quatrefoil oculi. These are due to stonecutters working at a later period than those active at the Doge's Palace at the height of the fourteenth century. This is attested also by the large windows, almost identical, of Bishop Pietro Miani's chapel, also in the Frari, the building of which had been decided in 1434 and whose capitals are already of the type with thick asymmetric leaves in use in the fifteenth century[65].

Finally, it should be pointed out that this great architect gave the trefoiled inflected arch a shape of great elegance, but that there is nevertheless an archaic trend in it, already noticed, towards giving the central foil a more expansive, heart–like form. The idea of a multifoil placed between the Gothic arches is very ancient and already widespread in France in the second half of the twelfth century, and the quatrefoil oculus is also of ancient date. It appears in France in the second half of the twelfth century as well, and reaches perhaps its most elegant expressions in the first half of the thirteenth century in France and in England. The fact remains, however, that at this date, about 1350, the inflected arch did not exist in France and the inspiration could therefore come only from England. The same may be said of the balustrade with colonnettes alternating with small trefoiled arches, certainly among the most ancient in Venice, of the same character as the 'bands' on Ponte della Paglia, which was built in 1360[66], widened last century and showing signs of some restoration, but substantially legible; and which, considering the broad and firm course of the profiles, may have been designed by the same architect as the Doge's Palace[67]. Again, the abacus of the corner capitals, of larger size, is used chiefly for placing the well–known sculptures; at the corner of the portico towards the Piazzetta the *Original Sin* and above it, at the corner of the loggia, the *St. Michael*; at the corner towards the Ponte della Paglia *Noah's Drunkenness*, and above it *St. Raphael*. And these sculptures fit well under the jutting out profile of the cornices on high pedestals covered with thick leaves as in a niche, because they represent also a solution for the corner where the arches fall, above and below, in the middle (or nearly) of the capitals, so that the quatrefoil oculus in the loggia is thereby halved. The expedient intended to avoid problems in the choice of a harmonious solution for the difficult problem becomes, as often happens with great artists, a brilliant—indeed indispensable impulse. This is particularly proved by the two archangels, splendidly fitted in, a living part of the architecture.

Such a building could not avoid provoking a great deal of argument. When, after the fire of 1577, a decision was required on whether to rebuild or demolish the old palace, and the best architects were consulted, Cristoforo Sorte had this to say... 'that he did not in any way approve of putting the Most Serene Lordship in the great danger of inhabiting a palace built in the air'[68], implicitly condemning it. Goethe also speaking of St. Mark's found nothing better than to compare it to a 'roast lobster'.[69]

Until the eighteenth century, this architecture was called barbarian or German (*tedesca*). A gradual understanding of medieval art has led since the beginning of the last century not only to an increasingly widespread and enthusiastic love for these aspects of the medieval city, which in fact goes back to the eighteenth century (it is enough to mention Canaletto and Francesco Guardi), but also to a critical appreciation which precedes the exegeses of the great foreign historians of architecture. It is surprising to read in Leopoldo Cicognara's pages of 1838 on the Doge's Palace 'one of the greatest architectural monuments of the fourteenth century'[70], remarks which in a nutshell contain much, if not everything, of what was written later. It is enough to quote two phrases:

About the tracery of the loggia on the first floor: 'If, in particular, one looks at the build-

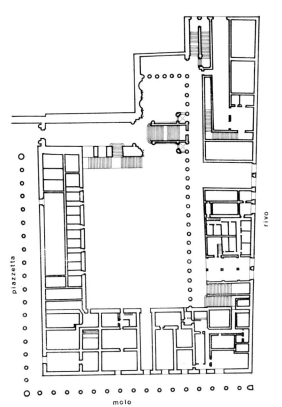

*The Doge's Palace. Plan of the ground floor according to a drawing of 1580 (from Paoletti)*

ing in perspective through the corner, it produces a marvellous effect, because of the air which interposes itself together with the light.'[71] The remark is surprising and penetrating in that, if we are not mistaken, no one has ever mentioned this aspect of the building, preferring instead to insist on those values of unbroken coloured areas which indiscriminatingly characterize the whole of Venetian secular Gothic. A façade which bends in a right angle, like this one, generating such a lively contrast between light and shadow, had never been seen before on the lagoon and was never to be repeated.

'The incrustation of the high walls' (Cicognara) 'with the alternate variety of colour in the stones produces a very great effect, removing from the high and vast mass all that is heavy and monotonous.'

In 'height', in 'mass', as well as in 'incrustation' and 'merlons', Cicognara sees connections with Islamic art, an idea which, as far as mass and height are concerned, has never been seriously examined[72]. Selvatico also expresses opinions which in 1847 could surprise; when he writes of the Doge's Palace loggia that it is '...of such harmonious elegance as to leave nothing more to be desired', he anticipates with a sentence that may now seem banal a quality judgment which today only an exact comparison with the whole of this artistic patrimony shows to be exact[73]. Ruskin[74] also insisted on the unique character of the Doge's Palace, seeing[75] in the 'breaking' of the angle a peculiarly Gothic principle (arising out of the necessity of strengthening the sides of enormous buildings or by that of compensating 'the meagreness of effect in buildings which admitted large surfaces of wall'). He concludes that 'the Ducal Palace, in its acknowledgment of this principle, makes a more definite concession to the Gothic spirit than any of the previous architecture of Venice'.

Burckhardt is inclined to criticize the proportions of the Doge's Palace, and it is a criticism which, being the consequence of a classical education, could be equally extended to the whole of Venetian Gothic architecture. In the purely qualitative evaluation, however, Burckhardt is right. The loggia 'has no equal in the whole medieval art'. And he is equally correct when he writes, purely by intuition: 'This marvellous palace is partly a derivative, partly an anticipation of a remarkable lay architecture which flourished in the middle of the fifteenth century'[76]. The opinions of Ruskin and Burckhardt, reflecting the position taken by the romantic criticism of the middle of the century, met with the resistance of reactionary criticism, of which we find an echo, again, in Selvatico, who in 1856 unconditionally praises the architecture of the Doge's Palace 'letting the horrified teachers by precepts cry "scandal"'[77].

Another German scholar with a classical bias, Kugler, though he also falls under the spell of the building, does not fail to remark in 1858[78] that he does not find in it 'relations of full rhythmic clarity'.

Cicognara's first happy intuition found a complete formulation a few years later in Schnaase[79], who, starting from the premise that 'there are few buildings which arouse so powerfully their own image even in the souls of those who are laymen in matters of architecture' and though dating to about 1424 the present appearance of the palace, notes that the architect has lightened with appropriate decoration the upper wall mass, the diagonals cancelling the feeling of verticality, and that the upper part is not even divided into smaller sections. It stands on its own, is clearly divided from the lower part, and weighs on it 'like an alien cube', so much that everyone feels this disproportion. '...But precisely because this is expressed in such a strong and strange manner, it cannot be considered an error, but something deliberately willed by the master, whose boldness imposes itself on the observer and whose importance fascinates and interests like an enigma. Unwittingly the fancy considers together this building and the republic which sheltered in it that high government whose presence in history seems no less unusual and mysterious.'

The appreciation of the irrationality of this façade becomes from now on current coin for

Hare[80], who follows Ruskin's guidelines, and for Pauli[81].

After Venturi[82] whom the belief in a Lombard influence on this architecture perhaps prevented from grasping its most intimate significance, the merit of understanding its sense completely fell to Toesca[83] '...The lower part of the façade, which should appear as a solid base for the mass of masonry above, is all lightness and slenderness; two deep galleries in which the lower columns without bases, the Gothic traceries above, seem to wish to draw attention to their insufficient ability to carry the great weight of the cubic pile above. The inversion of common constructional logic is so strong as to appear deliberately pursued...

...and that apparent absurdity of structure is one of the means towards the magic effect on the senses and the imagination. In the vaporous air of Venice, where the architecture can be seen only in the changeable relations of light and colour, the deep shadows of the galleries form a more than sufficient base for the mass above, which for the eye has no weight, is not material, but only an uncertain appearance of lights and tints, changing at each moment the colour which both forms and clothes it'.

'...Hues of white, of pink, of grey, not spread but minutely divided in little marble pieces arranged like a chequerboard, as in the illuminated frontispiece of a Byzantine Gospel, in order to multiply their vibrating quality and the better to perform, also on the marble, the continuous miracle of Venice, of forms changing colour between the reflections of the water and the mists of the sky, the vast mural curtain, in this way transformed into a mobile veil of colour, lighter than the dense shadow of the upper gallery, where the intricate Gothic tracery is like the first loosening of the movement which higher up changes into airy hues[84].' This is the only time when a passage from Toesca (a scholar whom I have revered as my master) is quoted extensively, because the words really correspond here to the facts. Certainly the 'small marble pieces arranged like a chequerboard, as in the illuminated frontispiece of a Byzantine Gospel' may have suggested the motif of the great white and pink wall, but to it may have contributed also certain decorative motifs which were widespread from one end of the Islamic world to the other (from the Gaun' al Kabir twelfth-century minaret in Mossul to the fourteenth-century tower of the Al-Mansurah mosque in Algeria and to the 'minor' arts in which the decorative pattern of lozenges in diagonal is very frequent).

It may be interesting at this stage to review the opinions concerning a possible architect of the palace and to re-examine the oldest evidence.

Paoletti found in an old *Mariegola* (register) of Scuola Grande della Carità, which goes as far as 1344, a *Henricus Taiapietra* (stonecutter–without any other indication). He then mentions two other documents, one of 1351 which names one *Mr. Henricus protomagister palacii* and one of 1356 in which reappears a *Magistrum Henricum protomagistrum nostri Comunis*.[85]

When one considers the date 1344 which evidences the beginning of the building, one cannot ignore this indication. Was this Master Henry the planner of this palace, indisputably coherent in the whole of its architectural framework?

We cannot say so with certainty, because the date of 1344 may well refer to some other person.

A document of 23 September 1361[86] speaks of a *quondam Petri Baseio magistri prothi Palatii nostri novi*[87]; it appears from it that *quondam* Filippo Calendario had looked after the interests of the three children of Baseggio.

Filippo Calendario is the name most often mentioned as the architect of the Doge's Palace.

Let us summarize what we know of this person who, even if he still eludes us, must have occupied a not unimportant place in the Venetian artistic milieu of the fourteenth century and was executed in 1355 for having taken part in the Marin Faliero plot. The year of his death would, to begin with, exclude his participation in the building of the Grand Council

Hall, erected in 1301–9 according to Sansovino[88], next to the tower (evidently the corner one) which the Barbo chronicle attributes to Calendario. Cadorin[89] argued that the structures near the tower also were the work of Calendario, but he is rather imprecise in reporting this information. Cadorin also reports the evidence of Egnazio, Caroldo, the Agostini chronicle, of Sanudo, of Sabellico[90], etc. Sabellico, Egnazio and Caroldo attribute to Calendario the façade on the quay and mention him in 1354, a year before his death, as the architect. Egnazio[91] designates Calendario *Marini Faletri principatu statuarius, et architetus insignis*, who *forum columnis intercolumnisque sic ornavit, sic ab omnibus spectandum cinxit, addito etiam cornitio maiore, in quo patres convenire possent;* an unclear phrase but not enigmatic to the point of denying that Calendario was considered also a sculptor and that the forum ornamented with columns refers to the Doge's Palace in *quo patres convenire possent;* and he does not even forget to mention the great cornice[92].

The Barbo chronicle also mentions him as an able sculptor, greatly esteemed by the Signoria; Sabellico mentions him as sculptor and architect; the Agostini chronicle[93] as sailor and architect. It seems to us that his description as sculptor, indeed as *fenissimo maistro tajapietra* (excellent master stonecutter)[94] is an important clue to follow.

That before his activity as sculptor and architect in the service of Faliero he may have followed to the wars the captain of the Venetian troops, Marino Ruzini[95], is a piece of information which does not clash with what was said or suggested above. Cadorin also quotes the document of 1361 in which Calendario is mentioned as testamentary executor for Baseggio's sons[96].

Calendario's paternity as architect of the new palace is accepted as undisputed by scholars of the nineteenth century, such as Bettio[97], Ermolao Paoletti[98], Cicognara[99], Selvatico[100] and, after them, Burchkardt[101], Lubke[102], Amico Ricci[103] and Kugler[104]. Zanotto[105] associates Baseggio with Calendario. In 1868 Lorenzi republished the important document of 23 September in which Filippo Calendario is mentioned as having been the delegate of the sons of Pietro Baseggio *olim magistri prothi Palacii nostri novi*[106]; other documents were published by Cecchetti[107], from which, in 1341 and 1343, Calendario appears to have been the owner of boats, but is also said to be a stonecutter at S. Samuele. A few years later the same author gives him another passing mention[108]. An article by Vittorio Lazzarini[109] on Calendario supplies information confirming what we already know. Calendario was a 'stonecutter' and owner of boats for the carriage of stones. But, as we know, the occupation of stonecutter does not at all exclude that of architect. Very often these masons were also architects, and vice–versa. Lazzarini finds no evidence of Calendario as architect; he finds instead, in 1351 and 1356, mentions of a certain master Enrico as *protomagister Palacii* and *protomagister Communis* and in 1355 of Pietro Baseggio as *magister prothus palatij novi*. But, observes Lazzarini, as the documents of those years speak of many protomasters (master–builders), one can reach no certain conclusions as to the name of the Doge's Palace architect.

Baseggio, already dead in 1354 (a year before Calendario) and mentioned in 1361 as master builder *palatij nostri novi*, is entirely ignored in the oldest chronicles as architect of the palace; and this, it seems to us, has an indisputable weight. If there were many master–builders, it is without doubt Calendario who, through the centuries, won the greatest fame. But Baseggio too had his supporters. Zanotto names him as architect of the palace, but in a confused manner and with mistakes in the dates[110], Ruskin and Fulin–Molmenti[112]. Most recent critics prefer not to take up a position. *Henricus protomagister palacii* mentioned in 1344, 1351 and 1356[113] is even less probable. In the present state of our knowledge, we have therefore three architects who, around the middle of the fourteenth century, could be connected with the building. But we know too little to choose with confidence any one of them.

The fourteenth–century southern façade was completed by the construction between

1400 and 1404 of the great central window, the decorative structures of which rise above the terminal cornice, interrupting on the upper side the line of merlons and on the lower side the upper cornice of the loggia.

A document[114] of 22 July 1400 notes that the *locus in que ordinatum fuit fieri podiolum qui respicit versus sanctum Georgium manet cum deformitate maxima tante sale* (of the Maggior Consiglio) *e pro fama et honore nostri dominij et civitatis nostrae, quod fiat dictus podiolus in forma qua jam diu depictus et designatus est... vel alia sicut melius et pulcrius videbitur domino*; wherefrom it appears evident that the important proposal of the Grand Council does not refer to the whole great enterprise (as critics currently maintain) but only to the balcony. Another document confirms that work was being done on the balcony in 1402 and that the sum allowed for it was increased[115].

A third document, discovered by Paoletti, of the 2 October 1400, although not actually naming the window, refers explicitly to it and bears the name of the artist—Pier Paolo dalle Masegne—who undertakes to *facere laborare et fabricare unum opus et hedificare in una carta membrana dessignatum, cum figuris ymaginum tresdecim*[116].

This date is supplied by the inscription on the spot, on the side of the extrados: *Mille Quadrigenti–currebant quatuor anni–hoc opus illustris Michael dux stellifer auxit*[117]. In 1405 work was completed[118].

The great window has the same dimensions as those next to it, but is open at a somewhat lower level and this in order to allow the harmonious placing within the high wall of the decorative complex which is, without doubt, one of the rarest and most singular works that Venice possesses.

Columns instead of the usual posts sustain the arch flanked on each side by a taller, ringed column, while with a marked and picturesque irrationality, the two outside 'pillars' rise level with the abaci of those columns and contain within canopied niches the statues of SS. George and Theodore. The four aediculae above the abaci of the columns and pillars contain the statues of the cardinal virtues, and continue in four equal spires which surpass the terminal cornice of the façade. These spires framed a remarkable but disorganized group of sculptures. At the sides of the oculus tangent to the vertex of the arch (originally, perhaps, a quatrefoil), there are two female statues supposedly Faith and Hope; immediately above, St. Mark's lion, now vanished; and, finally, a crowning device with truncated cusp and three aediculae containing the seated figures of SS. Mark, Peter and Paul. At the very top, well above the line of the upper cornice, the merlons and the spires, is the great statue of Justice.

This striking decorative complex, in which the various structures do not seem to be based on any framework of line or masses, is not the work of an architect but, evidently, that of a sculptor who does not achieve the right rhythm and harmony desirable in a façade which is the masterpiece of an architect of extraordinary coherence. One should consider the solid, well–linked structures which, while giving the freest rein to the decorative impulse, will be displayed some decades later by works as complex as Porta della Carta by Bartolomeo Bon or the portal of S. Francesco alle Scale in Ancona by Giorgio da Sebenico. When critically analysed, this insertion into the fourteenth–century façade of the Doge's Palace reveals at once a conflict, long since healed however by the patina of time and by the air of the city.

Of the statues, St. Theodore has revealed the hand of Pier Paolo[119]; the *Justice* was made by Vittoria in 1579 to replace the one which fell in the earthquake of 1511; *Charity* was placed there in 1577, after the well–known fire, probably replacing an older figure, since this would explain the thirteen statues mentioned in the document; St. George was made in 1767 by Alvise Pellegrini[120]. All the other statues were made at the same time as the building[121].

The balustrade is not of the type usual in Venice, with colonnettes or small pilasters; it is an elegant work with traceried panels and supported by strong corbels[122].

In the second half of the fourteenth century and the first decades of the next, the fourth order increasingly assumed more regular forms, which should distinguish such examples from those, more irregular, of the first five decades of the fourteenth. A swarm of buildings arises in Venice from 1440 on, to which belong many of the most famous examples of the mature and late Gothic. But the fourth order in its most simple forms was to persist even then in very numerous buildings of lesser importance, and it is precisely from the middle of the fifteenth century that it began to spread in the lands under Venetian dominion. It is not easy to identify buildings which belong to the second half of the fourteenth century, the more so in that the style they demonstrate oversteps the limits of the century and, with the enlargement of the period, the difficulties of any criticism which would attempt to establish a clear succession of artistic facts increase.

A fine and complete façade of a certainly fourteenth–century house is to be found in calle Cicogna (Castello 6219) at S. Maria Formosa. Two two–light windows in line are on the left while four single windows (two and two) flank them on the right, a regular arrangement, developed in height, which cannot have been unusual even in the Romano–Byzantine period. The attribution to the fourteenth century is confirmed by the flat profiles of the arches with a simple torus along the edge and a Byzantine dentil ornament along the moulding, as well as by the octagonal base of the column[123].

The few who have examined it assign to the fourteenth century the beautiful five–light window of the Palazzo Viaro–Zane in campo S. Maria Mater Domini (S. Croce 2123); Lorenzetti places it at the beginning of the century, Maretto in the second half.

The principle here is akin to that of Palazzo Agnusdio: a three/five–light window with two lateral windows wider and separated by two pilasters from the central three–light window; the moulding of the trefoiled arches, containing a plain dog–tooth ornament (a unique example); the round paterae at the points of the arches, as in other examples of the early fourteenth century; the marble parapets with a sill cutting the columns intact and two original plutei; the capitals with caulicoli; the marble–incrusted rectangle above, outlined by a cornice. A whole, proportioned and elegant in every part, with the arches on a by now regular geometric course[124], without any abnormal element, which should be placed in the middle of the fourteenth century.

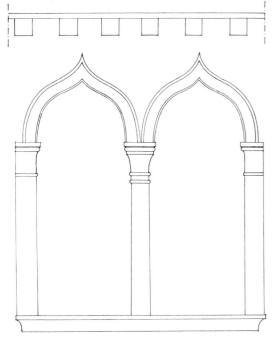

A sector which has preserved relatively ancient remains is that part of the S. Giovanni Crisostomo quarter which surrounds the corte degli Amadi, corte dei Morosini and corte Seconda del Milion. For the Palazzo of the Morosini we have a date; it is found on an eighteenth–century stone fixed in the wall at the bottom of a staircase at no. 5825 of corte Morosina, on which it is recorded that the foundations of the house were laid in 1369 by Marino Morosini. The Gothic façade, however, on rio del Fontego dei Tedeschi, does not seem to correspond at all to that date but to be later by a century, as it contains Renaissance elements[125]. There are, however, in corte Morosina (Cann. 5825) five single windows (of which one with simple inflected arch, not trefoiled) which could well be considered of the late fourteenth century because of the presence of that archaic element, together with the two doors side by side surmounted by two openings with segmental arches[126], while the well parapet with shields and two–handled vases[127] is certainly of the fourteenth century.

The so–called house of Marco Polo in corte Seconda del Milion (Cann. 5845) has, besides older remains, undoubted traces of the fourteenth century. There remains a very simple door, surmounted by a rectangular opening and, higher up, a three–light window on low columns with decidedly archaic capitals, forming a single body with a window of larger dimensions on the left (following a pattern which we have already seen elsewhere). Five paterae are placed in line with the vertices of the arches, of regular form and modelled with a profile which will be infinitely repeated later[128]. Mention should also be made of Palazzo Magno–Bembo (calle Magno 2893), almost unanimously attributed to the fourteenth century, well-known for the courtyard where a tall ringed column supports the upper storey, as in Palazzo Ariani, with a wooden architrave with owls' beak; and for the beautiful exterior staircase, supported by round arches, with astragals along the handrail (of the end of the fourteenth century) and the faces of the steps with torus cornices. Cylindrical elements replace the colonnettes (as in Palazzo Priuli at S. Severo). On the landing there are two rectangular doors with posts with smooth torus (next to them there is a two–light window with rosette capital, the abacus with plain dog–teeth and torus). The grille is still in place[129].

Another complex which may be considered of the fourteenth century is a building (preserved in part and whose external aspect it is difficult to reconstruct) situated on the fondamenta Gherardini al Carmine (Dorsoduro 2824–6), of which various elements remain, such as the two four–light windows of type four with fourteenth–century columns and capitals, single windows (one of which is provided with a balcony almost certainly of the fourteenth century) and a very simple staircase in the courtyard[130].

We have quoted examples of houses which, because of sure signs of an archaic style, must be considered of the fourteenth century, in which is typical, in addition, the irregularity in the distribution of the openings as well as the differences of levels (in particular, the house in salizzada S. Stae 1988, and the Venier house on rio dell'Arco). Other façades which we present here show some of those characteristics and may also be considered of that period. Of a façade in calle dei Botteri (S. Polo 1617–20), there remain only the first floor, a door on the extreme right (rectangular with, above, an opening with segmental arch) and the upper cornice. As in the house in salizzada S. Stae, a window of larger dimensions flanks a three–light window with low columns and fourteenth–century rosette capitals; spread at a lower level, the four windows of the wings frame the multi–light window; on the portal there is a shield with an angel of fourteenth–century workmanship[131].

A very similar motif (two–light window flanking a larger single window) is found in calle dei Botteri (S. Polo 1552), in the remains of a small but remarkably interesting complex.

A house in calle dei Mercanti (S. Croce 1828–9) should provide confirmation that these forms belong to the fourteenth century, namely the three–light window close by the side of a window with balcony, from which it is again divided by a pilaster. In the house in calle dei Mercanti a four–light similar window is placed in line with another, similar but belonging to the more archaic third order. We have thus confirmation that the latter survived long enough to appear together with the fourth order, about the early appearance of which early in the fourteenth century there can be no doubt[132]. We find the same motif again on the façade of a house in rio dei Miracoli, with capitals with caulicoli, and a round–headed water–gate, also like the multi–light window of the fourteenth century. Also to the fourteenth century is attributed by the Elenco (list) and by Lorenzetti, the small Palazzo Sansoni at Ponte Raspi (S. Polo 898). Its multi–light windows (one of them of a later period) displace the axis to the right, where we see above the usual three–light window by the side of the larger window sheltering under the cornice. The lower part has openings (doors and windows) of a fourteenth–century cut, but is divided from the upper part by a fascia, sculptured with jutting–out leaves, similar to those seen already in thirteenth–century palaces, which bends in a right–angle in order to accommodate the relieving arch on the portal already opened towards the bridge. This is a complex held to be (except for the two–light window) all of the same period, even in the 'irregularities' due to practical reasons. The edge, reinforced by Istrian stone quoins (a motif which in the fifteenth century will assume an aspect marked by a taste for regularity) is also remarkable. Toesca attributed to the fourteenth century a

house in Piscina S. Zulian (S. Marco 550) where the four–light window and the three–light window, perhaps in the centre of two wings which have since disappeared, the squat columns without bases, and other signs, confirm this dating[134]. To the second half of the fourteenth century must belong whatever Gothic can be seen in the Zuane Contarini Hospice, founded in 1378[135] on the fondamenta delle Terese (Dorsoduro 2209). One sees there a three–light window of the fourth order, displaced to the right and, on the left, three single windows of the same type.

The original façade of Palazzo Quartieri on rio della Guerra must have been delightful. Only the water–gate, of the usual type with two centres, and the second floor remain. (The first floor has been modified.) This second floor has a four–light window of the fourth order including a pilaster, and a window of larger dimensions on the right. The four–light window is not in line with the four single ones on the sides and is carried close to the upper cornice. These are archaic elements which (with capitals of a fourteenth–century type) would point to the second half of the fourteenth century[136].

The buildings we have mentioned may almost certainly be assigned to the fourteenth century. There are, however, very many others (or important parts of them) which it is possible to ascribe to that century only with great caution.

Taking first those with the greater probabilities in this respect, we shall mention now the beautiful Palazzo Da Pozzo in Cannaregio on four floors, with two four–light windows displaced to the right, two axes of single windows on the left, mezzanine with smaller windows at the top, rosette capitals, two small paterae 'loose' between the arches of the larger four–light window[137]; the three–light window (with the single window higher but close) in calle dei Sansoni (S. Polo 890)[138]; the Amadi houses at S. Giobbe (Cann. 652–57) where what restorers have left intact is, even if surmounted by a single long upper cornice, distributed in remarkable disorder (however, undeniably with fourteenth–century elements; even the coat of arms in the first floor wall)[139]; the Venier house in fond. Lizza Fusina (Dorsoduro 1844–5), with the three–light window on short columns, not in line with the four windows in the wings, rectangular portal surmounted by the usual opening with segmental arch and cornice, an already rigorously symmetrical complex[140]. Another façade with the three–light window in the centre between two wings (one window each side), colonnettes on high plinths and a square door with an upper rectangular opening[141], and rhomboidal paterae between the arches[142] is in calle Racchetta (Cann. 3789).

We cannot at all exclude the possibility of other buildings being of the end of the fourteenth or the beginning of the fifteenth century. We shall list some examples, leaving aside a problem that may remain subject to argument. A complete façade is the one which we can see in calle dei Botteri at S. Aponal (S. Polo 1565), the palazzo of which we have already considered the façade on rio delle Beccarie; namely a central portal with terracotta lunette, two floors of single windows of the fourth order and, under tne Gothic cornice, a mezzanine with small, rectangular windows following a scheme with a certain regularity recalling mainland models. However, we must question whether those mezzanines on the top floor may also be considered Gothic, even if the windows—of a purely 'functional' character—reappear in the same form in later periods. The many examples already seen, and the absolute uniformity of workmanship, would tend towards a positive answer[143].

Mention should also be made of Palazzo Badoer at S. Giacomo dall'Orio (S. Croce 1662) of which there remains a five–light window with archaic capitals with 'caulicoli'[144]; the remains of the two wings of the façade and the portico on the ground floor of the small Palazzo Costantini in rio Terrà Catecumeni (Dorsoduro 70)[145]; Palazzo Pisani Revedin at ponte di S. Paterniano (S. Marco 4013) with a beautiful façade on the canal, complete, with three floors (if all the elements seem referable, at least in style, to the fourteenth century, the central balustrade, supported by brackets with maned lion heads, appears to be of the end of the fifteenth)[146]; Palazzo Surian (S. Marco 456)[147]; Palazzo Zacco on rio di S. Marina at S. Canciano, with an ample, unorganic façade, with multi–light windows not coordinated on any central axis, 'fourteenth–century' capitals on the third and fourth floors, arches of type four with their vertices at different heights but, also, with Renaissance elements which seem to be contemporaneous with the Gothic ones, and concur in placing the whole complex in the late fifteenth century[148]. A beautiful anonymous example is that in calle Piacentini (Castello 4395a) where the two floors (fourth order) have fourteenth–century elements but the dentil ornament is doubled and the capitals with thick leaves could place this façade even in the fifteenth century[149]. The house in calle della Fava (S. Marco 5249), with a loggia on the second floor without any functional character (an archaic recollection) is almost certainly fifteenth century.

The remarkable façade in campo dei Do Pozzi (Castello 2611–13) may perhaps be contained within the fourteenth century: two floors, with a four–light and a three–light window, accompanied, without too much rigour, by various windows (the axis is diplaced to the left), upper cornice and beautiful ancient round chimney[150]. This house has supports of an archaic type, fourteenth–century, with rosette capitals. This, the fourth order with a rosette capital, is a combination which, when any sign of floriated Gothic (capital with thick leaves, flower–finials, cable cornice) is lacking, may make one think of the fourteenth century. The presence of pilasters in the body of the multi–light windows may also be an archaic indication. However, these forms may be entitled to a transfer to the first half of the following century[151].

The fourth order, as we said before, was to enjoy a great spread in Venice and on the mainland. It was the simplest and most rapidly adopted formulation of Venetian secular Gothic for over two centuries, and it is found in the great patrician houses as well as in the minor buildings. Such a vast spread, however, raises difficult, sometimes insoluble problems of chronology. It would seem likely, however, that its spread on the mainland did not occur before the conquest of those territories by the Serenissima a little before the end of the fourteenth century, so that it occurs then in the Treviso March and after about 1405 in the Western Veneto.

The Estuary centres, which had been bound for a long time to the chief city, must however be considered in respect of the development in time of those forms on a par with Venice.

Equally, the house on fondamenta Navagero (no. 51–51a) in Murano, where the five–light window has the characteristics of many Venetian houses already considered, must also be of the fourteenth century[152]; and, because of the obvious irregularities, Palazzo Corner (at nos. 70–71) and the Obizzi Sodeci house at nos. 4–6, both on fond. Manin in Murano, may be of the same century. Both have an irregular distribution of the windows on a single storey, above a portico with architrave (of a rather infrequent type)[153]. In Chioggia, what remains of the ancient part of the small Palazzo Renier may also belong to the fourteenth century[154].

The cinquefoiled inflected arch is very rare in Venice and on the mainland. We can mention a window of the house by ponte dei Fuseri, probably of the fifteenth century[155]. Another example may be seen in the Serena Cisterna house at Spilimbergo, together with others of the fourth type, certainly of the fifteenth century. Another is to be found on a sarcophagus in the cloister of the former Carmine convent in Venice. The windows of S. Stefano in Venice (of the early fifteenth century) are also cinquefoiled, as is the aedicule above the Frari façade. We have already mentioned the two–light window of Angera Castle.

The motif is of English origin, with very many examples, beginning in the thirteenth century (the tomb of Hugh of Northwold at Ely (1229–54), the tomb of Thomas de Cantilupe in Hereford Cathedral (1282–4)[156], in Guisborough Abbey, at the end of the thirteenth

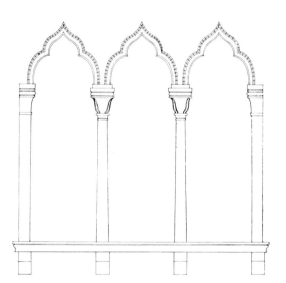

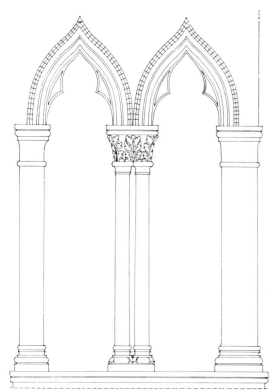

*Two-light window of a house on Piazzetta dei Leoncini*

century[157]; in the large windows at Ely (1325-50)[158], at Exeter, Winchester, Wells, etc., at Castle Ashby[159], Malvern (Worcs.), Edington (Wilts)[160], in Bristol Cathedral, of the early fourteenth century[161]). It may well be that the taste for these cinquefoiled arches came to the English from Spain, where the most magnificent example is found in the Cordoba Mosque (of the tenth century)[162].

Significant here, because it confirms the persistence of elements of style of specifically English taste, conditioning to a large extent the character of the secular architecture of the Lagoon, is the unique door of S. Stefano. Of a purely Venetian character in the rich modelling of the square opening and in the lunette with pinnacles and crockets, it is distinguished by a complex play of arches in the intrados, which in turn include smaller trefoiled arches. There are good reasons to ascribe this very beautiful portal to the first half of the fifteenth century: the affinity of its pillars to those of the door of the Corner chapel and that of the Frari façade and the foliage along the extrados similar to that which crowns the façade of St. Mark's would suggest a date around 1420[163]. The same motif reappears—a unique instance in Venice—in two windows opened in the terracotta structure behind the church, beside the campanile, towards the rio di S. Stefano. The multifoiled arches of this rich and articulated type originate, however, again in England, where their abundance from the end of the thirteenth century onward could surprise only the observer unable to connect them with the sumptuous wealth of the *decorated style*[164].

Ruskin classified as fifth order of Venetian secular Gothic the one characterized by a trefoiled inflected arch contained within a larger archivolt, inflected with four centres.

This form, more complex than the fourth order, might also suggest a later period in time. An examination, however, of the examples to be found in Venice would indicate that it too was born in the first half of the fourteenth century, although during this century the examples are numerically inferior to those of the fourth order.

A sarcophagus in the courtyard of Palazzo Contarini del Bovolo bears perhaps one of the oldest examples in Venice of an arch of that form. It crowns, in the middle of the front, an image of the Virgin. On the sides there are equilateral crosses inside quatrefoils, while the edges are marked by spiral colonnettes. If one recalls the most ancient examples of this type of sarcophagus in the Veneto (those outside S. Lorenzo in Vicenza, datable within the first two decades of the fourteenth century), this dating would appear correct[165]. In this respect, two windows in ramo Terzo del Mosca (S. Croce 56) which display the model discussed here, but profiled in an archaic manner with a single torus element along the edge (otherwise smooth), are very important, and perhaps of the first half of the fourteenth century.

Remains of one of the most ancient examples of the fifth order must be represented by a two-light window and a single window on the Piazzetta dei Leoncini (S. Marco 289-305). The two-light window is borne by two coupled colonnettes with capitals with truncated cubes (one wonders whether these are not re-used materials). The greater part of the building was still standing in the eighteenth century, as shown by a drawing of Canaletto (now in an unknown private collection) from which, however, the strongly shortened façade (even then already altered) is not quite legible[166].

There is certainly no lack in Venice of other confirmations, and quite impressive ones, of the early appearance of this type of order: as, for example, that offered by the southern front of the Doge's Palace, where this motif is displayed in the loggia.

Another reliable point of reference is provided by the small façade of the Abbey of S. Gregorio on the Grand Canal, erected around 1340, where a three-light window on short columns shows this motif fully developed in the moulding of the two arches (the simple and the trefoiled) spaced on two planes in depth, united by a soft chiaroscuro effect. There is, in this play, undoubtedly a 'progress' from the fourth order, and the prototypes, again, must be sought in the Gothic from beyond the Alps and beyond the Channel.

If it has been possible to find some points of reference for the fifth order in the first half of the fourteenth century, in the second half of the century and beyond, until the beginning of the third decade of the fifteenth century (when work was in progress on Palazzo Barbaro and the Ca' d'Oro) there are no dates, to our knowledge, which may indicate a succession or an unambiguous stylistic development.

A terminus *ante quem* is, however, constituted by what are properly the beginnings of the floriated Gothic, by the appearance of flower finials at the top of the arches, of cable ornaments along the posts, of a different balance, of new rhythms in the distribution of volumes and voids, and of other details to be defined later. All this happened at the beginning of the fifteenth century, or the end of the fourteenth.

In reality if, as it seems (but is not at all certain), the fourth order appears somewhat before the fifth, the two forms continue together throughout the fourteenth century, sometimes even in the same building, within a general scheme of architecture which is certainly more sober and more severe than that which will be presented by fifteenth–century buildings. The fourth order will then assume (in the fifteenth century), particularly in large buildings, a secondary role which will characterize some more modest parts of the buildings, while the fifth order, in increasingly sumptuous forms, will appear in the 'nobler' parts. On the other hand, the fourth order will appear very frequently in the 'minor', less pretentious buildings, spreading on to the mainland, where on occasion it will even assume the lead (for instance, in Verona). The time limits being thus defined, it will not be difficult to recognize in many Venetian buildings which display the distribution and particular characteristics of the fourth order, elements of the fifth order which can be placed in the second half of the fourteenth century.

A very important example of the early appearance of the fifth order, clearly marked by archaic elements certainly not retarded but bound together in a coherent synthesis which places them well into the fourteenth century, is that of the large façade of Palazzo Moroni, on fond. della Fenice (S. Marco 2557). We find here, in the stern five–light window, the austerity of early Venetian Gothic, with fourteenth–century capitals and pilasters, small, loose paterae inserted directly into the wall and the trefoiled arch still a little stunted, surviving elements of the fourth order on the second floor and the large spacing between the single–light windows[167]. It is not difficult to find virtually anywhere in Venice instances which reproduce the irregularities and the uncertainties noticed in so much of the 'minor' architecture of the fourth order. One can in fact say that we are dealing with those same architectural formulations, incompletely realized, of the fourth order in which appears, instead, the fifth order.

A modest house in salizzada Streta (Castello 105–108) displays fourteenth–century patterns[168] in the windows sheltering under the cornice (with lion-heads), in the three–light windows on the right with the largest window in the middle and in the (reconstructed?) doors. A four–light window with short columns on high pedestal in campo del Traghetto at S. Maria Zobenigo (S. Marco 2465) flanks windows of the fourth order[169]. The sequence on a first floor in fond. Zen at the Gesuiti (Cann. 4935) with a four–light window (two columns and an inserted pilaster) and two further windows[170] is another example, as are the Gothic remains of Palazzo Dolfin at S. Tomà in calle del Traghetto Vecchio (S. Polo 2878–9)[171] (a five–light window with traces of the original plutei); a six–light window made up of a four–light flanked by two windows connected with it by a pilaster, after a pattern we shall soon find again on fond. di Cannaregio at no. 1298. These are all fragments (or 'minor' features) which repeat arrangements already discussed, in which the presence of fourteenth–

century capitals (but we should notice that those with thick leaves, absent in these examples, appear in Venice already around the middle of the fourteenth century), the cornice overhanging the multi-light windows, the absence of finials or cable mouldings and, in general, the rather dry character of the forms, argue for the fourteenth century.

This is confirmed also by a remarkable complex, namely Palazzo Querini in Piscina S. Samuele (S. Marco 3431), perhaps once consisting of four floors, now mostly reconstructed. Of the façade, there remains the left side of the mezzanine and, on the *piano nobile*, the central three–light window and the left wing, all with capitals and shaped impost stones pointing to the fourteenth century[172]. The near–by Palazzo Pisani, also in Piscina S. Samuele (S. Marco 3395) seems to have been tampered with as well, but is none the less of some significance. The robust five–light window is in reality a three–light window flanked by two single windows (from which it is separated by pilasters). The second floor is furnished with the fourth order and is one of the earliest examples of the use of that order in a secondary part[173].

It is particularly in the case of 'minor' structures that one can deduce a fourteenth-century dating when the two orders, fifth and fourth, appear mixed together without any organized aesthetic criterion (apart from the cases difficult to decide, in which the distribution of the openings is dictated by chance, or by practical considerations). This is because a tighter organization of the wall surface comes into being gradually as one proceeds towards the fifteenth century. On the other hand, the structures (whole or dimidiate, or surviving in the fragments which we are studying), where the two orders mix together, have, save for that difference in the tracing of the arch, the same elements[174]. Examples of still complete structures are not lacking either. They follow regular and at times symmetric patterns, and are of notable size. This will happen increasingly in the fifteenth century.

A building in salizzada S. Basegio at S. Sebastiano (Dorsoduro 1651), also of four floors, in deplorable condition but with its structure intact, has two four–light windows, not at all in line, and the (vanished) balcony supported by lion–shaped corbels which will become more frequent in later times[175]. Another façade is that of a house on rio di S. Polo[176] (on the ground floor the usual door with pointed arch and four rectangular windows with relieving arch, in brick; on the first floor a four–light window with a pilaster associated with the columns; an upper cornice).

At this point, it is easier to understand what is left of the small Palazzo Semitecolo on the Grand Canal, where it is not improbable that, owing to one of those caprices one often encounters in these façades, the beautiful six–light window is contemporaneous with the scattered fourth–order windows of the second floor. In the six–light, the fourteenth-century practice of the larger window being divided by a pilaster is followed. Here it produces a four–light window between two single windows, thus creating a beginning of symmetry. The string course touches the inflected vertex of the water-gate while the solid wall shrinks to allow the opening below of the loggia on the canal, an infrequent occurrence[177]. Some interesting organic complexes of façades lead us towards the fifteenth century, but may yet be considered of the preceding century. To put them side by side, to assemble them in groups, may help us to understand them better and to define more closely the character of the architecture of the second half of the fourteenth century. It is precisely to these decades that we should refer since because of their own characters or by exclusion, these structures which are no longer characterized by the uncertainties or the abnormal forms recalling the Romanesque of the early fourteenth century, are yet far from the regular but increasingly sensitive, rhythmic and chromatic floriated Gothic.

The advance towards more regular forms and towards more organic (and sometimes imposing) masses becomes increasingly marked in a series of palaces which we propose to place at the end of the fourteenth century and which combine all the characters so far met

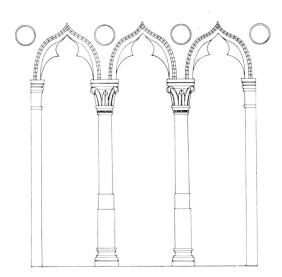

with, increasing the mass to unusual dimensions. A typical example of the way in which the Venetian façade is becoming organized (if we are at the end of the fourteenth century) may be provided by the large apartment house of five floors at the ponte dell'Ojo on rio del Fontego dei Tedeschi at S. Giovanni Crisostomo (Cann. 5788). The façade is symmetrical, with three two–light windows in line on the second, third and fourth floors, flanked by two axes of single windows (but those of the second floor are connected by two pilasters to the two–light window). The last floor, a mezzanine, has smaller windows with segmental arch, which always represent an archaic form. All the apertures are of squat proportions, the capitals 'fourteenth–century' with rosettes. The whole, however regular, is unusual and does not yet achieve the neat, compact, eurhythmic structures of the more mature Gothic.

It is precisely this symmetry which could make us doubt that we are dealing with a structure of the beginning of the fifteenth century. There was certainly a balcony on the third floor.

Remarkable also is Palazzo Gritti Loredan on rio dei Greci, rising on a high base not in line with the upper part (a high, singular portal, round-headed on pillars, opens on the water). The two floors above, mostly unaltered, reveal the striking height of the rooms inside. The *piano nobile*, of the fifth order, contains a great four–light window on short columns and purely fourteenth–century capitals. The second floor, also very high, of the fourth order, is in line with the first (the mezzanine and the cornice are of later date). The inner courtyard, though spoiled, displays on the eastern and southern sides, in great abundance, elements of the fourth and fifth order, clearly fourteenth–century, with the typical 'archaic' anomalies. The building has been for centuries the so–called Ospizio degli Esposti (Foundling Hospital). Founded in 1348 by Fra Pieruzzo d'Assisi, it passed in 1353 under ducal patronage and was enlarged in 1388[178]. Enough evidence is available to attribute the above structures to the fourteenth century[179].

In Palazzo Marcello on rio di S. Luca, of more complex mass, we find an unusual enlargement of the façade. If, in fact, the two three–light windows (one above the other) and the main portal represent one axis of an arrangement of the building which is in itself striking, this effectively fuses, on the right, with two other supplementary axes, where the accent falls on two two–light windows (one above the other) and on the smaller portal, creating, perhaps, the first example of its kind in Venice. Of the Gothic elements in fourteenth–century style, there remain the first and second floors, besides the water-gates with simple inflected arch. The dating, however, is not absolutely certain[180].

Of more modest bulk, but remarkable for its two surviving floors, the Palazzo Dolfin Bollani Erizzo on the Grand Canal develops in the seven–light window on the second floor and the pseudo six–light on the first the motif already noticed in Palazzo Semitecolo; that is, the tendency towards a loggia which traverses the façade from one corner to the other, with the insertion of pilasters at the ends, offering a more solid surface (almost the appearance of more solid structures) in contrast with the fleeting chiaroscuro of the shafts of the columns. The arches are designed with elegance, alternating with paterae[181].

A well articulated façade on the Zattere (Dorsoduro 920–921a) is also entirely devoid of elements specific to the floriated Gothic and displays the two orders (fifth and fourth) with a certain rhythmic regularity which we shall find again in much minor fifteenth–century building; but this is not enough, however, to convince us that it is of very advanced date, especially when we look at the three–light window of the second floor. But this, too, may be a case of retardation[182].

An unexpected solution, unique in Venice (but one we have already seen in Murano) is that realized in Palazzo Benedetti at S. Sofia (Cann. 4172–3). The two floors on rio Priuli stand above an architraved arcade with buttresses supported by five pilasters. The whole façade is now elaborated with absolute symmetry. The composition is compact, the *piano nobile* is at secondary level with the cornice immediately above. The profile of the buttresses with owl's beak and the string course with cable moulding are elements already common in the floriated Gothic. It is reasonable to believe, however, that this house does not go beyond the end of the century, as the two sides on rio di S. Sofia and on the ruga dei Due Pozzi seem to confirm, with elements which correspond to fourteenth–century forms. The side on the *ruga* (shopping street) is pierced by windows of the two orders, distributed without any rhythm and with the typical carelessness of Venetian builders. Every architectural balance disappears and the wall becomes a purely chromatic element[183]. A better known palace is the Grifalconi at S. Zanipolo in calle della Testa (Cann. 6359) whose façade gives on the rio dei Mendicanti (a four–light window in the middle under the cornice, as in Palazzo Benedetti, and two single windows on each side). This small palazzo is characterized by an outer staircase built against the southern side instead of in the courtyard. The arches which support it are round–headed; the banisters of the type of those of the Doge's Palace loggia and the Ponte della Paglia—findings which do not oppose an ascription to the second half of the fourteenth century[184].

We are inclined to place at the end of the fourteenth century also Palazzo Gritti in campo Bandiera e Moro (Castello 3608), however an examination of the imposing façade of four floors does not as yet reveal those qualities of organic balance which characterize the buildings of the fifteenth century.

Wise restoration could bring to light sundry new elements but would certainly not eliminate the absence of a harmonious axis, for instance between the large multi–light windows. The upper one, indeed, with the usual larger aperture forming body with the three–light window and the very high framing (common also to the single–light windows of the second floor, where also the paterae are placed very high up), reproduces motifs which we have already noticed in fourteenth–century buildings. (We should remember also the older of the Palazzi Soranzo in campo S. Polo.) That second floor argues for the same epoch as the first, where, however, the presence of fourteenth–century capitals and the trefoiled element above the frame with the eagle relief prevent a fifteenth-century ascription, a charming licence which joins in breaking the structural harmony with a splendid note of colour and a striking chromatic taste which alternates also with the colours of the columns of the five–light window, made in turn of red and grey marble, while the red shafts have white capitals and the grey ones red capitals. The seven–light window of the mezzanine, consisting of low, architraved lights is, however, in the middle of the building, away from the axes of the two multi–light windows. Flower finials appear on the vertices of the arches, alternating on the five–light window with human heads, chiselled away (it seems) on the second floor, and this may well be one of their first appearances at the end of the fourteenth century. No traces of string courses are noticeable however, and it is unnecessary to point out that the distribution of the windows does not display an absolute regularity or homogeneity, thus again confirming the ascription of this complex to the end of the fourteenth century. This is supported by an examination of the other sides of this magnificent building[185].

Judging by what remains, the Palazzo Gritti façade must have been one of the most brilliant examples of Venetian Gothic architecture, particularly if it offered itself as a large field of action for the painting which certainly took advantage of the vast expanse of wall. This façade excited the enthusiasm of Ruskin who placed it in 1310–20 and called it 'a magnificent example'. But later, in 1877, he remarked '...restored and destroyed', and this was later echoed by Hare who called it 'infamously modernized'. Paoletti speaks of mural decorations 'now perished'. Those who spoke of it later placed the building in the fourteenth century and lately, in the fifteenth[186].

Besides the examples discussed, there are obviously many buildings which may with some probability be attributed to the fourteenth century, and others which, more prudently, can be placed between the end of the fourteenth and the beginning of the fifteenth century.

A palace which should not cross the limits of the century is the one in rio Terrà Catecumeni (Dorsoduro 140), with the façade almost intact and, in the middle, the three/five–light window (with two pilasters). No symmetry is respected but note should be taken of the four–light window with segmental arches of the mezzanine up above and the solution of the two corner windows connected by a pilaster, which repeat, in a poorer way, the famous solution of the corner of Ca' Priuli, believed to be later in time[187]. For this reason, an attribution to the end of the fourteenth century seems to us possible. The Leoni House also (a rare case of a Venetian building showing two 'organized' façades, one on rio Pesaro, the other on calle della Chiesa, at S. Maria Mater Domini) shows archaic elements worthy of consideration (S. Croce 2180–1). The canal front (two three–light windows, one above the other, flanked by a simple window on each side) is of the fourth order, except for a fifth order light incorporated in a three–light window. The three–light windows are supported only by pilasters. The street front presents three multi–light windows in line, where one recognizes the usual elements of fourteenth–century extraction (columns on high plinths, pilasters for the internal support of the multi–light windows, promiscuity of the two orders)[188].

Another façade of more elegant proportions is that in campiello S. Maria Nova (Cann. 6024–5), with a four–light window displaced to the left, no respect for the level of the openings, and, important, rectangular windows of the mezzanine (and of the same period as the oldest part)[189].

The front of Palazzo Cappello in rio de la Panada (Cann. 5400) has a symmetrical layout, dominated by the two large four–light windows in the middle, in which the strong shafts of the columns play a dominant part (without, any longer, the high pilasters typical of the early fourteenth century). One should note in this new rhythm of the multi–light windows referable, like this one, to the end of the fourteenth century (and which will last into the first decades of the fifteenth, as the five–light window in the entrance courtyard of the Ca' d'Oro demonstrates), the contrast between these round and robust supports and the relative slenderness of the inflected arch, a contrast underlined in Palazzo Cappello by the fourteenth–century capitals. This comparison is not useless here for underlining the passage from the dry fourteenth–century structures to those, more florid and luxurious, of fifteenth–century floriated Gothic[190].

Finally, with reservations, a large structure like Palazzo Talenti in rio delle Oche (S. Croce 1033) may be placed at the end of the century, since though without the greater rigour of some large fifteenth–century buildings, it is a clear anticipation of them. A string course defines in the upper part a high base marked by two mezzanines which have small windows with segmental arches, and by the high corner column incorporated in the edge, a common feature in the fifteenth century. The middle axis is marked by two four–light windows with massive columns like those of Palazzo Cappello and 'fourteenth–century' capitals, while three axes on each side provide at substantial intervals the rhythm of the large wings. The order is the fifth everywhere. The third mezzanine, with detached windows in line with the openings below, stands under the ancient upper cornice. The façade, strong and well finished, with a water–gate with inflected arch, is the work of a builder whose spirit is very clearly evident and shows a firm mastery of space, and not the work of conservative masons, still involved in fourteenth–century ways. This would lead us to think of the end of the fourteenth century or, perhaps at most, the first decade of the fifteenth[191].

And, to conclude this list of architectural structures which so vividly recall each other, mention should be made of an apartment house, modest but not without grace, in calle dei

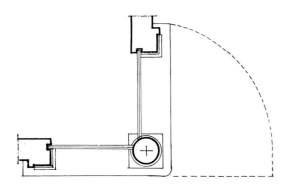

Meloni (S. Polo 1412–15), of a more 'middle-class' character, with two long rows of windows where the two orders alternate[192].

There remain, to finish, scattered fragments with the fourth and fifth order mixed together, which may well go beyond the end of the century and reach into the first half of the fifteenth, always remembering, however, the tenacious vitality of these forms in Venice. To mention them here does not commit us to any rigorous chronology[193].

The tall and thick columns (of various colours) of the large four–light window in Palazzo Tron, contrasting with the trefoiled arches which thus appear almost diminished (also owing to the proximity of the strong voluminous capitals) lead me to place this building at this point of time. Though much tampered with, it displays, in the older parts, some archaic accents[194].

A first floor at S. Zulian (S. Marco 555) with a beautiful three–light window of archaic layout, and of the fifth order, is flanked on each side by two single, third–order windows (not, however, of a 'Byzantine' type but Gothic, with four centres and five mouldings) and not improbably belongs to the fourteenth century. We give in a note other examples of the fifth order with archaic capitals[195].

*The transition to the floriated Gothic; further aspects of the Venetian architecture of the late fourteenth and early fifteenth centuries (until about 1420)*

The transition to the floriated Gothic in Venetian architecture does not entail substantial modifications in the structure of the buildings, which cannot therefore provide any indications for establishing a chronology or the development taken by the forms. But useful clues are, on the other hand, provided by decoration which—between the end of the fourteenth and the beginning of the fifteenth century—covers with ever richer forms the wall surfaces, the mouldings, the windows, the staircases and the well–curbs. The most conspicuous example of this change is represented by the Ca' d'Oro, begun in 1424, but judging by many signs, such as the use of cable mouldings which bring a new chromatic vibration into the string courses, the jambs, the use of flower finials on the vertex of the extrados and that of the capital with thick leaves, the change could precede that date even by decades. As noted previously, the capital with thick leaves appeared in Venice around 1340.

As for the flower finials, present in major French architecture already in the first quarter of the fourteenth century (Laon, Chartres, Amiens), they are found late in Venice, not before the end of the fourteenth century. The presence of a flower finial on one of the windows of the oldest part of the Doge's Palace, giving on the rio di Palazzo, must be considered an exception. The flower finial appears, however, almost certainly in buildings considered of the second half of the fourteenth century. A typical case may be presented by the Palazzo Bembo Boldù (Cann. 5999), where the four-light windows have capitals with rosettes and an incorporated pilaster while the upper arches have a still archaic outline, and a narrow, compact façade between the edges and the upper cornice, where everything (including the ground floor) recalls the late fourteenth century, with exuberant tufts on the first floor windows[196].

Another characteristic case—perhaps earlier than the preceding one—may be seen in the façade of the small Palazzo Conca at SS. Apostoli. Two floors remain, with a clearly archaic three–light window on the first floor in which the arches do not touch, supported by short fourteenth–century columns.

A smaller three–light window on the second floor is of the fourth order. These elements, together with the somewhat uncertain cut of the arches and the rather flat profile, indicate an ascription to the end of the fourteenth century[197].

Quite different, and very significant if we are indeed dealing with a fourteenth–century work, is the small palazzo on rio della Pietà (Castello 3616). Here appears to be already in its essential characters the definitive aspect of the floriated Venetian Gothic: a four–light window framed with flower finials and paterae. But all the elements are timid and archaic, from the capitals to the rosette ornament which frames the multi–light window, the usual pilaster, etc. A dating to the late fourteenth century is therefore not excluded[198].

It is unlikely that the floriated Gothic came to Venice only with Raverti and his apprentices; other Lombards too, from the last quarter of the fourteenth century onwards, could have introduced it. This is yet to be proved by documents.

We are considering, in fact, Ruskin's so–called sixth order.

As mentioned in connection with the Ca' d'Oro, in 1426 Matteo Raverti was asked by Marino Contarini to '*compir due piane con i suo mudiony le qual dovea andar ai laj la suo balchonada lavorado per tutto chome sie quele dela chasa de ser Nicholo moresinji fo de miss. Gasparin del suo soler de erto*' (mak etwo landings with their brackets which should reach the sides of the gallery: the whole worked out like those of the house of Ser Nicolò Morosini, son of Sig. Gasparino, on his *piano nobile*)[199]. The *piano nobile* mentioned here is easily identified as the second floor of Palazzo Sagredo, which is certainly later than the beautiful Romano–Byzantine first floor of which we have already spoken, and is therefore earlier than 1426.

It is reasonable to assume that the four–light window on the façade of Ca' Sagredo, with the three single–light windows on the right and the other one on the left, belongs to the years between the fourteenth and fifteenth centuries. We see again, in addition to the archaic capitals, the somewhat depressed and irregular trefoiled arches and the small paterae. On the whole, this is a rather cramped and contracted style, to which a singular note is added by quatrefoils clearly imitating those of the Doge's Palace but separated here by a horizontal ornament from the arches underneath them, with whose vertices they are in line. We have perhaps here the first timid attempt to imitate the splendid but misunderstood prototype, the Doge's Palace[200].

The four–light window vividly recalls the one which dominates the lower part of the Palazzo Gabrieli façade on riva degli Schiavoni, which some have already justly assigned to the end of the fourteenth century. The fourth order dominates in a rather wide façade, in which the central multi–light windows are subject to a rigorous arrangement not respected in the wings, the whole under a single upper cornice. The low balustrades of the lower four–light window are remarkable. The fifth order appears here and there and the tops of the arches are not at the same level[201].

We have already mentioned Palazzo Priuli and the part which we have assumed to be of the fourteenth century. It is mentioned again now because it offers a sure chronological foothold.

We saw how in 1431–4, while work was going on at the Ca' d'Oro, Marino Contarini attests that '*maistro Nicholo romanello tajapiera... me tolse a far i miei tre pergoli de la mia chaxa del mio soler da basso de piera viva...: tutj tre die esser a muodo de quelo de la chasa fo di ser Chostantin de priolj quelo e suso al chanton inverso sam Zacharia*' ... (Master Nicolò Romanello, stonecutter, undertook to make the three large windows on the lower floor of my house of new stone... all three must be of the kind of that of the house of Sig. Costantino Priuli, that on the side towards S. Zaccaria). Paoletti[202] correctly identified the example mentioned by Marino Contarini with the corner two–light window of Palazzo Priuli, at the confluence of rio dell'Osmarin with rio di S. Severo (but neither the 'large window' of Palazzo Priuli nor those of Ca' d'Oro exist any longer).

The beautiful two–light window is therefore anterior to 1431; perhaps, precisely, of the first thirty years of the fifteenth century and, notably, it does not appear at all aligned with the fourteenth-century part towards ponte del Diavolo, but rather with the window which follows on rio S. Severo, a clear sign that at the beginning of the fifteenth century this substantial building had been enlarged towards rio di S. Severo. The two–light window strikes a new note, inspired by the specific style of the Doge's Palace and by a number of essential motifs on the corner between the Piazzetta and the quay. The vigorous modelling of the tracery with the trefoil oculus on the axis between the two inflected arches (the protrusions between the foils are also traceried) is firmly contained by the strong cornice within a rectangle of which the lower limit is at the level of the abaci. The corner of the upper part is marked by a spiral colonnette. The taut, sharp profiles, the balance of the firmly calibrated parts, the brilliant 'invention' itself, everything betrays the hand of a remarkable architect, not unlike in spirit to (though distant in time from) the one who conceived the Doge's Palace.

According to Tassini, Palazzo Navagero on the riva degli Schiavoni, near ponte del Sepolcro (Castello 4146) dates from 1438. The only thing of interest here is the first floor with a three–light window in the middle and the usual two single–windows on the sides (two give on the rio). The date confirms the persistence of archaic forms in that period[203].

Additional examples may be quoted, and it seems useful to do so here in order to elaborate a first ordering of certain buildings erected approximately between 1375 and 1430. However, in the absence of realiable data, this can often be done only by way of exclusion. On a more attentive examination one may even meet with surprises. Some buildings, owing to the conservative spirit of which we have had notable examples, may turn out to be much later in time. However, it is not entirely useless to have placed together–the chronology notwithstanding–buildings showing stylistic affinities.

These are, for instance, Palazzo Contarini at S. Canciano (Cann. 5549–50) with a rectangular door of archaic profiles, three–light windows with flower finials and rosette capitals[204]; Palazzo Falier at S. Vitale (S. Marco 2906–14) which also heralds the canonical formulations of the late fifteenth century but nevertheless, because of certain details and certain irregularities, cannot belong to a very mature period[205]; Palazzo Gherardi at S. Canciano (Cann. 5575)[206], perhaps of the beginning of the fifteenth century; the former Palazzo Pisani in Lista di Spagna (Cann. 117–19) with a graceful five–light window surmounted by flower finials and with two inserted pilasters[207].

To the fifteenth century may be attributed the beautiful building on fondamenta della Misericordia (Cann. 2528), with two beautiful slender four-light windows one above the other and with some archaic elements. It heralds in its general harmony the best buildings of the middle fifteenth century[208].

Particular cases are presented by Palazzo Donà Calle Larga (S. Marco 383)[209] and Palazzo Condulmer Da Lezze on the Grand Canal. The splendid four–light window of the first (supported in the middle by a pilaster) remains; one may consider a date in the first quarter of the fifteenth century. The second (S. Marco 3319) has a symmetrical balanced front, with large flower finials at the top of the four–light and single windows; but the promiscuous use of the fourth and fifth order, the different levels of the openings and the archaic capitals, are elements which make one think of the first half of the fifteenth century, perhaps the first three decades[210].

On the façade of Palazzo Zatta on fondamenta Labia, the *piano nobile* is of the sixth order, the second floor of the fourth and fifth orders, the door rectangular. This is a very homogeneous complex, with archaic capitals, making one suspect the early appearance of the sixth order between the fourteenth and fifteenth centuries[211].

Very often the early fifteenth century has an archaic–like appearance. Ancient remains of a structure, perhaps of the early fifteenth century, have been integrated into the pseudo–Gothic palace which at present shelters the Bauer Grunwald Hotel (erected in 1901), as, for instance, a good part of the first floor which gives on rio di S. Moisè, though with corrections and adaptations (the masonry is ancient). The five–light window on the Grand Canal is certainly ancient, of the second half of the fifteenth century, but it too contains corrections and adaptations.

Among the works which, in spite of certain signs of archaism, may be considered of even later period, may be listed a five–light window in campo S. Silvestro (S. Polo 1125), the remains of a Palazzo Bernardo (?). It is remarkable because it reproduces, at the base of the internal balustrade, a motif of the Doge's Palace loggia where the 'stylobate' continues, in the moulding, the bases of the pilasters. The colonnettes support, however, a horizontal architrave[212]. The small and charming house on fondamenta S. Alvise (Cann. 3233) with a door and five windows (fifth and sixth orders)[213] and the other small house, with two simple lines of windows, in fondamenta de le Grue (S. Croce 2009) are two examples of 'minor' architecture exemplarily brought up to the level of the 'major' one.

Finally, two examples which might be brought forward in time: the first is Palazzo Maffetti at the Giudecca (fond. S. Biagio 786), a construction with the regular and bold cut of the buildings of the late fifteenth century, but whose details could all derive from the second half of the fourteenth (from the cut of the corbels to the absence of string courses, from the type of the capitals to the timid profiling of the trefoiled arches[214]). The second building is the large house which rises in campo de la Pescaria (S. Polo 327–30) on four floors, also on the pattern of fifteenth–century palaces (two coats of arms of the middle of the fifteenth century are walled in the façade): the geometrical distribution of the openings is now stereotyped, but there are archaic elements which do not exclude some hint of the floriated Gothic (but this is not a reason for considering buildings of this kind anterior to, say, about 1430)[215].

The Palazzo Vendramin at the Giudecca (fond. S. Zuane 13) has some archaic characters (only two flower finials surmount the two windows which, at a considerable distance, flank the slim four–light window, following a distributive–proportional conception which we have seen applied in fourteenth–century buildings) but one cannot help hesitating about its placing in time (rather late than early)[216].

*The exterior staircases, the portals, the battlements and the well-curbs, from the thirteenth to the early fifteenth centuries*

External staircases distinguished the dwellings of the wealthier classes from the fourteenth, perhaps even the thirteenth century onwards[217]. The problems involved in their dating are similar to those which make so difficult the chronological and stylistic ordering of the buildings, namely the conservative spirit of this architecture which makes great caution necessary. We shall only mention a few typical examples such as the remains of a staircase in corte Morosina (Cann. 5827) which point to a still Romanesque type, very simple with roll mouldings and arch of brick voussoirs (*bardellone*), one could even consider it of the thirteenth century[218], and the one, restored and disfigured, of Palazzo Lion in corte del Remer (perhaps of the early fourteenth century)[219].

The beautiful staircase of Palazzo Priuli at S. Severo is certainly of the end of the fourteenth century. Its dating is derived more from the sculptures which adorn it than from architectural elements, such as the cylinder colonnettes which are found also in later works[220]. That of Palazzo Donà in campo S. Polo[221] and that of Palazzo Goldoni[222] may be considered near it in time. That of the house on fondamenta Gherardini at S. Barnaba[223] is perhaps also of the end of the fourteenth century or the beginning of the next. The staircase of Palazzo Magno–Bembo, one of the best known in Venice, is similar in some of its elements to that of Palazzo Priuli[224].

The presence of elements belonging to the floriated Gothic such as, for instance, the leaves adorning the faces of the steps, would seem to associate the staircase of Ca' d'Oro and that of Palazzo Contarini Porta di Ferro at S. Giustina. However, restorations make difficult a judgment on the Ca' d'Oro staircase. It is not to be excluded that, at the last restoration, it should have been made to resemble that of Palazzo Contarini. This last, however, certainly belongs to the first half of the fifteenth century (although Ruskin attributed it to the fourteenth century)[225].

Whoever now considers the steep archaic staircase of Palazzo Priuli, where every detail recalls the fourteenth century, cannot fail to notice in Palazzo Contarini the presence of the floriated Gothic of the first half of the fifteenth century, together with motifs (in the small arches) recalling the beautiful balcony of Palazzo Bragadin Carabba which is certainly of the middle of the fifteenth century. To that time, and to the decades immediately following, must be attributed some of the most magnificent examples of those staircases which assume an ample and decidedly monumental rhythm—as for instance that of Palazzo Bernardo on the Grand Canal (of the middle of the century)[226], that of Palazzo Morosini at S. Giovanni Laterano, where the two types of banisters alternate (those with small arches for the level stretches, those with cylindrical shafts for the flights of stairs to be attributed to about 1450–60)[227]; or the two which, in two contiguous courtyards, serve two *piani nobili* at different levels of Palazzo Soranzo–van Axel, with colonnettes with trefoiled arches built some thirty years later.

Among the creations of Venetian secular Gothic born at the same time as the architecture of the buildings but which, as types, detach themselves from it and assume their own characteristics due, essentially, to their location which is not subordinated to the rhythm of those structures are the portals, the battlements (and roof parapets) and the well–curbs.

The water portal is often modest, as it gives access to the ground floor entrance hall *(portego)*. The access to the *piano nobile* which was the living area, was by means of an external staircase which started from the *corte* (courtyard). The well–curb was free of any architectural subjection, and although its structure was, substantially, inspired by that of a capital, it underwent nevertheless a fairly independent development. It became a valuable element in the context of the *corte*, an environment treated, each case on its own, with incomparable picturesque freedom, unencumbered by more or less obligatory rhythms. The well–curb, whether simple or elaborate, was the subject of particular attention and often became a real masterpiece of architectural sculpture. But equally the portals giving access to the courtyard, not tied to the building itself, often opened in the walls which surrounded the courtyard, and were treated independently. In time, they assumed their own characteristics, for which reason they will be treated separately with regard to their succession in time.

Nor can one ignore their Romanesque precursors if one wishes to ascertain the first appearance of Gothic elements. And also here (and more than in connection with thirteenth–century palaces) the qualification of Romanesque is clear and explicit. The first portals are, in fact, of the twelfth century and are entirely Padan Romanesque. Their ornaments point to examples of Lombard and Veronese sculpture between the eleventh and twelfth centuries[228].

Oldest of all is the one in the corte Seconda del Milion, of the first half of the twelfth century[229]. The one walled up in corte Bottera, in which one sees also a second archivolt moulding and a dentilled cornice, is perhaps of a later date[230]. The beautiful water–gate at the ponte di S. Tomà is visibly related to the two above-mentioned portals but, at the same time, diverges from them. The knotting of the twining scroll *(girale)* in the moulding does not produce *rotae* (contiguous roundels) but a freer, flowing disposition of the decoration, which is already flatter and more colourful between two large torus profiles surrounded by an ornament of palm leaves and dentils[231].

The Byzantine infiltration attested by some of these elements, and the hesitant hint of a pillar in the course of the arch, might suggest here an even later dating, since, after the fall of Constantinople, the arch on pillars spreads in Venice (where, in any case, it had precedents in church architecture). These elements would be of the first half of the thirteenth century as the great resemblance with the ground floor arcades of Ca' Da Mosto also suggests. The animals (like griffins), no longer isolated inside roundels, move here freely through the foliage.

*Well-curb in Campiello Ca' Zen.*

At this point, a series of similar arches sculptured in bas-relief increasingly confirm the presence in Venice of a stonemason's workshop of clearly Romanesque inspiration. The Romanesque door at ponte di S. Tomà is part of the Palazzo Bosco complex. It predates, however, the windows with simple inflected arch of the first floor, confirmation of which is provided by the Romanesque ornament through which they clearly cut and which is obviously related to the water–gate. We are at the end of the twelfth or the beginning of the thirteenth century.

The arch nearest to the Palazzo Bosco door is without doubt the one above the door (external, on the first floor) of Palazzo Lion in corte del Remer. We find there again many of the elements of the door at ponte di S. Tomà, with the sole difference of the archivolt moulding which, in Palazzo Lion, is an imitation of a classical acanthus scroll. But it is certain that the two round–headed upper sections are the work of the same team. The ascription of this series of arches to the thirteenth century is confirmed at Palazzo Lion by the fact that it is an organic part of a complex born at the same time, connected through moulded fascias to windows on both sides showing doubled and inflected arches which one cannot avoid dating to the mid–thirteenth century. Another of these arches, with a looser interlacing of the scroll, has been used in the building of the Servi church about 1333[232], the surviving door of which it still decorates.

Yet a further very similar one is incorporated in a work which can be dated with certainty to the thirteenth century and is coeval with the one just mentioned. It is an integral part of the remains in the garden of Palazzo Da Mula in Murano. A decoration similar to that of Palazzo Da Mula can be seen on the moulded archivolt of the Grand Canal portal of Palazzo Barzizza (where the underside of the arch is also richly decorated). As in Palazzo Bosso, the archivolt moulding is contained between two robust *tori*. The fact that the profile of the two impost stones is identical to the one visible on the upper floor of the palace, which all critics agree to assign to the thirteenth century, is proof that this is a thirteenth–century work (the two re–used columns should not deceive us). Another example, also akin to the Palazzo Bosso portal, is offered by the modified arches of the portico of the already mentioned Ca' Da Mosto. The magnificent arch on pillars of Palazzo Contarini Porta di Ferro at S. Giustina is also related to the Palazzo Bosso type.

It is not to be excluded that arches on pillars existed in the secular architecture of Venice also in the twelfth century, even if we do not have examples, since all the Romano–Byzantine buildings erected in Venice are attributed to the thirteenth century.

Also in the case of the Palazzo Contarini arch, given the clearly Romanesque character of the elegant scroll in which lurk, in a remarkably plastic relief, the usual animals with almond eyes recalling twelfth-century sculpture, an attribution to the first half of the thirteenth century is possible[233].

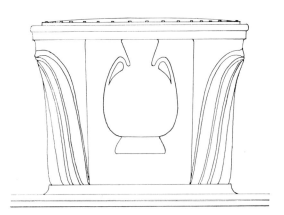

There are also some cases of the use of elements of these portals in the fourteenth century, in which, however, the integrity of the more ancient work is not respected as it is in the Servi portal. The first instance concerns the portal of Palazzo Cappello Malipiero at S. Samuele, mentioned by Cattaneo, who noted that the parts making up the archivolt moulding displayed sudden interruptions. This undoubtedly attests to the forced adaptation of an older work to a fourteenth–century portal. Where we do not agree with Cattaneo, however, is in the dating (around 1000!) of these reliefs, which have a mature Romanesque character and undoubted correspondences with arches which are integral with architecture decidedly later than the beginning of the eleventh century (such as the remains of the small Palazzo Foscolo at S. Pantalon, and those in the courtyard of Palazzo Da Mula in Murano and Palazzo Lion). But there is more. The vertex of the moulded archivolt of the arch in Palazzo Cappello Malipiero is of one piece and provides undoubted evidence that the older arch was not round–headed but with two centres, Gothic, and therefore not earlier than the thirteenth century[234].

The second example is provided by the fourteenth–century side door of Palazzo Agnusdio, where pieces of an ancient Romanesque archivolt moulding are re-used (of the thirteenth century, according to Lorenzetti). All these examples reconfirm the dating already sugges-ted by others (and here re-offered) to the twelfth century in the case of the more ancient examples, and to the thirteenth century of the others subsequently mentioned.

The simple pointed uninflected arch of western origin had obviously already arrived in Venice in the thirteenth century, and must certainly have appeared in portals of that century even if, as a rule, the use of this type of arch is rare in the secular architecture of the Lagoon. And we do not find in Venice, except for those rare ones on pillars, portals which reflect the successive transformations of the Byzantine–type arch, with the simple or repeated Islamic cusp on the vertex. There is, instead, between the thirteenth and the fourteenth centuries, a direct passage to the western type with pointed arch, or to the rectangular portal, and these are two types for which it is difficult to find reliable evidence in the thirteenth century.

For the first type we can refer to the portal on the bridge of Casa Bosso (not to be confused with the one on the canal) which is certainly among the oldest—if we do not separate the actual true portal (with strong mouldings of late Romanesque character) from the lunette above it, which is fourteenth–century and in Padan style (the emblem must be of an even later period)[235]. Another example, commonly attributed to the thirteenth century, is the portal of Palazzo Donà in campo S. Polo (S. Polo 2177) with a curious decoration of dogs chasing hares and antelopes (not of high quality and with deep Gothic mouldings). These are perhaps already of the fourteenth century[236].

We are, however, inclined to place in the late thirteenth century a singular type of portal, the surviving examples of which give ingress to courtyards or straddle the entrance to streets, namely those in which the lunette is surmounted by a high, triangular tympanum. Again, it is singular how they stand alone, unconnected to façades. They represent a fascinating interpretation of the tympanum, of the Gothic gable flanked by pinnacles (*wimperg*), created in France in the middle of the thirteenth century.

Typical of these doors is the refined treatment of the terracotta, making the vast surfaces vibrate, subtly wrinkled by decorations recalling late Padan Romanesque. Thus a door like that of Casa Magno at S. Luca (S. Marco 4038) is transformed by the tall tympanum, inside and outside; the small Islamic cusp on the extrados of the archivolt is quite typical of the thirteenth century[237]. Of a somewhat later period, and more modest, is the similar portal on ramo rimpetto Mocenigo (S. Croce 2054)[238]. A similar structure surmounts the entrance to corte di Ca' Pisani (S. Croce 1177) and is, perhaps, already of the fourteenth century, uti-lizing older elements (the two lions under the architrave)[239]. A beautiful example of a lunette in terracotta is found in calle dei Proverbi at SS. Apostoli (Cann. 4564), obviously recalling Veronese work[240].

The rectangular doorways seem to be typical of the fourteenth century and naturally those with uninflected pointed arch continue to appear. A typical rectangular portal is that of the S. Gregorio Abbey on the Grand Canal, of around 1340, which is of elegant proportions

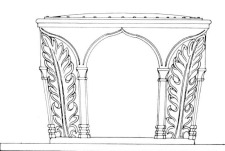

with remarkably great use of the *twisted stick*[241], i.e. spiral (cable) forms. On this basis it may be that the doorway formerly in S. Nicolò della Lattuga, founded in 1332, and now the entrance to the Frari cloisters (S. Polo 3003) should be considered of the fourteenth century. Note should be taken, however, that from now on the Venetian doorway follows the same or a similar fashion in palaces and in churches[242].

Following this trail, it is possible to find other rectangular doorways attributable to the fourteenth century. The oldest of all, which are the two of the older of the two Palazzi Soranzo in campo S. Polo, contain two bas–reliefs with a female bust between two wild beasts (of the fourteenth century). The more current types are those marked at most by a simple torus profile already seen in houses attributed to the fourteenth century[243] and, in addition, that of Palazzo Querini in calle dell'Arco (Castello 3520) with the external dentil profile and surmounted by a fourteenth–century shield[244]; the one in calle della Chiesa (S. Polo 2343) with cable ornament of simple elegance[245] is not unlike another one in calle del Padiglione (Cann. 4712)[246]; that in calle dei Forni (Castello 2187) with dentil border and internal torus profile[247]; that on fondamenta S. Zuane at the Giudecca (nos. 23-25)[248]. (The type then continues into the fifteenth century, as in Palazzo Zaguri on fondamenta Corner.)

The portal in calle del Cafetier at S. Zanipolo[249] is of uncertain dating. Nor should the ever rarer appearance of the round–headed lunette of Romanesque origin be ignored–a magnificent and unique example being that of Casa Corner at S. Margherita (already considered) with the emblem in the centre (the figures are typically fourteenth-century), chequered background of transalpine miniature inspiration, and highly decorative archivolt moulding.

In the fourteenth century the upper structures show an alternation between uninflected and inflected pointed arches and (less frequently and later, contrary to what happened in other sectors of fourteenth–century architecture) trefoiled inflected arches.

This list of fourteenth–century portals is arranged by types, for ease of exposition, and not in rigorous chronological order. Among the first may be counted the one with the Zorzi coat of arms in ruga Giuffa, near Palazzo Zorzi Bon at Castello, where the light shatters itself on the dense mouldings with dentils, cable, and plain dog–teeth[250].

More refined, the portal of Palazzo Agnusdio makes use of an older Romanesque moulding for a simple pointed arch which encloses the shield with three angels. To the soft relief of the figures stand in contrast the Byzantine dentils of the archivolt and the framing which, on the geometric carvings, dryly reflects and divides the light.

That the great portals with inflected arch should go back as far as the early fourteenth century cannot cause surprise when one considers the splendid portal of Palazzo Tron (?) in calle Tiossi (S. Croce 2084), whose inflected archivolt moulding, surmounted by a large flower finial, encloses scrolls of vine in relief coming out of two vases–elegant transposition into a freer fourteenth–century version of a motif already seen in the Romanesque portals of the thirteenth century[251]. It may well be that this portal is of the same time as the beautiful four–light window on fondamenta Pesaro, already discused. The lunette is here also clearly distinguished from the jambs, which are defined by a torus profile and a large fascia.

This distinction between the two parts is characteristic of the most ancient portals of this type. In the Gothic portal of Palazzo Raspi (S. Polo 1557), the lunette with inflected arch is, at the base, of substantially lesser width than the rectangular portal[252]. The same clear separation between the upper and lower sections is visible in portals which already anticipate the fifteenth–century type, like that of Corte delle Muneghe with the coat of arms of the Amadi (perhaps around 1400)[253], that of Casa Grifalconi (believed to be of the fourteenth century), framed by a mighty Byzantine dentil ornament, that of calle Renier at S. Margherita (Dorsoduro 3434) with the typical fourteenth century angel on the shield[254], and others. Portals, aediculae, lunettes with hut–like slopes above the entrance to lanes, do not seem anterior to

the fourteenth century and therefore constitute an architectural episode typical of that century. Among the first manifestations of this kind is the aedicule with the Madonna (of later date) on the 'granary' of Chioggia, bearing the (transmitted) date of 1322.

In Venice itself, the most ancient example is perhaps that provided by the lunette above the entrance to corte Morosina, with the arch still on pillars and an ornament in relief of Muslim style of the beginning of the fourteenth century, a fairly rare echo of the intervention of the Islamic style in certain parts of St. Mark's[255]. To confirm the early appearance of the inflected arch is the entrance to the Carità cloisters, of around 1345, the recollection of which has been transmitted by Grevembroch[256]. The arrangement of the aedicule with the sacred image sheltered under the two sloping eaves and flanked by two spiral columns (which we have already seen on the door of S. Gregorio), repeated also by the portals, is confirmed by the relief with the Virgin, dated to 1345, at present above the entrance door of the former Scuola della Carità. It is clear, therefore, that the portals displaying this characteristic must be considered of the fourteenth century, as also the one in calle della Testa (Cann. 6218 and 6227) with inflected arch under the tympanum[257] (among the most typical in Venice), and the partially preserved one in calle della Furatola (S. Polo 1495)[258].

We are unable to give a reason, not just practical but aesthetically valid, for the fact that the fourteenth century (and also the fifteenth century) Venetian portal does not adopt the trefoiled inflected arch but instead constantly adheres to the simpler formula, while, from the beginning of the century, that arch is very common in windows.

Mention has been made of the ground–level Trevisan tomb of 1338 with the inflected trefoil. In the last quarter of the century, however, there are not a few tombs of this type in Venetian churches, as attested by Grevembroch's drawings (and the upper foil is almost always crushed, as in English perpendicular Gothic)[259].

As for the portals, however, the two examples presented here show the trefoil motif very particularly. One of them is the portal of the Misericordia Abbey, and the other that of via Garibaldi (Castello 1310). But in both these complex works, placed by students of Venetian sculpture in the second half of the fourteenth century, the motif does not integrate the portal in its architectural structure; it appears, instead, rather as an elegant decorative accessory.

Numerous (as witness Jacopo de Barbari's landscape) terracotta battlements crowned the walls surrounding the courtyards of the more conspicuous Venetian houses since the fourteenth century. Quite a few remain, and many have been reconstructed in modern times.

They reflect the various trends current in Venice in two centuries of Gothic. A western type, perhaps still of the fourteenth century, is represented—to quote one example only—by the battlements still visible in calle della Balote at S. Salvador[260], with trefoil openings surmounted by a quatrefoil; this may be one of the most ancient types. The same type, with a profile in Islamic style in terracotta, is found in salizzada S. Canciano (Cann. 5549-50 – Palazzo Contarini). A late type is represented by the battlements with recesses with *pecten*, of which a preeminent example is that in corte degli Amadi (or delle Muneghe) at Miracoli[261].

Like the portals, the well–curbs also follow their own *iter*, although now and then harkening back to the form of the capital. The scarcity of dated pieces is compensated by the large number of products of high quality, which we follow here up to the beginning of the fifteenth century. Among the oldest, in the thirteenth century, should be counted those in the shape of truncated cubes, like the capitals initially studied. The corners are marked by a deep triangular hollow and on the lateral faces there is often carved, in relief, the clear symbol of the amphora.

Among the most beautiful is the carved one in the corte del Teatro Vecchio[262], another in Borgoloco S. Lorenzo and the better–known one in the Primiceri cloister at S. Apollonia. These are thirteenth–century works, and the trend continues into the fourteenth, characterized by two tall water leaves on the corners, while the amphora often alternates with a coat of arms[264]. Among the most ancient of this type is the one near the antiquary Minerbi.

Of a different character, the well–curb in corte del Remer reflects elements of thirteenth–century architecture, namely the octagonal colonnettes and the arches in Islamic style around the inside approximately indicate the middle of the century. A hexagonal one, formerly by the antiquary Carrer at S. Stae, sold some time ago, also had small arches with Islamic cusps[265].

To 1344 was dated a well–curb known from a reproduction by Grevembroch. There the eight sides in which the external area was divided were organized in simple inflected arches[266].

Quite exceptional, because containing figures and dating to 1325–50[267], is the remarkable well–curb of the Budapest Museum, with young men and women holding hands carved in relief round the almost circular well-mouth, alternating with shields (chiselled away) and rosettes on a smooth background, with French and Italian stylistic elements. It originated in a Grand Canal palace.

Yet another very widespread type is characterized by a cylindrical trunk on top of which is a square element with projecting arcading and truncated corners (certainly fourteenth century). We find it in corte di Palazzo Magno Bembo, in corte delle Muneghe (Amadi), in calle larga S. Rocco, in corte del Tintor at S. Bartolomeo, in the Glass Museum of Murano and in campo S. Stefano; and there was once one, with an inscription, in S. Paterniano in Venice. But the most frequently represented type is perhaps the one which imitates the rosette capital, with square abacus, where the water leaves end in a volute folding under the cornice. Of this type[268] is the well–curb in campo dell'Angelo Raffaele, on top of the well built by Marco Ariani and dated 1342, so that it is a valid reference point; although not of particularly high quality, it signals the establishment of the typical capital 'with rosettes' which predominates in the fourteenth century[269]. Another date confirming the spreading of this type at that time is that of 1331 affixed to a well–curb at S. Fiorenzo del Pasenatico in Istria[270]. Closely connected with the previous one is a type derived from the octagonal capital used in religious buildings and in the Doge's Palace, with eight (or six) sides, achieving effects of exquisite elegance derived from the greater concentration of the surfaces, the nimbler rising of the dividing vegetable elements, and in which appears as a decorative element, alternating with the armorial shields, the helmets and the amphora, the great rosette which will predominate in the fifteenth century. Perhaps these octagonal well-curbs are better placed in the second half of the fourteenth century, also because of their clear kinship with the more ancient capitals of the portico on the southern façade of the Doge's Palace, a kinship which is particularly striking (human heads alternating with large corner foliage) in one of the well–curbs at present at Fondaco dei Turchi.

The most remarkable are one in the Glass Museum of Murano (hexagonal, with human heads), one in corte delle Strope at S. Giacomo dall'Orio, one in Palazzo Soranzo at ponte dell'Angelo[271] (now in the Jacquemart André Museum in Paris), as well as two other octagonal ones preserved in the same museum (the one with children's heads reproduces the capitals—of the simplest type—of the Doge's Palace portico by the quay), another, classically balanced, in corte Correggio at S. Cassiano[272], another, formerly in calle Cavallerizza and now at the Correr[273], yet another in a house on fondamenta S. Felice[274], a further one at Correr (formerly in the prison building) and, finally, plastically the most remarkable, the well–curb now in calle Larga 22 Marzo (formerly in Palazzo Pesaro at S. Beneto)[275].

Well–curbs richly ornamented with figures in high relief are found at the end of the fourteenth century. Perhaps the most important, still bound to the fourteenth–century complex with which it was created, is that of Palazzo Priuli at S. Severo[276]. Very dilapidated, but still legible in the sculptures (certainly allegories), executed by an artist who, in the Venice of the end of the century was a vivid personality, it stands alone. This well–curb is also remarkable because in the cornice (with abacus and cable ornament) and in the large corner leaves, it anticipates a type which will be very widespread until the middle of the fifteenth century. Another well-curb, with figures, formerly belonging to the Ongania family at S. Leonardo, may be considered of the early fifteenth century[277], as also the one at the Misericordia which records on the four sides the two brother-members who governed the pious association[278].

**1.** On the *Palatium ducis* anterior to the present one see: Lorenzetti, 1956, p. 230; Lorenzetti, 1933, p. 38; Ongaro, 1935, p. 9; according to Bassi (1962, I, p. 31 et seq.) the *Palatium Comunis Venetiarum* faced the Quay, while the *Palatium ad jus reddendum*, detached from the first-mentioned one, faced the present Piazzetta. There are sure traces of a corner tower towards rio di Palazzo (cf. Bassi-Trincanato, 1960, p. 10); a document of 1355 attests that Calendario, involved in the Marin Faliero plot, was hanged from the red columns towards the Piazzetta (Zanotto, 1853, I, p. 61) and a subsequent document of 1412 records that *ad columnas rubeas Palatij ad quas stat Serenissimus dominus Dux ad videndum festa super plateam* was hanged the traitor Francesco Bolduyno; these two items of evidence prove therefore that there must have been a loggia attached to this *palazzo 'della Ragione'* before it was replaced by the present wing of the Doge's Palace (Lorenzi, 1868, p. 54). Nothing remains that could give us even an approximate idea of the aspect of the Doge's Palace before the Gothic reconstruction. The miniature found in an Oxford codex is, in our modest opinion, too far from any reality, true or presumed, to afford us any elements useful for a reconstruction; my impression is that it is a record made from the memory, perhaps at some distance in time; and that it is not, therefore, very reliable (Bodleian Library no. 264; published by Parker in *National Miscellany*, London, November 1853; echoed in *Mitteilungen der K. K. Central-Commission etc.* Vienna, I, 1856, p. 183; Zanotto, 1853, I, pp. 193, 198, 199 and note 7 to the plates; *Bulletin Monumental* 3me série, Tome 2, Paris 1856, p. 66 et seq.; Kugler, 1859, II, p. 41, no. 1; Schnaase, 1876, V, pp. 225–36; reproduced by Pignatti, 1956, p. 7; Bassi, 1962, I, p. 34). Parker used this miniature in order to contest Ruskin's opinion, which we believe correct, that the Doge's Palace was created in one effort by a single artist; according to Parker, to the loggia and portico of the fourteenth century was added in the sixteenth (nothing less!) the great upper wall; a hypothesis which the documents and the subsequent researches have completely demolished. Schnaase also deduced a difference in time between the loggias and the upper construction, which

he puts at 1424, thus increasing the confusion. Zanotto and Kugler rightly note the inconsistencies in the Oxford miniature, which do not permit any secure critical deductions.

**2.** Lorenzi, 1868, pp. 26–7.

**3.** The document of the 28 December 1340 (published by Zanotto, 1853, I, pp. 46 and 48, no. 26, and more correctly by Paoletti, 1893, p. 9) ordains that the great hall *superrime construenda debeat construi super sala. Dominorum de nocte in hunc modum videlicet, quod fieri debeat tantum longam, quantum est ipsa sala Dominorum de nocte, et tanto pluris quanto distat camera Officialium de Cataveri ab ipsa sala Dominorum de nocte* (that much more, that is, that the Cattaveri room is distant from that same hall, which practically means, up to the corner of the Palace)... *et lata tantum, quantum est ambulum existens super colonis versus canale respicientibus* (and as wide as the ambulatory contained by the columns below, which face towards the canal). *Caeterum quamquam magistri praescripti asserant quod dicta sala erit fortis non ponendo collonas super sala Dominorum de nocte* (and though the said masters assert that the hall to be built would be strong enough without the need to erect columns in the hall of the Night Lords to support the one above), *consulunt quod pro majori firmitate dicte sale nove ponantur super praefata sala Dominorum de nocte ton colone quod necesarie videbuntur.*
This refers to columns still in existence in the sala del Piovego, undoubtedly of the middle of the fourteenth century. See also: Zanotto, 1853, I, p. 58 et seq. The Night Lords dealing with crime, and other important offices, occupied the rooms of the southern wing of the palace adjacent to the Foscari loggia, on the floor of the loggias (cf. Zanotto, 1858, III, p. 27). See also: Lorenzi, 1868, p. 27.

**4.** Zanotto, 1853, I, p. 59.

**5.** Paoletti, 1893, p. 9.

**6.** Thode, 1895, p. 87.

**7.** Lorenzi, 1868, p. 32.

**8.** Zanotto, 1853, I, pp. 54–5.

**9.** Lorenzi, 1868, p. 34.

**10.** Lorenzi, 1868, pp. 34, 35.

**11.** Zanotto, 1853, I, p. 72, note 25.

**12.** Lorenzi, 1868, p. 38.

**13.** Zanotto, 1853, I, p. 63.

**14.** Sanudo, *Vite dei Dogi*, col. 664; Sansovino, 1563, p. 123; Toesca, 1950, pp. 150, 151.

**15.** Lorenzi, 1868, pp. 38, 39.

**16.** Cf. Ruskin, 1886, II, p. 286.

**17.** Ruskin, 1886, II, p. 295.

**18.** Zanotto, 1853, I, p. 50.

**19.** Paoletti, 1893, pp. 9, 10.

**20.** Zanotto, 1853, I, p. 79. See in this connection also: White, 1966, p. 79. p. 355 et seq. (with interesting observations).

**21.** Cicognara, 1838, I, pp. 56, 57.

**22.** Cicognara, 1838, I, pp. 57, 125 et seq.

**23.** Selvatico, 1847, pp. 109, 125 et seq.

**24.** Selvatico, 1847, p. 134; Idem, 1852, p. 48.

**25.** Zanotto, 1835, I, p. 66.

**26.** Selvatico, 1856, II, pp. 220, 221.

**27.** Ricci, 1858, p. 341.

**28.** Kugler, 1852, II, p. 575 et seq.

**29.** Dall'Acqua, 1864, p. 25 et seq.

**30.** Schnaase, 1876, p. 229 (who attributes, however, the façade on the Quay to Giovanni Bon).

**31.** Venturi, 1924, p. 283; even more singular is the statement by Lavagnino (1936, p. 527) who, following Venturi, says that the reconstruction of the palace began in 1422 and adds that Pier Paolo delle Masegne gives 'the tone to the whole building'; and of Serra (1949, p. 4) who strangely affirms that the loggia and the windows have been remodelled.

**32.** Bettini, 1953, p. 54.

**33.** Belvedere (1960) ascribes the exterior to 1424.

**34.** Ruskin, 1886, II, p. 282 et seq.

35. Paoletti, 1893, I, p. 10.

36. Della Rovere, 1880, p. 2.

37. Pauli, 1898, p. 36.

38. Molmenti, 1910, pp. VI, VIII.

39. Folnesics, 1914, p. 35 (to the end of the fourteenth century).

40. Ongaro, 1937, pp. 7 and 9 (erring only in believing that the southern façade was begun in 1309).

41. Lorenzetti, 1956, p. 231 et seq.

42. Toesca, 1950, p. 154.

43. Pignatti, 1964, pp. 7, 8 (sees a unitary project, not a restoration of older structures, 'creation of a single artist'). See also Hubala, (1966, pp. 632, 633: the southern wing ascribed to 1340–1400).

44. Toesca, 1950, p. 154. And for this hypothesis also Mariacher, (1950–1, p. 241).

45. Toesca, 1950, p. 152.

46. Lorenzi, 1868, p. 32, doc. 89.

47. Cattaneo (1881, p. 205) quotes from the Contarini chronicle (Marciana, 61, VII, Cod. 95): 'ancora in lo dito mileximo fo schomenzado i capiteli che xe sora la jexia de San Marco la ò che sona le ore per mezo la jexia de San Basso en 1385, e un altro capitolo suxo l'altro canton' (also in the same year, 1385, were begun the aediculae which are on the church of St. Mark's where the hours are rung towards the church of S. Basso, and another aedicule on the other corner. It is to be noted that in Venetian, even in present-day speech, the word capitello means aedicule; and, says Cattaneo, under the aedicule erected on the S. Alipio corner there is a bell with the date 1384. Another chronicle affirms that 'en 1415 fo fati i capitelli in la glesia de San Marco inver San Basso e fo fato le figure che è dentro... e scomenzado a meter le foie de piera atorno i archi' (in 1415 were made the aediculae in the church of St. Mark's towards S. Basso and were made the figures inside... and begun the placing of stone leaves around the arches) (Archivio Veneto, T. XVII, p. II, p. 325).

48. Cattaneo, 1877–87, p. 205.

49. In '1388 adì 13 Decembrio fo fatto quelo lavorier de intagio davanti el Corpo de Cristo in la jexia de San Marco dalo ladi del altar grando' (the 13 December 1388 was made that intaglio work in front of the Lord's body (the Tabernacle) in the church of St. Mark's, by the side of the main altar). Cattaneo identifies it with the tabernacle on the left (p. 205) of the Contarini chronicle. I think that the one on the right must be considered almost coeval.

50. Venturi, 1924, p. 294.

51. See Enlart, 1894, p. 72 et seq.; Bulletin Monumental, 1922, p. 202.

52. For this iconographic part, which is outside the limits of our work, the reader is referred to Zanotto's pages (1853, I, p. 209 et seq.) to the well-known ones of Ruskin and to Didron-Burges in Annales Archéologiques, Vol. XVII, Paris 1857, p. 68 et seq. and p. 192 et seq.; a brief description is in Lorenzetti, 1956, p. 235.

53. Venturi, 1908, p. 27 et seq.; 1924, VIII, 2, p. 288.

54. Toesca, 1950, p. 416 et seq. and note 161.

55. Pope-Hennessy, 1963, pp. 57, 58.

56. If, in respect of these sculptures, Toesca kept within a Venetian ambit of the end of the fourteenth century but avoided mentioning any name, and if Venturi had thought of an artist akin to Michelino da Besozzo, the other attributions put forward diverge considerably from those indications. It seems opportune to bear in mind in this connection that, even leaving aside the capitals connected to those sculptures and the other sculptures, which Toesca relates to those of the Doge's Palace, the understanding of this important unknown, on the critical plane, should be greatly facilitated by an obvious observation: that the Progenitors, Noah, the two archangels towards the quay and Venice are undoubtedly by the same hand.
Leaving aside, then, an old, untenable attribution of Noah to Marco Romano (Della Rovere, 1880, p. 2), we recall that Noah was attributed by Planiscig (1921, p. 11) to Bartolomeo Bon. Muraro (1953, p. 95) more prudently, thinks of a Venetian of the beginning of the fifteenth century. Mariacher (on several occasions) and Pignatti (1956, p. 24; 1964, p. 9) think for the two groups of 1410–20 and of Raverti (or his workshop). Pope-Hennessy has already been quoted. Pignatti (cit. p. 10) considers 'perhaps' by Antonio Bregno the three archangels (i. e. also Gabriel near the porta della Carta).

57. The Relief of Venice as Justice. One of the masterpieces of the Venetian sculpture at the end of the fourteenth century. For the exact reading of the inscription cf. Bettio, 1837, pp. 10, 11; who, rightly, puts a comma after Furias. There is a French reflexion in the seat formed of lion limbs. (See a miniature by Jean de Joinville in the Bibliothèque Nationale of Paris, an artist who died in 1317; see a coloured illustration in Le Muse, VI, p. 149, Novara 1966).

58. The Sages capital (second on the quay from the Piazzetta corner) bears on Pythagoras' open book the clear date of 1344. Paoletti who, I believe, was the first to discover it, (1893, I, p. 10) saw in it the proof that the portico capitals were of the fifth decade of the century (but, mistakenly, described this capital as the second from rio di Palazzo). If the date is very clear, good reasons are lacking for taking this capital out of a series which the most qualified scholars accept as of the end of the fourteenth century; when they did not think, as we saw, of a later time. Paoletti, therefore, given the coherence between this sculpture and others marked by the same stylistic tendency, placed them all in the middle of the fourteenth century (see Paoletti, 1893, I, p. 16).
The coexistence of the Venetians and the Lombards is generally accepted in these sculptures, as is their dating to the end of the century. See: Lorenzetti, 1956, p. 235; Mariacher, 1950–1, pp. 239, 242 (Michelino is also mentioned, besides the Venetians); Bassi-Trincanato, 1960, p. 13; Arte Veneta, 1962, p. 34 (where Raverti is again, unduly, mentioned); Pignatti, 1964, p. 8. We are inclined to exclude the name of Raverti (whose documented Venetian activity is of a later period) from all these sculptures of the Doge's Palace.

59. Lately Wolters (1965, p. 113) has taken up again as valid the date of 1344 on the well-known capital and, increasing the confusion, places in 1340–65 the great statuary groups.

60. The capital in situ is a copy of the ancient one, at present in the Palace Museum.

61. In the vast literature on the subject see: M. Aubert, La sculpture française sous le règne de Saint Louis, Paris 1929, II, Plates 41, 45, 48, Clemen-Meyer, Gotische Kathedralen in Frankreich, Freiburg i. B., 1951, Plate 155; etc.
See also for kinship with the capitals in question: Bond, 1913, II, p. 507 (capital at Woodstock). Mariacher (1939, pp. 31, 32; 1950–1, p. 239) and Pignatti (1964, p. 9) attribute these capitals to Raverti's workshop.
The sixth capital from the corner under the Progenitors towards the Piazzetta was remade by Bart. Manopola (Temanza, Vite, 1778, p. 504; Zanotto, 1853, I, p. 146).

62. See it reproduced in: D. Schlumberger, Les fouilles de Qasr el-Heir el-Gharbi, in Syria, XX, 1939, p. 195 et seq., Plate XXVII; and in: Studies in Islamic Art etc. in honour of K. A. C. Creswell (K. Brish, Zum Bab - Wuzara der Hauptmoschee von Cordova, p. 44).

63. Ruskin, 1886, II, p. 234.

64. Sartori, 1956, p. 9; Bassi, 1965, p. 198 (of about 1420).

65. For the dating see: Thode, 1895, p. 85.

66. Ponte della Paglia. Remember Lorenzi's (1868, p. 37) document: 3 May 1360. Ordinatum est de refficiendo pontem que est apud Palacium nostrum. Zanotto (1856, 162) says that it was 'widened and restored' in 1847; the Elenco (1905, p. 7, no. 80), I do not know on what grounds, remade in 1854; the old parts are, more than is thought, still quite recognizable today.
Cf. also: Fulin-Molmenti, 1881, p. 153 ('it is said to be the first built in Venice'; which we consider not improbable); Paoletti, 1893, I, p. 6, note 2; Douglas, 1925, p. 24; Lorenzetti, 1956, p. 283.

67. Balustrades. Their forms derive, with great delay, from the French and English Gothic, in which, as in the Doge's Palace, they very frequently have small trefoiled arches (see those of Clermond-Ferrand Cathedral; cf. Bandot-Perraul-Dabot, Les Cathédrales de France, I, Paris n. d.).
In Venice, the dwarf balustrades between the columns of multi-light windows are not uncommon. The most beautiful example is perhaps offered by Palazzo Pesaro Orfei. Even more ancient, those of Palazzo Gritti at S. Giovanni in Bragora, perhaps of the fourteenth century. Then those, perhaps remade, of Palazzo Bernardo on the Grand Canal, of Palazzo Dandolo-Danieli, of Palazzo Gritti at S. Angelo, of Palazzo Molin at the Zattere, of Palazzo Molin in Frezzeria, of Palazzo Priuli at S. Severo; and others.

68. Cadorin, 1838, p. 104.

69. In the Tagebücher. Cf. B. Tecchi, Goethe in Italia, Vicenza 1967, p. 18.

70. Cicognara, 1838, p. 53.

71. Cicognara, 1838, p. 60.

72. Cicognara, 1838, pp. 55 and 68; Ruskin too (1886, II, p. 241 et seq.) has some useful considerations on the Islamic character of these battlements (parapets); and also Burckhardt (1925, p. 149) and Kugler (1858–9, III, p. 77).

73. Selvatico, 1847, p. 126.

74. Ruskin, 1886, II, pp. 233, 234.

75. Ruskin, 1886, II, pp. 304–6.

76. Burckhardt, 1925, pp. 148, 149.

77. Selvatico, 1856, p. 224.

78. Kugler, 1858, II, p. 576.

79. Schnaase, 1876, p. 226 et seq.

80. Hare, 1884, p. 33.

81. Pauli, 1898, p. 36.

82. Venturi, 1924, p. 288 et seq.

83. Toesca, 1950, p. 155; for a similar interpretation see: Bettini, 1953, p. 55.

84. A general restoration of the two façades was carried out (with some arbitrariness) between 1873 and 1889. See: Trimarchi, 1889, p. 428 et seq.

85. Paoletti, 1893, I, p. 10, note 1.

86. Lorenzi, 1868, p. 37, doc. 102.

87. Baseggio is thought to have died in 1354. See on Baseggio: Cadorin, 1837, p. 127; Zanotto, 1853, I, p. 47, note 9 and p. 56, note 11; Lazzarini, 1894; Thieme-Becker, II, 1908, p. 595 (with bibl.); Lorenzetti, 1956, pp. 230–1.

88. Sansovino, 1563, p. 123.

89. Cadorin, 1837, pp. 6, 9.

90. Sabellico, dec. III, libr. III, p. 321.

91. Egnazio, VIII, p. 275.

92. Zanotto (1853, I, p. 51) denied that this passage referred to the Doge's Palace.

93. See the evidence quoted in: Zanotto, 1853, I, pp. 45, 56, note 12.

94. Zanotto, 1853, I, pp. 51, 56, note 12.

95. Cadorin, 1837, p. 159; Zanotto, 1853, I, p. 68, note 9.

96. Cadorin, 1837, p. 127; Zanotto, I, 1853, p. 47, note 9.

97. Bettio, 1837, pp. 9, 12.

98. E. Paoletti, 1837–40, II, p. 52.

99. Cicognara, 1838, I, p. 56.

100. Selvatico, 1847, p. 106 et seq.

101. Burckhardt, 1925, p. 148.

102. Lübke, 1858, I, p. 499.

103. Ricci, 1858, II, pp. 333, 334. Ricci also, on the evidence of Barbo, attributes the tower to Calendario.

104. Kugler, 1858–9, II, p. 575.

105. Zanotto, 1853, I, pp. 60, 61.

106. Lorenzi, 1868, p. 37, doc. 102.

107. Cecchetti, 1887, p. 64.

108. Cecchetti, 1884, pp. 294, 295.

109. Lazzarini, 1894; for further information see: Paoletti, in Thieme-Becker, V, 1911, p. 388.

110. Zanotto, 1853, p. 51; 1856, p. 120 (the façade would be by Pietro Baseggio and then, after 1309 (!) by Calendario).

111. Ruskin, 1886, III, p. 212 (considers him chiefly responsible).

112. Fulin-Molmenti, 1881, p. 113.

113. Paoletti, 1893, I, p. 10, note 1.

114. *The large central window on the quay.* Lorenzi, 1868, p. 48, Paoletti, 1893, I, p. 1.

115. Lorenzi, 1868, p. 49.

116. Paoletti, 1893, I, p. 3.

117. Paoletti, 1893, I, p. 2.

118. Paoletti, 1893, I, p. 2.

119. See: C. Gnudi in *Critica d'Arte*, February 1937, p. 35.

120. Paoletti, 1893, I, p. 2.

121. *Large central window on the quay.* In addition to the authors quoted cf. also: Cicognara, 1838, p. 60 (one sees, in accordance with current opinions on the late date of this façade, the style of Bartolomeo Bon); Zanotto, I, 1853, p. 202; Ruskin, 1886, II, p. 296; Selvatico, 1847, pp. 122–3 (he is the first to see, shrewdly, the intervention of the Dalle Masegne); Paoletti, 1893, I, p. 2 (the figure of Faith reminds him of Nicolò Lamberti); Venturi, 1908, VI, p. 19 (faithful to his opinion on the late date of the façade on the quay, he places the balcony—contrary to the documents already known—in 1420–30); Lorenzetti, 1956, p. 235; Toesca, 1950, p. 151; Bassi-Trincanato, 1960, pp. 17, 18; (saying that the original profile of the window was perhaps changed in 1579 by Vittoria); Bassi, 1962, II, p. 43; Pignatti, 1964, p. 7.

122. We are doubtful about Paoletti's assertion that the *pergoli* (balconies), at first strictly limited by regulations, became, after the balcony of 1404, increasingly numerous in Venice (Paoletti, p. 93). All one can say with certainty of these balconies is that those with colonnettes or small pilasters with architrave take us away from the fourteenth century; and, moreover, that those with carved cherubim in Tuscan style are certainly later than about 1460 (typical the beautiful balcony, certainly ancient, of Palazzo Bragadin-Carabba). The balconies of Palazzo Foscari on the Grand Canal, unless we err, are later than 1452. And those on Fondamenta del Dose, of Palazzo Barbaro at S. Vidal, of Palazzo Duodo Balbi Valier, of Palazzo Gherardi, of Palazzo Giovanelli on the Grand Canal, of Palazzo Mastelli, of Palazzo Pisani Revedin may be considered ancient. And there are others, naturally, which may be missed by an insufficiently minute enquiry.
Ruskin dealt with this subject (1886, II, p. 244 et seq.; according to whom not one of these balconies remains in Venice that is earlier than the fourteenth century); see also: Viollet-le-Duc, II, p. 67 et seq.; Wiener, 1929, Plates 120, 121; Trincanato, 1948, p. 86.
The fourteenth-century loggias of fra Giovanni degli Eremitani in the *Salone* of Padova have colonnettes with architraves.

123. *House in calle Cicogna.* Elenco, 1905, p. 60, no. 537.

124. *Palazzo Viaro-Zane.* Zanotto, 1856, p. 384; Elenco, 1905, p. 140, no. 197 (to the thirteenth century); Tassini, 1879, p. 290; Lorenzetti, 1956, p. 467; Muratori, 1960, p. 81; Maretto, 1960, pp. 9 and 41; Hubala, 1966, p. 904 (to the fourteenth century) - Maretto gives the plan with the two courtyards and assumes a two-families house. The five-light window, if the façade had some unity, appears displaced to the right. In the courtyard towards the campo there is a fourteenth-century external staircase (balustrade remade?). The façade on rio della Pergola has a five-light window with Ionic capitals, substituted when part of the house was remodelled in the sixteenth century.

125. *House of the Morosini.* Tassini, 1863, 1915 ed., p. 486; Idem, 1879, p. 262. The capitals are quasi Bramantesque; the impost stones have classical-looking dentils.

126. These low windows with segmental arches (which are found also atop the rectangular portals) are common in the mezzanines of the Venetian palaces. I do not quite know when they began. Those of the Hospice of S. Giovanni Evangelista, begun in 1414 (Paoletti, 1893, I, p. 31) must be of that time and perhaps even earlier.

127. *Corte Morosina.* Elenco, 1905, p. 100, no. 590 (to the fifteenth century); Lorenzetti, 1956, p. 392 (to the fourteenth century). Worthy of note an external staircase, partly remade (no. 5827), of Romanesque type, with arches of brick voussoirs (Bardelloni).

128. *The so-called House of the Polo.* Elenco, 1905, p. 100, no. 596; Lorenzetti, 1956, p. 355 (to the fourteenth century); Toesca, 1950, p. 150 (to the fourteenth century). A useful set of plans of the so-called house of the Polo may be seen in: Muratori, 1960, pp. 50, 51.

129. *Palazzo Magno-Bembo.* In calle Magno 2893, Castello. Selvatico, 1852, pp. 134, 135 (to the fourteenth century); Ruskin, 1886, III, p. 279 (to about 1330); Zanotto, 1856, p. 234 (of the fourteenth approx.); Tassini, 1879, p. 240; Fulin, 1881, p. 240 (the staircase to the fourteenth century); Elenco, 1905, p. 40, no. 174 and p. 184; Lorenzetti, 1956, p. 368 (to the fifteenth century); Trincanato, 1948, p. 104; Maretto, 1960, pp. 9, 41 (to the second half of the fourteenth century because of the plan in double L already encountered in the Viaro-Zane house, 'one of the most singular and accomplished creations of the Venetian Gothic'); Muratori, 1960, pp. 108, 109 (to the fourteenth century).

130. *House in fondamenta Gherardini.* The lower four-light window, with colonnettes and dwarf pilasters, is certainly of the fourteenth century. The single windows are in line with one of the third order; the balcony with small trefoiled arches and small fourteenth-century capitals recalls the already mentioned balustrade of the Doge's Palace and that of the ponte della Paglia of 1361. To see into it more clearly, a good survey of the whole complex would help. See: Elenco, 1905, p. 164, nos. 292 and 293 (mentions a coat of arms of the fifteenth century).

131. *Calle Botteri.* Elenco, 1905, p. 115, no. 128. Calle dei Botteri, 1552, with shop on the ground floor, two-light window, with a larger window next to it, on the first floor and another two-light window on the second may, because of the similar characteristics, be considered of the same time (Elenco, 1905, p. 115, no. 120) as the preceding one.

132. *House in calle Mercanti.* Elenco, 1905, p. 138, no. 170.

133. *Palazzo Sansoni.* Elenco, 1905, p. 111, no. 6 (to the fourteenth century); Lorenzetti, 1956, pp. 464–5 (to the fourteenth century).

134. *Piscina San Zulian, 550.* Elenco, 1905, p. 5, no. 36; Toesca, 1950, p. 150. Interesting the door

with segmental arch, flanked by two windows also with segmental arches: an element which, as we saw, now appears quite frequently.

**135.** *Ospizio Zuane Contarini.* The date is obtained from Vucetich (1896, p. 12). See also: Elenco, 1905, p. 161, no. 231; Trincanato, 1948, p. 278 (to the fourteenth century).

**136.** *Palazzo Quartieri.* On rio della Guerra. Elenco, 1905, p. 4, no. 20; notices the Anzeleri coat of arms on the entrance door, refrains from assigning a date.

**137.** Elenco, 1905, p. 72, no. 99; Fondamenta Cannaregio 1291.

**138.** Elenco, 1905, p. 110, no. 58.

**139.** *The Amadi houses at S. Giobbe.* Elenco, 1905, p. 70, no. 68 (to the sixteenth century); Lorenzetti, 1956, p. 441 (beginning of the fifteenth century).

**140.** *Casa Venier in Lizza Fusina.* Vucetich, 1896, p. 10; Elenco, p. 160, no. 212 (notices the sixteenth-century coat of arms and well-curb). Dorsoduro, fondamenta Lizza Fusina, 1845.

**141.** *House in calle Racchetta.* Elenco, 1905, p. 85, no. 336.

**142.** Always of the fourth order, the following could, with many reservations, be included in the fourteenth century: the beautiful four-light window in calle de Ca' Businello (S. Polo 1209) which the Elenco, 1905, p. 112, no. 84 assigns to the fifteenth century; the other four-light window, with rosette capitals, in calle dei Corli at Frari (S. Polo 2977–8) which the Elenco, 1905, p. 124, no. 260, assigns to the fifteenth century; the windows scattered in calle Drio la Sagrestia (Castello 4499–500) together with others, more archaic, of type 3; the graceful façade of a small house in rielo all'Angelo Raffaele (Dorsoduro 1871) (two-light window with column on high plinth and archaic shapes with simple torus archivolt, Elenco, 1905, p. 160, no. 214): surely fourteenth-century; the disorderly façade of palazzo Da Lezze, in Lista di Spagna (Cann. 134a) in spite of undoubted restorations still legible (see the 'uncoupled' three-light window), but given to the fifteenth century also by the Elenco (1905, p. 68, no. 26) and by Lorenzetti (1956, p. 449); the little that remains of the canal façade of palazzo Soranzo at ponte dell'Angelo: two windows and the beautiful relief, surely fourteenth-century, of the angel in the aedicule with sloping roof; the fourteenth-century elements which appear to have been used in the house at Malcanton (Dorsoduro 3547) reconstructed after the 1916 bombardment (see: Elenco, 1905, p. 168, no. 357 which declares it 'modern'; and Torres, 1937, p. 16, with plan); and one may doubt that the large house at no. 3580 of campo S. Angelo (S. Marco), or at least the openings of the first and second floor, belong to the fourteenth century; the axis is displaced to the left and the vertical alignments are not entirely regular; the portal is fifteenth-century (Elenco, 1905, p. 12, no. 175); the seven single windows in ramo Cappello 3113 at S. Margherita, on the top floor, with flat profiles. Doubtful chronologically, Palazzo Pisani (S. Polo 2709) with four-light window, three-light windows and two single windows in rio Terrà dei Nombali (Elenco, 1905, p. 122, no. 231). As for flat profiles surrounded by a single dentil ornament, they are not frequent and it is doubtful in some cases whether they

are fourteenth-century products or later, economical solutions: see the windows in calle dei Bombaseri (S. Marco 5101–2) or those of Borgoloco S. Lorenzo (Castello 5076) (Elenco, 1905, p. 53, no. 401).

**143.** *House in calle Botteri* 1565. Elenco, 1905, p. 115, no. 123; Lorenzetti, 1956, p. 464. The window in the middle of the first floor is of the fifth order. A façade of this house gives on rio delle Beccarie; it is the one with the five-light window of the second order (Romanesque-Byzantine) of which we have already spoken.

**144.** *Palazzo Badoer in calle Larga.* Elenco, 1905, p. 137, no. 148 (S. Croce 1662). Two single windows on the right remain, of the fourth order. The left wing was reconstructed in the sixteenth century, some archaic capitals remaining. The five-light window gives the impression of having been inserted by breaking into the wall.

**145.** *Palazzetto Costantini.* Elenco, 1905, p. 147, no. 10 (to the fifteenth century); Trincanato, 1948, p. 279 et seq. (the porch to the fourteenth century, with plans and useful information). The surviving windows are in sandstone, with flower finials.

**146.** *Palazzo Pisani Revedin.* Tassini, 1879, p. 259; Elenco, 1905, p. 20, no. 339. The axis is displaced to the right; four-light window in the centre; two axes of windows on the right and four on the left. On the ground floor windows with segmental arches.

**147.** *Palazzo Surian.* Tassini, 1879, p. 253 (erected in the fifteenth century by Giacomo Surian). Elenco, 1905, p. 4, no. 23 (to the fifteenth century). The rear gives on corte del Forno, where there are interesting remains of a warehouse (*fondaco*) (doors surmounted by openings with segmental arch; various windows of the fourth order; a three-light window; high opening with wooden architrave, corresponding to the canal door).

**148.** *Palazzo Zacco.* Calle dei Miracoli, Castello 6097; Tassini, 1879, p. 277; Lorenzetti, 1956, p. 327 (to the fifteenth century).

**149.** *House in calle Piacentini* 4395A. Elenco, 1905, p. 49, no. 324 (to the fifteenth century).

**150.** *House in campo Do Pozzi* 2611. Elenco, 1905, p. 40, no. 166; Lorenzetti, 1956, p. 368.

**151.** *The fourth order with rosette capital* is frequently found: fondamenta Briati (Dorsoduro 2531–3): two floors with two three-light windows in the middle (Vucetich, 1896, pp. 8 and 9: *palazzo Angaran* at the end of the fourteenth century, says the balcony disappeared not long ago; Elenco, 1905, p. 162, no. 258); fondamenta Ca' Venier (Cann. 336–7): two floors with two three-light windows displaced to the extreme left; calle del Campaniel and campiello Bruno Crovato (Cannaregio at S. Canciano): scattered windows and a three-light window; calle del Campaniel (S. Polo 1757): two floors with two two-light windows on the extreme right and a shop on the ground floor (Elenco, 1905, p. 116, no. 133); calle Castelli (Cann. 6097): two three-light windows one above the other and a portal (Elenco, 1905, p. 102, no. 636: Palazzo Zacco); campo Do Pozzi (Castello 2609–10): two two-light windows displaced to the extreme left and four single windows on the right (Elenco, 1905, p. 40, no. 164); campo Do Pozzi (Castello 2599); façade (remade) with two-light window in the middle, of a pleasant, flowing

aspect (Lorenzetti, 1956, p. 368: to the fourteenth century); house at ponte della Furatola at S. Polo: two floors with a three-light window in the middle of the first; four-light window with flower finials in rio Terrà dei Assassini (S. Marco 3695) (Elenco, 1905, p. 12, no. 184); calle del Teatro della Commedia (S. Marco 4606): three-light window with pilaster included, the remainder is imitation (Elenco, 1905, p. 23, no. 383); calle della Madonna (S. Marco 3613–17): remarkable are the two three-light windows one above the other and a corner shop with a wooden cable ornament (Elenco, 1905, p. 12, no. 180); calle della Malvasia (Castello 4330–1): a four-light window with inserted pilaster on the first floor, on the second a three-light window with single windows; campo dei Mori (Cann. 3373): a three-light window flanked by two windows on each side, of dwarf proportions and archaic capital with caulicoli (Elenco, 1905, p. 81, no. 272); fondamenta di Borgo (Dorsoduro 1317–18A): a three-light window and various windows, string-course with plain dog-tooth and colonnette on the edge (Elenco, 1905, p. 157, no. 160); piscina S. Moisè (S. Marco 2060): four-light window with columns alternately white and red, and two windows (Elenco, 1905, p. 9, no. 126); fondamenta della Sensa (Cann. 3319): a three-light window (Elenco, 1905, p. 81, no. 266).

A peculiar case is presented, on the same fondamenta della Sensa, (Cann. 3355) by a façade with two three-light windows one above the other, of which the lower has Romanesque capitals with truncated cubes (taken from elsewhere and re-used?) (Elenco, 1905, p. 81, no. 270; ascribed to the end of the fifteenth century).

We list some other fragmentary manifestations (either fourteenth-century or with retarded fourteenth-century characters) which could be included in this particular inflexion of the Venetian Gothic language; the Gothic remains of Palazzo Calbo Crotta at the Scalzi (Cann. 112b) (Zanotto, 1856, p. 611; Elenco, 1905, p. 68, no. 24; Lorenzetti, 1956, p. 450): of the fifteenth century, of fourth and fifth order, with smooth arch and torus profile; fondamenta della Sensa (Cann. 3248–52): first floor with five-light window and two windows on each side, and the nature of the arches, all walled-up, is not clear (Elenco, 1905, p. 81, no. 262); calle Verdi (Cann. 4343b): multi-light window with pilaster included and windows; fondamenta del Banco Salviati (S. Polo 1501): two windows one above the other with paterae and flower finials (Elenco, 1905, p. 114, no. 112); calle dell'Agnello (S. Croce 2159 and 2282–4): house with three-light window decorated with capitals of the fourth order with caulicoli, almost certainly fourteenth-century, and other windows of the fourth order: whence originates the wooden staircase now at the Ca' d'Oro (Elenco, 1905, p. 143, no. 227); fondamenta dell'Alboro (S. Marco 3896): a two-light window and four windows; rio di S. Giovanni Crisostomo (Cann. 5701–11): three-light window with pilaster included, surmounted by a cross in relief; rio del Cappello at ponte dei Dai (S. Marco): various windows on two floors ('Evangelical Church'); the Gothic elements (two-light windows, etc.) of the corti Coltrera and Contarina (Castello 1972–5) pertaining to a complex of minor architecture studied by Maretto (1959, p. 63) who rightly considers it of the fourteenth century; calle Centopiere (Dorsoduro 1199): a three-light window and windows (a damaged complex) (Elenco, 1905, p. 156, no. 148); calle del Dose da Ponte (S. Marco 2691): single windows with plain dog-tooth ornaments on the jambs and sills, certainly an archaic indication; fondamenta dei Frati (S. Marco 3824): single windows of the fourth order and, together, one with inflected arch, not trefoiled, with a patera on the vertex (the three-light window in the centre is reconstructed): of the fourteenth century? (Elenco, 1905, p. 18, no. 294: *Palazzo Paruta*); campo and rio della Guerra (S. Marco 513–14): various windows and three entrance doors to a warehouse (*fondaco*), similar to those in corte di Palazzo Surian (Elenco, 1905, p. 4, no. 30); calle Larga S. Marco, 420: various windows (the profiles cut away); calle dei Muti o Baglioni (S. Polo 1752): various windows (Elenco, 1905, p. 116, no. 132); sottoportico della Pasina (S. Polo 1120–2): various scattered windows, Byzantine-like cross, rectangular door with opening with segmental arch (Elenco, 1905, p. 111, no. 75: Palazzo Vendrame); calle de Ruga (Castello 160): a two-light window and windows (Elenco, 1905, p. 32, no. 25); rio Terrà S. Aponal (S. Polo 941–2): single windows, in part walled-up; interesting the jutting-out of the two chimneys on the façade, supported, above, by the Gothic cornice, as often in Venice; rio Santi Apostoli: two wings with four windows (the centre remade during the Renaissance); campo S. Maria Zobenigo (S. Marco 2471–2): on the first floor three windows and a three-light window, with pilasters instead of columns (Elenco, 1905, p. 11, no. 153); campo S. Sofia (Cann. 4204): beautiful three-light window on the extreme left and two windows on the noble floor, the second floor perhaps restored or remade (Elenco, 1905, p. 88, no. 388); of the early fifteenth century; campiello Testori (Cann. 3847): house with single windows on the two sides and a shop on the corner (Elenco, 1905, p. 85, no. 346: a shield of the end of the fifteenth century); Palazzo Pisani in calle del Scaleter (S. Polo 2237–40): there remains only one four-light window (Elenco, 1905, p. 118, no. 180); fondamenta Maravegie (Dorsoduro 1058: 'Pensione Accademia': on the first floor, on the inner garden, a three-light window and various windows (shafts and capitals remade?), rio di Noale (at the outlet of rio Trapolin): a first floor with a three-light window and four windows.

**152.** *House in fondamenta Navagero in Murano.* Notice the employment of the plain dog-tooth ornament, also in the moulding of the pilasters.

**153.** *Casa Corner and Casa Obizzi Sodeci in Murano.* The columns of the Casa Corner porch were remade in a later epoch; the porch of the other house is, however, the original one, with profiles, at the earliest, of the end of the fourteenth century. Lorenzetti (1956, p. 788) puts Casa Obizzi Sodeci in the fourteenth century.

**154.** *Palazzo Renier in Chioggia.* In Corso del Popolo, 1262. The second floor is imitation; the remainder much restored; the porch seems ancient.

**155.** *House at ponte dei Fuseri.* Elenco, 1905, p. 22, no. 364 (S. Marco 4363). Three single trefoiled windows. Plain dog-tooth ornament on the jambs imposts and the sill.

**156.** Stone, 1955, fig. 118 a.

**157.** Webb, 1956, p. 120.

**158.** Webb, 1956, fig. 125.

**159.** See: Bond, 1913, II, pp. 632, 633, 637.

**160.** Bond, 1913, II, pp. 653, 662, 663.

**161.** Cf.: D. E. W. Harrison, *The Pictorial History of Bristol Cathedral*, London 1962, p. 13.

**162.** On the oriental origin of the multifoiled arch read the article of the always very accurate Ph. Heliot (*Les portails polylobés d'Aquitaine* in *Bulletin Monumental*, 1946, p. 63 et seq.).

**163.** *S. Stefano.* Sansovino says it was completed in 1325 but, as Paoletti has remarked, this could refer only to a previous church. Selvatico (1847, p. 121; 1852, p. 80) follows Sansovino but considers the 'stupendous' door to be the work of the Dalle Masegne, extolling its beauty. Paoletti (1893, I, pp. 57, 58) considers the apses, the façade, the side on the campo and some of the ornaments to be of the first half of the fifteenth century. The Elenco (1905, p. 18, no. 285) gives them to the fourteenth. Apollonio (1911, p. 6) says that work was going on there throughout the fourteenth century until 1394 and that the building was still going on (or reconstructions were proceeding) in 1407; that the convent was being built in 1434; and puts the portal in the first half of the fourteenth century. Venturi attributes the portal to the two Bon (1924, p. 301). Lorenzetti (1956, p. 497) hesitates in the dating of the church between the fourteenth and the fifteenth. Lavagnino (1936, p. 481) is for 1325, Bassi (1965, p. 198) attributes the portal to Bartolomeo Bon. One of the most brilliant examples of the systematic application of the cinquefoiled arch is the rose window once in S. Pietro in Trieste (begun in 1367), now on the façade of the church of Barcola (information kindly supplied by A. Rusconi). A more detailed examination would obviously exceed the limits of this work. It will become possible only when the Venetian church Gothic will come to be studied; and the dating, acceptable, to the first half of the fifteenth century does not contradict what we try to demonstrate here.

**164.** I shall mention only a few: the canopy on the tomb of the bishop de Luda at Ely (1290–9), the Crouchback († 1296) tomb at Westminster (*Bulletin Monumental*, 1909, p. 247); that of William de la Marche at Wells (1293–1302), the very rich Choir Screen of Lincoln (1300–20), the tomb of Eleanor Percy at Beverley († 1328), that of Aymer de Valence at Westminster (cf. *Apollo*, June 1962, p. 285), that of Richard Stepeldon at Exeter († 1326), that of Edward II († 1327) at Gloucester, one of the most imaginative creations of the English Gothic; the stalls of Chichester; the canopies of the tomb of William Turre in the rear choir of Lincoln; the three singular tombs in St. Mary of Bristol, enriched with rather original cornices; the tomb of Hugh Despencer (of 1349) at Tewkesbury and very many other examples in tombs, canopies and the crowning parts of doors.
The happy decorative inspiration of these singular multifoil arches had great success on the continent, already in the first half of the fourteenth century in Germany (in the Freiburg spire; in St. Martin of Braunschweig; in Cologne), in France (Brun tomb, d. 1349, in Limoges cathedral; Béthisy; Saint-Martin; Chaumont-en-Bassigny), in Spain (Arroyuelo tomb in Burgos cathedral), in Italy (the tomb of Mary of Hungary in S. Maria Donna Regina, by Tino di Camaino; the monument to Robert d'Anjou in S. Chiara of Naples by Gio-

vanni and Pacio da Firenze; the windows in the courtyard of Pavia castle; the vestibule arcade of Giovanni da Campione in S. Maria Maggiore of Bergamo).
The quite exceptional spread of this motif in England between the end of the thirteenth and the middle of the fourteenth century justifies the impression that it indeed originated there.

**165.** See: Arslan, *Vicenza, Le Chiese*, Rome 1956, p. 123, (lists 822–5 and Plate LXV).

**166.** *Palazzetto in piazzetta Leoncini.* Elenco, 1905, p. 3, no. 11; W. G. Constable, *Canaletto*, Oxford 1962, Vol. I, fig. 154; Vol. II, pp. 446, 447. no. 541.

**167.** *Palazzo Moroni.* As far as I know, this building has not stimulated any particular interest: its position, though, seems to me important, like that of so many, too many, other Venetian houses.
See: Elenco, 1905, p. 11, no. 167. On the side in calle del Piovan, three surviving windows of the fourth type.
On the façade a smooth arch of the third type, certainly anterior to it.

**168.** *House in salizzada Streta.* Elenco, 1905, p. 32, no. 22.

**169.** *House in campo del Traghetto at S. Maria Zobenigo.* Elenco, 1905, p. 11, no. 150.

**170.** *House in fondamenta Zen at the Gesuiti.* Elenco, 1905, p. 94, no. 491.

**171.** *Palazzo Dolfin at S. Tomà.* Elenco, 1905, p. 123, no. 254 (mentions a coat of arms of the end of the fifteenth century); Lorenzetti, 1956, p. 622. The five-light window was obviously part of a large complex, mostly reconstructed, which we need not consider further.

**172.** *Palazzo Querini at S. Samuele.* Elenco, 1905, p. 17, no. 269; Lorenzetti, 1956, p. 490 (to the fifteenth century).

**173.** *Palazzo Pisani at S. Samuele.* Elenco, 1905, p. 17, no. 263; Chiminelli, 1912, p. 232; Lorenzetti, 1956, p. 490 (to the fifteenth century).

**174.** Numerous examples of this type of architecture can be quoted; on the whole almost certainly more advanced in time than those listed above, on p. 20 ff.; thus the already mentioned house on rio dei Miracoli, where the four-light window 'lives together' with windows of the fifth order, and another house on the same rio; the sequence of a three-light window (with an arch of the fifth order and two of the fourth) and other windows on fondamenta S. Barnaba; the delightful house, also at S. Barnaba (Dorsoduro 2776–80) of the fourteenth century, described by Trincanato (1948, p. 267; Elenco, 1905, p. 164, no. 289); a house in ramo Corazzeri (Castello 3844–6) (Elenco, 1905, p. 47, no. 298: to the fifteenth century); the already mentioned complex of fondamenta Gherardini; the very long sequence on the first floor of the façade of *Palazzo Magno Manolesso* in calle Magno (Castello 2687) (Elenco, 1905, p. 40, no. 173; and p. 184); Palazzo Sagredo in calle del Teatro (S. Croce 2288) with façade on rio delle due Torri, with many refashioned profiles (Elenco, 1905, p. 143, no. 228; to the beginning of the fourteenth century); a house in calle del Piovan at S. Maria Zobenigo (S. Marco 2546 a), the complex façade in rio Terrà del Bagatin (Cann. 5564), with its own particular arrangement on an interesting plan (Elenco, 1905, pp. 97 and 555: to the fifteenth century); at the Carampane (at S. Polo 1513*b*); the rear of Palazzo Duodo on the Grand Canal (S. Croce 1958); Ca' Malipiero at S. Samuele; a house in calle della Ca' d'Oro (Cann. 3937) with cable ornaments along the edges; a house in calle Longa at S. Barnaba (Dorsoduro 2686–8) (Elenco, 1905, p. 164, no. 279); a three-light window, including the usual larger window, in marzaria del Capitello (S. Marco 4943) (Elenco, 1905, p. 25, no. 423: Giustiniani coat of arms of the fifteenth century; Lorenzetti, 1956, p. 324); a house in calle Cappella (Dorsoduro 3113–14; Elenco, 1905, p. 165, no. 310); a house on rio dei Mendicanti (Calle Gallina at S. Zanipolo) with a four-light window (on later pilasters) of the fourth order and two of the fifth order, with the usual Gothic door with two centres on the water; a façade on rio della Panada (Cann. 611; calle delle Erbe) where one can see four windows, two of the fourth order and two of the fifth, wrought in pink Veronese limestone: the Byzantine dentil ornament forming border is not followed, in the moulding, by a cyma but by the jamb at right angle, with cable ornament along the edge (which is, precisely, a characteristic of the Veronese civil Gothic); a *piano nobile* recently recovered in a house on the Grand Canal contiguous, on the left, with Palazzo Tiepolo Passi (a two-light window of the fifth order flanked by two smaller windows of the fourth order; all once walled-up); a graceful façade of a middle-class house, without preoccupations for alignment or symmetry in fondamenta Vendramin (Elenco, 1905, p. 78, no. 205; Cannaregio 2394) of the fifteenth century.

**175.** *House in salizzada S. Basegio.* Elenco, 1905, p. 158, no. 189.

**176.** *House in rio di S. Polo.* Elenco, 1905, p. 119, no. 190; Muratori, 1960, p. 39, Plate X.

**177.** *Palazzo Semitecolo.* Quadri, 1834, p. 3 (notice the original windows of the mezzanine); Zanotto, 1856, p. 580 (to the fourteenth century); Elenco, 1905, p. 149, no. 25; Lorenzetti, 1956, p. 614 (to the fifteenth century). The Gothic balconies appear remade.
Other examples, worth mentioning, of the fifth order: the great façade with three- and single-light windows on corte Morosina (Cann. 5820–7) next to the houses of the Amadi; the beautiful façade (with recent balconies and the axis displaced to the right) in fondamenta Cannaregio 1273 (Elenco, 1905, p. 72, no. 98); *Palazzo Zorzi* at S. Marcuola on the Grand Canal, with two three-light windows of the fifth order flanked by a single-light window on each side and the top floor altered (Cann. 1760–2); fourteenth-century capitals without rosette (Tassini, 1879, p. 269; Elenco, 1905, p. 73, no. 134 and p. 185); what remains of Palazzo Colombo in the street of the same name (S. Croce 1639–43) (Elenco, 1905, p. 137, p. 146–7); the façade, developed in height, of the house in calle dei Botteri at S. Polo (no. 1573) 'recently reconstructed' (Elenco, 1905, p. 115, no. 125); the two dwarf windows in Marzaria del Capitello (Elenco, 1905, p. 25, no. 421; S. Marco 4924); the façade in calle della Pietà (first floor) (Cann. 3628–9); the three-light window described by Ruskin (1886, II, p. 266) in campiello delle Strope at S. Giacomo dall'Orio, who praises its singular purity (S. Croce 1011 and 364–5; Elenco, 1905, p. 135, no. 108).

**178.** Tassini, 1863, 1933 ed., p. 538.

**179.** *Palazzo Gritti Loredan.* Elenco, 1905, p. 47, no. 289; Tassini, 1879, p. 236; Lorenzetti, 1956, pp. 292–3. In sestiere di Castello at nos. 3698 and 3702. On the restorations see: *La nuova sistemazione*, 1932. A three-light window of the fourth order on the eastern façade of the courtyard, not reproduced here, carries capitals and shafts perhaps of the fifth century.

**180.** *Palazzo Marcello Moro in rio S. Luca.* The entrance is from calle della Verona (S. Marco 3667). Lorenzetti, 1956, p. 506 (to the fifteenth century). The balustrades of the multi-light windows on the first floor and of the last window on the right are Renaissance; the two of the left wing seem to be of the fourteenth century. On the floor which gives on rio della Verona two windows of the fourth order are flanking the two of the fifth order. The windows of the ground floor are Renaissance. The upper mezzanine is reconstructed; the upper cornice Gothic. In the whole of this façade there is no element that could be referred to the floriated Gothic. It poses no problem of rhythm and it follows a plan very freely interpreted and dictated by practical requirements (the alignment of the windows is not always respected).

**181.** *Palazzo Dolfin at SS. Apostoli.* Lorenzetti, 1956, p. 631 (to the fifteenth century). The recessing façade, on the right, has windows of the fourth order with depressed arch, level with that of the façade discussed in the text; the string-courses also (at least on the ground floor) seem to mark the same level. The top floor, transformed in the seventeenth century, is also the same on the three sides.

**182.** *House on the Zattere*, nos. 920–1a. The ground floor is entirely reconstructed. The columns of the four-light window are of alternate colours. Elenco, 1905, p. 154, no. 110.

**183.** *Palazzo Benedetti.* Tassini, 1873, p. 105 (erected by the Benedetti); Tassini, 1879, p. 187; Elenco, 1905, p. 87, no. 378. This building is one of the many that are neglected, almost ignored, sharing in this the fate of the greater number of these Gothic buildings: admired after a fashion by the ordinary tourists and neglected by the qualified critics. On the façade there is the coat of arms, with lozenges, of the Benedetti.

**184.** *Palazzo Grifalconi.* Tassini, 1879, p. 244; Elenco, 1905, p. 67, no. 8 and p. 185; Chiminelli, 1912, p. 228; Paoletti, 1920, p. 93; Molmenti, 1925, p. 297 (fourteenth to fifteenth centuries); Lorenzetti, 1956, p. 332 (ascribes everything to the fifteenth century); Trincanato, 1948, pp. 48 and 633.

**185.** The other two visible sides (Palazzo Gritti) confirm the utter indifference towards any architectural organization. On that in salizzada S. Antonin there is a row, devoid of rhythm, of single windows of the fourth order below and another, of the fifth order, above. On the rear façade there is a beautiful three-light window (fourth order) on the second floor.

**186.** *Palazzo Gritti at S. Giovanni in Bragora.* Visible in the *View* by J. de' Barbari. Fontana, 1845, Plate 16; Zanotto, 1847, pp. 425–6; Selvatico, 1852, p. 101 (to the fourteenth); Ruskin, 1886, III, pp. 277, 278, I, Plate VIII; Zanotto, 1856, p. 218 (to the fourteenth century; notices the arms of the Badoer; 'at present in course of restoration' and the remains of old 'ornamental' paintings around the windows are being removed 'to be replaced by a compartment painted with
white and red squares'; he deplores this interference); Mothes, 1859, I, pp. 213, 214 (to 1300–40); Tassini, 1863, 1915 ed., p. 488 (the fourteenth-century coat of arms is that of the Gritti, who in that century dwelt in the parish of S. Giovanni in Bragora; he denies that the Badoer had ever owned the palazzo; idem, 1873, pp. 100, 101; Paoletti, 1893, I, p. 31; Marini, 1905, p. 82 (to the fourteenth century); Elenco, 1905, I, p. 289 (to the fourteenth century); Molmenti, 1925, I, p. 289 (to the fifteenth century); Lorenzetti, 1956, p. 294 (to the fifteenth century).

**187.** *House in rio Terrà Catecumeni.* Elenco, 1905, p. 148, no. 15 (to the fifteenth century). The capitals are of fourteenth-century type; with rosette.

**188.** *Casa Leoni.* Elenco, 1905, p. 141, no. 206; Lorenzetti, 1956, p. 467 (to the fifteenth century). S. Croce, 2180–1, Calle della Chiesa.

**189.** *House in campiello S. Maria Nova.* Elenco, 1905, p. 102, no. 623; Maretto, 1960, p. 20 (to the fourteenth century).

**190.** *Palazzo Cappello at ponte della Panada.* On the water, door with inflected arch; on the first floor, the four-light window flanked by two windows on each side (fifth order); on the second floor, of smaller proportions but still conspicuous, a fifth order four-light window flanked by four other windows (some of fourth order); the cornice remade. Elenco, 1905, p. 96, no. 531 (to the fifteenth century).

**191.** *Palazzo Talenti.* Elenco, 1905, p. 136, no. 121. The edges of the façade are marked by Istrian stone quoins for the whole height; but their course is quite irregular. The central balcony is obviously Renaissance.

**192.** *House in calle dei Meloni.* Elenco, 1905, p. 113, no. 100 (S. Polo 1413); Maretto, 1960, p. 65 ('three cells organization in one block' type as 'one-family independent building units'; with excellent plans).

**193.** Scattered examples, and more definitely fifteenth-century, of buildings with the fourth and fifth orders, can be found everywhere in Venice. We mention: a top floor in fondamenta Ormesini (Cann. 2687) in which the two orders are represented and a three-light window with round arches (perhaps of later date) has fourteenth-century capitals and columns on high cylindrical plinths (it is *Palazzo Gatti*: Elenco, 1905, p. 79, no. 236); a house in rio Priuli and rio della Ca' Dolce (Cann. 4174–5) where there remains a first floor with a three-light window in the centre (fourth order) and two windows on each side (fifth order) and the side on the ruga dei Due Pozzi with scattered windows and an interesting rectangular gate (Elenco, 1905, p. 87, no. 379); what remains of *Palazzo Cappello Malipiero* at S. Samuele, that is, the door (of which we shall speak elsewhere) and the windows, partly in pairs, partly single, of the top floor on campo S. Samuele and on calle Malipiero, under the Gothic cornice, of the fourth and the fifth and even the first order (of which we have already spoken); it must have been an imposing mass and must have had, also on the façade on campo S. Samuele (rare example in Venice) a certain architectural ordering which, naturally, cannot have been missing in the façade on the Grand Canal either, rebuilt in 1622 (Zanotto, 1856, p. 587; Tassini, 1863, 1915 ed., p. 413; Idem, 1879, p. 212; Elenco, 1905, p. 16, no. 243; Lorenzetti, 1956, pp. 490 and 619). We leave for the end the Palazzi Cendon at S. Giobbe (Cann. 434 and 435 a), the first of which carries on the outside a coat of arms with the date 1437. The two small palaces are noticeably different from each other: the one at no. 434 has windows with badly traced Gothic arches, still surmounted by 'cusps' of Islamic origin, combined with three-light windows with simple inflected arch, not trefoiled, with other characteristics which make one think of the early fourteenth century. The second building (no. 435 a), as our illustration shows, also has fourteenth-century characters, but of a later date; and in those times the upper cornice extended, perhaps, identical over the two houses. Nothing prevents that coat of arms (the presence of such coats of arms is often misleading) from having been affixed later (Tassini, 1863, 1915 ed., p. 178: to the fifteenth century; Elenco, 1905 p. 70, nos. 60 and 61: the second palace is placed at the beginning of the sixteenth century; Lorenzetti, 1956, p. 444: ascribes the two houses to the fourteenth century). I should be inclined to date to the fifteenth century Palazzo Da Lezze at the confluence of rio di Noale and the Grand Canal, with two façades forming an angle, the one on the Grand Canal more regular, the other with openings scattered without any order; with windows all of the fourth order (Cann. 3673) see: Quadri, 1834, p. 26.

**194.** *Palazzo Tron on the Grand Canal.* Elenco, 1905, p. 20, no. 322; S. Marco 3949, corte Tron; Lorenzetti, 1956, p. 625 (to the fifteenth century). The ground floor has been remodelled. Reconstructions, at least partial, also on the first and third floors. The upper cornice is, perhaps, at the original height. Of about 1440. The adjoining palazzetto Tron (Memmo) is a nineteenth-century imitation. The original building was quite different (Quadri, 1834, Plate 30). This is mentioned also by Zanotto (1856, p. 595) who says that it was altered 'in the subsequent reductions'.

**195.** *House in piscina S. Zulian, 555.* Elenco, 1905, p. 5, no. 38. Other elements of the fifth order, scattered over Venice, with capitals, if any, of archaic type: house at ponte della Malvasia, with single windows of the fifth order (S. Marco 2593; Elenco, 1905, p. 12, no. 169); second floor in fondamenta Di Canal, Cann. 2380–1, of the fifth order, with half walled-up four-light window (Elenco, 1905, p. 78, no. 203 (to the fifteenth century); scattered windows and two-light windows in campo U. Foscolo (Cast. 3206); large three-light window of the fifth order in fondamenta di fronte l'Arsenal (Cast. 2427 d), certainly late; house in calle Orsetti (S. Croce 1415–17) with fifth order windows (Elenco, 1905, p. 136, no. 130); three-light window (fifth order) in calle del Ravano (S. Croce 2191; Elenco, 1905, p. 141, no. 208); small house in rio Malpaga at S. Barnaba (Dorsoduro 2780–2; Elenco, 1905, p. 164, no. 289); three-light window and simple windows in campiello Marcona (Dorsoduro 3885; Elenco, 1905, p. 170, no. 379).

**196.** *Palazzo Bembo Boldù.* Ascribed to the fifteenth century by the Elenco (1905, p. 101, no. 618) and by Lorenzetti (1956, p. 331). At the rear, in calle del Forno (Cann. 5974) windows of the fifth order and door similar to that on the façade.

**197.** *Palazzetto Conca.* Not mentioned by the guide-books.

**198.** *Palazzetto in rio della Pietà.* Elenco, 1905,

p. 46, no. 280; Maretto, 1960, p. 42 (notes the archaic plan and attributes it to about 1350).

**199.** Paoletti, 1893, I, p. 22.

**200.** *Palazzo Sagredo Morosini at S. Sofia.* Fontana, 1845, Plate 22 (almost identical with its present state); Zanotto, 1847, pp. 424, 425; Ruskin, 1886, III, pp. 343, 344 (to the early fourteenth century; among the most beautiful windows of the fourth and fifth order); Burckhardt, 1925, p. 150; Mothes, 1859, I, pp. 67, 217, 219 (to 1340–70); Kugler, 1858–9, III, p. 578; Paoletti, 1893, I, p. 22 (the palazzo is mentioned in 1426 as an example to imitate for certain works at the Ca' d'Oro); Lorenzetti, 1956, p. 633 (to the end of the fourteenth century); Hubala, 1966, p. 763 (to the fourteenth century).

**201.** *Palazzo Gabrieli.* Quadri, 1834, p. 41 (shops on the ground floor); Tassini, 1863, 1915 ed., p. 303 (notes the Gabrieli coat of arms on the façade and on the well-curb); Idem, 1879, p. 235; Elenco, 1905, p. 48, no. 303 (to the fifteenth century); Douglas, 1925, p. 28; Lorenzetti, 1956, p. 298 (to the end of the fourteenth century); Maretto, 1959, p. 36 (to the end of the fourteenth century; notes the plan in L). In the courtyard (the building is now a hotel) a three-light window of the third type (transferred?).

**202.** Paoletti, 1893, I, p. 25.

**203.** *Palazzo Navagero.* According to Tassini (1879, p. 130) who transmits the date, confused with the neighbouring house where Petrarch lived (Palazzo Molin dalle Due Torri); Selvatico, 1852, p. 108; Elenco, 1905, p. 48, no. 305; Douglas, 1925, p. 27; Lorenzetti, 1956, p. 29 (fifteenth century).

**204.** *Palazzo Contarini at S. Canciano.* Elenco, 1905, p. 97, no. 551 (to the beginning of the fifteenth century); Lorenzetti, 1956, p. 353 (to the fifteenth century); Maretto, 1960, p. 16.

**205.** *Palazzo Falier at S. Vitale.* Quadri, 1834, p. 33 (the two *liagò* may be seen); Ruskin, 1886, II, p. 262, Plate XVII, no. 9, erroneously located in front of Ca' Foscari (notes, in the five-light window, the increased size of the lateral windows in comparison with the central ones); Elenco, 1905, p. 14, nos. 220 and 221; Molmenti, 1925, p. 298; Torres, 1937, p. 15 (considers the two *liagò* added later); Lorenzetti, 1956, p. 619 (to the fifteenth century); Hubala, 1966, p. 775 (to the fifteenth century; an example unique of its kind). (The *liagò* are small covered balconies, enclosed by a grating.)

**206.** *Palazzo Gherardi.* Three-light window with rosette capitals; flower finials, original (?) balustrade. Tassini, 1879, p. 275 (belonged perhaps to the Moro in 1336); Elenco, 1905, p. 97, no. 553; Lorenzetti, 1956, p. 353; Maretto, 1960, p. 38.

**207.** *Palazzo Pisani (Hotel Terminus).* Elenco, 1905, p. 68, no. 23 (to the fifteenth century).

**208.** *Palazzo on the fondamenta della Misericordia at the Madonna dell'Orto.* Elenco, 1905, p. 79, no. 226; Maretto, 1960, p. 50 (with plans; to the fifteenth century).

**209.** *Palazzo Donà; Banco S. Marco.* On rio di Canonica. Elenco, 1905, p. 3, no. 15 (to the fifteenth century). Has undergone reconstructions. The plan is interesting.

**210.** *Palazzo Da Lezze formerly Condulmer at S. Samuele on the Grand Canal.* Tassini, 1879, p. 258; Elenco, 1905, p. 16, no. 251; Zanotto, 1856,

p. 589 (to the fourteenth century); Tassini, 1879, p. 258; Elenco, 1905, p. 16, n. 251; Marini, 1905, p. 82 (to the fourteenth century); Lorenzetti, 1956, p. 621. Another multi-light window in the courtyard.

**211.** *Palazzo Zatta.* Elenco, 1905, p. 69, no. 44; Cannaregio, fondamenta Labia 330–1. The axis of the two three-light windows is entirely on the right together with the portal; on the left, single-light windows on two axes. Pleasant façade of minor architecture.

**212.** *Palazzo Bernardo (?) at S. Silvestro.* Elenco, 1905, p. 112, no. 76.

**213.** *Small house in fond. S. Alvise.* Elenco, 1905, p. 81, no. 260 (to the fifteenth century).

**214.** *Palazzo Maffetti.* Elenco, 1905, p. 176, no. 45; Lorenzetti, 1956, p. 759.

**215.** *Large house in campo de la Pescaria.* Quadri, 1834, p. 11. The ground floor shops demonstrably remodelled. The three-light windows are divided by pilasters.

**216.** *Palazzo Vendramin at Giudecca.* Elenco, 1905, 173, no. 2. A two-light window but, this, certainly fourteenth-century, with two Gothic inflected arches, not trefoiled, gives on the garden at the rear. Born with the remainder of the palazzo?

**217.** In the more ancient buildings the stairs were probably internal (see: Trincanato, 1948, p. 73) and internal they were, naturally, in the more modest houses; sometimes in wood. Of these last, the only remaining example is the one now preserved in the Ca' d'Oro, originating from the house of the Dell'Agnella at S. Maria Mater Domini (see: Tassini, *Curiosità*, 1863, 1933 ed., p. 212; Molmenti, 1925, I, p. 296: according to Molmenti the wooden stairs preceded in Venice those of stone; Paoletti, 1920, p. 96; Trincanato, 1948, pp. 101 and 105). See also on the subject: Mothes, 1859, p. 215; Paoletti, 1893, I, p. 27; Trincanato, 1948, p. 98; Bettini, 1953, p. 39.

**218.** *Staircase of corte Morosina.* Elenco, 1905, p. 100, no. 589; Lorenzetti, 1956, p. 355.

**219.** *Staircase of Palazzo Lion.* Chiminelli, 1912, pp. 218–19; Toesca, 1950, p. 675, (perhaps of the fourteenth century).

**220.** *Staircase of Palazzo Priuli at S. Severo.* Elenco, 1905, p. 53, no. 392; Chiminelli, 1912, pp. 225–6.

**221.** *Staircase of Palazzo Donà at S. Polo.* Chiminelli, 1912, p. 228; Maretto, (1960, p. 46 and Plates XIII and XIII bis) on the basis of considerations derived from the plan, ascribes it to the end of the fourteenth century.

**222.** *Staircase of Palazzo Goldoni.* Chiminelli, 1912, pp. 227–28.

**223.** *Staircase in fondamenta Gherardini, Dorsoduro* 2824. Chiminelli, 1912, p. 231.

**224.** *Staircase of Palazzo Magno-Bembo.* Selvatico, 1847, p. 118; Chiminelli, 1912, pp. 224, 225. Lorenzetti and Trincanato (see above) attribute it to the fifteenth century.

**225.** *Staircase of Palazzo Contarini Porta di Ferro.* See next chapter.

**226.** *Staircase of Palazzo Bernardo on the Grand Canal.* Maretto, 1960, p. 46, Plate XIII bis. Of this palazzo we shall speak later. With more archaic structures, the remains of the exterior staircases of Palazzo Flangini Fini (Grand Hôtel) at S. Moisè (Chiminelli, 1912, p. 232) and of fondamenta Minotto (S. Croce 151); certainly fifteenth century the remaining arches of that of Palazzo Molin at S. Fantin (Mothes, 1859, p. 148; Elenco, 1905, p. 9, no. 121; Lorenzetti, 1956, p. 504); among the most elegant, placed by the side of the façade, that of Palazzo Grifalconi.

**227.** *Staircase of Palazzo Morosini at S. Giovanni Laterano.* Ruskin, 1886, III, p. 307 (to the beginning of the fourteenth century); Elenco, 1905, p. 61, no. 550; Chiminelli, 1912, p. 230. Cannaregio 6396.

**228.** See on this particular subject my article *Portali romanici a Venezia* published in 'Festschrift Ulrick Mitteldorf', Berlin 1968, p. 15 et seq.

**229.** *Portal in corte del Milion.* Selvatico (1852, p. 138) attributed it to the eleventh century, as also Zanotto (1856, p. 369) and Cattaneo (1889, p. 193). Gabelentz (1903, p. 117) moves the date to about 1100; the Elenco (1905, p. 100, no. 598) puts it in the twelfth century, as do Molmenti (1925, I, p. 275), evidently reflecting the opinions current in his time, and Marzemin (1912, p. 333). Lorenzetti (1926, p. 344) is for the eleventh to twelfth centuries. Toesca (1927, p. 895, note 32) is for the twelfth century, as is Salmi (1936, p. 50). Bettini (1953, fig. 35) gives it to 'the eleventh'.

**230.** *Portal of corte Bottera at S. Zanipolo.* Given to the thirteenth century by the Elenco (1905, p. 61, no. 540); is not considered older than the twelfth century, if we understand him correctly, by Fiocco (who in this judgment involves also that of corte del Milion) (1930, p. 67) and is taken by Trincanato (1948, p. 152) to the twelfth to thirteenth centuries.

**231.** *Portal at ponte di S. Tomà.* For Ruskin (1886, III, p. 350) 'probably of the twelfth century'; for Gabelentz (1903, p. 117) of the twelfth; for Molmenti (1925, I, p. 278) and Lorenzetti (1926, p. 547) of the thirteenth. Bettini (1953, fig. 33) gives it to the eleventh century.

**232.** S. Maria dei Servi was begun around 1333 (see: H. Thode, 1895, p. 89).

**233.** *Portal of Palazzo Contarini Porta di Ferro.* The ascription of this arch (with its framing) to the thirteenth century is unanimous: by old Selvatico (1852, p. 134) to Zanotto (1856, p. 233), Tassini (1879, p. 176), Molmenti (1925, p. 279), Lorenzetti (1926, p. 369). Bettini (1953, fig. 37) gives this carved arch to the eleventh century.

**234.** *Portal of Palazzo Malipiero at S. Samuele.* Cattaneo, 1877–87, p. 146 (to the tenth century circa); Gabelentz, 1903, pp. 116–17 (to the first half of the eleventh century); Marzemin, 1912, p. 333 (to the tenth to eleventh centuries); Lorenzetti, 1926, p. 467 (to the thirteenth century).

**235.** *Portal of Casa Bosso.* See: Ruskin, 1886, III, p. 350 (early Gothic) .

**236.** *Portal of Palazzo Donà in campo S. Polo.* Zanotto, 1856, p. 481 (to the thirteenth century); Tassini, 1863, 1915 ed., p. 578 (to the thirteenth century); Idem, 1879, p. 279 (to the thirteenth century); Elenco, 1905, p. 118, no. 174; Lorenzetti, 1956, p. 569 (to the fourteenth century).

**237.** *Portal of Casa Magno at S. Luca.* Elenco, 1905, p. 21, no. 344 (to the twelfth century); Molmenti, 1925, I, p. 280 (to the thirteenth to fourteenth centuries); Lorenzetti, 1956, p. 486 (to the thirteenth century); Fiocco, 1930, p. 79.

**238.** *Portal at S. Croce 2054.* Elenco, 1905, p. 140, no. 186; Trincanato, 1948, p. 93 (end of the thirteenth century).

**239.** *Entrance to corte di Ca' Pisani.* Elenco, 1905, p. 135, no. 114 (to the thirteenth century; but considers the Pisani coat of arms of later date; we think it was built with the lunette).

**240.** *Lunette in calle dei Proverbi.* Elenco, 1905, p. 90, no. 430; Lorenzetti, 1956, p. 393 (to the thirteenth century).

**241.** Dudan, 1921, I, p. 183.

**242.** *Portal formerly in S. Nicolò della Lattuga.* See: Elenco, 1905, p. 124, no. 266; Lorenzetti, 1956, p. 573.

**243.** I recall here that of the already mentioned Casa Ottoboni (Cast. 5136) at S. Severo, the architrave of which carries a fourteenth-century sculpture.

**244.** *Portal at Castello 3520.* Elenco, 1905, p. 46, no. 46.

**245.** *Portal at S. Polo 2343.* Elenco, 1905, p. 119, no. 191 (to the first half of the fifteenth century); Maretto (1960, Plate X), on data derived from the plan, puts this house (reconstructed anyway) in the first half of the fourteenth century.

**246.** *Portal in calle del Padiglione.* Half of it has disappeared. Elenco, 1905, p. 91, no. 454.

**247.** Elenco, 1905, p. 38, no. 134 (carries the three coats of arms of Mocenigo, Boldù, Erizzo).

**248.** It is the entrance to corte Mosto. Elenco, 1905, p. 173, no. 4.

**249.** *Portal in calle del Cafetier:* Castello 6480.

**250.** *Zorzi portal in ruga Giuffa.* Tassini, 1863, 1915 ed., p. 40; Elenco, 1905, p. 53, no. 387. A fourteenth-century portal, tampered with, is on fondamenta Venier (Dorsoduro 707).

**251.** *Portal in calle Tiossi at S. Maria Mater Dei.* Gabelentz, 1903, p. 231; Elenco, 1905, p. 140, no. 193.

**252.** *Portal of Palazzo Raspi at S. Polo.* Lorenzetti, 1956, p. 464 (to the fifteenth century).

**253.** *Portal of corte delle Muneghe.* Elenco, 1905, p. 102, no. 634 (beginning of the fifteenth century); Lorenzetti, 1956, p. 329 (to the fifteenth century).

**254.** *Portal of calle Renier at Dorsoduro.* Elenco, 1905, p. 168, no. 345.

**255.** *Lunette over the entrance to corte Morosina.* Cattaneo, 1877–87, p. 193 (of the eleventh or first half of the twelfth, with elements of the fourteenth century); Elenco, 1905, p. 99, no. 587; Molmenti, 1925, I, p. 278 (to the thirteenth century); Lorenzetti, 1956, p. 355 (to the thirteenth to fourteenth centuries).

**256.** Museo Correr, Cod. Gradenigo-Dolfin, no. 228/III, Plate 25.

**257.** *Portal in calle della Testa at Cannaregio.* Elenco, 1905, p. 67, no. 4 (to the fifteenth century).

**258.** For other examples of this kind, but concerning aediculae (with tympanum in hut form, carried by two colonnettes, mostly spiral) cf. Grevembroch's drawings in Museo Correr (Cod. Gradenigo-Dolfin, no. 228/III, Plate 4: of 1347; Plate 15: of 1354; no. 228/II, Plate 53; no. 228/III, Plate 24: of about 1391).

**259.** Cf. the Falier tomb in the Frari, of 1374 (Cod. Gradenigo-Dolfin, no. 228/I, Plate 37), the similar Foscarini tomb (Plate 25), the tomb of Franciotto degli Abbati, of 1382 (Plate 42); that of Bartolomeo Boateri in S. Giorgio Maggiore of 1381 (Gabelentz ,1903, p. 250; Cod. Gradenigo-

Dolfin, no. 228/I, Plate 43); that of Vettor Pisani, with canopy, of 1380, as reproduced by Grevembroch in its original location (no. 228/II, Plate 74); the pensile urn of Jacopo Cavalli in SS. Giovanni e Paolo, of about 1384; that, at ground level, of Giovanni de Santi, of 1392 (no. 228/I, Plate 47; Cicogna, II, p. 277, no. 45); and finally, that of Nicolò Cornaro, at the Frari, of 1400 (Cod. Gradenigo-Dolfin, no. 228/I, Plate 53).

**260.** See: Paoletti, 1893, I, p. 30 (Ca' Foscari).

**261.** Selvatico, 1847, pp. 115, 116; Paoletti, 1893, I, pp. 30, 31; Idem, 1920, p. 92. See also on the subject: Ruskin, 1886, II, p. 241 et seq.; Paoletti, 1920, p. 94; Trincanato, 1948, p. 95.

**262.** *Well-curb in corte del Teatro Vecchio.* Elenco, 1905, p. 116, no. 137 (ascribed to the fifteenth century).

**263.** *Well-curb in Chiostro dei Primiceri.* Ongania, 1889, Plate 40 (to the thirteenth century); Lorenzetti, 1956, p. 317.

**264.** See that of S. Servolo (Ongania, 1889, p. 246); of the Torcello Museum; at S. Lorenzo; in corte Morosina at S. Giovanni Crisostomo; in front of the Arsenal; in Palazzo Tron at S. Stae; at S. Silvestro; at S. Provolo; in corte dietro il campo della Lana at S. Croce.

**265.** *Well-curb formerly Carrer.* Ongania, 1889, Plate 37.

**266.** Was once in Scuola della Carità (Ongania, 1889, Plate 232: there remains Grevembroch's drawing). The record of another, similar, once in campiello delle Mosche at S. Pantalon is transmitted by the same Grevembroch (Ongania, 1889, Plate 214) and similar examples are seen in the fourteenth and fifteenth centuries (in corte del Capellan at S. Francesco: Ongania, 1889, Plate 25; another, of Revedin ownership, at S. Polo (Ongania, 1889, Plate 122). And again: Ongania, 1889, Plate 248.

**267.** *Well-curb with figures of Budapest.* For the history of this impressive well see: J. Balogh, in *Acta Historiae Artium, etc.*, XII, 1966, p. 238 et seq.

**268.** *Ariani well-curb.* See: Tassini, 1863, 1915 ed., p. 30; Ongania, 1889, fig. 188; Vucetich, 1896, p. 15; Lorenzetti, 1956, p. 545.

**269.** Examples in Palazzo Sagredo at S. Ternita (Ongania, 1889, Plate 120; Cicogna, VI, p. 923), in corte del Volto Santo (Trincanato, 1948, p. 111), in corte Perini at S. Lio, in corte Locatello, in calle delle Ballotte, in Palazzo Contarini alla Madonna dell'Orto, in campiello S. Marina (Elenco, 1905, p. 59, no. 516; Castello 6058).

**270.** See: Ferrari-Antoniazzo, 1955, p. 88.

**271.** Ongania, 1889, Plate 192.

**272.** Ongania, 1889, Plate 135.

**273.** Ongania, 1889, Plate 143.

**274.** Ongania, 1889, Plate 116.

**275.** *Well-curb in calle Larga XXII marzo.* Ongania, 1889, Plates 189, 190; recorded in a drawing of Grevembroch.

**276.** *Well-curb of Palazzo Priuli at S. Severo.* Ongania, 1889, Plate 243; Paoletti, 1893, I, p. 23, note 1 ('very much decayed').

**277.** *Ongania well-curb.* Ongania, 1889, Plate 56.

**278.** *Well-curb of Misericordia.* Ongania, 1889, Plate 196.

90-91. *Abbey of S. Gregorio. Cloister capitals.*
92. *St. Mark's. Capital of tabernacle by the main altar.*
93. *St. Mark's. Pinnacle with 'Our Lady of the Annunciation'.*

97. *Doge's Palace. Detail of the external facing of the façade.*
98. *Doge's Palace. Façade on the Quay from Riva degli Schiavoni.*
99. *Doge's Palace. Foreshortened perspective of the multi-light window.*

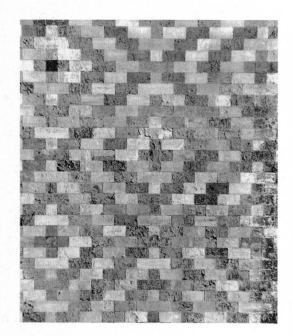

100. *Doge's Palace. Gallery seen from Riva degli Schiavoni.*
101. *Doge's Palace. Corner sculpture. 'Noah's drunkenness'.*

102. Doge's Palace. Corner sculpture. 'The Archangel Raphael and the younger Tobias'.
103-105. Doge's Palace. Corner motifs.

109. *Doge's Palace. Fourth capital of southern portico. Childhood.*
110. *Doge's Palace. Fifth capital from Ponte della Paglia.*
111. *Doge's Palace. Fifth capital from Ponte della Paglia. Detail.*

114. *Doge's Palace. Capital representing the Crusader's family. Detail.*
115. *Doge's Palace. Sixth capital from Ponte della Paglia.*
116. *Doge's Palace. Sixth capital from Ponte della Paglia. Detail.*
117-118. *Doge's Palace. Sixteenth capital from Ponte della Paglia and detail.*

119. *Doge's Palace. Corner towards the Piazzetta.*
120. *Doge's Palace. Sculpture of the corner towards the Piazzetta: 'Adam and Eve'.*
121. *Doge's Palace. Corner sculpture with 'Adam and Eve'. Detail.*
122. *Doge's Palace. Corner sculpture with 'Adam and Eve', with St. Mark's in the background.*

125. *Doge's Palace. Western façade. Details of the large windows.*
126. *Doge's Palace. Western façade. Detail of 'Justice'.*
127-128. *Doge's Palace. Perspective view of the western façade portico.*

*129. Doge's Palace. Twenty-seventh capital from Ponte della Paglia.*     *130. Casa Viaro Zane at S. Maria Mater Domini.*

131. *Three-light window in Calle Piacentini.*
132. *Marco Polo's house in Corte seconda del Milion. Detail.*
133. *Murano. Small Gothic house on rio dei Vetrai.*

134. *Palazzo Zacco on rio di S. Marina.*
135. *Palazzo Zacco on rio di S. Marina. Small corner balcony on the rio.*

136. *Palazzetto Benedetti on rio Priuli.*
137. *Palazzo in Salizzada S. Baseggio.*
138. *Palazzo Marcello at S. Luca seen from Ponte della Cortesia.*

*139. Palazzo Badoer in Campo Bandiera e Moro.*
*140. Examples of windows with trefoiled arch of the end of the fourteenth century (from Ruskin).*

141. *Palazzo on rio della Misericordia from Ponte di S. Marziale.*
142. *Palazzo del Banco di San Marco on rio di Palazzo.*

*143. Palazzo Bembo in Calle Magno. Small courtyard.*
*144. External staircase of Carlo Goldoni's house.*

148-150. *Open staircase in the courtyard of Palazzo Contarini Porta di Ferro.*

*151-152. House of Marco Polo in Corte del Milion. Details of the portal.*
*153. Palazzo Bosso at S. Tomà. Portal.*

154. *Palazzo Contarini della Porta di Ferro.*
*Lunette above the portal.*
155. *Casa Magno at S. Luca. Detail of portal.*
156. *Palazzo Agnusdio. Lunette above the door.*

157. Well-curb in Corte Morosina at S. Giovanni Crisostomo.

158. Well-curb in a courtyard in Calle delle Balote.

159. Well-curb in Campo Teatro Vecchio.

160. *Well-curb in Campiello del Remer, Cannaregio.*

161. *Well-curb in Istrian stone. Private collection.*
162. *Well-curb formerly at S. Paterniano.*
163. *Well-curb in Borgoloco S. Lorenzo.*
164. *Well-curb in Casa Correr.*

165. *Well-curb of the Scuola della Carità (from the Gradenigo-Dolfin Codex).*
166. *Well-curb in Campo S. Raffaele.*
167. *Well-curb in the courtyard of Palazzo Priuli, S. Severo.*
168. *Well-curb in the Budapest Museum.*
169. *Well-curb in Fondaco dei Turchi.*

# Chapter IV  GOTHIC ARCHITECTURE THE FLORIATED STYLE

*The Ca' d'Oro, Palazzo Barbaro and buildings of the first half of the fifteenth century*

A happy find of documents relating to the building of the Ca' d'Oro, by Cecchetti in 1886[1] and Paoletti in 1893[2], brought into focus the very singular character of a building which, in the closely woven fabric of Venetian secular Gothic architecture between the fourteenth and fifteenth centuries, stands quite alone, even if it is connected with it through the internal 'distributive' character and the aspect of the façade (certainly Venetian). However, its singularity consists in the documented intervention of Lombard master–workers, as well as in the particularly luxurious character of the whole building, which prevents its being placed 'in series' with whatever else was being built in Venice in the first half of the fifteenth century.

Initial criticism (the nineteenth–century guides, etc.) was quite unsparing in its admiration of this extraordinary building, but did not go beyond this. Without reliable data on its origins, opinions varied concerning the time of its erection, and even its name was misquoted. Ignored by Sansovino, it was accurately reproduced by Diedo and by Cicognara in 1820 and 1838, the last–named advancing the hypothesis of a project, left unfinished, which would have provided also for a left wing[3] of which, with so many examples of asymmetric façades, we certainly do not feel the need today. For Fontana, in 1845, it is *Palazzo Doro*[4] and this name, which appears in many old Venetian guide-books, is not really absurd because, as Molmenti[5] has shown, a Doro (Aurei) family did in fact exist and owned houses since the twelfth century precisely at S. Sofia—although it remained evident to Molmenti that the name Ca' d'Oro was acquired by this building through the great use of gilding. The old form, already corrected by Tassini, is still used by Pauli[6].

Selvatico[7] was the first to notice that the profiles of Ca' d'Oro were 'very far' from those of the Doge's Palace and he rightly assigns it to the fifteenth century. Zanotto, in 1847[8], speaks of the 'restoration which recently took place'; we shall speak of this later. According to Burckhardt[9], the Ca' d'Oro 'indicates in what dimensions this style shows itself most happily efficient'. Naturally, Ruskin[10] also speaks of it, noting the beauty of the first floor capitals, evidence of the most 'glorious' sculpture of the fifteenth century but displaying some uncertainty in his critical judgment; he says it was 'destroyed by restorations' and describes the havoc made under his eyes. Zanotto[11] returns to the subject of restorations and records the loss of the 'cornice going round under the battlements' (but considers it anterior to 1310).

After the middle of the century, appreciation of the Ca' d'Oro, as of the whole of Venetian

Gothic architecture, becomes somewhat more positive, thanks to Kugler[12] and, above all, Mothes who, taking up one of Selvatico's ideas again, puts the accent on the differences between the Ca' d'Oro and the Doge's Palace. It is remarkable that Mothes, naturally ignoring the specific Lombard contribution, speaks of traceries more advanced than those in the Doge's Palace and finds the cornices *kecker profiliert* in comparison with those of the latter[13]. This observation is, however, sufficient for Mothes (as later for Schnaase)[14] to put the Ca' d'Oro among the latest in time of the Gothic palaces—later, that is, than the Giustiniani, Foscari and Bernardo palaces. He was unable to imagine that the diversity was not imputable to 'progress' but to the intervention of non-Venetian workers. In 1868 and in 1870, Tassini[15] confirmed the attribution to the fifteenth century. In 1903 Raschdorff recorded in a survey the state of the building which lacked the arcading under the battlements[16].

The studies of Cecchetti and Paoletti have restored to this building an established position in the history of Venetian architecture, the former publishing chiefly the contracts between the employer Marino Contarini and Giovanni and Bartolomeo Bon, the second producing the documentary evidence of the intervention of the Milanese Matteo Raverti with his large team of stonecutters and other artists. The work went on from 1424 to around 1437.

The Ca' d'Oro is not very unlike other Venetian buildings in the distribution of its enclosed spaces, though there are some small not very substantial differences, namely a store on the ground floor, with rooms for offices, and a courtyard with an uncovered staircase; on the second floor a hall which, in its plan, reproduces the store, with the usual dwelling rooms, while the third floor reproduces the second floor. Not even the façade would show, at first sight, any innovations in respect of the distribution of the parts. However, the ground floor portico and the two loggias above do not appear as such, but instead as a row of closed windows. Large rooms open in fact behind this portico and the two six-light windows reproduce a motif which was already peculiar to Romano-Byzantine buildings (Ca' Farsetti, Fondaco dei Turchi, etc.). The motif of the entirely open loggia is not, in fact, encountered in Venetian Gothic buildings, except in the Doge's Palace, and the one in Ca' d'Oro is perhaps the only one drawing inspiration—as a general constructional idea only, and not as a particular elaboration of taste—from the Doge's Palace loggia.

Continuing meanwhile a review of opinions on this monument based on a better critical vision, mention should be made of the observations of Giacomo Boni—made before Paoletti's studies—on the polychrome decoration[17].

At that time—1887—the state of preservation was undoubtedly better than at the time of Ruskin, but the building had undergone restorations which had deformed its aspect. Acquired in 1847 by the Countess de Voisins (the ballerina Maria Taglioni), it was restored by G. B. Meduna, and it suffered a second restoration in 1865 following a new change of ownership. In 1894 it became the property of Baron Giorgio Franchetti who, having bought back from a German antiquary in Paris Bartolomeo Bon's well-curb, made a gift of the palace, in 1916, to the Italian State, after which he went on, until his death in 1922, with a more rational renewal. These last restorations, though more scrupulously carried out than the previous ones, could not, naturally, bring back the palace to its primitive integrity. We are now obliged to judge with proper reservations those parts (above all the external staircase and the street gate) which were made good and reconstructed. There is some evidence that in 1905 the external staircase 'no longer existed'[18]. Molmenti, an attentive witness to what was being done at the Domus Magna, gave an account of it in 1910: 'The battlements (roof-parapet) with the arcading underneath them have been put back, reproducing for this detail a small original arch found in the wall above the street.' (We are to understand here that the battlements—clearly visible in the oldest graphic evidence—were restored, or remade.) According to Molmenti, furthermore... 'all the balconies, copied from two old examples found in the palace' were replaced; 'the street gate was reconstructed, making use of parts of it found in the courtyard'. Finally, Franchetti decorates 'the entrance hall by the (canal) landing so as to moderate... the effect... of modern workmanship' and has the walls 'inlaid'[19].

The name of Matteo Raverti and of his team had meanwhile brought to light the Lombards' intervention, at the same time provoking statements about the Ca' d'Oro which appear questionable today: according to Adolfo Venturi (in 1924) the Ca' d'Oro was a 'typical model of Venetian floriated Gothic' and Raverti the 'proclaimer' in Venice of the 'floriated Gothic of Lombardy' ... 'The work was principally carried out by Matteo Raverti of Milan with a team of assistants from Milan and Como'[20] (Venturi)—which is true up to a point. Even the crowning part is attributed by Venturi to Raverti, whereas we know from documents that Giovanni Bon had a hand in it. The very scarce knowledge of Venetian secular Gothic, perennially confused between the fourteenth and fifteenth centuries, is an attenuating circumstance for such statements. In 1924–25 Giacomo Boni reproduces again the contracts of April 1430 and September 1431 with erudite observations on the final colouring and gilding[21]. Molmenti[22] starts again from the beginning but without saying anything new. He is followed by Boschieri with a very useful study, including the history of the palace and a mention of Lavagnino[23]. Toesca discerns in the Ca' d'Oro[24] a later development of the Doge's Palace. For Bettini, Raverti 'must be deemed the true architect of the palace...'[25].

A careful examination of the monument and a scrupulous reading of the documents published by Paoletti, bearing in mind, however, what was being achieved in Venice in the first half of the fifteenth century, may help us to understand this architecture, to distinguish the various developments in taste and also, but only up to a limited degree, the various hands.

For many years the Lombard and Venetian teams worked side by side. The Lombards prevailed numerically. It is with them that the munificent employer, Marino Contarini, treats right from the beginning. The first contracts are in fact made in 1421 with Matteo Raverti of Milan and Marco di Amadio, the former a stonecutter, the latter a master–builder[26] who, we should note, was already in Venice in 1410[27]. But the first contract with Giovanni Bon, his son Bartolomeo and two apprentices, is of 1422; it deals, however, only with the terms of payment, without mentioning the work[28]. Work begins only in 1424, when the two Bons with the two assistants, Zane and Rosso, reappear[29]. In 1425, Marco di Amadio works on a well and there appear, in addition, Stefano Fasan, stonecutter, with his son and two others, all Venetians, under the orders of Marco[30].

The first really concrete notice (in 1425) concerns the external staircase, finished in 1426, to which had applied themselves Matteo Raverti and his Lombard and Venetian assistants[31]. These are Antonio Busato (Paoletti considers him Campionese but he is certainly Venetian, and is found again in Dalmatia)[32], Antonio Foscolo (Venetian), Marco of Segna, Paolo (certainly Paolo Bregno), Gasparino Rosso of Milan[33], Giacomo[34] and Giorgio of Como, Niccolò degli Angeli (called Romanello), Antonio da Rigezo of Como (Bregno)[35], Pietro 'of the Comacene Frisons, Frison with his brother Martino and Guglielmo his servant, Giovanni Frison and an Antonio Frison, son of Guglielmo of Milano', all working with Raverti[36]. With the two Bons were working the apprentices Rosso and Giovanni (the first mistaken for Nanni di Bartolo!), Luca, servant of Giovanni, Antonio Buranello of Murano, Michele, Cristoforo (Orsini?) and a certain Master Curim[37]. It is, however, opportune to insist that one should not, like Paoletti, rigorously maintain this division by schools and tasks because these stonecutters were the executants of the designs of the one or the other master.

In 1426, of the great door 'there is still to finish the *champanilej*, the opening with the angel and arch, the foliage going up on the arch'[38]. On it are working with Raverti, Antonio

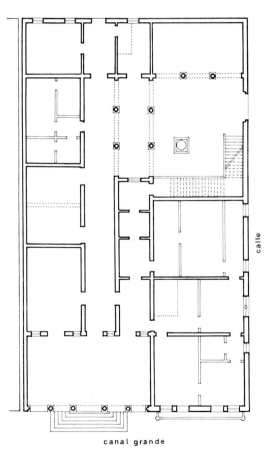

canal grande

calle

235

Busato and Antonio Foscolo[39], both undoubtedly Venetian, along with Gasparino Rosso of Milan and Giacomo of Como, two Lombards occupied on the *champanilej*; according to Paoletti, these are the pinnacled turrets hanging on the sides of the door. The flower was carved by Niccolò Romanello[40].

On 4 April 1426 the carriage of 'the great door from the house of Master Matteo'[41] is paid for; the arch on the door is set up, however, only in 1431 by Antonio di Martino and Giovanni Benzon, both Venetian[42], while it appears that, in the same year, Gasparino Rosso, a Milanese, has bought from Raverti 'a piece of stone—to put the backing of the arms on the tympanum'[43], which means on Contarini's coat of arms.

An opinion on this door is made difficult by the present restoration. As Paoletti[44] observed, the *campaniletti*, the flower, the foliage on the extrados, as well as the green marble of the tympanum, have all disappeared.

In these years—in 1425–26—Antonio and Paolo Bregno of Righeggia are working by the side of Raverti, and are later to be active on the Doge's Palace and at the Frari[45]. These are two artists whose work cannot again be concretely identified in the Ca' d'Oro.

In 1432 Cristoforo Orsini of Milan, with his brothers Rigo and Ambrogio, builds the battlements on the courtyard wall[46], which have also vanished. Paoletti attributes to Raverti also the internal row of windows 'on the colonnade with marble columns and wooden architraves with buttresses, of larch, profiled in the shape of owls' beaks'[47]. In 1427 Bartolomeo Bon is paid for the well-curb.

Boschieri[48] tells us about the demolition of the external staircase, which occurred in 1847, and the dispersal of its marble, without, however, giving any information about style and epoch. A direct examination would demonstrate that the stairs (and the step faces) are not genuine; the handrail (with plain dog-teeth and cable moulding, as in Bartolomeo's well-curb) appears to be partly remade and the landing balcony entirely new; even the supporting arches appear largely reconstructed. If Raverti was really the author of the staircase as documents maintain, we must agree that he adapted himself to entirely Venetian models. Paoletti attributes to Raverti also the staircase of Palazzo Contarini Porta di Ferro, which was, according to him, the model for the reconstruction of the one in Ca' d'Oro[49]. It may be, however, that Contarini had, as was his wont, pointed out the staircase of Palazzo Contarini as a model to imitate. This does not really throw any new light on Raverti's authorship of the Ca' d'Oro staircase, which would appear to be entirely Venetian. These external staircases are not unlike those in the Sicilian palaces (e. g. that of Palazzo Bellomo in Syracuse) of the early fifteenth century[50].

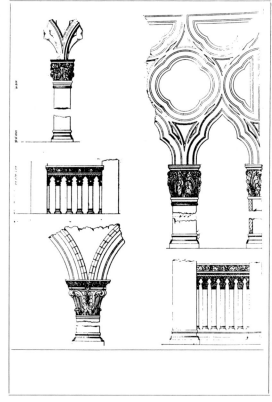

Less embarrassing is a commentary on the portal giving onto the street. According to the documents, coming from Raverti's workshop, they were the same on both sides–on the street and on the courtyard.

The opening is architraved, with a spiral moulding inside and Byzantine dentil ornament outside. Over a dense horizontal foliage ornament rises the great inflected arch, marked on the intrados by a foliage surmounted by crockets and a large flower finial, flanked by two spires (the *campanili*) with two floors and a pinnacle. The type recalls the portals of Venetian churches (Frari) and the quay-side balcony of the Doge's Palace. In the centre of the lunette, in relief, is an angel with the coat of arms which, damaged, was 'piously put together again in the restoration'[51]. The spires and the great arch with crockets seem also largely reconstructed.

Concerning these two works which, according to the documents, originate in Raverti's workshop, it is likely that their form should not be ascribed to him, but only the direction of the work, executed on an unquestionably Venetian design. It may be possible, with more evidence, to find precise characteristics which are not entirely Venetian in the magnificent façade, even if the distribution and the cut of the forms obey specific traditional criteria peculiar to Venice. And it must be readily admitted that it has not really in its particular interpretation of the traditional forms (the trefoiled inflected arch, the traceries, etc.) anything in common with what has been so far discussed, neither with the Doge's Palace nor with whatever was erected later.

The ground floor portico opening with five large arches towards the water is certainly a recollection of the more ancient house of the Zeno, on the site of which Contarini raised his *Domus Aurea;* though certainly not faithful to an original rhythm, it nevertheless recalls the portico on the water of the thirteenth-century Ca' da Mosto. This part of the Ca' d'Oro does not offer therefore important novelties. On these arcades were working in 1425 Giovanni and Antonio Frison[52], and in January 1426 there is also mention of Bartolomeo Bon, Giacomo Passerotto (a Lombard?) to whom is due the round-headed central arch, and a certain Andrea of Milan[53], perhaps the same—unidentified—artist who worked on the Doge's Palace capitals.

Still on the façade, Giorgio of Como works on the bases of the columns and at the 'triple string-moulding of a *corner* of the ground floor', the other being carved by Antonio Buranello, while the foliage of the ground floor cornice is by Martino, brother of Fison[54]. Here it should be noted with Paoletti that the cable mouldings along the edges of the façade are akin to elements which can be found in the Duomo of Milan and therefore allow an attribution to Raverti[55]. However, one must also deduce from the documents that Venetians and Lombards were working closely together if one of these cable mouldings was entrusted to Antonio Buranello—an indication of how much one can trust documents which name the executants, not the conceivers, of these 'decorative' and not pre-eminent parts on which the Lombard and Venetian stonecutters were working side by side in accordance with drawings provided by their chiefs. Again, in December 1429, Giovanni Bon *conzò ij lidi de marmoro che ando a le cholone grandj de soto de la riva*[56] (prepared the marble capitals which were put on the great columns below, on the water side) which are in fact the ancient ones, belonging to the old house of the Zeno.

The magnificent six-light window, closely flanked by two single windows with balcony on the first floor is quite different. The names of the two stonecutters associated with Raverti, namely Gasparino Rosso of Milan and Giacomo of Como, are mentioned in connection with the tracery completed in 1426, while the 'flowers' (finials) were executed by the Bons.[57] One cannot doubt that the design was provided by Raverti himself, who produced a very personal interpretation of the motif inaugurated by the anonymous master of the Doge's Palace, in the famous loggia. But also the capitals, entirely new, are by a Lombard; Nicolò Romanello, a companion of Raverti, carved four of them in 1428, while the fifth was the work of Raverti himself[58].

It is worth transcribing two documents from Paoletti: *1428, 19 giugno maistro Nicholo dito romanelo me die far i lidi de la balchonada da basso che die far maistro Mattio; 1429, 17 settembre — si pagano a nome di m.o mattio di reverti ducati 20 a Maistro Nicholo romanelo per 4 lidi... andò in la... balchonada del primo soler.* (19 June 1428, master Nicolò alias Romanello must make the capitals for the lower balcony which is to be made by master Matteo; 17 September 1429—on behalf of master Matteo di Reverti twenty ducats are paid to master Nicolò for four capitals placed on the first floor balcony.)

The sense is very clear. As Paoletti observed, the last capital on the left 'carved by a different hand and resembling those of the courtyard' had already been executed by Raverti[59]. The other four are therefore by Romanello. Paoletti rightly sees in these capitals 'an example of a school other than the Venetian'. On our part we would add that Nicolò Romanello (given the frequency and importance of his interventions) must have really been the number two of the Lombard team.

On 4 April 1426 the carriage of the *straforo de la balchonada granda* is paid for. The traceries of the balconies (by which almost certainly are meant the windows provided with outjutting balconies at the sides of the multi–light window, which is always called *balchonada*) are also by the Milanese Gasparino Rosso and by Giacomo of Como, while the flowers hanging at the centre of the traceries of those balconies (a motif which will enjoy a certain fortune in Venice) are entrusted in 1426 to the two Bons.[60].

In 1429 the Venetian *m.o Pantalon Taiapietra* (Master Pantaleone, stonecutter) is paid for stairs and 'plates', two of which are used in the *pergolj de portego del primo soler*[61] (balconies of the first floor portico). The person in question is Pantaleone di Paolo whom we shall find working on the Doge's Palace, by the side of Bartolomeo Bon.

And it is again Nicolò Romanello, stonecutter, companion of Raverti, who from 1431 to 1434, writes Contarini, *ne tolse a far i mie tre pergoi de la mia chaza del mio soler da basso de piera viva dagandoli mi piere e malmorj: tutj tre die eser a modo de quelo de la chaza fo di ser Chostantin de priolij quelo e suso al chanton inverso sam Zacharia*[62] (undertook to make the three balconies of the first floor of my house, in new stone, I giving him stone and marble; all three to be like that of the house of ser Constantin de Priuli, the one on the corner toward S. Zacharia).

It was intended, as Paoletti correctly saw, to take as model one of the corner two–light windows of Palazzo Priuli at S. Severo. Unfortunately, neither the balconies of Palazzo Priuli, nor those being discussed at the Ca' d'Oro (the single windows of the first floor) exist any longer; and at the Ca' d'Oro they were replaced by others, not inspired by any established prototype. And, moreover, almost all the lions carved for the balconies have disappeared[63].

Passing now to the second floor, Paoletti's document seems, again, sufficiently clear; according to Contarini, Raverti in 1426 was to *compir ʃ cholone lavorade e fregade de piera de ruigno a longeza e grossezza de quele se in la mia balchonada grande del primo soler; Item... compir ʃ soche de piera da ruigno per far i lidi va suso le dite cholone; Item... compir due piane con i suo mudiony le qual dovea andar ai laj la sua balchonada lavorado per tuto chome sie quele dela chasa de ser Nicholo moresinij fo de miss. Gasparin del suo soler de erto*[64] (execute five columns, worked out and polished in Rovigno stone, of the length and thickness of those on my great balcony on the first floor; Item... make five blocks of Rovigno stone for the capitals of the said columns; Item... make two shelves with their brackets which must reach the sides of the balcony; all worked out like those of the house of ser Nicolò Morosini, son of Sig. Gasparino, on the upper floor).

Paoletti believes the last named building to be Palazzo Sagredo at S. Sofia. We shall see later to what extent this second six–light window should be considered Raverti's work.

The capitals of this second balcony were also made by Nicolò Romanello[65]. Later, in 1434, he was to be employed also for making the balconies *(pergolij)* of the windows of the second floor, with the instruction (and Raverti's guarantee) to make the capitals and bases *(i lidij e le sopede)* the same as those of the balustrade of the outside staircase[66].

It seems that in the meantime (7 July 1426) the masonry work of the house had been entrusted to the two Bons, because they oblige themselves to *chompir la chaza del dito miss. contarini* (finish the house of the said Master Contarini[67].) In the same year *m.o Bortolomio di chozi* of Milan and a *m.o Cristofaro* (perhaps Cristoforo Orsini) begin work on *le pinze de marmori* (the marble discs) of the façade[68]; from 1426 to 1427 a 'Zuan Piero' carves nine corbels with lion heads to support the floors of the balconies[69], and a certain Antonio Buranello of Murano, under the orders of the Bons, works on the mouldings of the arches of the windows with balconies[70]. Even in these rather vague indications, and even if all the lions carved for the balconies have disappeared[71], the third document confirms

that the Bons and their workshop are the makers of the 'balconies', i.e. the windows with balustrades[72].

Continuing the examination of the façade, we find that from 1427 to 1428 Cristoforo, assistant to Giovanni Bon, works on the *finestre del mezado*, i.e. the two smaller windows of the ground floor[73]. This part of the building was completely altered by Meduna but, at the last restoration, reinstated on the basis of an old engraving[74]. However, it would be hazardous to express a judgment, except to observe that an original solution was applied which unites within the dentilled border the dwarf window with the underlying framing. Four lion heads of these windows were by Romanello[75].

As we shall see, the Lombards continued for some years to work on the Ca' d'Oro. From 1427 onwards, the documents give, however, more striking evidence of the contribution of the two Bons, father and son. On 9 April 1427, they are paid *per parte del pozal el qual mi Bortolamio i die far per soldi 20 al di* (for part of the well-curb which Bartolomeo must make for twenty soldi a day); this sculpture was therefore unfinished and, indeed, on 9 November 1427, there is a mention of *Rosso (fante che fo del Zane bom) che feze le soaze del pozal* (Rosso, servant of Zane bom, who made the cornices of the well–curb) which is valued in order to pay the balance due[76]). We are considering the famous well–curb which we have already mentioned. A year after Matteo Raverti and his assistants had finished the multi–light window and the second floor balconies, on 30 June 1429, Giovanni Bon is paid for *il bordonal* (the architrave) *de piera viva che va (soto la loza) a la porta di la riva* (of new stone to be placed under the loggia at the water–gate), namely, above the four–light window opened in the part which separates the portico over the canal from the inner one; a document which would have great weight if it fixed for these years the physiognomy of the two Venetians' art[77]. On 3 December 1429 *Maistro Zane Bom taiapiera* (Master Zane Bom stonecutter) has not yet finished *el straforo da soto al bordonal di piera viva de la loza* (the tracery under the new stone architrave of the loggia); it will be finally in place in February 1431[78]. Many and varied, even if not always clear, are the interventions of Giovanni Bon in 1429 and 1430. In 1429 Giovanni makes the *gorne intaiade* (carved gutters), with large rectangular tips, on the calle della Ca' d'Oro side[79]. In addition, he executes the cornices on the corners of the first floor *(soler da basso)*, the red 'slabs' *(piane)* of the upper floor *(soler de sora)*, the two windows of the *soler de soto* (ground floor, already discussed), the capitals over the corners *(chantoni)*, namely those crowning the two cable ornaments along the edges of the façade and also the corner towards the courtyard so that its 'table which binds the old cornice' *(tola che liga la chornixe vechia)* becomes more outjutting, starts work on that same old cornice and *sel besognasse chonzar alguna chossa de la dita... hover che el ge manchasse... de conzar e compir*[80] (if anything of it needs restoring... or is missing... to restore and make).

This last commission deserves closer examination. We are dealing with the great corner capitals, with thick leaves, the abacus of which is not in line with the 'old cornice' *(la chornixe vechia)* that is, a cornice of simple profile, dentilled and with a row of rosettes which runs immediately under the trefoiled arcading of the crowning and which is called old because it is one of the elements of the old house of the Zeno (of the end of the thirteenth or the beginning of the fourteenth century, re–utilized by the builders)[81]. It is, indeed, re–instated, restored and, where necessary, completed.

Other works demanded of Giovanni Bon are, in the contract of 1430, the arcading of the crowning, for which Paoletti transmits the very detailed instructions, followed very precisely 'as in the drawing' *(chome sé el disegno)* made, evidently, by Bon himself[82]. 'On the said corners' *(suxo i diti chantoni)*, writes Contarini again, and that means the horizontal terminal cornice with cable moulding—'I want a lion seated with my arms in its paws, as large as

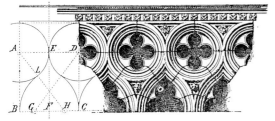

Quadrato di base $ABCD$; $AE = HF = AL = \dfrac{BC}{2} = 2\,BG = 2\,HC$; $BH = HL$.

could go into those arches' *(voio uno lion sentado chon la mia arma in le zafe tanto grando quanto el pora vegnir in li diti archeti)*[83]. Of these lions, pointed out Paoletti, there remains one; the other is a copy. In May 1431 steps are taken to complete the marble revetment for the two *piani nobili*, and this is entrusted to Gasparino Rosso of Milan and two Venetians, Antonio di Martino and Giovanni Benzon, who put in hand also the marbles of the large balcony towards the courtyard[84]. Finally, there is the contract of 15 September 1431 with Giovanni of France, a painter whose presence in Venice for at least twenty-six years is attested by the documents produced by Paoletti, to paint in gold, ultramarine blue and red the more outstandingly decorative parts of the façade; all those in Siena marble (in red), the paterae, the corbels between the arches of the water-side portico, the cornices and even the thirteenth-century decorations; and, finally, in gold, in ultramarine, in black—the whole of the complex crowning. The work was completed in 1434[85].

There is nothing else of importance except the mention of two chimneys ordered from Pietro di Nicolò, also known as il Pela, but not executed because of the artist's death[86], and Nicolò Romanello's activity which continues until 1440[87], which is the year in which the Ca' d'Oro—as far as the architecture is involved—may be considered completed[88].

It is not possible to make a really profound aesthetic evaluation of the Ca' d'Oro without an elementary distinction between the hands which have worked on it. Such a distinction, which will finally bring us onto a critical plane, is made possible not only by an attentive reading of the documents published by Paoletti, but also by a better knowledge of Venetian secular Gothic, of which this is the best known and most conspicuous example.

The documents published by Cecchetti and Paoletti do not clarify the genesis of the whole structure but do define some essential points and, above, all, and definitively, Raverti's (and, generally, the Lombards') authorship of the first floor six-light window, and Giovanni Bon's authorship of the four-light window on the ground floor (between the water-side portico and the internal one), of the crowning and, it seems, of the single windows with balconies. All the other testimonies are made uncertain by two considerations, namely that the works mentioned in Contarini's papers have been demolished and remade (like the external staircase and the great portal) and, also, that in other parts of the building the collaboration between Venetians and Lombards took place in a manner which prevents us from seeing clearly to whom their conception is initially due.

The house structure in Ca' d'Oro, the courtyard, the staircase and all the rest fit easily into schemes, into modes of expression, into solutions which, *mutatis mutandis*, are also repeated elsewhere in Venetian building practice, and are, on the whole, part of a tradition. One should consider the interest, documented by his very numerous instructions, of Marino Contarini, to whom, even if only hypothetically, should be credited decisions and interventions which could only with difficulty have come from one of the two groups led by Raverti or Giovanni Bon. It should not be forgotten that the old palace of the Zeno, which stood on the site on which was built the *Domus Aurea*, had been sold in 1412 by the Zeno to Contarini who in 1406, at the age of 20, had married Soramador Zeno, who died in 1417. Soramador did not see the new palace, begun in 1424, in which Marino Contarini wished to preserve some souvenirs of the certainly luxurious structure of the Zeno, demolished to make room for a building of unusual richness. In 1437, when work was still going on at the Ca' d'Oro, Contarini married Lucia Corner; he died in 1441.

The portico on the water side is certainly a recollection of that of Palazzo Zeno, since it is quite improbable that the master masons invited to erect the *Domus Aurea* would have conceived such an archaic and conservative solution. Equally, it is only the new owner who could have decided to re-use the thirteenth-century ornaments of various sizes, in particular the one on the right wing, in line with the coat of arms, which must have been placed vertically also in the older palace. This is a unique example among all those known to us. We do not know how harmoniously it fitted with the previous vanished architecture[89]. We can, therefore, hazard the guess that the will of the client made itself felt even where the presence of the artists working for him was well attested. That Marino Contarini may have been the architect of his own palace has already been asserted by Molmenti, when he says that this Procurator of St. Mark's was 'very expert in design', and a 'skilful builder' and affirms 'that he conceived and erected his graceful house'[90]. Boschieri[91] also suggests that it was perhaps Contarini who conceived it. The source of this information, given with such confidence, remains uncertain. The fact remains, though, that an open–minded examination of the building, in the framework of Venetian Gothic architecture, does not put these two historians in the wrong. The façade of the Ca' d'Oro is much too different (except in its general arrangement) from other Venetian palaces of the fourteenth and fifteenth centuries to allow us to believe that the artists involved could have wanted on their own initiative to diverge in such striking, indeed such capricious ways.

The fact remains that in the six–light window of the first floor and the four–light window of the ground floor portico, Matteo Raverti and Giovanni Bon gave their own personal interpretation of the loggia conceived in the fourteenth century by the great architect of the Doge's Palace. The six–light window dates from 1426 and the four–light from 1429. It should not be forgotten that new work was in progress at the Doge's Palace, and that two years before, it had been decided to continue towards the Basilica the same façade already in existence on the quay. Meanwhile Raverti introduces a novelty of his own. While, as we saw, the Doge's Palace loggia is firmly closed by a simple and vigorous horizontal cornice above the neat and firm circles enclosing the quatrefoiled oculi, at the Ca' d'Oro Raverti introduces a whimsical variation by placing, above the quatrefoils, in line with the vertices of the arches, some half–quatrefoils[92]. The powerful balanced architectural effect of the Doge's Palace is annulled by this fanciful play, not contained by a solid frame, and aiming only at a stranger chiaroscuro effect on the surface which the Lombard artist further stimulates by means of dense mouldings, tending to avoid any firm coagulation of the mass, which dissolves in twistings which lead astray the eye, where the light shatters and all structural consistency disappears.

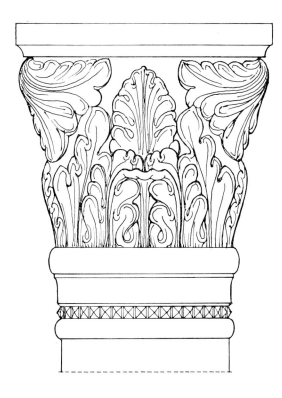

It may be appropriate here to remember that in the tomb of Alessandro Borromeo (the record of which is transmitted by Grevembroch) dated to 1430, Matteo Raverti repeats, precisely in the cornice, a play of quatrefoils alternating with half–quatrefoils which directly recalls the six–light window of the Ca' d'Oro. The capitals, executed by Nicolò Romanello (but perhaps designed by Matteo), help in this effect by offering a very lively original interpretation of the decoration, with thick leaves spiralling round the bell somewhat tumultuously, breaking the symmetrical arrangements still valid in Venice at the beginning of the fifteenth century.

Even the balustrade between the columns does not have the simple and balanced structure of the one in the Doge's Palace, but is marked by a more conspicuous decorative spirit.

Giovanni Bon's four–light window is also the work of an artist who has the motif of the Doge's Palace in mind, but his language is here quite other than that of Raverti. Two quatrefoils instead of one are placed on the extrados of the inflected arches but, in the space underneath, in line with the column, there is a piercing in the shape of a cross with its arms consisting of inflected arches—a motif inspired by the large fourteenth–century windows of the Doge's Palace, which are recalled also by the slender, spiral double columns of Campionese memory. The magnificent work appears timid, even irregular in its execution, of rather delicate and uncertain gracefulness.

Now the tracery of the six–light window on the upper floor of the façade recalls, in reality, although earlier by three years, much more this work of Bon's than the six–light window underneath made by Raverti (whose participation in the making of the columns and capitals cannot be put in doubt either through the documents or by a direct comparison). The upper six–light window repeats the motif of the half–quatrefoils cut from the cornice.

It must be admitted that the image of Matteo Raverti as a sculptor is due far more to happy intuitions than to concrete references: and, particularly for Venice, we lack a capital work like the Borromeo tomb in S. Elena, which is of 1422 when the Lombard was already in touch with Marino Contarini. For the architecture we lack all valid means of comparison and it seems therefore hazardous to accept the Ca' d'Oro as an architectural work of Raverti's, aside from the fact that some parts are certainly due to Giovanni and Bartolomeo Bon and that there is some well–founded suspicion that Contarini's interference was greater than is thought. The only architectural work which can be attributed with certainty to Raverti in Venice is therefore the six–light window on the first floor of Ca' d'Oro, which being, as we saw, profoundly different from all Venetian works of the kind, is recognized as an essentially Lombard product, precisely of Raverti, head of the team working at Ca' d'Oro.

The chief of the Venetian stonecutters working at Ca' d'Oro requires, however, a different discourse. Born perhaps a little before 1360[93] and living until 1443, Giovanni Bon headed a very active enterprise. His personality, however, as Planiscig pointed out, 'disappears completely in the activity of the workshop'[94]; and this will be the case from time to time also for Bartolomeo. If, however, it is possible to extract from the whole set of works produced in Bartolomeo's workshop a certain number of sculptures sufficiently connected and coherent to construct the *facies* of a well–defined personality, this does not apply to Giovanni Bon. In the Ca' d'Oro itself, two sure testimonies of his work, the four–light window of the ground floor portico and the crowning of the building, demonstrate this point. The beauty of the battlements (roof parapet), dissolving the chromatic restlessness of the façade, seems to have nothing in common with that four–light window carved with an at times quite clumsy timidity, and someone[95], certainly with exaggeration, has even spoken of the 'dull embroidery of the second loggia'.

As we saw, an important novelty are the single windows of the *piano nobile*, in which the inflected arch encloses traceries recalling those introduced in the fourteenth century by the Campionese in the great windows of the Doge's Palace, to which is added the peculiarity of the large flower suspended in the centre. It appears from documents that Bon's workshop had a part in them. The motif was to enjoy a certain fortune in Venice in the fifteenth century, but more in sacred than in lay architecture. In the latter, the most striking example is to be seen in the central windows of the two Giustiniani palaces, next to Ca' Foscari.

The motif of the pendant capital is found in the Scuola Vecchia della Misericordia, dated between 1441 and 1451[96] (Bartolomeo Bon was working here as a sculptor). The great single–light windows which light the building are based on the principle of the pendant double arch surmounted, as in the Ca' d'Oro, either by a complex tracery or by quatrefoil oculi. The variety noticeable in the more nervous modulation of the framework at the Misericordia may be attributed to the intervention of many hands within the ambit of a busy building site. The motif is not very widespread. We mention here only the two–light window of the chapel of S. Girolamo in the Duomo of Traù, built in 1458 by M. Gruato and N. Racic. Gruato, belonging to a well–known family of Venetian stonecutters, certainly had contacts with the workshops of the Bons at a time when they dominated all the main undertakings in Venice, around the middle of the fifteenth century.

Another decorative element by which the Ca' d'Oro stands out among the other Venetian

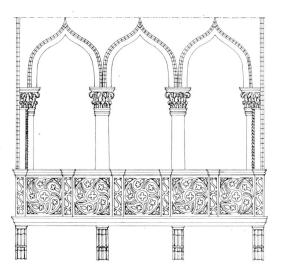

*Plan of Palazzo Soranzo Van Axel at Miracoli*
*(from Maretto)*

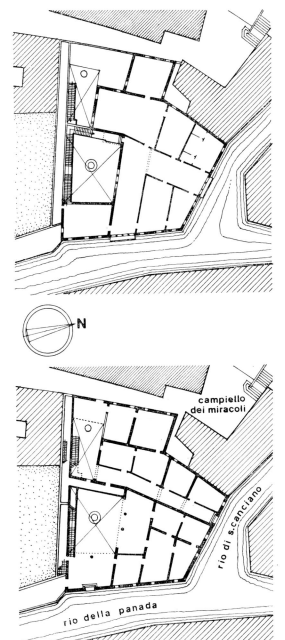

buildings is the double cable (spiral) ornament which runs along the two edges of the façade without, however, connecting with the crowning. The whole façade indeed, if one looks carefully, is of a structural incoherence without its like even in those Venetian Gothic buildings where the search for colour effects prevails over architectural requirements, and this is not due to the intervention of different teams of workers but to an extraneous factor which must be looked for in Contarini's interference.

To it are certainly due other incongruities as, for instance, the centre line which passes through the last arch on the right of the portico and through the middle of the two windows above, but does not coincide with the centre line of the cresting, marked by the three higher central pinnacles, which, in turn, are themselves not exactly in the centre of the rich cornice.

We have then, contrasting with the left wholly traceried side, the right side, with too large intervals between the windows, intervals in which are planted smaller, square windows. We should also note the misalignment, strange in Venice at this time, of the second floor row of windows, with the over-high framing of the single windows and, in addition, the fascia with the coat of arms and the vertical decorations (re-used) which accompany it.

The placing of this fascia is, evidently, dictated more by considerations of practical convenience, or of prestige, than by aesthetic motives or even the desire for a colour effect. The Ca' d'Oro façade is, in the end, the result of very diverse, even conflicting, components, not of a definite aesthetic intention or a calculated distribution of colour and chiaroscuro. If any part of it is capable of giving some balance to such a restless surface, we must certainly look for it in the great cornice (it has no equal in Venice) which forms a single body with the high and fanciful roof parapet, the only element elaborated with a certain continuity from one corner to the other of the façade beneath, which it undoubtedly dominates and conditions.

One must refer this roof parapet to the Doge's Palace. Apart from the crestings, still partly in existence, on the walls closing the courtyards (*corti*), there must have been in Venice other crestings on top of buildings, as would seem to be demonstrated by a small palace formerly in campo S. Polo (with a six-light window) visible in an engraving by Visentini[97]. Some can also be seen in Jacopo de Barbari's landscape.

The Venetian miracle is at work on the Ca' d'Oro. The changeable atmosphere, varying at every moment, and the unstable reverberations of the water, render acceptable and even precious these traceried and ornamented marble surfaces, even if not set up 'according to the doctrine of ancient Vitruvius, from whose rules the best architects are not allowed to depart' (Sansovino)[98].

A few more words about the façade on the courtyard. Its five-light window is attributed by Paoletti to Raverti, but, in truth, the only concrete mention of this most beautiful part of the building in the documents is the one which speaks of the two Venetians, Antonio di Martino and Giovanni Benzon, who were preparing the marbles for the *balchonada* (the long balcony).

Now this beautiful five-light window (with an included pilaster, columns with thick shafts and the capitals not yet in floriated Gothic style) has nothing whatever to do with Raverti and is in every detail quite Venetian—of the years around 1425. Equally Venetian is the four-light window of the second floor, where also a three-light window flanks and, in an archaic manner, connects with a window which is a little higher.

The collaboration—or competition—between the Venetian and Lombard masons and stonecutters in Venice (and on the mainland) is an area of study which we have not tackled because of the lack of fundamental stylistic or documentary data. And we also noted, when speaking of the Ca' d'Oro, the complexity of such an undertaking.

That all was not always sweetness and light between Venetians and Lombards can be guessed from relatively late documents, brought to my knowledge by my pupil, Luisa

Cogliati Arano. A document of 12 October 1486 and one of 25 October 1491, in which the apprehension of the Venetians faced with an invasion of 'foreigners' is evident, and the 'Statute of the Art (Guild) of Stone-workers' in Venice reflect the situation.

Only a careful study of individual monuments, together with the discovery of new documentary evidence could, however, throw light on this complex question[99].

That the work of the Bons and their workshop was in accord with the whole of Venetian Gothic architecture is proved by a palace which can be attributed to Giovanni Bon, namely the house of the Barbaro at S. Vidal.

A document revealing this authorship has been made known some time ago by Paoletti[100]. Marino Contarini, in the summer of 1425, deducts certain amounts from the account of Giovanni Bon and his assistants: 'Master Zane Bon because he works at Ca' Barbaro... in all five ducats. Zane and Rosso his assistants who also work at Ca' Barbaro... in all ten ducats.'

Paoletti also tells of another undertaking of Giovanni Bon, who was working with his team on the building of Palazzo Baseggio (no longer in existence) at S. Marciliano[101]. We find engaged on this building with Giovanni and Bartolomeo Bon, from 1437 to 1447, the stone-masons already active at Ca' d'Oro, namely Pantaleone, Vito, Andrea di Antonio (of Milan?) and Antonio Foscolo. Planiscig is not without reason of the opinion that the Bons were perhaps engaged on many buildings in Venice in the first half of the fifteenth century[102].

This is also our opinion and it confirms the attribution to Giovanni Bon and his workshop of Palazzo Barbaro, which is very important because it has a firmly established date: 1425.

One observes from the façade that presumably also for Giovanni Bon the traditional module does not undergo changes such as would alter its customary layout. Archaic accents of a fourteenth-century derivation may be discerned in the higher dimensions of the second floor and in the presence, on that same floor, of inflected, non trefoiled arches on high columns and capitals with thick leaves (of note, the Renaissance water-gate).

Worthy of notice, in correspondence with the Ca' d'Oro, is the presence of half-quatrefoils on the lower four-light window. The flower finial on the vertices is in use everywhere[103].

It may be useful to consider buildings which show certain affinities to Ca' Barbaro—even without any claim to identify thereby the participation of Giovanni and Bartolomeo Bons' workshop. The reference will, at most, lead to their less uncertain attribution to the first half of the fifteenth century.

If it is possible to find such affinities, they are to be discerned in the rather high modulation of the column shafts, which gives a slender aspect to the beautiful multi-light windows. This modulation, together with capitals of an archaic character (with rosette and also with thick leaves), contributes to give a striking appearance to these façades. To realize this, it is enough to compare them with a work which is certainly of the eighth decade—Palazzo Soranzo-van Axel, and with related buildings (of which we shall speak later) and to note how this slenderness diminishes with time. The capital, in these works of the late fifteenth century, appears much better integrated with the multi-light windows (between the solid and the void), and in a closer, more harmonious interplay than, for instance, at Palazzo Zeno Pizzamano at ponte degli Scudi[104]. Here the great bulk of the floriated capital brusquely breaks the line running from the arches to the verticals of the long shafts (in comparison with the more fluid expression achieved in Palazzo Soranzo-van Axel), thus achieving a decidedly more archaic effect.

A building not out of keeping with this time and with this style is the Casa del Tintoretto at Cannaregio. It is fairly organic on the *piano nobile*, with the three-light window of the sixth order displaced to the left and enclosed in a frame (with capitals with thick leaves),

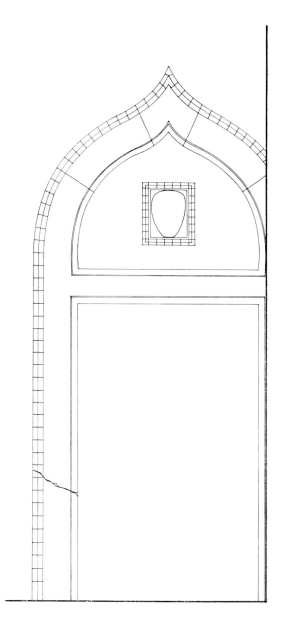

while the four windows of the upper floor are uncertainly disposed and unequal, were it not for the Renaissance–type openings in the mezzanine beneath. This was perhaps a current arrangement in other times[105].

If, in Palazzo Zeno Pizzamano, the resemblances to Ca' Barbaro allow one to assume only a proximity in time, excluding constructional affinities, these cannot be denied in the case of Palazzo Goldoni at ponte S. Tomà[106]. On the façade, the axis of the four–light window (closely flanked by two single windows) is displaced to the left, and the other wall is noticeably bent in order to follow the canal. The columns are of the elongated type and the capitals have rosettes. Internal elements, beside the façade, make one think that the building cannot be later than, perhaps, 1440.

A substantial development of the windows in a vertical direction is visible also in the façade of Palazzo da Mula at S. Vio[107], with capitals of a fourteenth–century type, and in Palazzo Michiel del Brusà[108] (similar also in the general arrangement to Ca' Barbaro). Analogous considerations can be advanced also in respect of the imposing Palazzo Zaguri at S. Maurizio[109], where the two façades—one in campo S. Maurizio, the other on fondamenta Corner—are conspicuous examples of that moment, around 1425, which precedes the establishment of the floriated Gothic. The façade on fondamenta Corner is particularly remarkable for the large four/six–light window divided by three columns with rosette capitals and two pilasters, the whole framed by a Byzantine dentil ornament, certainly coeval with the other façade with a three/five–light window repeating the same motifs between single windows of smaller dimensions. We find these again, shortened, on the second floor (where the five–light window has columns on high, square plinths). This is a complex which, owing to the number of 'archaic' indications, may be considered earlier than Ca' Barbaro.

This manner of ordering the façade of the Venetian Gothic palace will persist in time, parallel with other patterns effecting, as we saw, a more intimate fusion between capital, arch and column (we have mentioned Palazzo Soranzo–van Axel). These buildings go beyond the middle of the century, though remaining anchored to 'superseded' forms.

The beautiful Palazzo Sanudo at ponte Bernardo[110] appears more ancient than the adjoining Palazzo Bernardo (of which we shall speak later). Neither cable ornaments nor thick–leaved capitals appear here, but rosette capitals, plain dog–tooth ornaments and certain less flexible forms (the arches of the upper four–light window) which must not deceive us into believing the palace to be anterior to about 1450.

The small refined façade of Casa Amadi on rio del Fontego dei Tedeschi must be considered entirely apart. This is made up of two three–light windows, one above the other, enclosed by a Byzantine dentil ornament into a single large rectangle in line with the simple, pointed water-gate. There are two wings with the usual couples of single windows, two on each side, of which those on the second floor have been preserved. Over this floor the cornice, supported by brackets placed with a certain irregularity (as in the most ancient fourteenth–century examples of modest houses), hangs very close. Everywhere here there are archaic elements (traceried trefoils) but the capitals with thick, wavy leaves cannot take us before 1430-40, and the tall, slim columns mark a rhythm which we have seen in the cases immediately preceding. The big discs have with the remainder a relation similar to that seen in Palazzo Bernardo at S. Polo and in Palazzo Zorzi Liassidi, both erected around the middle of the fifteenth century. This is visibly the work of a stonemason–architect who places the sculptural–decorative values before those of pure architecture. All the mouldings (even those of the abaci) are richer than is usual. The strong plastic values which knit this central rectangle make one think of the work of a stonecutter[111].

Finally, one cannot fail to mention Palazzo Contarini Porta di Ferro at S. Giustina[112], of which is left only the entrance to the courtyard (namely a beautiful thirteenth–century gate) and the remains of a four–light window of type five on the first floor, the Gothic cornice and, in the courtyard, reached through a long entrance–lobby, the external staircase.

This last has already been pointed out by Paoletti as the example from which Matteo Raverti and his collaborators drew inspiration for the outside staircase of Ca' d'Oro. In the staircase of Ca' Contarini could be seen, during Paoletti's time (1920) as now, the same diminishing arches, with about the same shapes, then walled up, as the balustrade was walled up. The colonnettes have disappeared but the faces of the steps, adorned by a plant ornament, are intact. The staircase arches are of Istrian stone, the parapet of pink limestone, the hand–rail has plain dog–teeth and a cable ornament. A surviving very ornate small arch on the upper landing recalls those of Palazzo Priuli at S. Severo (of the fourteenth century). The sculptures here also suggest the end of the fourteenth or the very beginning of the fifteenth century.

To the middle of the fifteenth century, with clear signs of the floriated Gothic in the beautiful six–light window and the water–gate, may be assigned what is left of Palazzo Barbaro at S. Vio, on the Grand Canal, with the balcony serving only the four central openings[113].

*The completion of the west side of the Doge's Palace in the early fifteenth century. The Porta della Carta and the Foscari Colonnade.*

The Doge's Palace had already been finished when, on 27 September 1422, the Signoria, noting that *Palacium nostrum deputatum ad jus reddendum, ut evidenter apparet in dies minetur ruinam et tam ob necessitatem predictam quam pro providendo opportune quod dictum Palacium fabricetur et fiat in forma decora et convenienti, quod correspondeat solenissimo principio nostri Palacji novi*, orders the required appropriation of money to the Salt and Rialto officers and to the Procurators of St. Mark's (these last were later replaced by one or two nobles nominated by the Signoria)[114].

The *Palacium ad jus reddendum* was the ancient palace of the Ziani, the Palace of Justice, by the side of the Government Palace. The demolitions began, however, only on 27 March 1424[115]. The Sivos chronicle also is quite definite on the subject: 'The Palace on the piazza being very old and almost ruined, it was decided to make new all that part and to continue it like that of the Great Hall, and thus on Monday 27 March 1424 began the demolition of the said old Palace from the side which is towards the bakery, that is, of the Giustizia, which is in the oculi above the columns as far as the Church, and the great door was also made, as it is now, with the Hall which is called the Library[116].'

We do not know exactly who was the architect entrusted with the new work, and it is only relatively important to know this because from the appearance of this façade it appears that an absolute fidelity to the fourteenth–century prototype was certainly enjoined on the executors, and even though only within certain limits (and with certain exceptions), on the sculptors of the capitals.

However, Cadorin[117] already considered 'reasonable to attribute (to Pantaleone and Bartolomeo) the continuation of the façade of the Palace' and also the Sala dello Scrutinio, the rooms beneath, and the Foscari stairs and arch, asserting that most of the work had been done by 1463. This is an opinion shared by Selvatico[118], Ricci[119], Della Rovere[120], Planiscig[121], Fogolari[122], and Ongaro[123]. We also accept it.

Between 1438 and 1442, the Bons were working on Porta della Carta. It may be assumed that the new façade had been completed by the first–mentioned date. The corner capital towards the Porta della Carta, signed by Piero di Nicolò Lamberti and Giovanni di Martino of Fiesole, is reasonably dated to about 1424[124]. A year before, the two had signed and dated the Mocenigo monument in SS. Giovanni e Paolo, and the correspondences, at least for Lamberti, are such that the two works must be considered virtually contemporary. If this is not the most likely date for the completion of the new façade, it may be admitted with some probability that this and other capitals had been executed before the façade had reached that point. The façade and the parts immediately behind it must have been completed by 1438, because in the contract for the erection of the Porta della Carta, concluded in that year, it is said that it should go, in width, from the 'church of the Lord St. Mark to the Palace'[125] *(giexia di Missier Sam Marcho per fino al palazzo)*.

On 13 May 1442 the palace was already built, if we are to believe a passage of the 'Zancaruola' chronicle affirming that on that day Francesco Sforza was offered hospitality in the 'new' palace[126].

Zanotto believes that in 1452 work was still in progress on the new façade, because the square was being cleared of the stones intended for the building in preparation for the arrival of Frederick III[127]. But work continued until 1463 at least.

Little remains to be said on the architectural structure of the palace, which was continued without change up to the Porta della Carta in a strangely conservative spirit. Fires destroyed the great central window, which was almost entirely remade at the time of Andrea Gritti (about 1536). As Trincanato rightly points out, the only fifteenth-century element (useless for our purposes) left in these parts is the pointed arch with its capitals. The great window must have more or less reproduced the one on the quayside.

In the loggia were reproduced the two red columns which had existed in the palace of the Ziani[128]. The enlargement of the building certainly changed the peculiar aesthetic effects of the fourteenth-century structure, even if the plastico-spatial element, which determines the aspect of the palace, had already been settled by the fourteenth-century architect when he built the corner on the Piazzetta for the whole width of the Council Hall. The new façade took in these six arches of the portico, the part of the loggia and the corresponding part of the great wall above and continued northward, repeating the distributive scheme typical of the southern façade.

The effect, thus duplicated, of the two façades meeting at an angle is among the most charming in the history of architecture. In the highly mobile light of Venice, the two façades reflect the constantly changing effects of light and deep shadow, and, even more, of colour. The dream of the fourteenth-century architect is thus unexpectedly amplified. The two prospects merge in a single vision and a new, magnificent back-drop towards the Piazzetta is created, which with the traceried 'wall' made by the two columns of Marco and Todaro has only to await the brilliant solution imagined with the Library façade by Jacopo Sansovino, in order to bring to life a new space effect determined by a practically unlimited number of lines.

Strange to say, the Tuscan architect, much more than the Gothic builder of the Doge's Palace, renounces precisely that which in his own land, or in Rome, would have been absolutely obligatory, namely a symmetrical axis visibly marked by a body and by a different central opening.

Nor did a different criterion inspire the two long sides of the adjacent larger square, the old Procuratie of Coducci and the new, continued by Scamozzi on the pattern of the Library and heightened by one floor. Thus the portico and loggia of the Gothic palace, bent in a right angle and offering to the eye long perspectives in depth, are accompanied, on the other side of the Piazzetta, by a similar motif. And as the first guides the eye from the open surroundings of the quay, from the view of the basin (where, even in ancient times, the architectural elements rose from among the dominating waters but were certainly not overwhelmed by the waters or the sky) towards well-defined architectural surroundings, thus also the ground floor colonnade of the Library brings it without sharp change into the great space of the square, enclosing the visitor in an unchanged continuity of spatial forms of virtually unending rhythm, not tied to any predetermined measure or balance, to any catalytic centre or to any obligatory terminating point.

As in the fourteenth-century section, the plastic decoration (capitals and major sculptures) completes and integrates the architectural substance. Thirteen large capitals crown the columns of the ground floor portico, and double that number those of the loggia. The first of the ground floor capitals at the corner by the Porta della Carta is justly famous, and is the work of two 'Florentine associates', that is, of Piero di Nicolò Lamberti (also called Pela) and, less certainly, of Giovanni di Martino of Fiesole, who in 1423 sign and date the monument to Tommaso Mocenigo in SS. Giovanni e Paolo. Like all the other capitals on this side, beginning with the seventh column, the one signed by the two Tuscans repeats in the profiles of the abacus and in the vast vegetation which covers the bell the fourteenth-century elements of the columns on the quay.

Venturi had attributed to the two Tuscans all of the nine capitals of the portico, starting from the Porta della Carta[129], and later had extended this attribution up to the capital under the roundel with the *Justice*[130]. Fiocco also sees the two Tuscan workmates employed, together with the Lombards, on the capitals of the new façade[131].

The last-named scholar[132], however, and with him Planiscig[133], justly and more exactly see in the capital with the Virtues (the eighth from the Porta della Carta) the work of Piero di Nicolò. This would appear indeed to be disclosed by the characteristics peculiar to this Florentine, namely a somewhat thick-set and sturdy approach. This was a craftsman who, without doubt, brought to Venice in 1416 the voice of the Renaissance, and one whose importance is to be found not so much in his art but in the new Word of which he made himself the preacher. The work of Piero di Nicolò has been unduly extended by the critics, but what can be attributed with certainty to him—the Mocenigo tomb (1423), the Fulgosio monument in the Santo at Padova (1429) (with a collaborator), the two capitals of the Doge's Palace (about 1424—with the reservations on his collaborator on the Justice capital who, much too carelessly, has been identified as Giovanni di Martino), the Annunciation in Orsanmichele in Florence, the upper central arch in St. Mark's in Venice[134]—reveal a spirit endowed with a certain plastic liveliness but which on occasion is a little clipped, undecided and stiff in form—and therefore very far from that extraordinary master who sculpted, in Venice, the *Judgment of Solomon* which is placed, in the Doge's Palace, right above the Justice capital. This was a powerful sculptor to whose hand are rightly attributed also the beautiful statues of the Evangelists, of the Virgin and of Gabriel in the aediculae crowning the western façade of St. Mark's. If, however, Planiscig recognized the hand of Piero di Nicolò in four of the eight figures appearing in the Justice capital, he nevertheless did not feel bound by the inscription — DUO SOTII FLORENTI — (two Florentine workmates)—to consider the other four little scenes the work of Giovanni di Martino of Fiesole (who appears in the Mocenigo monument with his own, distinct features) and attributed them to a follower of Andrea of Pontedera[135].

The hand of Piero di Nicolò is, however, clearly visible in the *Virtues* capital (the eighth from Porta della Carta). As for the other capitals up to the thirteenth (from Porta della Carta), it should be pointed out that they are almost all copies of fourteenth-century examples on the quayside. There must have been, in this respect, very precise instructions from the Signoria (or the officials in charge of the new building) even if Piero di Nicolò, and some other sculptors, were exceptionally allowed to insert compositions of their own invention in the predetermined scheme.

In fact, capital no. 2 (*Childhood*) is a copy of no. 4 counting from Ponte della Paglia;

no. 3 (*Birds*) is a copy of no. 11 (as above); no. 4 (*Vices and Virtues*) is a copy of no. 12 (as above); no. 6 (*Music*) is a copy of no. 8 (as above); no. 7 (*The Sins*) is a copy of no. 10 (as above); no. 9 (*Virtues and Vices*) is a copy of no. 7; no. 10 (*Fruits*) is certainly derived from a fourteenth–century prototype; no. 5 (*Thinkers*) and no. 11 (*Ladies and Knights*) are not derived from any known prototype, but it seems difficult to see in them independent examples of early fifteenth–century sculpture; and this is even more noticeable in no. 12 (*The Months*) and no. 13 (*The Family*) which, though an integral part of the new façade, seem to be works antedating its beginning.

We know also of a certain Andrea of Milan who was working on the capitals of the Doge's Palace in 1426, but nothing very precise[136].

The capitals of the loggia, on the new façade, when considered with some attention and compared to those on the façade towards the quay, show on the whole a more noticeable diversity. The forms, unquestionably more rigid, archaic and symmetrical, which characterize the fourteenth–century capitals, make way here for a freer, more agitated treatment of the swollen foliage, of which the capital nearest to the Porta della Carta, very similar to certain Venetian well–curbs of the same time, is a very beautiful example. And the same turgid plastic exuberance marks a good number of those that follow—all works of the same team, which includes on the four sides, above among the foliage, half figurines of considerable worth which it would be useful to examine in connection with the Lamberti circle. There follow then, up to the *Justice*, other capitals of the same type but less exuberant and also less harmonious.

Sculpture, indeed two sculptures, could not fail to be here again an integral part of this façade, at the corner towards the Basilica: below, where the arcades of the portico meet in a right angle, the group with the *Judgment of Solomon*; above, between the quatrefoils of the loggia, the Archangel Gabriel. On the famous group of the *Judgment of Solomon*, much has been said.

It is not possible to put a definite date to this sculpture, but it must certainly be placed between 1424, the year in which the new façade was begun, and 1438, the year of the contract for the Porta della Carta. Considering, not without good grounds, thàt sculptures of this kind, executed separately and for which a place was reserved perhaps only after many years, are not always necessarily tied to the date of the buildings, they could be placed between about 1425 and 1430, when concrete signs of the Tuscan Renaissance are already present in Venice.

Venturi attributed it in 1908 to Nanni di Bartolo[137] who, as we know, was living in 1432–5 in Venice, from where he sent sculptures for the portal of S. Niccolò at Tolentino. But the restless Tuscan, whose vision was troubled by contacts with Jacopo della Quercia and with Donatello, does not seem to us, neither at Tolentino, nor in the *Abdia* of the Florentine campanile (a statue now in the Museo dell'Opera del Duomo), nor in the Brenzoni monument in Verona, to have anything in common with the calm grandeur of the *Judgment of Solomon*. This is a complex sculpture. If from one point of view it integrates the architecture in that it is less subordinated to it than the other sculptures towards the quayside, none the less it emerges with a powerful plasticity, generating a new space, multiplied volumes and deep shadows. After Venturi, Fiocco[138] saw in it the work of Piero di Nicolò Lamberti, associating it with the statues under the tabernacles of the main façade of St. Mark's. If this association is correct and illuminates the figure of a powerful artist with his own peculiarities (and the Marcian aediculae completed around 1415 justify the appearance, after some years, of the *Judgment of Solomon*), the true Piero di Nicolò appears entirely different. In the works which are unquestionably his (the Legislators' capital, the Mocenigo tomb, the Fulgosio tomb—and always in collaboration with a different 'associate') Piero di Nicolò reveals a plastic restlessness akin to that of Rosso (which must certainly have struck the Venetians) but is very far from the serene grandeur of this group, bound as it is to a lively but somewhat unequal realism. And it must also be noted that too many other attributions have helped to deform the fairly clear vision of Piero's art (the lunette of the Corner chapel in the Frari, the statues of the Porta della Carta, etc.). In disagreement with Fiocco, Planiscig resolutely denied the famous group to Piero di Nicolò[139] and attributed it to Bartolomeo Bon, an artist whom Planiscig had certainly the merit of putting in a better light than did those who were extolling Lamberti at the expense of the Venetian, but who, even in his late Gothic nobility (when he works alone, without the intervention of his team) never seems to reach this height.

The scene is caught at the moment when the soldier is about to strike the child the fatal blow. His attitude is firm, crystallized as it were, almost an abstraction, without troubled movements, without signs of ferocity. On the left Solomon is seated, listless, with a magnificent head, and looks in front of him as if absorbed and indifferent to the scene. On the right the mother displays a forward movement of the body, almost imploring, but without passion, in her form contained and defined by the magnificent folds of the mantle; behind stands the other mother, immobile, she too enclosed in solemn draperies. The three figures appear close together, joined in the same movement of mass and of spirit, which leads them together towards the naked child, suspended in mid-air, while Solomon stands isolated, separated by pools of shadows and only puts his left hand on the soldier's arm, arresting his action.

A complex of restrained, controlled movements, in a highly dramatic action which appears undramatized thereby, sublimated in a rarefied atmosphere, where the eloquence of the plastic values is raised to the utmost in the quiet solemn apparition, where one would find it hard to admit, in reality, a cry or a voice.

Neither Nanni di Bartolo, nor Pietro Lamberti, nor Bartolomeo Bon have ever achieved so much strength and such pregnancy. Who may have been the masterly author of this work, it is difficult to say. The same must be said of the very beautiful statues under the aediculae of the main façade of St. Mark's and of the Baptism group on the Beato Pacifico monument in the Frari[140]. Mariacher[141] has ascribed the beautiful Archangel Gabriel to Antonio Bregno. We shall speak of this again in connection with the Porta della Carta.

At a meeting held on 8 July 1966 in the gallery of the Venice Academy, Cesare Gnudi expounded his new critical interpretation of the *Judgment of Solomon* and of the sculptures more or less connected with it. Linking in his turn the group of the *Judgment* with the *Virgin* and the *Angel* in the aediculae on the main façade of St. Mark's (and we agree that they are of the same hand), he considers that the statues on the façade have been made by Jacopo della Quercia between 1405 and 1408 and the *Judgment* by the same Jacopo around 1412–13. To about 1420, and to the same artist, Gnudi assigns the four 'gargoyles' on the northern façade of the Basilica, towards S. Basso.

If this supposition was favourably received in Venice, other, non-Venetian scholars appear less well disposed towards it, least of all the Tuscans.

We have seen that the *Judgment* must have been created between 1424, when the new wing of the Doge's Palace was begun, and about 1438 when the Porta della Carta was put in hand, perhaps between 1425 and 1430. These dates, however, do not allow us to see Jacopo della Quercia working in Venice, and therefore lead Gnudi not only to propose a much earlier date for the *Judgment*, not far from that of the *Madonna* of Ferrara, but also to formulate a bold hypothesis. The *Judgment* group had been located on the third corner of the fourteenth-century palace, completing the two groups of the *Ancestors* and *Noah* and once the new side of the palace, towards the Piazzetta, was erected, had been transferred to the new corner, by the Porta della Carta.

In our view, one must not forget that until 1422 the old palace, erected by Ziani in the second half of the twelfth century, was still standing, and that this was truly and properly the Palace of Justice *ad jus reddendum*, detached from the fourteenth–century palace on the quay, seat of the Government, which was finished in the first decade of the fifteenth century. We do not know what the corner towards the Palace of Justice of the last–named building may have looked like until 1422. We only know and are convinced that owing to its content the *Judgment* group must have been meant for a Palace of Justice and must have been originally placed, if anywhere, on the palace of Ziani and not on that of the Government (which had been barely finished). Does it not seem more probable that once the demolition of the old palace of the Ziani had been decided, and the new wing had been extended with the intention of gathering in one single formal seat the political and judicial powers, it was found desirable to indicate on the Piazzetta wing, with a solemn sign, both the old and the new destination? In this case, however, the attribution to Jacopo della Quercia cannot be justified because neither his 'curriculum' nor the style allow it.

Hence Gnudi's hypothesis, which dates the *Judgment* to 1410–12 and sees in the famous group the expression of a humanism nourished by a naturalistic late Gothic spirit, widespread at the time in the most advanced European sculpture (Sluter). In the *Judgment* and in the six statues on the façade of St. Mark's (four of which he attributes to Nicolò di Piero) he sees the 'solemn dignity of the antique statuary clearly evoked, but expressed in a language still rich with Gothic desinences', announcing perhaps Nanni di Banco.

The *Judgment of Solomon* would therefore be situated at the beginning of that change of course which, through the statues of Fontegaia, leads to the dramatic sequence of the Bolognese cycle.

The *Judgment* of Venice certainly shows some relation with the art of Jacopo della Quercia, but is a work of such complexity that it could also be considered that of a great sculptor who (much more than the Sienese did) looks to the fascinating production, between 1380 and 1420, of the Salzburg sculpture, to the authors of the so–called *schöne Madonnen*. Indeed, the mantle folds of these madonnas are sometimes very much like those of the two mothers in the Venetian group (the Madonna of Altenmarkt, of the end of the fourteenth century). Nor should we, when considering the connections between Sienese sculpture and Venice, forget that the resumption, around 1420, of Venetian Gothic elements in his art leads Jacopo directly to the Trenta altar in S. Frediano of Lucca, where the crowning of the niches, with mixtilinear arches, are of clear lagunar derivation and entirely new in Tuscany in 1422.

It is also difficult to imagine the coexistence of the roundel with *Venice as Justice* which also clearly alludes to the Palace's destination *ad jus reddendum* and of the group with Solomon in such close neighbourhood, when the building on the quay had been completed (and the Palace of Justice erected by Ziani was still in existence). The roundel now fills one of the quatrefoils of the loggia, and precisely the one which, at first, was cut from the corner of the Government Palace towards the Basilica. While we must discard, because absurd, the hypothesis that the Solomon group had been intended for the corner towards the quay of the old Palace of Justice a few years before its demolition, we agree on the other hand with Gnudi in considering the *Angel* and the *Annunciation* of St. Mark's the work of the same master who made the *Judgment*—a link already made by Fiocco. The aediculae are to be placed between about 1385 and 1415. It would be rash, however, to consider them as exactly contemporaneous with the sculptures, which we believe not far from 1415 but which Gnudi places around 1405.

We agree, however, with Gnudi in seeing another hand in the *Evangelists* of the Marcian aediculae, which he attributed to Nicolò di Piero Lamberti, while seeing the hand of Jacopo della Quercia in the four gargoyles towards S. Basso (between 1419 and 1424).

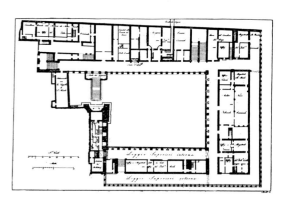

The work of a great master, the *Judgment*, which fits so happily in the corner of the new wing above the well-known capital of the *Justice* (which also clearly alludes to the original destination of the palace) remains for us a great mystery.

On 10 November 1438 Giovanni and Bartolomeo Bon undertake to make within eighteen months the great gate of the Palace, later called Porta della Carta. With them are the stone-cutters Filippo Correr, Andrea Zulian and Bertuccio di Jacobello, all evidently Venetian[142]. After forty months the work is still not finished and the time is extended until 1442. Giovanni, as a document of 17 April 1442 attests, was then still alive, but he dies in 1443[143]. The tops of the pillars, as well as the three angels supporting St. Mark's bust were yet to be made, but within two months 'the piercing' and 'the other figures'[144] were to be completed. The statue of Justice on the vertex was already in place in October 1441[145]. The Porta della Carta is rightly considered the work of Bartolomeo Bon, whose signature (*Opus Bartolomei*) can be read on the architrave[146]. The fact that the surviving documents do not speak of the four statues of Virtues in the lateral niches has been seen as confirmation of their stylistic lack of connection with the remainder of the monument and they have been rightly attributed to another hand.

The structure is well developed in height. The rectangular doorway, flanked by two pillars enriched by the four splendid aediculae and crowned by the high pinnacles, recalls similar portals in Venetian churches. The idea which transforms the wall above the gate is new, even if its individual components recall motifs already known in Venice. Above the great sculpture (now remade) with the Doge kneeling before St. Mark's lion, there is a remarkable window clearly inspired, in its proportions, by those of the neighbouring palace, but it is made quite different by the great tracery with quatrefoil oculi of vigorous profile (with a trefoil inserted in each foil).

These are from the fourth decade of the fifteenth century, but recall the English Gothic of a century before. The trefoils enclosed in the arches of the quatrefoil oculus are found in England already around 1300[147]. They are found towards the middle of the fourteenth century at Beverley, in the cathedral[148], with forms very similar to those later adopted in the Porta della Carta, also in respect of the unusual ogee arches which can also be seen at Ely[149].

The mixtilinear crowning, springing up to support the figure of *Justice*, is not a novelty in Venice. Of Islamic origin, it is found crowning pictures of the first half of the fourteenth-century. In Venice it appeared on the façade of the Church of the Cappuccine of S. Maria delle Grazie[150]. It was developed on a large scale by Jacobello and Pier Paolo dalle Masegne on the façade of the Mantova Duomo (1396–1401), now no longer in existence[151]. It appears again on the tomb of the Dogaressa Venier († 1411) at SS. Giovanni e Paolo, and the examples nearest to Porta della Carta are certainly those displayed by the polyptych carved in the Mascoli chapel (1430) and by the portal of S. Nicola at Tolentino, executed in 1432–5 by Nanni di Bartolo. Here, probably, this Florentine resident of Venice is also responsible for the architectural project so largely inspired, particularly in its uppermost part, by the lagunar spirit[152].

In the terminal crowning with little angels among large leaves, where Bartolomeo and his assistants emulated the crownings executed a quarter of a century earlier by the Tuscans and the Lombards on the three façades of St. Mark's, the effect is wholly and skilfully obtained by the alternation of the solid flesh of the lively little angels with the exuberant, indented and traceried crockets. There is a triumphal and almost resounding finale around the bust of the Evangelist which is truly unique in Venice. In the shield-carrying little angels *imbaroccati* (given a baroque aspect) at the base of the pinnacles Adolfo Venturi saw, not unreasonably, the hand of the young Giorgio da Sebenico, at the time *habitator venetiarum* and recalled on 22 June 1441 to Sebenico in Dalmatia to become overseer of works at the cathedral[153]. In the Porta della Carta (already praised by Cicognara, 'a model of lively grace' for Selvatico[154]), Bartolomeo's figure must be reappraised, particularly in consideration of a workshop which was popular and very active. His work must therefore be considered item by item, on the basis of the quality of the sculptures which may or may not be believed his. Born around 1409, at about twenty Bartolomeo was working on the Ca' d'Oro well–curb. If it is an exaggeration to put him, as did Venturi, by the side of Jacopo della Quercia[155] who was more than twenty years older—it is yet certain that there is in those *Virtues* carved on the well–curb a taut and austere strength attesting a vigorous personality, undoubtedly the most vigorous in the 'transitional' sculpture of Venice. The remarkable *Charity* of 1437 on the portal of the Scuola di San Marco is certainly his; the admirable lunette, however, with the Evangelist among the brotherhood members, has seemed above him (but the attribution to Piero di Nicolò has, justly, been dropped) and there has even been talk of a 'reworking' by the Lombards when the whole portal was restored by them. One must ask oneself, however, how it is possible to see in this exceptional bas–relief of such accomplished coherence (and in which, indeed, one sometimes feels the concentrated strength of Jacopo della Quercia) the intervention of Pietro Lombardo.

The group of the Doge kneeling before St. Mark's lion, destroyed in 1797[156], must be dated to about 1440.

In 1441 the beautiful *Justice*, Bartolomeo's authorship of which cannot be doubted[157], is already in place on Porta della Carta. Of those years, or thereabouts, is also the Madonna on the Frari portal.

These are the best achievements of Bartolomeo, whose somewhat massive Gothic charm, at the limits of the Renaissance, will not rise any higher after the years around 1440. After the success achieved at the Doge's Palace, Bartolomeo became increasingly absorbed in works of great architectural and plastic complexity. From 1437 to 1447, he worked on Palazzo Baseggio (no longer in existence)[158]; the Madonna of Udine is of 1448; the complex work at the Scuola della Misericordia is of 1451 and in 1461 Bartolomeo is asked by Francesco Sforza to prepare a project for a large palace on the Grand Canal[159].

To this must be added the many years of Bartolomeo's activity on the new wing of the Doge's Palace, to which undertaking he was suddenly recalled in 1463.

It seems clear then that the artist immediately after his thirtieth year was absorbed by his workshop, which rarely allowed him to express himself in this genuine vein. This is particularly so in the case of Porta della Carta (where the little angels have already a Renaissance character) to which other hands have contributed[160], and also in the lunette of the Carità, where the contribution of another artist is quite recognizable. While the *Madonna della Misericordia* in the Victoria and Albert Museum has been unduly underestimated in the past in order to extol the work of Piero di Nicolò, Sansovino had noted in this work 'the well–conceived clothes' and it reveals, in the group of brotherhood members, affinities with the lunette of the Scuola di San Marco such as to make us consider the possibility that Bartolomeo, in the years of his youth, had indeed in a happy moment created that masterpiece.

This discussion of the Porta della Carta cannot be concluded without mentioning the colonnade to which it gives access and with which it is closely connected. On 28 January 1438 Stefano Bon, a Cremonese, undertakes to build four of the six vaults (still in existence)[161].

This is an organism which proceeds in the spirit of the Porta della Carta, in which the elements defining the space (cornices, vaulting ribs, etc.) predominate to the point of depriving, on the aesthetic plane, the walls and the vaults of all bearing or limiting value, overwhelmed as they are by the decoration. This is particularly demonstrated by the rich cornice with putti heads which, in line with the capitals[162], is superimposed on them, adding an abundance of foliage and cables to the pilasters, the transversal arches and the ribs. These last, applied to the not very high vaults with pointed arches, attract the attention and break the monotony and solidity of the load–bearing elements, fragmenting their volumes and reducing their functional appearance. An entrance porch like this, though intended as a continuation of the ground floor portico of the Doge's Palace, is unique in Venice, where the entrance porches of even the most luxurious private palaces have a flat roof. For this reason, probably, Bartolomeo sent for a Lombard to build the vaults.

*Buildings with quatrefoiled traceries. Work at the Doge's Palace up to the arrival of Rizzo.*

The superb motif introduced by the Doge's Palace Loggia, created in the fourteenth century (and continued in the following century), became fashionable in Venice only in the first half of the fifteenth century. If we look at the dates, it cannot have appeared much before about 1440 (namely when the new wing of the palace was being finished); and it is anyway indubitable that its flourishing occurred around the middle of the century.

We are dealing with outstanding buildings, the most impressive ornaments of that wealthy city, erected everywhere in competition, but chiefly along the great waterway on which the most important buildings of previous epochs, and of course the Ca' d'Oro, have their façades, the Grand Canal. An important precedent for the use of the quatrefoil oculi may be seen on the *piano nobile* of Palazzo Sagredo (already mentioned), where they are placed in line with the openings of the four–light window, which may well date from the end of the fourteenth century.

We believe, however, that the introduction of the quatrefoil in the tracery of loggias and windows on the example of the Doge's Palace occurred in the fifteenth century.

The first still surviving building in which this stylistic principle was used is perhaps Palazzo Bernardo on the Grand Canal, already erected according to Paoletti in 1442. The imposing façade is dominated by the great six–light window of the second floor, in which the trefoiled arch (with the upper lobe somewhat slender) surprisingly resembles that of the Doge's Palace loggia; and we find here again the lion heads in the triangles between the arches, and the rosettes in the triangles between the quatrefoils, while the dwarf balustrade appears to be typical.

The single windows on the same floor have interesting traceries with interlacing arches, very similar to those of the single windows of the Ca' d'Oro which at the time had barely been completed. The small differences (the small arches are here cinquefoiled, and the inter-lacing arches are semicircular) do not preclude us from thinking that Bon's workshop may have participated here. The first floor is not aligned with the second (the six–light window is displaced towards the right). The edges of the façade, besides being decorated on the example of the Ca' d'Oro with spiral columns (one for each of the four floors), also have a vertical fascia of alternating quoins, which strongly and with strikingly picturesque effect enclose the vast area on the sides. The cornice is not particularly well developed. The base is marked by a torus element and the alignment of the string courses with the window ledges is not rigorous.

Even with this obvious irregularity, this great page of architecture is alive with those picturesque suggestions present in so many fourteenth–century buildings, in the unconstrain-ed and inspired grandeur which emanates from it, almost intolerant of any ordering[163]. It is, however, uncertain whether this façade was not erected over two distinct periods of time. It has been noted[164] that this palace represented a 'two–families unit' with two

254

*piani nobili*, two courtyards and two entrances, by land and water. The large courtyard, with the uncovered staircase climbing to the second floor, splendid well–curb and a porch supported by two columns with thick leaves, is one of the most beautiful and best preserved in Venice.

Of the Corner Contarini dei Cavalli palace at S. Benedetto on the Grand Canal, begun, according to a document, in 1445, there remains only the *piano nobile* (a six–light window flanked by a single one on each side)—but this is enough to suggest the idea of a new firmer rhythm, determined by the rectangle framing the great multi–light window, by the two single windows and by the intervals. In this sense, Palazzo Cavalli represents a great novelty which already in the last century struck the more attentive observers. The Gothic cornice certainly marks the height of the original palace.

Without doubt the architecture of this building has also been directly influenced by the Doge's Palace. In the one–light windows, the motif of the quatrefoil cut through by the frieze, already appearing in the Doge's Palace, assumes here an independent value[165].

But it is not only the example of firmness and of a clear structure imparted by the loggias of the Doge's Palace that contributes to this, until now unknown effect. The repercussions of a rhythm already established for some time in the mainland buildings, particularly in Tuscany, are evident here. There is an echo of the theory and practice of Alberti and Brunelleschi in the proportions, already displayed beyond the Appenines in buildings dominated by a symmetry and harmony of which, as we saw, there is no trace in the Domus Magna of Contarini.

The two Giustiniani palaces, begun, according to Tassini, immediately after 1451, are a unique example in Venice of a large wall, almost an immense backdrop, arranged on two great axes whereon are centred the two six–light windows, very much like those of Palazzo Cavalli. By the side of, and in line with the larger mass of Ca' Foscari, they are certainly calculated to impress the viewer who, coming from Rialto, reaches the 'turn of the Canal' and finds himself at a distance enabling him to take in the immense façade at a glance.

Two façades in one, but each so ordered as to give an appearance of unity to the whole vast area. If the centre line of the two façades passes through the water-gate and determines the arrangement of the ground, first and third floors, the second floor on the other hand, namely the *piano nobile* and the one most developed in height, carries the two six–light windows aligned on a different axis. They thus appear as if prolonged towards the centre, which is characterized by two single windows larger and richer than the others, with quatrefoiled tracery like that of Porta della Carta and small pendant arches like those in the single windows of Ca' d'Oro. The whole surface of the two palaces is thus uniformly animated, while the two multi–light windows thus brought near each other and the two richer single windows in the middle join, almost imperceptibly, in creating a certain unity. If the six–light windows still recall the Doge's Palace loggias, the two traceried single windows suggest the intervention of Bartolomeo Bon's workshop[166], which seems confirmed by the presence of heads in the capitals. The edges of the double structure, in Istrian stone quoins of alternate size, together with the long cornice and the base, provide a frame which will become typical of many of these buildings.

The largest and showiest of these buildings is Ca' Foscari. There are notices of a building on this area going back to Sansovino '... which building belonged once to the Giustinian family, one of whose members, Bernardo, a most eminent man, sold it in 1428 to the Senate, which gave it to the Marquess of Mantova, but having returned to their ownership and been sold by auction, Prince Foscari bought it and built it higher, so that it should no longer look like part of Giustiniani's house'[167]. These notices, misinterpreted[138], were thought valid until Tassini[169], who established the building's place in the history of Venetian art by confirming its date of inception in 1452 on the evidence of the genealogist Girolamo

Priuli, according to whom the old building passed in 1452 into the ownership of Doge *Corner two-light window in Palazzo Giovannelli*
Francesco Foscari 'who rebuilt it in a more magnificent manner' transferring it 'from the place where there is now the courtyard to the corner of the rio, over the Grand Canal, leading to San Pantalon where it is seen now, leaving behind the courtyard where the house was before'[170]. This massive building, placed in a position dominating a long stretch of the wonderful waterway, in line with the two Palazzi Giustiniani, was always given its due importance, even if not understood in the spirit which, in the middle of the fifteenth century, makes it one of the main reference points in the development of Venetian Gothic architecture. Ruskin[171] had already called it 'the noblest example in Venice of the fifteenth–century Gothic, founded on the Doge's Palace'; Mothes[172] had pointed out the play of the crossed inflected arches, seeing in this type of tracery the one most suitable to connect with the framing (but this observation is equally valid for Palazzo Cavalli and for the Doge's Palace, which is at the origin of this style). Kugler[173] calls it the last Gothic palace displaying a 'grand and excellent richness'. Paoletti[174] remarks on the similarity of its tracery to that of the Doge's Palace and Ca' d'Oro and praises its proportions.

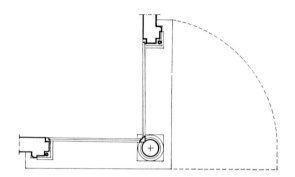

In its effects this great mass is quite unitary, the expression of a clear mind inspired by a canon of proportions reflecting certain preoccupations of the most inspired of the architectural styles current in the Peninsula. The façade is a rectangle very near a square, in which is placed the rectangle formed by the two eight–light windows, one above the other. The second floor uses the motifs already seen in Palazzo Cavalli (windows with two halved quatrefoils), while on the top floor reappears the even more complex motif already noticed in the multi–light windows of Ca' d'Oro, perhaps an invention of Raverti. The rich four–light window on this top floor is separated from the lower part by a soberly sculptured fascia, with the emblem in the middle and, on the sides, the four shield–supporting putti, certainly of antique inspiration. To the high base in Istrian stone, to the alternating quoins along the edges, to the particularly well developed cornice, is entrusted the task of firmly framing the great area, provided with its rhythm by the string courses (which also mark the height of the corner columns incorporated in the edges) and by the colour zones (white and brick-red) which share the surface. If we pay attention to the first floor balustrade, already Renaissance in style, and to the sculpture of the fascia with putti, we must conclude that the building work took a considerable time[175].

The style of these buildings, inspired by a balance of forms and a symmetry recalling the examples of the mainland, was to last at least until about 1470, as may be deduced from the presence of Renaissance elements. A typical instance, certainly of later date, is the Ambassador's Palace (Loredan) where the presence of the two statues of shield–carrying pages in niches cannot antecede the arrival of Pietro Lombardo in Venice. The wonderful façade, of more modest proportions than that of Ca' Foscari, is here also based on the principle of the straightforward central square ornamented with traceries nearly at the crossing of the diagonals. The framing of the façade is carried out in the same way as at Ca' Foscari. In addition, the base is marked here by a torus moulding and there are spiral columns on the edges[176].

These elegant buildings, in which the use of the multi–light window with quatrefoils in imitation of the Doge's Palace is typical, may therefore be dated between about 1450 and 1470. The examples already adduced provide some *point d'appui* for an attempt at chronology.

Palazzo Giustiniani Faccanon is perhaps later than Ca' Foscari, of which it repeats the distribution of the façade openings. As in Palazzo Bernardo on the Grand Canal, the two six–light windows are on different axes. There are not many changes, except in the attic which destroys the effect of the upper part. There are spiral columns along the edges[177].

A palace which in grandeur, and perhaps also in the distribution of the apertures, must have rivalled Ca' Foscari, was Ca' Brandolin, on the Grand Canal opposite Ca' d'Oro. It had, in fact, also a third floor, demolished around the middle of the nineteenth century. What is left is (except for some retouching on the ground floor) marked by a strong regularity[178].

As against the above–mentioned buildings, Palazzo Dandolo (now Hotel Danieli) appears developed in width. Even the sketchy engraving of it made by Coronelli leaves no doubts about the changed aspect of the present mezzanine. It was, in fact, characterized by two 'dwarf' five–light windows located at the two ends of the façade. The windows one sees there at present have suffered alterations and displacements, caused also by the modern door inserted in the centre of the façade. Also the present ground floor, reconstructed to bring light to the hotel premises, has nothing to do with the original, perhaps entirely occupied by a row of shops (as would appear from Coronelli). The two upper floors, occupying two thirds of the façade, are still in a good enough condition to maintain to a large extent the peculiar charm of this building.

We find here again almost all the elements already noticed in the preceding palaces. In the original disposition, the two low five–light windows of the mezzanine undoubtedly also helped to emphasize the horizontal direction peculiar to this façade, which in a way displays the very spirit of the Doge's Palace. Above the beautiful six–light window of the first floor stands the eight–light window of the second. The regularity of the distribution of its parts is perfect and allows us to date this building also, with spirals on its edges, to the middle of the fifteenth century. The window balconies are obviously a later addition[179].

The Gothic façade of Palazzo Contarini degli Scrigni is characterized by slender trefoiled arches, like those of Palazzo Bernardo on the Grand Canal. Many other characteristics place it with the buildings already mentioned (besides, of course, the use of the quatrefoil oculus), but there are signs of uncertainty (zones too tall and unsettled above the lateral windows; less rigour in the overall framing) which prevent a more exact dating[180]. The façade of Palazzo Erizzo alla Maddalena on the Grand Canal, where the only thing worthy of notice is the five–light window on an axis displaced to the left with slender trefoils like those of Palazzo Bernardo (in the usual firm framing), to be placed around the middle of the fifteenth century[181], follows a somewhat obsolete and more banal scheme.

That the quatrefoil motif, in the hands of stonemasons devoid of the required architectural balance, could undergo changes, even abnormal ones, may be readily admitted (as shown by Palazzo Mastelli (del Cammello) on Fondamenta Contarini, where the more showy second floor displays a four/six–light window with unusual deformations in the use of the quatrefoils, while the corner windows drew their inspiration partly from those in Palazzo Foscari and partly from the well–known corner window of Palazzo Priuli). The whole is turned out without any firm coordination, with antique balconies supported by leonine corbels and a cornice also on leonine brackets[182].

Quite different, for balance as well as for a certain refinement in the different relationships (discernible in spite of the poor state of preservation) is the small Palazzo Cavazza on rio della Fava, where the fifteenth–century set–up of the simple, harmonious façade is enriched, in the middle, by the very beautiful strongly framed three–light window, an almost unknown jewel in the heart of Venice, worthy of a place in the circle of palaces inspired by the Doge's Palace, with subtle outlines recalling those of the Bons[183].

A different type of tracery is displayed in Venice by three notable fifteenth–century buildings: Palazzi Giovanelli, Franchetti and Pisani–Moretta. The use of the quatrefoil is modified here so that it no longer forms one body directly with the inflected trefoiled arch but is placed on the vertex and the axis of the arch. The arch itself, however, is no longer inflected but is generated by an interlacing of round–headed arches, resulting in simple trefoiled arches between which are inserted trefoiled piercings, *mouchettes* (daggers). On the points of intersection of the round–headed arches and on the vertices of the trefoiled arches are placed, in a row, the quatrefoil oculi.

The motif of the round–headed arches which, by interlacing, generate pointed arches, is quite common in Italian Gothic architecture of the thirteenth and fourteenth centuries (it is enough to mention here the papal loggia in Viterbo of 1267, the small terracotta arcadings very frequently found in the Po valley, and one of the large windows in the Doge's Palace). The quatrefoil on the point of the arch is also known in Venice (the Frari apse; the S. Gregorio apses), in Bergamo (on the façade of S. Agostino, now rightly dated to the second half of the fourteenth century) and, much earlier naturally, in France (Albi cathedral, S. Germer de Fly, the very beautiful S. Sulpice–de–Favières; all of the thirteenth century). We have not found the two motifs fused together in the precise form displayed by the three Venetian palaces elsewhere.

We know that the present aspect of Palazzo Giovanelli at S. Fosca does not exactly coincide with the old one. Zanotto[184] reports that G. B. Meduna had aligned on a vertical axis the central body of the palace, without telling us how, precisely, this modification was carried out. The very rich motif of the central seven–light window finds further application in the lateral and corner windows, which recall those of Palazzo Priuli at S. Severo. The period must be around the middle of the fifteenth century.

The façade of Palazzo Cavalli Franchetti at S. Vidal[185] must have been a masterpiece capable of rivalling Ca' Foscari (and still is, for whomever can ignore the alterations and deplorable additions made by Boito). The guiding motifs of the floriated Gothic in the middle of the fifteenth century are there fused together in a new conception. Almost undifferentiated, the two *piani nobili* of equal height are adorned with two splendid five–light windows, the lower one with the interlacing arches motif, the upper one with the other exuberant motif originating perhaps with Raverti which appears also on the topmost floor of Ca' Foscari. The various sequences are more scattered over the vast area in a lively, sonorous musicality at Ca' Foscari. At Palazzo Cavalli they are more concentrated and compact, as in a single, low chord. Here also, the rhythm of solid and void is firmer in the admirable pauses of the wings enhancing the value of the central, almost wholly traceried body, closed above, with exact relations in the overhang as well as in the intervals between the corbels (too close in Ca' Foscari) by the cornice. We should note, moreover, the abandonment of single windows surmounted by semi–quatrefoils, replaced here by entire quatrefoils, the sobriety of the second floor windows in contrast with the five–light window, and the use of the torus profile as a chiaroscuro structural element. The contacts with Ca' Foscari would also indicate the sixth decade of the fifteenth century for this miracle of architecture. Third in this series, Palazzo Pisani Moretta repeats to some extent the arrangement of Palazzo Cavalli Franchetti, taking however the motif of the interlacing arches to the second floor, while the six–light window on the first reproduces that of the Doge's Palace loggia. It marks, however, certainly a later moment in time owing to the clear presence of Renaissance elements. To the lateral framing of Istrian stone quoins pilasters are here substituted, which are divided up by squares, with capitals in classical style. The string courses and balcony plates too have Renaissance outlines. Most notable, however, are the balconies with small very elegant spindle pilasters, of Tuscan origin, which were to have a great vogue in Venice, and which must here be considered to have been created with the building, not added later.

A remarkable and infrequent element are the coupled water–gates. The date of the building cannot be far from about 1470[186].

Next to these examples, where the motif of the loggia with quatrefoils plays an essential part, it is appropriate to mention a lesser building which has in common with the previous ones a peculiar distributive harmony, almost Renaissance in spirit. This is the small Palazzo Contarini on the Grand Canal[187], not far in spirit from Ca' Foscari and perfectly symmetrical. And, finally, we shall mention a Palazzo Donà at S. Vio, of which a record has been preserved in the Bertarelli Album in the Milan Civic Museum[188]. On the water–level floor is a portal with inflected arch between two Gothic windows. Above these are two roundels flanked by two windows on each side; on the *piano nobile* a central five–light window and four single ones are symmetrically placed. On the top floor a five–light window with quatrefoiled arches between four single windows is symmetrically placed. It is difficult to express a confident judgment, because the building has been demolished, but one could argue for a dating around 1450–70.

It appears from a document of 1463 that Bartolomeo Bon was threatened with severe sanctions for having neglected work at the Doge's Palace, and peremptorily urged to 'extend' this 'over the square' to make it possible to 'go in comfort to the very recent hall'[189].

The document is not very clear, but it could refer only to the work on the access to the 'very recent' hall, namely that of the *scrutinio*, which, with the façade to the west, was therefore ready by then. The stones which in 1452 were cluttering up the Piazzetta and had to be removed for the arrival of Frederick III[190] may well have been meant for the work in progress on the interior of the palace; and, anyway, the façade on the Piazzetta must already have been finished in 1463 if one of the dates which can be read on the Foscari loggia recording the entrances of the Dogaresses is 1462[191], and if in 1463 Girolamo Valeresso was hanged between the red columns[192].

It is interesting to note that in the document of 1463, Pantaleone di Paolo is named first and, after him, Bartolomeo Bon. As we have said before, Pantaleone is still an obscure figure[193]. It is to be assumed, therefore, that at that time the façade of the Palace towards the Piazzetta was finished and that Bartolomeo Bon and his team, heavily committed also elsewhere in Venice, had worked on it after the death of Giovanni Bon—which occurred in 1443[194]. On the participation of the Bons as architects in this part of the palace, all scholars are in agreement[195]. That, in fact, the so–called Foscari arch opposite the Giants' staircase had been finished while Bartolomeo (and his associate Pantaleone) were still alive, is suggested also by the coats of arms placed there of the two Doges, Francesco Foscari (1433–57) and Cristoforo Moro (1462–71)[196]. Bartolomeo died between 1464 and 1467[197].

We learn from a document of 8 December 1450 that another masterworkman, Picino, actively engaged at the Doge's Palace, is already old and as he cannot *ut opus esset servire*, he is to be assisted by *unum alium ingeniarum* and *coadiutorem*. Master Pincino, as he is called in various other documents, was Engineer of the Republic, but we have no idea what his work at the Doge's Palace may have been. We shall find him again in Dalmatia[198].

Of the Foscari arch, which faces the Giants' staircase and which the older critics attributed to Bartolomeo[199], it should be said that it is strikingly related to Bartolomeo's work of which it is clearly a development.

The Foscari arch is one of the somewhat hidden, forgotten marvels of Venice. Begun at the time of Francesco Foscari (1433–57), certainly not before 1440 (when the arcade must have been completed), it was finished in the time of Cristoforo Moro (1462–71); the coats of arms of the two doges are in fact visible on the façade towards the Giants' staircase, while the side towards the courtyard bears the coats of arms of the Mocenigo Doges (1474–6; 1478–85)[200].

The project certainly goes back to Bon and his school (Pantaleone di Paolo perhaps played a part in it which cannot so far be precisely defined). But, as we have noticed already, there are some recollections here of the Foscari tomb in the Frari, and therefore of the art of Antonio Bregno.

A strange construction, the Foscari arch is divided into two parts by a graceful Gothic balustrade with trefoiled arcading, not unlike the one adorning the outer loggia of the Doge's Palace (or the Ponte della Paglia). In the lower part there opens the great arch of the arcade which leads to Porta della Carta, while the walls flanking it are marked by two orders of columns with late Gothic capitals framing niches which seem to make some concession to a rhythm of volumes of Renaissance style (a motif repeated in the small southern façade). The upper part is dominated by a large and deep niche delimited by a segmental arch and flanked by two lateral square bodies surmounted by pinnacles and in line with corner columns, which also carry pinnacles with statues. Above the great niche are two large bases, also adorned with statues, marking the passage to a pyramid crowned by a statue. The southern side, smaller and altered in its lower part by the monument to Francesco I della Rovere, has a round–headed arch in place of the niche, above which there is a pyramid similar to the one already mentioned, but lower.

A fanciful, not really organic complex which only in the façade towards the Giants' staircase achieves an undoubted harmony, not only of colours but also of chiaroscuro, determined by the deep, shady cavities of the portico and niche and by the balustrade on brackets providing a robust horizontal accent.

This lively crossing of vertical and horizontal rhythms, together with the strong projections and deep shadows, recalls, even more than the Porta della Carta, the magnificent portal of S. Francesco delle Scale erected by Giorgio Orsini in Ancona; and it is certainly not pure chance that, just while he was working with the Bons on the Porta della Carta, Orsini was called to Sebenico.

The uncovered staircase called Foscara must have been built at the time of Doge Foscari. One passed from the courtyard to the first floor of the western loggias over this. It was later eliminated following the work carried out under Manopola. And, also, the loggia Foscara, where the oldest record of entrances of Dogaresses relates to the wife of Cristoforo Moro (1462). These dates are beside the emblem of the swordmakers, on the spot allotted to the representatives of these craftsmen, together with the other corporations of arts and trades on those solemn occasions. The date of 1471 records the entrance of the Dogaressa Tron, that of 1475 of the Dogaressa Malipiero.

Loggia Foscara is characterized, a little to the rear of the line of the outer loggia which gives directly onto the square, by columns supporting carved architraves, making an easier passage from the outer loggia to the courtyard. It demonstrates the participation of Bartolomeo and his team[201] (a typical product of the Bon school—as in the decoration of the Foscari arcade or in Palazzo Barbaro at S. Vidal) in the capitals with human heads among thick leaves.

The western and southern loggias overlooking the great inner courtyard must have been completed by 1468[202], when the Sala dello Scrutinio was already in use[203]. The pointed arches which distinguish these two loggias are borne by pilasters—no longer by single columns—in which are combined together four sheaf columns, representing the last manifestation of Bartolomeo's school. The long–established fourteenth–century motif which characterizes the exterior of the new wing gives way here to a richer variant, one more in keeping with the late Gothic of the second half of the century. The quality of the capitals, still with thick leaves and small heads, is here somewhat inferior to that of similar artifacts of the loggia Foscara[204].

The eastern loggia, however, was rebuilt by Rizzo after the fire of 1483[205] 'alike in everything to that which bears the hall' (of the Maggior Consiglio), but he gave the portico a definitely Renaissance expression[206].

Further changes in the appearance of the courtyard were to be successively made at the beginning of the seventeenth century by Bartolomeo Manopola. The lower part of the western and southern loggias (earlier than 1468) were in fact walled–up until 1602. Until then a simple wall surrounded the courtyard on these two sides, over which ran the loggia and, beyond the loggia, the walls of the two halls (of the Maggior Consiglio and Scrutinio). On the ground floor were the prisons[207]. In 1607 Bartolomeo Manopola, holding 'suspended in the air the whole fabric of the Palace on the southern side, that is to say the Sala del Maggior Consiglio, and demolishing the wall which was supporting it, replaced it by round arches'[208], like those of Rizzo on the eastern side. He thus demolished in 1608–10 the Foscari stairs on the western side of the courtyard and 'the wall underneath the Sala dello Scrutinio, and replaced it with round arches'[209]. The Ducal coats of arms which adorn these arches of Manopola's refer indeed to those times.

1. Cecchetti, 1886.

2. P. Paoletti, 1893, I, p. 20 et seq.

3. Cicognara, 1820, Plates 55, 56; Idem, 1838, I, Plates 100, 101. The original project, as imagined, by Cicognara, may be seen again illustrated in Lübke (1858, p. 499).

4. Fontana, 1845, Plate 10.

5. Molmenti, 1910.

6. Pauli, 1898, pp. 39, 40.

7. Selvatico, 1847, p. 112.

8. Zanotto, 1847, p. 422.

9. Burckhardt, 1925, p. 149.

10. Ruskin, 1886, III, p. 285.

11. Zanotto, 1856, p. 605.

12. Kugler, 1858-9, III, p. 578.

13. Mothes, 1859, pp. 223, 231 et seq.

14. Schnaase, 1876, p. 234.

15. Tassini, 1863, 1915 ed., p. 115; Idem, 1870, p. 25 et seq.

16. Raschdorff, 1903, Plate VI.

17. G. Boni, 1887, p. 115 et seq.

18. Marini, 1905, p. 84.

19. Molmenti, 1909, p. 8.

20. A. Venturi, 1924, pp. 277, 283 et seq. See also: Molmenti, 1925, I, p. 286 et seq.; Lavagnino, 1936, p. 528.

21. Boni, 1924-5, p. 481 et seq.

22. Molmenti, 1925, p. 286 et seq.

23. Lavagnino, 1936, p. 528 ('begun' by the Bon and 'continued' by Raverti).

24. Toesca, 1950, p. 155.

25. For Bettini (1953, pp. 53, 54) Raverti is the 'true architect of the palace'; and this also, in the light of the documents and following a more accurate critical investigation, cannot be accepted.

On the Ca' d'Oro see also: Lorenzetti, 1956, pp. 419, 633 et seq.; Decker, 1952, p. 48. For an extensive interpretation of the Lombard influence, see also *Arte Veneta*, XVI, 1962, p. 36.

26. Paoletti, 1893, p. 20.

27. Paoletti, 1920, p. 98.

28. Cecchetti, 1887, p. 63; Paoletti, 1893, p. 20; Idem, 1920, p. 97.

29. Paoletti, 1920, p. 97, Paoletti, 1893, p. 21.

30. Paoletti, 1893, p. 21.

31. Paoletti, 1893, p. 21. Raverti receives an advance of twenty ducats for the stairs; Paoletti, 1920, p. 98.

32. See also: Thieme-Becker, 1911, V, p. 278; Folnesics, 1914, p. 67, note 93.

33. There are indications of Gasparino Rosso of Milan being in Venice from 1416, when he was perhaps working with Pela at St. Mark's (Paoletti, 1920, p. 98; Thieme-Becker, 1935, XXIX, p. 58); A. G. Meyer, *Oberital. Frührenaissance* I (1897); Venturi, *Storia*, VI, 1908, p. 27.

34. Of him, perhaps working at St. Mark's with Pela, there are indications from 1418 (Paoletti, 1920, p. 98).

35. It is certainly Antonio Bregno who has been spoken of in connection with Porta della Carta. See also: Mariacher, 1937-8, pp. 584, 585.

36. Paoletti, 1920, p. 98.

37. Paoletti, 1920, p. 98.

38. Paoletti, 1893, p. 22.

39. Paoletti, 1893, p. 21.

40. Paoletti, 1893, p. 21; Idem, 1920, pp. 99, 100.

41. Paoletti, 1893, p. 22.

42. Paoletti, 1893, p. 25.

43. Paoletti, 1893, p. 25.

44. Paoletti, 1893, p. 22.

45. Paoletti, 1893, p. 20; Idem in Thieme-Becker, IV, 1910, p. 568; Idem, 1920, p. 98; Mariacher, 1937-8, pp. 584, 585.

46. Paoletti, 1893, p. 22; Idem, 1920, p. 101. The Borromeo chapel (1418-20) is by Cristoforo Orsini. In 1441 he built the campanile of the Udine Duomo. In 1443 he directed the work on the hostel of the Scuola della Carità (Paoletti, 1920, p. 101).

47. Paoletti, 1893, I, Plate 21; Idem, 1920, pp. 101 and 113.

48. Boschieri, 1933, p. 428. See also: Paoletti, 1893, I, p. 27; Chiminelli, 1912, p. 245 et seq. (the staircase demolished in 1847 was rebuilt—for the first time—by Meduna!); Paoletti, 1920, pp. 98, 99.

49. Paoletti, 1920, p. 99.

50. Venturi in *Storia dell'Arte*, VIII, 1924, fig. 77.

51. Mariacher, 1939, p. 37.

52. Paoletti, 1893, p. 21; Idem, 1920, p. 104.

53. Paoletti, 1893, pp. 21, 22.

54. Paoletti, 1920, p. 104.

55. Paoletti, 1920, p. 103.

56. Paoletti, 1893, p. 24; Idem, 1920, p. 106.

57. Paoletti, 1893, p. 21; Idem, 1920, pp. 104, 105.

58. Paoletti, 1893, p. 23; Idem, 1920, p. 105.

59. Paoletti, 1893, p. 22.

60. Paoletti, 1893, p. 22; Idem, 1920, pp. 104, 105.

61. Paoletti, 1893, p. 24. But they could also refer to the four-light window towards the courtyard; Idem, 1920, p. 106.

62. Paoletti, 1893, p. 25; Idem, 1920, p. 108.

63. Paoletti, 1920, p. 109.

64. Paoletti, 1893, p. 22; Idem, 1920, p. 108.

65. Paoletti, 1920, p. 105. A beautiful stray capital in corte Boldù may be compared with those of Romanello.

66. Paoletti, 1893, p. 26.

67. Paoletti, 1893, p. 22.

**68.** Paoletti, 1893, p. 22; Idem, 1920, p. 115.

**69.** Paoletti, 1893, p. 22; Idem, 1920, p. 108.

**70.** Paoletti, 1893, p. 22.

**71.** Paoletti, 1920, p. 109.

**72.** These balustrades had all disappeared already in 1846 (see ill. in Paoletti, 1920, p. 130).

**73.** Paoletti, 1893, p. 23; Idem, 1920, p. 105.

**74.** Compare the engraving anterior to 1846 (reproduced in Paoletti, 1920, p. 130) with the old Alinari photograph taken before the last restoration (Paoletti, 1920, p. 103) and with the present façade (Alinari, 12565).

**75.** Paoletti 1893, p. 23; Idem, 1920, p. 108.

**76.** Paoletti, 1893, p. 22.

**77.** Paoletti, 1893, p. 23. Idem, 1920, p. 107.

**78.** Paoletti, 1893, p. 24.

**79.** Paoletti, 1920, p. 107.

**80.** Paoletti, 1893, p. 24; Idem, 1920, p. 117 (reproduces the 'capital' towards the courtyard).

**81.** It is clearly visible in the drawing published by Paoletti (1893, p. 24) as fig. 28.

**82.** See these detailed instructions in: Paoletti, 1893, p. 24; Idem, 1920, pp. 111 and 128; Boni, 1887, pp. 125, 126; Planiscig, 1930, p. 92.

**83.** Paoletti, 1893, p. 24.

**84.** Paoletti, 1893, p. 25; Idem, 1920, p. 119.

**85.** Paoletti, 1893, p. 25 and note 3; Idem, 1920, pp. 119, 120; Fiocco, in *Rivista di Venezia*, 1927, p. 475 et seq.

**86.** Paoletti, 1893, pp. 14, 26; Fabriczy, 1902, p. 325; Paoletti, 1920, p. 124; Planiscig, 1930, p. 70; Fogolari, 1932, p. 29 et seq.

**87.** Paoletti, 1893, p. 26; Idem, 1920, p. 124.

**88.** Elusive figures are a Francesco da Padova, mentioned in 1430 in connection with some carved stones (Paoletti, 1920, p. 109) and a Pietro da Milano who in 1437 is working on certain balconies (Paoletti, 1920, p. 110), if he is not the same person as the one present from 1442 in Ragusa and then in Naples. On the work in the interior, we know that Stefano Fasan supplied ten doors in 1430 and that in 1431 Antonio di Martino and Giovanni Benzon were painting the walls (Paoletti, 1920, p. 116).

**89.** Fogolari, 1927, p. 16.

**90.** Molmenti, 1910, pp. 4 and 5.

**91.** Boschieri, 1933, p. 417.

**92.** Already Paoletti had clearly seen in the author of the six-light window 'a non-Venetian artist' (1920, p. 108).

**93.** The first notice is of 1382 when Giovanni is a witness (Paoletti, 1893, p. 39, note 2).

**94.** Planiscig, 1930, p. 89.

**95.** Mariacher, 1939, p. 37.

**96.** *Scuola vecchia della Misericordia.* See, for the date: Paoletti, 1893, I, p. 55. Ruskin (1886, II, pp. 305, 306) had already noticed the peculiar richness of the traceries of these windows. The attribution to the Bons is accepted by Venturi (1924, p. 294) and by Lorenzetti (1956, p. 400). The similarities with the rich traceries of the coeval Porta della Carta seem to me to confirm absolutely that authorship.

**97.** Visentini, 1742, III, 4. The same palace, with one floor with a six-light window in the centre, is visible in an engraving by Engelbrecht and in one by Canaletto.

**98.** Sansovino, 1581, p. 143.

**99.** Paoletti, 1893, p. 152 and note 8 which quotes from Lorenzi and Sagredo.

**100.** Paoletti, 1893, p. 21.

**101.** Paoletti, 1893, p. 39, note 2.

**102.** Planiscig, 1930, p. 91.

**103.** *Palazzo Barbaro.* Carlevarijs, 1703, Plate XCVI; Coronelli, 1709, II, Plate 23 (one can see the top floor, Gothic, now transformed); Quadri, 1834, p. 34 (proves that the Gothic arch on the ground floor, on the left, is later than that date). Zanotto, 1847, p. 430 (given to the thirteenth century!); Fontana, 1845, Plate 38.

**104.** *Palazzo Zeno al ponte dei Scudi.* Tassini, 1879, p. 240; Elenco, 1905, p. 40, no. 170 (Castello, 2654) and p. 184 (ownership passes, in the seventeenth century, from the Zeno to the Pizzamano); Lorenzetti, 1956, p. 368 (to the fifteenth century). Asymmetrical façade with a four-light window on the left and another four-light window, smaller, in line with the first; in the façade open the door on the bridge and that on the water. In the courtyard there is an uncovered staircase and a beautiful three-light window above a large, round archway with rosette capitals; above, there are two windows of the fifth order. (1440–50?).

**105.** *Casa del Tintoretto.* Fond. dei Mori, Cann. 3399; Elenco, 1905, p. 81, no. 278; Lorenzetti, 1956, p. 405 (to the fifteenth century).

**106.** *Palazzo Goldoni Rizzo Centani.* Mothes, 1859, pp. 214, 215 (to 1300–40); Elenco, 1905, p. 122, no. 240 (S. Polo 2793); Lorenzetti, 1956, p. 571 (to the fourteenth century); Toesca, 1950, p. 150 (to the fourteenth to fifteenth centuries); Miozzi, 1957, I, p. 437. In the courtyard, uncovered staircase and well-curb.

**107.** *Palazzo Da Mula at San Vio.* Quadri, 1834, 3 (not different from the present); Tassini, 1863, 1915 ed., p. 223 (the da Mula have lived at S. Vio since the fifteenth century); Marini, 1905, p. 82 (to the fourteenth century); Lorenzetti, 1956, p. 614 (to the fifteenth century). Notice the heads in the capitals, dear to the Bons.

**108.** *Palazzo Michiel del Brusà.* Fontana, 1845, Plate 53; Zanotto, 1847, p. 428; Idem, 1856, p. 603; Elenco, 1905, p. 88, no. 398 (Cann. 4390); Lorenzetti, 1956, p. 631. Interesting the greater dimensions of the lateral windows in comparison with the multi-light windows. Rigidly symmetrical structure. The name (Brusà) is due to a fire which broke out in 1774. Ruskin, 1886, III, p. 278 (early fourteenth century); Burckhardt, 1925, p. 149; Zanotto, 1856, p. 585 (to the fourteenth century); Tassini, 1863, 1915 ed., pp. 60, 61 (thinks it of the fourteenth century; acquired—but a previous building must be involved—in 1414 by Pietro Spera; restored by the Cavaliere and Procuratore di S. Marco Zaccaria Barbaro); Elenco, 1905, p. 14, no. 212; Marini, 1905, p. 82 (to the fourteenth century); Chiminelli, 1912, p. 231 (the staircase partly remade); Paoletti, 1893, p. 21; Venturi, 1924, p. 297 (to Giovanni Bon); Lorenzetti, 1956, p. 617; Lavagnino, 1936, p. 528 (to Giovanni Bon); Miozzi, 1957, I, p. 459 (one sees appearing the flower finial as a 'new element'). As we have said, the arch giving onto the canal is a later imitation. The notices on Zaccaria Barbaro go from 1441 to 1492 (information kindly supplied by P. Zampetti).

**109.** *Palazzo Zaguri.* Fontana, 1845, Plate 58; Zanotto, 1847, p. 429 (1300–50); Idem, 1856, p. 176 (1300–50); Mothes, 1859, pp. 208, 209 (1300–40); *Venise*, 1861, p. 126 (to the first half of the fourteenth century); Tassini, 1863, 1915 ed., p. 207 (says it was founded in the fourteenth century by the Pasqualini, as attested by the chronicles); Idem, 1873, pp. 104, 105 (confirms that the Pasqualini were the builders of the palace); Idem, 1879, p. 30 (repeats the above; on the façade and on the well, the emblem of the Pasqualini); Elenco, 1905, p. 13, no. 187 and p. 191 (S. Marco 2631 and 2668) (to the fifteenth century); Marini, 1905, p. 82 (to the fourteenth century); Chiminelli, 1912, p. 247 (the staircase was uncovered); Lorenzetti, 1956, p. 517 (to the fifteenth century); Toesca, 1950, p. 150 (not of the fourteenth but of the fifteenth); Maretto, 1959, pp. 21 and 68. The side, on calle de Ca' Zaguri, has been tampered with but has some surviving windows.

**110.** *Palazzo Sanudo at ponte Bernardo; S. Polo* 2165. Lorenzetti, 1956, p. 602 (to the fifteenth century); Maretto, 1959, Plate XIII (with plan; typical solid block house). The façade on the canal strictly symmetrical, with water-gate and four small windows with segmental arch; on the *piano nobile*, four-light window of the sixth order flanked by four windows; on the next floor, four-light window and windows of the fourth order; the mezzanine has been reconstructed; Gothic cornice. On the rear façade, the great, round-headed arch of the warehouse; above it, in line, two four-light windows of the sixth and fourth orders.

**111.** *Palazzo Amadi.* Tassini, 1863, 1915 ed., p. 16; Elenco, 1905, p. 99, no. 585; Lorenzetti, 1956, p. 392. Behind the palace, there is still the courtyard with the name of the Amadi, in which only two Gothic windows are left and the remains of an uncovered staircase (Cann. 5810–19). The Amadi came from Lucca to Venice in the thirteenth and fourteenth centuries.

**112.** *Palazzo Contarini Porta di Ferro at S. Giustina.* Zanotto, 1856, p. 233 (to the fifteenth century); Ruskin, 1886, III, p. 283 (staircase of c. 1350, one of the most richly and carefully wrought in Venice; the palace, *among the most magnificent in Venice*); Tassini, 1879, p. 176 (the staircase is attributed to the fifteenth century; Elenco, 1905, p. 43, no. 211 (beginning of the fifteenth); Paoletti, 1893, I, p. 27 (coeval with the Ca' d'Oro); Chiminelli, 1912, p. 223 (to the fifteenth century); Lorenzetti, 1956, pp. 373, 374 (the staircase attributed, with some doubts, to Raverti).

**113.** *Palazzo Barbaro at S. Vio.* Quadri, 1834, Plate 3 (only the six-light window is visible); Fontana, 1845, Plate 50; Zanotto, 1856, p. 580 (to the fourteenth century); Ruskin, 1886, III, p. 278, *good Gothic of the earliest fourteenth century type*; Lorenzetti, 1956, p. 614.

**114.** Lorenzi, 1868, p. 58, doc. 148; Paoletti,

1893, pp. 5, 6 (quotes also an anonymous chronicle of the fifteenth century, now at the Marciana, Cl. VII, cod. 2034). See also, on the matters dealt with in this chapter: Bassi, 1964.

**115.** Sansovino, 1581, pp. 119–25; Sanudo, *Vite*, col. 972; Cadorin, 1837, p. 13 et seq. and p. 46, note 12 (the story that the doge Tommaso Mocenigo had paid the thousand ducats fine provided the old palace were reconstructed remounts to a chronicle of the sixteenth century, preserved in the Museo Correr, no. 103, p. 253); Bettio, 1837, p. 28; Cicognara, 1838, p. 57; Ricci, 1858, II, pp. 335–7; Paoletti, cit., p. 6 (quotes the above chronicle of the Marciana: *adi XXVII marzo 1424 fu prinzipiado a gitar zoso el palazo vechio per refarlo da nuovo*—on 27 March 1424 began to be pulled down the old palace in order to remake it). See also: Zanotto, 1853–61, p. 76 and p. 81, note 5; Ruskin, 1886, II, p. 298 et seq., III, p. 215 et seq. The Sivos chronicle states that the demolition began *dalla parte ch'è verso panateria, cioè della Giustizia, ch'è nelli occhi di sopra le colonne fino alla Chiesa* (from the side which is towards the bakery, that is of the Justice, which is in the eyes above the columns up to the Church). (See: Ruskin, III, p. 216; Ricci, 1858, II, p. 337).

**116.** Quoted by Paoletti, 1893, p. 6.

**117.** Cadorin, 1837, pp. 114, 116.

**118.** Selvatico, 1847, p. 134.

**119.** Ricci, 1858, II, p. 341.

**120.** Della Rovere, 1880, p. 2.

**121.** Planiscig, 1930, pp. 74 and 92.

**122.** Fogolari, 1930, p. 457.

**123.** Ongaro, 1935, p. 10.

**124.** Fiocco, 1927–8, p. 364.

**125.** As Zanotto had already noted - 1856, I, p. 219.

**126.** Cadorin, 1837, p. 47, note 15; Ricci, 1858, II, p. 342.

**127.** Zanotto, 1853, I, p. 78. The argument, however, is not conclusive.

**128.** On the two red columns see Zanotto's useful digression (1853–61, pp. 61, 62).

**129.** A. Venturi, 1908, p. 226.

**130.** Venturi, 1924, p. 288.

**131.** Fiocco, 1927–8, pp. 363, 364. Pignatti (1964, p. 10) also believes the 'greater part' of the capitals of the new wing to be by Lamberti.

**132.** Fiocco, op. cit.

**133.** Planiscig, 1930, p. 75.

**134.** In 1419 Piero di Nicolò is working with his father on the great middle arch on St. Mark's façade (Meyer, 1889, p. 15; Paoletti, 1893, I, pp. 13 and 14; Fabriczy, 1902, pp. 322, 324; Venturi, 1908, p. 224). In 1423 he signs, with Giovanni di Martino of Fiesole, the sepulchral monument of Tommaso Mocenigo in SS. Giovanni e Paolo which Meyer (1889, p. 14) had already rightly called a 'mediocre work'. In these certain Venetian works, the Tuscan sculptor is certainly the transmitter of lively ideas which could interest the local late-Gothic circles, but does not reach the high level of the *Judgment of Solomon*. Planiscig (1930, pp. 57 and 87 et seq.) refuses to Piero the author-

ship of the two statues in Orsanmichele.

**135.** *The Justice (or Legislators) Capital.* Zanotto, 1853, I, p. 219; Meyer, 1889, p. 15; Paoletti, 1893, I, pp. 11, 12; Fabriczy, 1902, p. 325; Lorenzetti, 1956, p. 239; Fiocco, 1927–8, p. 363 et seq.; Fogolari, 1930, p. 428; Planiscig, 1930, p. 71 et seq.; Fiocco, 1930–1, p. 1041 et seq. (against the doubts of Fogolari and Flaniscig, read the inscription: 'DUO SOTII FLORENTI INC. SE.'); Gamba, 1930; Pope-Hennessy, pp. 58, 59. The inscription was discovered at the restoration of 1858.

**136.** Thieme-Becker, I, X. 1907, p. 459; Venturi, 1908, p. 32; Paoletti, 1920, p. 104.

**137.** *The Judgment of Solomon.* Venturi, 1908, p. 216 et seq. Molmenti, 1910, p. IX was thinking of a Tuscan. Venturi's ideas were adopted by Fogolari (1927, Plate 5) who, rightly, associated him with the terracottas of the Beato Pacifico monument, Mariacher (1950, pp. 20 and 21) and Pignatti (1964, p. 10; 1956, p. 27—with doubts).

**138.** *The Judgment of Solomon.* The first to propound the attribution to the two associates was Della Rovere (1880, p. 2), followed by Pauli (1898, p. 64), by Fabriczy (1902, p. 322: to Piero Lamberti; and quotes Gamba who is of the same opinion), by Reymond, with doubts (The tomb of O. Strozzi, in *L'Arte*, 1903, p. 14; denies this tomb, however, to Piero); by Ongaro (1923, p. 12). Fiocco (1927–8, pp. 364 and 368; 1931, pp. 271, 284 et seq.) fights resolutely for the attribution to Piero Lamberti; insisting (and in this we agree with him) on the affinities with the Beato Pacifico monument.
Serra (1949, p. 6) and Lorenzetti (1956, p. 237) hesitate between Lamberti's workshop and Nanni di Bartolo. Muraro (1953, p. 96) thinks of a Florentine sculptor of the fifteenth century. Bassi-Trincanato (1960, note 35).

**139.** *The Judgment of Solomon.* (Planiscig, 1930, pp. 75 and 108 resolutely denies it to Piero Lamberti; pointing out that at the beginning of the nineteenth century this sculpture was considered to be by the Bons); recently, with an ingenious and not entirely improbable formula, Pope-Hennessy (1963, p. 59) has spoken of a Tuscan artist associated with the workshop of the Bons.

**140.** *The Tomb of the Beato Pacifico* was attributed by Meyer (1889, p. 97) to the Florentine Rosso; and he is followed by Paoletti and by Planiscig, 1921, p. 19 et seq.; 1930, p. 84 et seq. Venturi, 1908, p. 116 et seq. has related it to the 'Maestro della Cappella dei Pellegrini'. Fiocco (1927–8) gave it to Piero Lamberti and saw in it contacts with the *Judgment of Solomon*; Fogolari (1929–30) demonstrated that 1437 is not the date of erection of the monument, which had been completed several years before, and confirmed the affinity with the *Judgment of Solomon*; this dating is accepted also by Fiocco (1930, p. 160).

**141.** Mariacher, 1950, p. 127.

**142.** *Porta della Carta.* Lorenzi, 1868, p. 68.

**143.** Planiscig, 1921, p. 3.

**144.** Paoletti, 1893, p. 37 et seq.; Planiscig, 1921, p. 3 et seq.

**145.** Paoletti, 1893, p. 39, note 1.

**146.** See also on the *Porta della Carta*: Cadorin, 1837, pp. 14 and 15 (quotes the Trevisan, Barbo

and Veniera chronicles, all in agreement to attribute to Bartolomeo the Doge and Lion group; Cadorin, 1845, p. 105 et seq. (with the documents of 1438 and 1442); Cicognara, 1838, I, p. 62, I, Plate 26; Selvatico, 1847, pp. 135 and 136; Zanotto, 1853, I, pp. 83 and 84, note 18; Ricci, 1858, II, pp. 341 and 342; Paoletti, 1893, I, p. 37 et seq.; Venturi, 1908, p. 987 et seq.; Molmenti, 1910, IX (the lion with the doge executed by Luigi Ferrari 'a few years ago'); Venturi, 1924, pp. 304 and 305 (sees in it the prototype of the one created by Giorgio da Sebenico: *S. Francesco alle Scale di Ancona*); Lorenzetti, 1956, p. 239; Fiocco, 1927–8, pp. 368 and 369; Fogolari, 1930, p. 457 et seq.; Planiscig, 1930, p. 92 et seq. and p. 100 et seq.; Fogolari, 1932, p. 33 et seq.; Bettini, 1953, p. 57; D'Elia, 1962, p. 213 et seq.
The statues of the four virtues on pillars are not mentioned in the documents. They were probably set up last, after (or within) 1442. Modern criticism identifies in them a different quality from that of Bartolomeo. In 1908 (p. 987 et seq.) Adolfo Venturi was still attributing it to the Bons. Planiscig (1921, pp. 30, 31) rightly attributes to Antonio Bregno (author of the Foscari monument at the Frari) the *Fortitude* and the *Temperance*, assigning the other two to the workshop; he is followed by Venturi (1924, p. 494) and by Lorenzetti. In 1927–8 (p. 368 et seq.) Fiocco attributes to Lamberti the two lower statues and, hesitatingly, to Giovanni di Martino the two upper ones. A little later Fiocco (reviewing Rigoni, 1930, pp. 156 and 159) reconfirms them to Piero Lamberti; and Planiscig (1930, p. 101) allows (but here he is less convincing) the two less beautiful virtues to Giovanni di Martino, assigning however the crowning of the door to another master. Fogolari (1932, p. 41) is even less convincing when he attributes these statues to Bartolomeo's hand. More recently Mariacher (1952, p. 26) discerned in the *Prudence* and in the *Charity* the hand of Bregno and in the others the hand of a Tuscan. Also *Gabriel* beside the Porta della Carta (above the capital of the 'associates') was considered by Mariacher (quoted pass.), by Bassi-Trincanato (1960, p. 36) with reservations and by Pignatti (1964, p. 10) to be by Antonio Bregno: an ascription with which we do not feel we can agree. As for the statues of the Virtues, the first distinction made by Planiscig still seems to me the most correct. To the critics, Antonio Bregno is by now a well-understood artist: in the Foscari monument his style is, indeed, very legible. We have met him already at the Ca' d'Oro where, however, it is not possible to follow his hand, which was very probably executing someone else's drawings. Still good, Paoletti's voice in Thieme-Becker, IV, 1910, p. 568.

**147.** Cadorin, 1845, p. 112.

**148.** At Beverly, St. Mary (Bond, 1905, p. 254).

**149.** Bond, 1905, p. 130.

**150.** Giampiccoli, c. 1782, Plate 39.

**151.** On the mixtilinear arch see: A. M. Romanini in *Venezia e l'Europa* 1956, p. 176 et seq. (the façade of the no longer existing S. Maria Maggiore of Milan was considered a copy of the fourteenth-century preceding one, demolished; but it nevertheless seems a different thing and one is left somewhat uncertain on what could have been its true dating. The Mantuan crowning, however, faithfully reproduces the upper part of the Porta della Carta.

**152.** C. V. Fabriczy, *Giovanni di Bartolo und das Portal von S. Nicolò zu Tolentino* in *Rep. für Kunstwissenschaft*, 1905, p. 96 et seq. (belongs only in part to Rosso); Frey, 1913, p. 107 et seq. (notes the mixtilinear Venetian crowning); Folnesics, 1914, p. 88; Venturi, 1924, p. 338 (erroneously given to Giorgio da Sebenico); Serra, 1929, pp. 220 and 221; Planiscig, in Thieme-Becker, XXIX, 1935, p. 59.

**153.** Venturi, in *L'Arte* 1908, p. 31; Idem, 1908, p. 996 et seq. (*Storia dell'Arte*); Idem, 1924, p. 310 et seq.

**154.** Selvatico, 1847, p. 135.

**155.** Venturi, 1908, p. 994.

**156.** The Doge's head, saved from the destruction, is now in the Doge's Palace Museum.

**157.** Fogolari (1932, p. 41) was oscillating between old Giovanni Bon, then on the eve of his death, and Bartolomeo.
This very beautiful sculpture is by an artist at his full maturity, working in Venice around 1440. And, we add, one of the highest and most significant of Bartolomeo, when he was working without assistance.

**158.** Paoletti, 1893, p. 39, note 2.

**159.** See: Franco, 1939, p. 271 et seq. and what was said on the subject in this penultimate chapter of this book. On Bartolomeo Bon's building activity see also: Bassi, 1965, p. 198 et seq.

**160.** A more balanced evaluation of Bartolomeo Bon (against the opinions of Fiocco, who tends to disparage his art in favour of Piero di Niccolò) was made by Planiscig, 1921, 1930, and by Fogolari, 1930, 1932. A separate problem, still unresolved, is raised by the work of Pantaleone di Paolo. He cannot have been a person of little account if his name, in the 1463 document, concerning the work at the Doge's Palace, is placed before that of Bartolomeo. Active from 1426 onwards, Pantaleone works by the side of the Bons at the Ca' d'Oro in 1429, on various works on the first floor openings (Paoletti, 1920, p. 106), and we then find him by the side of Bartolomeo on the works at the Carità (1442–50) and in Padova, where he estimates the Gattamelata, in 1453 (see also: Thieme-Becker, XXVI, 1932, pp. 203 and 204). Paoletti, (Thieme-Becker, XXVI, 1932, p. 203) proposes him as the author of a *Madonna with St. Peter*, now on the fondamenta Quintavalle, a damaged but very noble work which, however, does not exactly correspond with the document with which it is being connected.

**161.** *The Foscari Arcade* (*Porticato*), at the Doge's Palace. Gallo, 1933, p. 287 (the masonry of the arcade was reinforced in 1454 and in 1472). According to Lorenzetti (1956, p. 240) 'it seems' that this arcade was completed after 1440 by Antonio Bregno; according to Mariacher (1950, pp. 21, 22) Antonio Bregno had succeeded the Bons in these works on the arcade, and on the Foscari arch, after 1440. For Pignatti (1964, p. 10) after 1450. These assertions, based on a mention of Bregno as overseer of the palace works made by Sansovino, should perhaps be more carefully scrutinized. The dating of this arcade to 1430–40 has been confirmed again by Bassi-Trincanato (1960, p. 44 et seq.).

**162.** Venturi (1908, p. 994) had already recognized Bartolomeo's hand in this fanciful cornice.

**163.** *Palazzo Bernardo on the Grand Canal*. Visible in the *View* by J. de Barbari; Zanotto, 1847, p. 433; Selvatico, 1847, p. 116; Selvatico, 1852, p. 232; Burckhardt, 1925, p. 150; Ruskin, 1886, III, p. 279 (notes the 'rich and unusual' traceries and the derivation from the Doge's Palace; early fifteenth century); Zanotto, 1856, p. 594 ('a palace among the first of its style', fifteenth century); Mothes, 1859, p. 230; Tassini, 1879, p. 72 (gives hospitality to Francesco Sforza in 1442); Fulin-Molmenti, 1881, p. 281 (to the fourteenth century); Paoletti, 1893, I, p. 29 (notes that the traceries are the same as those of the Frari apse; already built in 1442); Marini, 1905, p. 84 ('preserved... in its full beauty and in the excellent regularity of its parts'; to the fifteenth century); Elenco, 1905, p. 117, no. 153 (S. Polo 1978); Lorenzetti, 1956, p. 624 (to *c.* 1442).

**164.** Maretto, 1960, Plate XIII bis (with useful observations).

**165.** *Palazzo Corner Cavalli*. Carlevarijs, 1703, Plate XCV; Ruskin, 1886, III, p. 283 (notes the derivation from the Doge's Palace; and the rich and beautiful capitals); Burckhardt, 1925, p. 149 ('particularly energetic in the structure of the windows'); Selvatico, 1852, p. 233 (to the fifteenth century); Mothes, 1859, p. 219 (to 1340–70); Kugler, 1858–9, III, p. 577 (*in kräftig edler Durchbildung*); Tassini, 1863, 1915 ed., p. 458; Idem, 1879, p. 227 (to the fifteenth century); Paoletti, 1893, I, p. 29 (specifies 1445 as the date of the beginning of the building); Elenco, 1905, p. 20, no. 331; Lorenzetti, 1956, p. 625 (to about 1445).

**166.** *The two Giustiniani Palaces*. Coronelli, II, 182; Fontana, 1845, Plate 45; Zanotto, 1847, p. 424 (where there appears the information, I do not know whether for the first time, that there had been three palaces because the third, where Ca' Foscari stands now, had been actually built; the organization of the two façades, as we have analyzed it, each completing the other, excludes however the possibility that a third façade was continuing on the right, towards the rio di S. Pantalon, the typical structure of the two at present in existence); Burckhardt, 1925, p. 149; Ruskin, 1886, III, p. 300 (mentions Lazari's statement that it had been erected before 1428; notes that it was founded on the Doge's Palace and that it has unusual traceries); Zanotto, 1856, p. 588 (to the fourteenth century); Kugler, 1858–9, III, p. 577; Mothes, 1859, p. 222 (to 1300–50); Tassini, 1879, p. 182 (on 29 October 1451 Nicolò and Giovanni Giustinian bought on a valuation a little low house which stood in the way of the building they had begun at S. Pantalon on the Grand Canal); Idem, 1863, 1915 ed., p. 347; Fulin-Molmenti, 1881, pp. 410 and 423 (says that the two palaces were acquired in 1429 and 1439 for Gianfranco and Francesco Sforza); Paoletti, 1893, I, p. 31 (accepts Tassini's date); Elenco, 1905, p. 166, pp. 321, 322 and 324; Marini, 1905, pp. 83 and 84 (to the fifteenth century); Chiminelli, 1912, p. 245 (both had uncovered staircases; that of the palace next to Ca' Foscari remade by Ing. Samassa); Lorenzetti, 1956, p. 620 (to the middle of the fifteenth century); Maretto, 1959, p. 56 (the great staircase of the larger courtyard climbs to the second floor, the small staircase of the lesser courtyard goes to the first floor; the multi-light windows are wider than the traversing halls).

**167.** *Ca' Foscari*. Sansovino, 1581, p. 149 et seq.

**168.** *Ca' Foscari*. Carlevarijs, 1703, Plate LXXVIII; Visentini, 1742, 1 and 2 (note the rectangular windows on the ground floor); Cicognara, 1820, Plate 57; Fontana, 1845, Plate 13 (makes Giovanni Bon the architect!); Zanotto, 1847, pp. 423 and 424; Selvatico, 1852, p. 230; Zanotto, 1856, pp. 588 and 589 (given to the fourteenth century; the last floor by the Bons); Mothes, 1859, p. 229 (to about 1438); Tassini, 1879, pp. 179, 180 and 182, note 1 (contests the dating to the fourteenth century, is for the fifteenth); Raschdorff, 1903, Plate IX (to the first half of the fourteenth century; the third floor of 1437); Marini, 1905, p. 83; Chiminelli, 1912, pp. 244 and 245; Folnesics; 1914, p. 52 (on the putti motif, taking its inspiration from an ancient relief); Miozzi, 1957, I, p. 441; Hubala, 1966, p. 773.

**169.** *Ca' Foscari*. Tassini, 1863, 1915 ed., p. 285 et seq.

**170.** *Ca' Foscari*. The rear part was rebuilt at the end of the seventeenth century and at the beginning of the eighteenth. Cicognara mentions it in 1838, I, p. 149 as a 'nest for owls and night birds and empty of inhabitants'. Ruskin, 1886, III, p. 290 calls it in 1845 a 'foul ruin'. In 1847 it was restored thanks to the Municipality of Venice which had acquired it (Tassini, 1879, pp. 179 and 180). According to Mothes (1859, pp. 222 and 223) the restoration was carried out in 1844–6 by L. Parravicini. In the nineteenth century it was enlarged towards the courtyard with additions and modifications, and the demolition of the uncovered staircase (Chiminelli, 1912, pp. 244 and 245), of which we have a record in an engraving by Coronelli (*Singularities of Venice*, Plate 170).
From Fontana's engraving it appears that the four present windows of the wings are imitations and that the whole floor on the canal has been remade.

**171.** *Ca' Foscari*. Ruskin, 1886, III, p. 290.

**172.** *Ca' Foscari*. Mothes, 1859, p. 229.

**173.** *Ca' Foscari*. Kugler, 1858–9, III, p. 578.

**174.** *Ca' Foscari*. Paoletti, 1893, I, pp. 29 and 30.

**175.** *Ca' Foscari*. See also: Burckhardt, 1925, pp. 149 and 150; E. Paoletti, 1837–40, III, p. 192; Sagredo, 1856, pp. 81 and 82; Fulin-Molmenti. 1881, p. 412; Lorenzetti, 1956, p. 620; Maretto, 1959, pp. 56 and 57.

**176.** *Palazzo dell'Ambasciatore*. Zanotto, 1856, p. 586; Tassini, 1863, 1915 ed., p. 17; Idem, 1879, p. 284; Paoletti, 1893, I, p. 32 (praises its proportions; notes that there are Renaissance elements in the lower cornice, in the door); Raschdorff, 1903, Plates XI and XIV (with plans); Elenco, 1905, p. 153 (calle dei Cerchieri, Dorsoduro 1262); Marini, 1905, p. 85; Lorenzetti, 1956, p. 618. The Renaissance windows of the mezzanine were perhaps cut into the wall later. The building was largely restored after a fire in 1891.

**177.** *Palazzo Giustiniani Faccanon*. Coronelli, Plate 43, Fontana, 1845, Plate 68; Zanotto, 1847, pp. 431 and 432 (to the fourteenth century); Selvatico, 1852, p. 115 (to the fifteenth century); Zanotto, 1856, p. 205 (to the fourteenth century); notes the 'charming quatrefoiled openings'); Mothes, 1859, p. 230; Ruskin, 1886, III, p. 290 (connections with the Doge's Palace); Marini, 1905, p. 84

(sees it akin to Ca' Foscari); Paoletti, 1893, I, p. 32, note 2; Elenco, 1905, p. 25, no. 426 (San Marco 5016); Lorenzetti, 1956, p. 324. A certain affinity, in some particulars, with Palazzo Caotorta makes one think of a same architect, if not a same team of workers.

**178.** *Palazzo Brandolin-Morosini.* Zanotto, 1856, p. 604 (the top floor 'demolished a few years ago'; to the fourteenth century); Tassini, 1897, p. 291 (reminders of the Doge's Palace); Elenco, 1905, p. 116. no. 138 (S. Polo, calle del Campanile 1789; to the fifteenth century); Lorenzetti, 1956, p. 632 with modifications to the fifteenth century); Maretto, 1959, p. 35 (considers that one of the two wings is modern).

**179.** *Palazzo Dandolo, now Hotel Danieli. Formerly Nanni Mocenigo and Bernardo.* Visible in the *View* by Jacopo de Barbari. Coronelli, Plate 69; Fontana, 1845, Plate 12 (says that the shops are of a later period; speaks of a 'radical' restoration and of a further restoration project by Tranquillo Orsi; Zanotto, 1847, p. 423 (speaks of the 'very modern entrance on riva degli Schiavoni' made, evidently, after the transformation of the building into a hotel; and judges favourably the courtyard and the staircases); Ruskin, 1886, III, p. 307 ('a glorious example of the central Gothic, nearly contemporary with the finest parts of the Doge's Palace'; purer than Ca' Foscari or Ca' Bernardo, quite unique in the delicate drawing of the cusps of the central windows, *which are shaped like broad scimitars*); Zanotto, 1856, p. 261 (comparisons with the Doge's Palace; 'courtyard and staircases considered very praiseworthy'); Mothes, 1859, p. 230 (deplores the restoration); Kugler, 1858-9, III, p. 578 (called Palazzo Barbarigo); Tassini, 1863, 1915 ed., p. 604 (founded in the fourteenth century; hotel since 1822); Idem, 1879, p. 143 (to the fourteenth century); Paoletti, 1893, I, p. 24, note I and p. 29 (refers to this palace one of the *marani*—boats loaded with stones—consigned in 1421-2 to Leonardo Dandolo; which does not fit very well our dating of Palazzo Dandolo); Elenco, 1905, p. 48, no. 309 (Castello 4191; to the fifteenth century); Idem, pp. 51, 350, 352 (three Gothic doors in calle delle Rasse; Castello 4566, 4579 and 4581); Marini, 1905, p. 83; Douglas, 1925, p. 25 (to the fourteenth century); Lorenzetti, 1956, p. 284 (to the fifteenth century); Miozzi, 1957, I, p. 446.—The interior has been entirely remodelled.

**180.** *Palazzo Contarini degli Scrigni.* Carlevarijs, 1703, Plate XC; Coronelli, 1709, Plate 171; Fontana, 1845, Plate 14 (the balcony of the *piano nobile*, which had also two coats of arms, is missing); Selvatico, 1852, p. 230 (to the fifteenth century); Zanotto, 1856, p. 586 (to the fourteenth century); Ruskin, 1886, III, p. 283 (founded on the Doge's Palace); Mothes, 1859, p. 230; Tassini, 1863, 1915 ed., p. 198 (to the fourteenth century); Elenco, 1905, p. 155, no. 127 (calle Gambara, Dorsoduro 1057-9); Lorenzetti, 1956, p. 618 (to the fifteenth century); Miozzi, 1957, I, p. 440.—At the rear there are two praiseworthy Gothic four-light windows with rosette capitals; in the perimeter wall towards rio S. Trovaso there are some quite interesting small Gothic windows and a Renaissance door perhaps of the middle of the fifteenth century; worthy of study.

**181.** *Palazzo Erizzo alla Maddalena on the Grand Canal, formerly Molin-Barzizza.* Fontana, 1845, Plate 32 without variations from the present state);

Zanotto, 1847, p. 430; Selvatico, 1847, p. 237 (to the fifteenth century); Ruskin, 1886, III, p. 289 (founded on the Doge's Palace, with *bold capitals*); Zanotto, 1856, p. 607 (to the fifteenth century); Mothes, 1859, p. 230; Tassini, 1863, 1915 ed., p. 251 ('would seem erected in the fifteenth century'); Elenco, 1905, p. 75, no. 163 (Cann. 2139; to the fifteenth century); Lorenzetti, 1956, p. 637 (to the fifteenth century).

**182.** *Palazzo Mastelli.* Selvatico, 1852, p. 156 (to the fifteenth century); Tassini 1870, p. 21 et seq. (to the fourteenth century); Idem, 1879, p. 78. (to the fourteenth century); Paoletti, 1893, I, p. 34; Elenco, 1905, p. 81, no. 273 (Campo and rio dei Mori, Cann. 3379; to the fifteenth century); Lorenzetti, 1956, pp. 400, 401 (to the fifteenth century).

**183.** *Palazzo Cavazza.* Tassini, 1863, 1915 ed. pp. 552, 553 (originally of the Cavazza, then bequeathed in 1461 to the Brotherhood of the Carità and by this sold in 1487 to Michele Foscari; in 1491 it passed to Mocenigo dalle Zogie); Idem, 1879, p. 93.—The motif of the two coupled windows of the mezzanine, with segmental arch, is worthy of note.

**184.** *Palazzo Giovanelli.* Bertarelli Album, *c.* 1750, Plate 111. See also: Coronelli, Plate 104; Fontana, 1845, Plate 75; Zanotto, 1847, p. 423; Selvatico, 1852, p. 150 (restored by Medina in 1847); Ruskin, 1886, III, p. 296 (founded on the Doge's Palace); Zanotto, 1856, pp. 362 and 363 (perhaps by Baseggio or by Calendario); Ricci, 1858, II, p. 339 (mentions 'a document said to have been recently discovered', which attests that Calendario was the architect of the palace); Mothes, 1859, p. 224 et seq.; Tassini, 1870, p. 12 et seq.; Idem, 1879, p. 109 (does not consider impossible Calendario's authorship, in that the palace, as it seems, was the property of the Venetian Municipality); Fulin-Molmenti, 1881, p. 253; Paoletti, 1893, I, p. 25 (notices the points of contact with Palazzo Cavalli); Raschdorff, 1903, Plate XII (to 1470-1500); Marini, 1905, p. 83 ('radically restored and tampered with'; on this occasion the uncovered staircase was removed); Musatti, 1905, p. 284 (restored by Meduna); Elenco, 1905, p. 77, no. 188 (Cann. via Vittorio Emanuele 2290-2); Lorenzetti, 1956, p. 436 (to the first half of the fifteenth century); Miozzi, 1957, I, p. 448.
The aspect of the façade before Meduna's intervention may be deduced from an engraving in the collection of 61 views of *c.* 1750: it was asymmetrical in that the corner balcony on the *piano nobile* and the two corner windows of the top floor were missing. Meduna reduced the façade to a symmetrical module, distorting the original characters. The nine-light window on the top floor is singular. The courtyard, with tall columns divided by a *collarino*, though much tampered with, still contains elements worthy of study.

**185.** *Palazzo Cavalli Franchetti.* Carlevarijs, 1703, Plate XCVI; Coronelli, 1709, Plate 23; Visentini, 1742, I and 3 (the ground floor is substantially as at present); Quadri, 1834, p. 34 (see also here the characters, not very different, of the ground floor); Fontana, 1845, Plate 19 (note: the Baroque balconies of the great windows on the ground floor; two coats of arms in place of the two small, square windows; a different portal); Zanotto, 1847, p. 422 (to the thirteenth century!; and recalling the Doge's Palace); Selvatico, 1847, p. 113; Idem, 1852, p. 231 (to the fifteenth century); Ruskin, 1886, III, p. 283 (of little merit in the details; good balconies of

a later Gothic type); Zanotto, 1856, p. 585 (is reminded of the Doge's Palace; '...exquisitely elegant, distinguished by the best proportions, the well arranged curves and the good placing of the accessory ornamental parts'); Mothes, 1859, p. 224; Tassini, 1863, 1915 ed., p. 770; Paoletti, 1893, I, p. 32 (praises the proportions; good capitals, akin to those in the loggia of the Doge's Palace), Molmenti-Mantovani, 1893, p. 108; Raschdorff, 1903, Plates VIII and XIV (with plans; given to 1370-84); Marini, 1905, pp. 82 and 83 (praised for its 'harmony'); Elenco, 1905, p. 14, no. 213 (S. Marco 2859); Musatti, 1905, p. 155 (mentions Boito's 'restorations'); Lorenzetti, 1956, p. 617 (connections with the Doge's Palace); Miozzi, 1957, I, p. 444; Hubala, 1966, p. 776. The modern side starts from the turn of the façade (only the first axis of windows belongs to the ancient part) and takes in also the grand staircase in the part jutting out towards S. Vidal; the whole is a lamentable work of the Paduan architect Camillo Boito, of 1896; the central balconies were also remade by Boito.

**186.** *Palazzo Pisani Moretta.* Clearly visible in the *View* by Jacopo de' Barbari; Carlevarijs, 1703, Plate LXXXI; Coronelli, 1709, Plate 151; Cicognara, 1820, Plates 53, 59; Idem, I, p. 120, Plates 103 and 404; Fontana, 1845, Plate 30 (one can already see the balustrade on the cornice certainly added shortly before); Zanotto, 1847 (is reminded of the Doge's Palace); Selvatico, 1847, p. 116; Idem, 1852, p. 232; Ruskin, 1886, III, p. 310 (notes the passage to the Renaissance); Burckhardt, 1925, p. 150; Zanotto, 1856, p. 592; Mothes, 1859, pp. 221 and 224 (later than 1370); Kugler, 1858-9, III, p. 578; Tassini, 1863, 1915 ed., p. 571 (of the beginning of the fifteenth century); Hare, 1884, p. 69; Paoletti, 1893, I, pp. 32 and 33 (later than the middle of the fifteenth century; notes the two doors and the recalls to the Doge's Palace) Raschdorff, 1903, Plates X and XIV (with plans); Marini, 1905, p. 85 ('the most beautiful example of the ogival architecture already feeling the influence of the Renaissance'); Elenco, 1905, p. 122, no. 235 (calle Pisani Barbarigo, S. Polo 2766); Lorenzetti, 1956, p. 622 (to about 1450); Miozzi, 1957, I, p. 447; Maretto, 1959, pp. 21 and 54 ('one of the highest achievements of the Venetian Gothic'; notes the two doors; the interior remade).

**187.** *Palazzo Contarini at St. Mark's on the Grand Canal.* Visible in the *View* by Jacopo dei Barbari. Quadri, 1834, p. 36 (the access to the ground floor differed from the present one, which is of more recent times); Zanotto, 1856, p. 581 (to the fifteenth century); Lorenzetti, 1956, p. 613. The first floor of the rear façade is intact, with a four-light window of the fifth order; some single windows remain on the second floor; only the ancient window-sills on the ground floor. Under the upper cornice, there is a walled-up, six-foiled eye, with torus mouldings inside a square, dentil frame, perhaps more ancient than the present palace (there is a similar one on fondamenta delle Convertite 689 at the Giudecca, in Veronese limestone). The remains of a large and singular building, pulled down in the last century, may be seen from the ponte di S. Cristoforo (calle di S. Cristoforo) by S. Gregorio and consist of an elaborate plinth with a cable ornament surmounting a line of dog-teeth; and a corner pilaster with cable, accompanied by alternate quoins also decorated with dog-teeth. This is Palazzo Venier delle Torreselle

(Dorsoduro 699) and it is difficult to say whether on this base, unique of its kind in Venice, there once stood a building similar to Ca' Foscari or Palazzo Cavalli Franchetti (Lorenzetti, 1956, p. 533). It is certainly of the second half of the century. A modest example of trefoiled window with small quatrefoil eyes, according to a pattern which we shall find again on the mainland, is on the façade of a house in rio di San Pantalon, with fourth order arches (cf.: Maretto, 1960, p. 33).

**188.** *Palazzo Donà at S. Vio.* Bertarelli Album, *c.* 1750, Plate 18.

**189.** Lorenzi, 1868, p. 83. See also, for the document of 1463: Cadorin, 1845, p. 108 et seq.; Zanotto, 1853, I, pp. 74, 79 et seq., n. 16 (with an inexact interpretation of it); Selvatico, 1856, p. 222; Ricci, 1858, II, p. 341; Paoletti, 1893, I, pp. 40 and 41; Thieme-Becker, XXVI, pp. 203 and 204; Planiscig, 1930, p. 93 recalls the Foscari arch.

**190.** Zanotto, 1853, I, p. 78.

**191.** Lorenzetti, 1926, p. 238.

**192.** Sanudo, *Vite*, col. 1174; Zanotto, 1853, I, p. 79.

**193.** We have seen Pantaleone di Paolo working by the side of the Bons at the Ca' d'Oro (Paoletti, 1920, p. 106), but his work there is not at all precisely traced (at the time he was certainly an executant of other people's designs), nor is it identifiable in the work carried out for the Scuola Grande della Carità, where almost everything is by now dispersed, and at S. Giovanni Evangelista. Pantaleone had worked also with the brothers Giovanni and Alvise in Ferrara; he died in 1465. He was of the same age as Bartolomeo and his faithful collaborator, but his figure still remains enigmatic (see also under this in Thieme-Becker, 1932, pp. 203 and 204).

**194.** Planiscig, 1921, p. 6.

**195.** Planiscig, 1930, pp. 74 and 92; Fogolari, 1930, p. 457; Ongaro, 1935, p. 10.
It is quite probable that to Bon was due also the so-called Scala Foscara, demolished by Manopola in 1618, which, climbing east to west from the courtyard, reached the level of the Loggia Foscara, skirting the outer wall of the passage between the Porta della Carta and the Foscari arch. Perhaps the modern authors give too much credence to Cesare Vecellio's engraving published in *Degli abiti antichi e moderni*, Venice, editions of 1590 and 1598.

**196.** Zanotto, 1853, Plate XVII, p. 4.

**197.** Paoletti, 1893, p. 41.

**198.** Lorenzi, 1868, p. 76, doc. 173.

**199.** Cicognara, 1838, I, p. 64.

**200.** *Foscari Arch.* Cicognara, 1838, p. 64; Zanotto, 1853, I, p. 166; Plate XVII, p. 4; Lorenzetti, 1956, p. 240; Fogolari, 1927, Plate 9; Gallo, 1933, p. 287; Mariacher, 1950, pp. 21 and 22. As we saw in connection with the Foscari arcade, Mariacher and Pignatti consider that Antonio Bregno replaced Bon after 1440 (or after 1450). According to Pignatti, Bregno had made 'the major part of the Foscari arch'; Bassi-Trincanato, 1960, pp. 44 and 46.

**201.** *The Foscari Loggia.* Zanotto, 1853, I, p. 159 et seq., Paoletti, 1893, I, pp. 6 and 8.
Recently (D'Elia, 1962, p. 217) the hand of Giorgio di Sebenico has allegedly been discerned in the capitals on the coupled columns towards the courtyard. He, however, had been invited in 1441 to build the Duomo of Sebenico and it is difficult to accept that these galleries on the courtyard are earlier than 1441, considering that for the nearby Foscari loggia a later date is very probable. Finally, the affinity between the heads of famous ornament of Sebenico and those of the Venetian capitals leaves us perplexed.

**202.** See: Cicognara, 1838, I, p. 57; and, in particular: Zanotto, 1853, I, pp. 79 and 80.

**203.** Corner, Eccl. Ven., Suppl. p. 416.

**204.** Paoletti, 1893, I, p. 17.

**205.** Zanotto, 1853, I, pp. 87 and 88.

**206.** Zanotto, 1853, I, p. 89.

**207.** See the exhaustive treatment of the subject in: Zanotto, 1853, I, pp. 164 and 165. A clear idea of the solid wall under the Foscari loggia is given in 1590 by the already mentioned engraving of Cesare Vecellio (reproduced in: Bassi, 1964, p. 184).

**208.** Zanotto, 1853, I, p. 163.

**209.** Zanotto, 1853, I, p. 164, (in opposition to Cicognara's assertions) Bassi, 1962, II, p. 49; Eadem, 1964, pp. 184 and 185.

*170. Palazzo Priuli in rio dell'Osmarin. Corner window.*

*171. Ca' d'Oro. Façade.*

173. *Ca' d'Oro. Multi-light window of the loggia of the third order.*

174. *Ca' d'Oro. Detail of the loggia of the third order.*

175. *Ca' d'Oro. Loggia of the second order.*
176. *Ca' d'Oro. Detail of the loggia of the second order.*
177. *Ca' d'Oro. Loggia of the second order from within.*

*178-179. Ca' d'Oro. Capital of the loggia of the second order.*
*180. Ca' d'Oro. Detail of the loggia of the second order from within.*

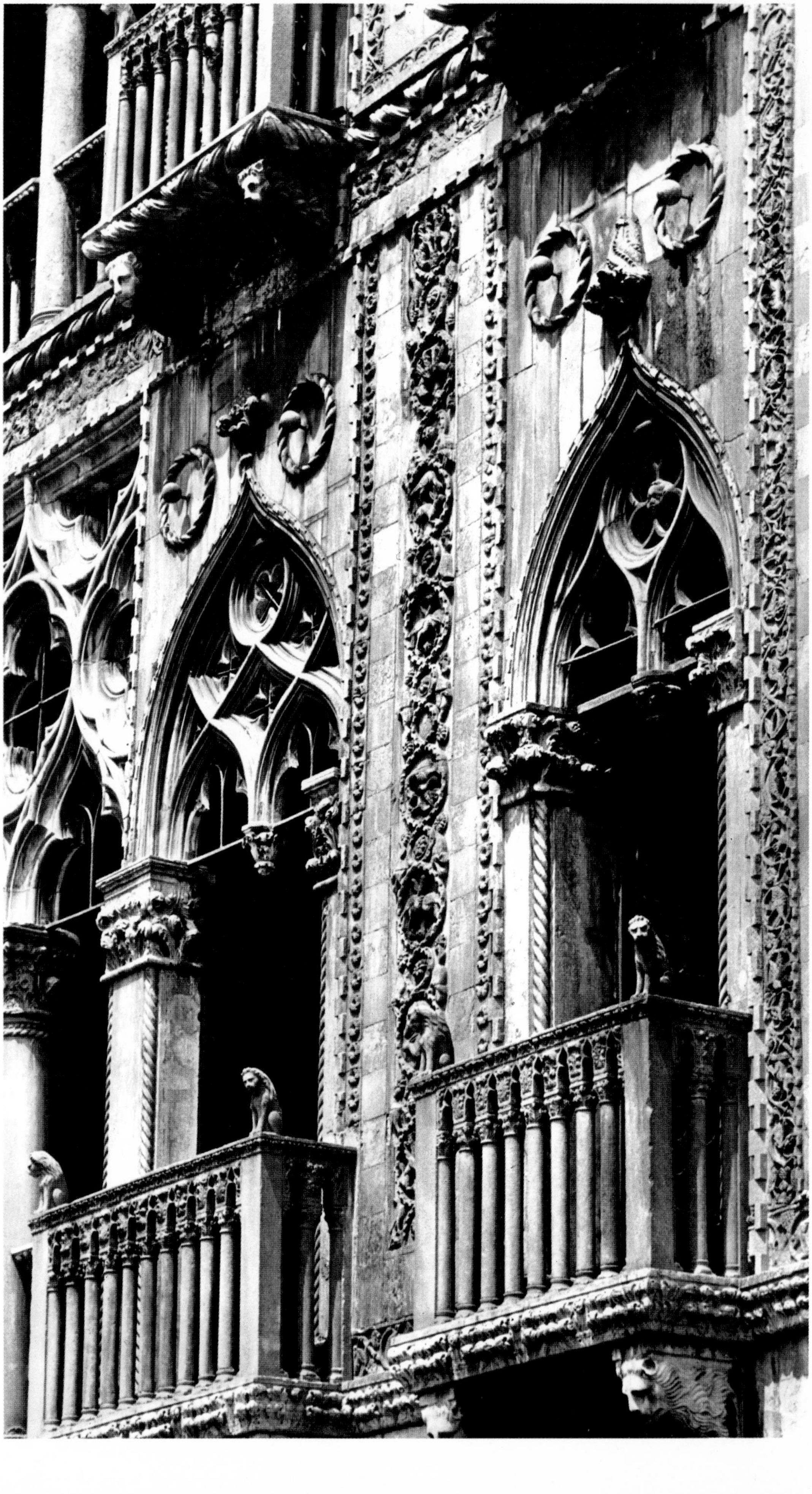

*181-182. Ca' d'Oro. Details of the right side of the façade.*

186. Ca' d'Oro. Courtyard ('cortile').
187. Palazzo Barbaro at the Accademia. Detail of the façade.

188. *Palazzo Barbaro at the Accademia. Façade.*

190. *Palazzo Zaguri. Façade on rio S. Maurizio.*
191. *Palazzo Zaguri. Rear façade on Campo S. Maurizio.*
192. *Tintoretto's House on Fondamenta dei Mori.*
193. *View of Gothic houses near La Salute, from the Ponte dell' Accademia.*

194. *Palazzo Barbaro and Palazzo Dario on the Grand Canal.*
195. *Palazzo Amadi. Detail of the façade.*

196. *The Doge's Palace. Western façade.*
197. *The Doge's Palace. Large window on the Piazzetta.*

198. *The Doge's Palace. Porta della Carta.*
199. *The Doge's Palace. Corner towards Porta della Carta.*
200. *The Doge's Palace. Detail of Porta della Carta.*

201. *The Doge's Palace. Porta della Carta.*
*Detail showing St. Mark.*
202. *The Doge's Palace. Porta della Carta.*
*Detail with 'Charity'.*

203. *The Doge's Palace. Passage into the courtyard.*

204. *Palazzo Corner Contarini dei Cavalli and Palazzetto Tron.*

205. *The Ca' Foscari complex.*
206-207. *Ca' Giustinian by Ca' Foscari. Details of the façade.*

*208. Ca' Giustinian. Detail of the façade.*

209. *Ca' Foscari on the Grand Canal.*

212. *Ca' Foscari. Detail of the façade.*
213. *Palazzo Loredan dell' Ambasciatore.*
214. *Palazzo Contarini-Corfù, also called degli Scrigni.*

215. *Palazzo Morosini Brandolin.*
216. *Palazzo Erizzo at the Maddalena.*
217. *Palazzo Giovanelli at S. Felice.*

218-221. *Palazzo Mastelli or del Cammello on rio della Madonna dell'Orto. Façade and details.*

*226. The Doge's Palace. Detail of the Loggia Foscara.*

*227-228. The Doge's Palace. Details of the gallery towards the courtyard.*

*229. The Doge's Palace. Internal portico towards the courtyard, on the western side.*

*230. The Doge's Palace. Capitals of the gallery towards the courtyard.*

233. *The Doge's Palace. The courtyard.*

# Chapter V
# BETWEEN GOTHIC AND RENAISSANCE - VENETIAN GOTHIC ON THE MAINLAND

*The buildings of the Floriated (Fiorito) Gothic from about 1450 to about 1480.*

Gathering together into a single vision the buildings inspired in some important feature by the Doge's Palace and having in common some significant traits which could make one think, if not of the same architect, then of the same team or related teams, makes less arduous the examination of the fifteenth–century buildings—some of them of great splendour—which arose all over Venice from about 1450 to about 1480.

It must be admitted that on the critical plane their study is very difficult today. One of the criteria adopted by Ruskin in order to define the 'evolution' of this lagunar Gothic was derived from the study of the trefoiled inflected arches. Now, if it is true that the so–called sixth order (trefoiled window surmounted by a flower finial and enclosed in a rectangular field) is an enrichment of the fifth order, the remains tend none the less to demonstrate that the two forms may have been born at the same time, and that after all the sixth order may have arisen earlier than is thought.

We have spoken of the spreading of the fifth order during the fourteenth century. This order continued into the first half of the fifteenth. Reliable data are lacking and our observations have therefore only the value of very cautious suggestions. We meet it (and we refer in this respect to the most archaic indications, which may yet prove fallacious!) with rosette capitals in calle delle Botteghe[1]; in a house at ponte di Ca' Balbi at St. Mark's (a three–light window and single window with rosette capitals); a three–light window in calle del Cristo at S. Moisè[2]; a house on calle della Madonna at S. Zanipolo[3]; and we have already mentioned a façade in fondamenta della Madonna dell'Orto in which a floor of the fifth order coexists with four Romano–Byzantine windows located below. But this seems above all the place to mention the large house in campo Bandiera e Moro (Castello 3626), with two four–light windows on the same axis as the four–light window of the upper mezzanine (with small rectangular windows, perhaps of the same epoch as the others and as those with segmental arches on the ground floor—with rosette capitals: not anterior to about 1450, but of an archaic type[4]).

As for the sixth order, there are elements to be accepted with great prudence which would support an early appearance, as for instance, the house on five floors in Marzaria S. Salvador, remarkably balanced in composition, with four two–light windows vertically aligned on the right (with rosette capitals) and an upper mezzanine with depressed arch, perhaps still of the first half of the fifteenth century[5]; the façade of the Salvadori–Tiepolo house on rio dei Barcaroli, with the axis of the two three–light windows displaced to the left (the lower one of the sixth order, framed, the upper one of the fourth order, and all the capitals with rosettes); the whole appears to be of the same period—the first half of the fifteenth century[6]; the small palace in fondamenta Minotto at S. Croce (façade with two Gothic floors, multi–light windows with rosette capitals, courtyard with external staircase—remade—trabeated portico with owl–beak brackets and rosette capitals, an archaic–looking three–light window of the fifth order)[7]; a house in fondamenta Misericordia[8]; the single window at ponte dei Miracoli with two paterae in the frame and a grating[9]; the large house, thought to have been the palace of Caterina Cornaro, situated between calle della Regina and rio Pesaro, which its remarkable façade overlooks—the apertures (two four–light windows in the middle, etc.) are all walled–up but were perhaps of the sixth order and the mezzanine, in the upper part, is of the most archaic type, with segmental arches[10]; the house of the Manuzio with the beautiful three–light window of the sixth order with flower finials on the vertices and framed by the usual Byzantine dentil ornament, but with archaic capitals and four axes of single windows of the fourth order[11]; Palazzo Sanudo on corte del Carro, with mixed elements of the fourth and sixth order and rosette capitals: an unusual ensemble which fits into the fifteenth century, with a beautiful five–light window[12].

Extending our examination to other elements capable of suggesting somewhat less un–certain locations in time, we realize that none of the many characteristics peculiar to these changes in taste are absolutely valid. Their validity has in most cases very elastic limits in time. Nor does the particular choice of taste or the fineness of execution count. Legions of master-masons and stonecutters were active all over the city. One should be careful not to confuse differences in taste and execution with distances in time. This premise stated, it seems appropriate, first of all, to make known two dates referring to two buildings erected in the seventh and eighth decades of the century, as a demonstration of a development of this style with time which imposes the greatest caution. It is, in fact, a mistake to believe in a development in time denoting a progressive infiltration of Renaissance modes and, as a consequence, a progressive decline of the Gothic style. The Renaissance was to prevail in the end, but not without repeated returns and unexpected revivals of 'out–of–date' forms.

One of these palaces is the Contarini Seriman at the Gesuiti built perhaps, according to Paoletti, under the direction of a certain Pietro of 'Como' (as it appears from a document of 1466[13]). It is of great constructional regularity, with capitals in the central four–light window in almost Renaissance style similar to those of the Foscari arch (Paoletti) and a curious string–course cornice not really Gothic in style, attesting a very definite personality. The date of 1466 and the authorship of the Comasque artist appear indeed surprising, as soon as one considers the Palazzo Soranzo–van Axel, built ten years or so later. But surprises of this kind are possible in Venice, when one thinks of the various 'firms' of builders, some more, some less conservative in matters of taste. By the side of Palazzo Contarini Seriman, Paoletti sets Palazzo Bragadin Carabba at S. Marina, noting the capitals which, here also, recall those of the Foscari arch, and the string–course cornice which is a repetition of that of Palazzo Contarini Seriman (suggesting perhaps the presence of the same architect). The cherubim adorning the remarkable balcony are also a clear Renaissance evidence. The façade, unchanged, is symmetrically arranged around the central axis, which also divides the water–gate[14].

Palazzo Soranzo–van Axel, however, is of 1473–9 yet in the ensemble of its characters, all integrally Gothic, would be thought earlier than the two buildings just mentioned.

It may be worthwhile, at this point, to add a few remarks on the particular aesthetic significance of the sixth order. The windows, the multi–light windows, are here strongly framed and undoubtedly represent the fullest maturity of Venetian secular Gothic,

*Gothic window at Ponte dei Miracoli*

increasingly frequent, as a luxury element in dwellings of various sizes, and particularly dominant in great residences. They are an expression of refined beauty and social prestige and represent on the whole a limit beyond which, for this very particular type of Gothic, there is no possibility of further development. With customary building plans, the Renaissance was to inherit also the distributive characters of the façade of the Venetian palace, but their interpretation will be entrusted to an entirely new vocabulary.

In conclusion, the manifestation of the sixth order in this last phase of settlement of the Gothic in Venice displays these openings as complexes isolated in the wall, which in consequence appears blind, without an architectural articulation of its own.

String–courses also are often missing in the fourteenth century and then appear in the fifteenth, still not quite regularly, as a stable element. On the second floors they are often entirely absent.

Thus, in the same way as Venetian builders avoid the overhanging of the roofs and give to the cornices a relatively flat and moderately thick character, the string–courses also are reduced to thin linear elements which disturb but little the powerful sense of isolation of the multi–light strongly framed windows, into which open zones of deep shadow. Even in the great fifteenth-century palaces the string–courses often pass almost unnoticed. Thus the character of this architecture, in no way tied to structures articulated and unified in all their parts (as is the case on the Continent) is reconfirmed, and the brick wall remains an excellent pretext for fresco decorations: such as very elegant plant representations, imitated from materials; or painted scenes, true 'pictures' with sacred and profane stories, allegories, etc., frescoes that have by now all disappeared (except on the mainland) because of the saltiness of the atmosphere.

The Ca' d'Oro, from about 1440 onwards, must have exerted a considerable influence (and we have already seen it in the two Palazzi Giustiniani and elsewhere). In a great building like Palazzo Bernardo at S. Polo we note the use of cable ornaments along the edges of the façade, along the string–courses and on the vertices of the window posts. These are subtle chiaroscuro values which, in the imposing façade marked by the three four–light windows on the central axis (the two larger ones are supported by tall columns) are contained by the bands of alternate quoins already noticed at Ca' Foscari, etc. The full maturity of this Gothic is revealed also by the large marble discs placed beside the flower finials, in perfect balance between the serrated ornaments and the extrados. An attribution to 1450–60 seems suitable for this building, spoiled within but with the façade in a good state of preservation and not disfigured by too violent intrusions[15]. It is one of the palaces which more completely realize the ideal of Venetian floriated Gothic in a strong and splendid measure.

One of the most refined and balanced examples of floriated Gothic, unthinkable without the precedent of the Ca' d'Oro, is what remains of Palazzo Caotorta on rio Menuo or della Verona, with two façades at an angle over the water, in which the refinement of the execution and the luxury of the details all contribute to a formal balance not far from that of the buildings near Ca' Foscari. One should note the water-gate, whose vertex joins the first string–course[16].

Even more imposing and similar in many of its features is Palazzo Pesaro Orfei at S. Beneto, particularly remarkable for the preservation of its vast bulk, with a façade on rio de Ca' Michiel and another, larger, on campo S. Beneto, while the long side gives on calle Pesaro[17]. The very long traversing hall (forty–five metres) connects the two façades and is flanked by two courtyards, of which the greater had an uncovered staircase, now badly tampered with.

The façade on campo di S. Beneto is one of the most complex of the Venetian Gothic. There are two large seven–light windows in the middle, a right wing with two axes of

windows (one of the axes very near the multi–light windows) and a left wing with the axes
of the two windows very far from the multi–light windows, the ground floor with a rectangular portal in the middle and small windows with very pointed and segmental arches;
the mezzanine under the strong cornice with a three–light window in the middle and other,
single apertures. The edges with quoins of Istrian stone of alternate size are associated with
spiral columns. The façade on rio de Ca' Michiel has on the first and second floors two four /
six–light windows (with two pilasters), on the third floor a dwarf four–light window,
all flanked by two axes on each side, and a water portal between four windows with segmental
arches (one of them walled–up). The enormous length of the traversing halls on the first
and second floors has required the opening of two large three–light windows, one above
the other, giving on the larger courtyard, and of two others on the smaller courtyard. On
the top floor there is a typical three–light window with surbased arches (towards the ramo
degli Orfei).

We are quite far from the architectural 'rigour' which characterizes Ca' Foscari or the
Ambassador's Palace. Here it is the purely Venetian, chromatic spirit of so many fourteenth–
century buildings which continues, reinforced by decorative exuberance and elegant
detail.

The sinuous half shapes of heavily maned lions which support the balconies evidence a
manifestly Gothic taste, surely imported from Lombardy. We are, in fact, reminded of
Giovannino de Grassi; the motif came perhaps to Venice with the Lombards working on
the Ca' d'Oro. It achieved a remarkable spread in the domain of the floriated Gothic[18].
An attribution of this building to the end of the fifteenth century has been insisted upon,
certainly based on the presence of four balconies with architraved colonnettes decorated
with cherubim, clearly in Tuscan taste.

We are convinced that a sharper definition of the limits between Gothic and Renaissance
in Venice would help to make the placing in time of many buildings more precise. Even
today, for architecture, one does not go below the limit (which has become a text–book
one) of 1465–70 (Porta dell'Arsenale; appearance of Pietro Lombardo). Why not assume
a more strictly chronological correlation between Renaissance painting and sculpture on
one side (which appear well before 1465 on the lagoon) and the architecture which surely
did not have to wait for that date either in order to show its first signs of life in Venice?
We have seen so far the portal of Palazzo Barbaro and that of Palazzo Contarini degli Scrigni
on rio di S. Trovaso, both probably not later than the middle of the century. The balconies
of Palazzo Orfei, with the Brunelleschian motif of winged cherubim, do not seem at all
inconsistent with the middle of the century.

Also not incompatible with the middle of the fifteenth century is a small building which
has indeed all the marks of the floriated Gothic (without Renaissance intrusions) and is,
of its kind, unique. This is the small Palazzo Contarini Fasan (which legend holds to be
Desdemona's dwelling). The limited area of the two floors, occupied by a splendid three–light
window below and two single windows above, is contained by the two indented edge
bands made of Istrian stone quoins, of alternate size, strong and very regular, placed in
contrast with the three beautiful balconies (whose brackets are, as has been noted, similar
to those of Palazzo Pesaro Orfei). These bands, which we have met in Palazzo Foscari and
in the group of palaces akin to it, are joined with the spiral colonnettes more common
around 1450, and are also in contrast with the gracefulness of the three balconies decorated
with wheel traceries whose direct connection with the Nordic style had already been pointed
out by Ruskin. This is a motif which, from the thirteenth to the early sixteenth century,
can be found in English and French Gothic architecture[19]; and also, for instance, in the early
fifteenth century, in the most ancient windows of the apse of the Milan Duomo. The small

pilasters between the 'turning wheels' are ornamented in Venice with waving scrolls; this also an entirely new element which, with the rest, makes one assume an exceptional creator, different in any case from the authors of the previous buildings. I should say of the middle of the fifteenth century[20].

Palazzo Bernardo Baglioni at S. Salvadore must have been a building of sumptuous and balanced richness. A remarkable three–light window of sturdy proportions framed by a Byzantine dentil ornament which adorns also the extrados of the arches, the wild exuberance of the thick–leaved capitals, the subtle balance with which the discs with the balls are placed on the marble plates, make this also an example of studied refinement, with an almost Lombard plasticity[21].

The most imposing façade among this series of buildings marked by the widespread use of spiral elements is that of Palazzo Contarini dal Bovolo on rio di S. Luca. Here, the central vertical axis is marked by the three five–light windows and is flanked at considerable intervals by three axes on each side. The two water–gates, symmetrically placed, are particularly well–made, with a large flower finial at the top. The kinship with Palazzo Caotorta seems indubitable. This façade, which cannot be seen unless one comes by water, is among the most remarkable ones of about the middle of the fifteenth century[22]. Next to it should be placed Palazzo Molin on rio dei Barcaroli, similar in organization and equally of large dimensions—which, in the middle, instead of the five–light window, has beautiful four/six–light windows with the wings, however, more restricted and with one axis only. There is a three–light window in the middle of the mezzanine, under the cornice, and also a central water–gate[23].

This great building, which Zanotto says was founded in 1468 (but we ignore where his information comes from), would raise, if that date were true, interesting questions, since it would appear to be later than the nearby Palazzo Contarini dal Bovolo.

Another palace of large size (perhaps the tallest in this group) existed once on the Grand Canal, where now stands the small pseudo–Gothic palace erected by Mme Stern. We are referring to Palazzo Balbi, later Michiel–Malpaga, a record of which has been preserved in an album of the Bertarelli collection in the Civic Museum of Milan and in a drawing by Francesco Guardi[24]. The water level floor is followed by a second floor with a five–light window flanked by a single window on each side, a third floor with another five–light window also flanked by a single window on each side and by two corner windows with balconies going round the corner, a fourth floor similar to the second, and finally, a mezzanine with a three–light window between single windows, one on each side.

This last detail, in these large palaces, is important because it leads one to think of a 'school', a workshop (which may perhaps also have been involved in the building of the Palazzo Pesaro Orfei). The corner balconies must have given a peculiar tone to the large mass, of which the Guardi drawing gives the measure, represented as it is at a short distance from Palazzo Rezzonico. One can see here that the two buildings reached about the same height.

This seems to be the best place to mention Palazzo Dolfin at S. Lorenzo, also rich in decorative elements of the floriated Gothic and characterized by windows in which a patera is inserted between the vertex and the finial, and by a double corner window (as in Palazzo Priuli)[25].

We should place in the second half of the fifteenth century, but in a period not too advanced —about ten to fifteen years after the buildings so far mentioned—a group of buildings connected by evident similarities of structure, as will at once become obvious if we compare two façades overlooking campi, such as those of Palazzo Donà in campo S. Maria Formosa and of Palazzo Gritti Morosini in campo S. Angelo. The former is asymmetric and indeed articulated by a free distribution of the openings, multiple and single. The latter is more 'symmetrical' but it too is animated in the lower part by windows (and by a four-light window) of dwarf proportions. It, too, has a grand portal, which is not usually found on façades overlooking the canals, in which these entrances are rather modest because the more formal entrance is always the land one, intended for pedestrians. In the two above-mentioned façades, however, the portal is, instead, included in the façade and is an integral element of it.

Palazzo Donà at S. Maria Formosa[26] has in the lunette of the portal a relief with putti supporting a coat of arms, of Renaissance character, which cannot be considered earlier than about 1460. Palazzo Gritti Morosini[27] repeats, simplified, the same form of portal in which the very pointed lunette is still clearly detached from the frame of the rectangular opening below.

Not distant in time from Palazzo Donà is the building next to it, at no. 6122, with a symmetrical façade which has been perhaps retouched in the right wing[28].

Akin to Palazzo Donà at S. Maria Formosa, but developed in width instead of in height like the two preceding ones, Palazzo Duodo, also in campo S. Angelo, may seem more archaic because of the lesser regularity of the second floor and the more cramped proportions of the central six-light window. But on a more careful examination, these different proportions appear in harmony with the development in width of the façade. The two pilasters, isolated at the two ends of the six-light window, reappear here as in Palazzo Donà; and in addition, the portal is one of those typical of the second half of the century, in which the external fascia of the jambs and of the architrave is extended in identical form around the lunette. Here also, an attribution not earlier than about 1460 could be given[29].

Also with a façade developed in width and with constructional details recalling the pre-viously considered group (one should look at the dwarf four-light window of the mezzanine, the portal and the general trend of the proportions) is Palazzo Marcello ai Tolentini. The façade, developed in placid rhythms, is asymmetric, with irregular intervals between the axes, whose vertical alignment is, however, respected[30]. Equally, Palazzo Bembo on riva del Carbon, which repeats the type of façade with two great axes centred on the double five-light windows, but also has a mezzanine with windows (and dwarf three-light windows) akin in spirit to those we saw at Palazzo Marcello, can be mentioned here. This palace is perhaps of about 1460[31].

With these examples, we could associate Palazzo Pesaro Papafava on the sacca della Misericordia. The base in Istrian stone and the two indented bands on the edges, interrupted on the second floor, would make us place it around 1450–60[32]; Palazzo Loredan Gheltoff with a beautiful six-light window reproducing those of Palazzo Duodo and Palazzo Donà at S. Maria Formosa (with pilasters isolated at the ends)[33]; the small Palazzo Foscari at the traghetto di S. Sofia on the Grand Canal, recently restored, whose six-light window reproduces exactly the type of those mentioned above[34]; the long first floor of Palazzo Molin at S. Maurizio with an articulation which recalls that of the two Palazzi Giustiniani (a central axis marked by two single windows and, at a considerable distance, two four-light windows) with a beautiful portal of the type of those already examined (at Palazzi Donà, Morosini, Marcello)[35]; the graceful Palazzo Longo at the Madonna dell'Orto, with a façade marked by a regular harmony of proportions (even if tampered with)[36].

An important building like Palazzo Soranzo-van Axel at the Miracoli gives, at this point, an idea of the difficulties of an acceptable chronological and stylistic ordering of these buildings of the second half of the century. The building dates are known—1473–9; but the elements which it offers to a careful examination are not such as to make us certain of that date were it not documented. It is a block built on an irregular plan, giving on rio della Panada, rio di S. Canciano, the street alongside the Miracoli church and also adjoining other properties, a free adaptation to the possibilities offered by an area which did not allow one of the more customary and regular solutions. The block presents, inside and out, a coherence such as to make us conclude that it was indeed erected in the years indicated by the documents, and this opinion is supported by the good state of preservation of the wall structures. The building was divided *ab antiquo* in two parts, with two sets of rooms intended for two families, two water and two land entrances, two courtyards, two wells, two staircases, one of which, reached from the more imposing entrance from fondamenta Sanudo, leads to the second floor, while the second, reached from the street along the church, leads to the first floor.

Of the two façades on the water, one gives on rio della Panada and is centred on two four–light windows between two unequal wings, and carries on top of the left wing an addition of certainly not much later date than the remainder; the other gives on rio di S. Canciano and has two three–light windows in the middle.

The halls of the two *piani nobili* are bent at an angle, benefiting in both parts from the light coming through the two multi–light windows.

The two uncovered staircases, though different in the different spaces in which they are inserted, and though perpetuating archaic characters, are among the most significant of the late fifteenth century in Venice[37].

Among the houses displaying with remarkable vitality the charms of the floriated Gothic, we should mention Palazzo Zorzi–Liassidi at ponte dei Greci[38]. The splendid four–light window is at the centre of two wings with three axes of windows each. While, however, the two single windows nearest to the four–light one are of the same sixth order and are enclosed in a single frame, even if separated by an interval, the two outside axes, on both sides, have windows of the fourth order, also surmounted by a flower finial, creating, in this apparent uniformity, a subtle and noticeable variety of accents which is further enriched by the large discs beside the finials (and on the water portal), placed in exquisite balance.

We add, further, Palazzo Contin on rio Terrà della Maddalena, with the two large six–light windows in the centre, framed but without finials, and the two ample wings where eight single windows are irregularly arranged[39].

Perhaps as complete examples of a more symmetrical style, we should mention here Palazzo Molin on the Zattere[40], whose ground floor has been very much remade, with a beautiful four–light window; the very similar Palazzo Corner della Frescada[41], with balcony and mezzanine already in Renaissance style on the façade over the canal, a rear façade with a four–light window and the traversing hall on the ground floor open with a large fifteenth–century arch on the courtyard bordering on the street, as well as a well–preserved floor; Palazzo Zen at S. Stin[42], with Renaissance balcony on the *piano nobile* and Ionic capitals on the second, certainly of the same period. A remarkable building with Baroque additions which have not subtracted from a regularly symmetrical character, with a strong rhythm in solids and voids in the firm framing of the bands of corner quoins integrated in the solid, smooth, tall corner columns, is Palazzo Pisani at S. Marina[43], a large block with three façades and courtyard (and with external staircase) separated by tall columns from the covered rooms forming the traversing hall on the ground floor. It is based on a principle similar to that applied in the fourteenth century, in Palazzo Ariani and, later, in Palazzo Bernardo on the Grand Canal; and was erected, probably, around 1460.

The solid, somewhat sturdy opulence of Palazzo Pisani is found again, unless we are mistaken, in the beautiful façade (the first floor remains) of Palazzo Correr at S. Fosca, where the six–light window (three columns and two strong pilasters) is modelled with a plastic assurance which is visible in the mouldings, in the splendid capitals and in the flower finials, and the motif is developed in width, with a fairly sure rhythm[44]. At this point we mention also the large Palazzo Cappello on rio di S. Lorenzo, with many walled–up windows but not altered in its main features[45].

To the long series of buildings with symmetrical façades may be added here Ca' Nani Mocenigo at S. Trovaso[46], characterized not only by a tendency towards a pronouncedly symmetrical balance of the façade but also by the placing of the great Gothic portal on its centre line. The reliefs of the profiles of the arches and of the dentilled cornices seem to tend towards becoming level with the brick surface; the two single windows flanking it seem associated in a single sequence with the four–light window (a single Byzantine dentil orna-ment separates the two fields); two coats of arms, in relief, are soberly placed in the two inter-vals remaining between the windows, and a subtle harmony of proportions governs this elegant façade. The date would be between 1460 and 1470 and is supported also by the main portal of a late fifteenth–century type.

The entrance hall on the ground floor communicates with the garden at the rear by way of a great round–headed arch (already seen in Palazzo Corner della Frescada). The rear façade carries two four–light windows with rosette capitals; the windows are in part walled–up, and there is a miserable remnant of external staircase.

Similar to Palazzo Nani for the regularity in the distribution of the apertures is Ca' Garzoni on the Grand Canal[47], in spite of alterations (the top floor and the cornice are the original ones).

Palazzo Giustiniani at S. Moisè, of 1474, on which worked a certain Master Paolo di Giacomo, is not so greatly altered as one would think by looking at Coronelli's print, where also the aspect of the tall and narrow building, with a different arrangement but connected by the same cornice and belonging to the same family (to be seen on the left) is not very unlike what it is at present. The rhythmic play of surfaces and windows is similar to that of Palazzo Nani, which we have attributed to this epoch[48]. Enriched by beautiful capitals with thick leaves, symmetrical and with seventeenth–century balconies, is the façade of Palazzo Salamon at S. Felice (the usual two four–light windows with single windows on the sides) overlooking rio di Noale[49].

With the great Gothic buildings, of between about 1450 and 1480, may be associated other, smaller ones, as well as some remarkable scattered 'fragments'. Among the buildings displaying a certain completeness (on the outside) is the small palace in campo S. Maria Formosa (nos. 6127–9), a little unbalanced, with some archaic accents, and windows made of tufa (infrequent in Venice) on the façade and at the rear[50]; the façade on rio di S. Marina of Palazzo Bollani Dolfin[51]; Palazzo Malipiero alla Feltrina (at S. Maria Zobenigo) with the squat columns of the end of the fifteenth century[52]; Palazzo Maravegia, with archaic accents (the depressed trefoiled arches) on the second floor and the axis displaced to the left, perhaps of 1470[53]; the small Palazzo Testa at S. Giobbe, symmetrical and with restorations on the *piano nobile* (where the capitals are in fourteenth–century style) but certainly not earlier than about 1460[54]; the small Palazzo Venier Contarini on the Grand Canal at S. Maria del Giglio, with asymmetrical façade and some irregularity in the forms which make the reading somewhat difficult (the first floor windows are round–headed), perhaps of the middle of the fifteenth century[55]; Palazzo Zorzi at the Zattere which, in spite of the 'fourteenth–century' rosette capitals, must be considered of the second half of the fifteenth century because of its great regularity and symmetry and the closeness of the lateral single windows to the four–light window, typical (but not always) of buildings of the second half of the century[56].

Venice offers many other examples of minor buildings in floriated Gothic style[57], and also examples of abnormal Gothic forms[58], and many other architectural fragments[59].

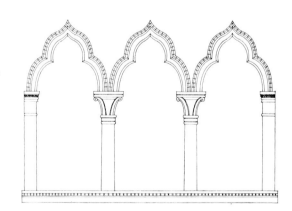

Resuming the examination of the portals of the beginning of the fifteenth century and the similar forms met with in the crowning of other works (arches on the streets, canopies on pendant tombs and carved reliefs on ground level tombs, etc.), it is possible not only to derive useful considerations, but also to discern the products of an imagination in harmony with this very singular city.

The rectangular gate clearly separated from the upper lunette with inflected arch, accompanied or not by dentil or cable ornaments, persists at the beginning of the fifteenth century, as for instance the portal of Palazzo Magno[60], that of the already mentioned Palazzo Dolfin at S. Lorenzo, with the openwork lunette, frame and two paterae, this last a rather infrequent motif as applied to portals (as in Palazzo Zorzi Liassidi) and some others.

One can see rich examples, based on the same principle, on fondamenta dell'Abbazia (Cannaregio 3456*a*) with the arch modelled in deep and involved profiles; that of Palazzo Donà at S. Maria Formosa (no. 6126) already considered, with three putti supporting a coat of arms in the lunette, standing out plastically in every part, the beautiful sculpture of which, not unacquainted with Agostino di Duccio, would take us to about 1450; the portal of the already mentioned Palazzo Marcello at the Tolentini (S. Croce 154); the very singular (for its wealth of plain dog–tooth and cable ornaments) portal of Palazzo Pisani at S. Marina (Cannaregio 6104)[61].

In the first half of the century the church portals are richer, and we mention them here only because they have some elements in common with the Porta della Carta, namely the employment of 'pillars' in particular, which had appeared already at the end of the fourteenth century in the two tabernacles in St. Mark's (at the sides of the main altar), obviously related to the aediculae (of distant French descent) which first appeared at the Doge's Palace and then, around 1400 on the façades of St. Mark's. Let us recall here the three portals of the Frari, that of S. Polo and the singular and very beautiful one of S. Stefano[62]. The motif of the crockets on the extrados of the arches is also of distant French descent[63].

Venice also takes up here the Gothic tympanum (or *wimperg*) of French origin to crown the entrance to calle del Paradiso, transforming the motif already employed to crown gates in the city. In the lunette, with simple pointed arch, is to be found the image of the Madonna di Misericordia surmounted by the high traceried cusp with a quatrefoil oculus, crowned by a flower finial. It is an idea which, although employing known elements, is outside the decorative schemes of Venetian building practice and must be considered to have been applied here at the beginning of the fifteenth century[64].

Passing to the second half of the century, particular attention should be given to the water portal of the already mentioned Palazzo Caotorta, where, with strong architectural sensitivity, the flower finial is united with the string–course cornice and the jambs are treated with an entirely new solution.

In the late Gothic portals, as Gabelentz had already pointed out, the doors remain rectangular and the jambs do not appear scaled in depth but continue identically in the architrave. The pointed arch above is in fact only a continuation of the lower part, with the same width and the same framework[65]. We mention from among the better known examples of this very widespread type, which perhaps began around the middle of the century, the one on the bridge of Palazzo Bernardo at S. Polo, that of Ca' Foscari (calle Foscari 3246) with the three putti supporting a coat of arms, and that of Palazzo Soranzo–van Axel (with original leaves)[66].

Special mention must be made of the beautiful frame on the small façade at no. 3381 calle dei Mori, between the very tall corner colonnettes and the portal without architrave but with two Byzantine paterae (at due distance); one of the rare cases where a certain proportional canon is deliberately applied[67].

It is remarkable that Venetian builders never use the trefoiled inflected opening for portals, but only for windows, though these are also found on ground level tombs, while the mixtilinear arch (we saw it in connection with Porta della Carta) is employed only as a crowning; and only on the Venetian mainland, exceptionally employed in windows.

The Venetian type of portal spread to a lesser degree than one was entitled to think on the Venetian and Friulan mainland (as we saw in the main cities). At S. Daniele del Friuli, in Istria, it is found on the church fronts. Special mention must be made of the portal on the façade of the Cividale Duomo, sculpted in 1476 by a certain 'Jacopo Tajapietra Vinizian' (Jacob, Venetian stonecutter), decorated with cable ornaments and bunches of foliage—important for the date. The Venetian portal appears, however, more frequently[68] along the Adriatic, in Dalmatia and on the western coast, where, incidentally, the reflections of Giorgio da Sebenico's art are always alive (the Monte di Pietà of Fermo)[69].

The fifteenth century sees a marvellous flowering of well parapets, parallel with the spread of the capitals with thick leaves.

The most famous is rightly the one which Marino Contarini wanted to have made by the young Bartolomeo Bon for his 'Domus Aurea'. It bears, as we know, the figures of Fortitude, Justice and Charity, seated on lions and surrounded by a swollen late Gothic foliage; and there are, on the corners, marvellous female heads with typical intense almond eyes. The upper cornice is made up of an abacus, a plain dog-tooth ornament, a cable ornament, a fillet and modillions of an already somewhat Renaissance aspect. The documents published by Paoletti[70] have disclosed, next to the name of Bartolomeo Bon, the name of an 'assistant of Zane Bon who made the cornices of the well', leading Planiscig[71] to believe that this person, pupil of Giovanni Bon, was Nanni di Bartolo. However, Fogolari[72], re-examining the books of Marino Contarini, made clear that Bartolomeo alone had worked from 7 January 1427 to 25 October 1428, in 203 work days, at the completion of the task, and that by 'well cornice' must be understood the modest work on 'the stone which on the ground protects the well parapet', which precludes seeing Nanni di Bartolo in Giovanni Bon's assistant[73].

Bartolomeo's work not only marks a milestone in this artist's development, here still tied to late Gothic expressions in almost Giovanni Bon style, but is equally important for the recognition and dating of similar works in Venice. The nearest is a well parapet known to me only from a photograph (Bohm 2431), considerably less rich than the one at Ca' d'Oro, but where there is a great resemblance between a female head at the corner and the similar ones on the well–curb at Ca' d'Oro. The cornice has a very particular profile.

Near to the Ca' d'Oro well–curb is without doubt the one which was once in corte Bressana. In Veronese red limestone it bears the coat of arms of the Contarini dalla Zogia, two half figures of Justice and Fortitude and a putto with a club. This well–curb is one of the highest expressions of early fifteenth–century Venetian sculpture. The blending of the human figures with the rich foliage enclosing them reaches a rare intensity. It is of a type similar to that of the Ca' d'Oro well parapet, even if it is not possible to speak concretely of any of the Bons, and it may well be thought to be of the second decade of the century. Sold in 1883, it is now in the Victoria and Albert Museum, London[74].

Tassini mentions, also in corte Bressana, another well–curb in white marble as being 'the work of Bon'. I think it is the one, now in the Venetian Civic Museum, where the mixtilinear framing of the coat of arms is quite similar to that on the London curb, with human and lion heads at the corners[75].

To this same period must be referred the well–curb in Palazzo Morosini at S. Giovanni

Laterano, with lion-heads at the corners and obvious iconographic recalls to the school of the Bons[76]. These are particularly elegant examples of a style which will not be lost in the second half of the fifteenth century, if to this period must be ascribed (because of the date transmitted with certainty of the erection of the building) the two in Palazzo Soranzo–van Axel. In the one remaining (the other has been sold), two–handled Donatellian vases and coats of arms of late fifteenth–century cut are joined with the very rich foliage, with the horizontal profiles in virtually Renaissance style[77]. Lion masks in a rich foliage are displayed by the well–curb of Palazzo Tiepolo Papadopoli at S. Polo[78]. The well–curb in corte della Malvasia, belonging to Palazzo Menor della Gatta, of which it carries the coat of arms flanked by the two she-cats in relief, with putti and allegories, is also of a very rich type and at the limits of the Renaissance (around 1480)[79]. Mention should also be made of a well–curb formerly in Palazzo Zaguri at S. Maurizio[80], with a strong and sober presentation of the heraldic element and of the usual amphora (in Donatellian style) with intervals which enhance the value of the plastic element.

There are also well–curbs of polygonal shape (hexagon, octagon), continuing a type already widespread in the fourteenth century, like the one in Palazzo Toderini, enveloped in thick leaves[81]; or the one, with large vertical acanthus leaves, of Palazzo Bernardo on the Grand Canal[82]; or the one originally in Palazzo Rizzo (Goldoni), now at the Correr, with eight lion-heads[83].

The passage to the Renaissance style occurred so gradually as to leave us, on occasion, somewhat perplexed. The 'Renaissance' examples of the late fifteenth century change in reality only their forms, but not their spirit. In these sumptuous products of the maturest Gothic, the passage to the new forms maintains an ostentation of display which is in clear contrast to the new architecture of Tuscan, Coduccian or Lombard inspiration Examples like the one, with festoons, in the courtyard of the Murano Museum, or the one (sold) of Palazzo Marcello ai Tolentini, or the one in campiello della Maddalena, or the one in corte Ca' Magno at the Barbaria delle Role (besides the impressive Lombard staircase), or the one at Jacquemart–André (formerly in a house by ponte delle Erbe), or the four superb pieces in existence at the old Scuola di S. Marco, at the Manin Institute at S. Geremia, in campo S. Giovanni Crisostomo (where the vertical line in the profile of the lion-heads excellently marks the spatial dimension), and the well–curb originally in S. Pietro in Volta and now at the Correr, in which the wear and tear have hardly diminished the sense of prodigious wealth controlled by a taste which in these stonecutters must have been inexhaustible, are proof of the persistence, even if in another guise, of this refined Gothic spirit which is at the base of Renaissance interpretations also. Equally the well–curb of Casa Giusti in Verona, a work dated with certainty, and through documents, to 1458 should be mentioned here, bearing in mind also that in Verona the appearance of Renaissance architectural structures occurred, in the fifteenth century, earlier than in Venice[84].

Beside these exceptional products, there were hundreds of well–curbs made for public and private use in Venice, in the whole estuary and, after the gradual conquest of the Venetian mainland and of the eastern shore of the Adriatic, wherever St. Mark's lion arrived. An exact computation of this enormous material, dispersed among the least thought–of places, would require very long researches which the limitations imposed on this study render inopportune. We shall only endeavour to define a few fixed points.

The type most frequently appearing during the fifteenth century is derived from the rosette capital, characterized more than by the rosette (which sometimes becomes a large flower), by a structure which will be consistently repeated, even if with variations. Of square shape at the top and circular at the base, it carries at the corners large leaves reversed under the cornice. On the four faces there are coats of arms, large roses, lion-heads, on occasion high

reliefs with figures. The cornice is marked by a torus and an abacus, divided by a plain dogtooth ornament.

We may cautiously suppose that this type (of which the examples are legion) arose at the end of the fourteenth century, as seems proved by the well–curb, already examined, of Palazzo Priuli at S. Severo, and by that of the former cloister of the Madonna dell'Orto, where the rigid spiral of the structure and the cut of the shields seem to indicate a relatively archaic period[85].

The use of thick leaves at the corners must have soon prevailed. These examples are very widespread.

We shall mention a few, more or less well known, like the one in Palazzo Loredan Mocenigo at S. Marina, dated to 1435[86]; the one of the early fifteenth century in Palazzo Gabrielli, perhaps earlier than the previous one[87]; the well–curb in corte Petriana at S. Polo, certainly from the middle of the century[88], characterized by the richness of the foliage and very similar to another in the presbytery of Dolo (Venice), of even higher quality, with the coat of arms of the Formenti who had their property[89] near Dolo (at Camponogara); the well–curb, simple and rich, in corte della Misericordia[90]; another one known to me only through three photographs by Bohm (2384, 2432, 2482); the one in campo S. Gregorio; the one in the former Scuola della Carità, bearing on its faces the emblem supported by two brothers of the order[91]; another in the Jacquemart–André Museum in Paris (with cable decoration). The type continues for decades, as is proved by the well–curb in campo S. Giobbe which Grevembroch says is of 1463[92]; the one, now in the Correr Museum, with the date of 1486; and the one transmitted to us by Grevembroch, who says it was perhaps by a certain Andrea Gabrieli who died in 1503, formerly in S. Francesco della Vigna[93].

A late example is represented by a well–curb in the Budapest Museum[94]. Of the second half of the fifteenth century, it is the well–curb with two shields already of Renaissance type, late Gothic foliage and four female heads at the corners, originating from Palazzo Testa at S. Giobbe[95].

Among the bridges remaining from the Gothic period, we should mention particularly that of the Frari, of 1428[96], the most remarkable after the Ponte della Paglia, with moulded arch marked by a Byzantine dentil ornament and the 'bands' made of plates of Istrian stone, richly moulded and perforated by rows of elongated hexagons.

### The 'rustic' Gothic in Venice and on the mainland

In addition to the Venetian architecture discussed so far which is chiefly marked by the marble and stone carved and worked by stonecutters and masons, and by the chromatic qualities of Istrian stone, Veronese limestone and re–used marble, mention should be made in Venice itself and in its dependent territories, of an altogether more modest architecture which finds its accent in the use of terracotta in the Lombard manner, or which simply repeats the forms of the architecture already elaborated in stone, by making use only of terracotta. It is a 'minor' architecture, unimportant in Venice itself.

We have in Venice (calle dell'Ogio and calle S. Aponal, in sestiere S. Polo; and on rio dell'Arco in sestiere Castello at nos. 2515 and 2517) examples of windows with trefoiled inflected arch simply cut out of the smooth wall, without the help of any stonecutters. One finds also in Venice the simpler Lombard type, with two centres and without trefoil, not only in many water–portals but also in windows with simple terracotta archivolts; in rio del Piombo, in campiello dei Orbi (four single–light windows with a terracotta archivolt bordered by a roll profile); in calle del Forno (Castello 6618) and in calle di Mezzo (with dentils and zig–zag motifs[97]) and in calle Dragan (Cann. 4398) with scrolls along the terracotta archivolt.

Ruskin had already drawn attention to a four–light window in campiello S. Rocco[98], as being *among the most ancient efforts of Gothic art in Venice*, placing it in the thirteenth century. It was an instance of trefoiled uninflected arches inside a larger two–centred arch (with torus profile) on columns with truncated cubes, an 'economic' type of the fourteenth century as the 'major' architecture shows. Similar structures may be seen in calle Contarina (Castello 1943–4), with two–and one–light windows decorated with small arches with thick leaves or scrolls, perhaps of the fifteenth century; in the crosera S. Pantalon (Dorsoduro 3854) a three–light window with uninflected trefoils and archivolts bordered by a Byzantine dentil ornament[99]; three richly moulded two–light windows in calle Zotti (Cannaregio 3905, 3907, 3908) with inflected arches, between the fourteenth and fifteenth centuries[100]; some windows of that type in calle del Forner (Castello 5995, 5996)[101] also with inflected trefoils within a two–centred arch, seen by Ruskin on fondamenta della Tana (Castello 1937)[102].

Two graceful two–light windows with arches shaped in terracotta and all the remainder in stone (but the arches are inflected) are found in salizzada del Pistor at SS. Apostoli[103]; it should be noted that both the list (Elenco) and Lorenzetti attribute them to the thirteenth century.

Of all these types, we find numerous examples on the mainland[104], by the side of the nobler forms. Near Padova, in the Marches, in Friuli, the trefoiled inflected arch, directly cut out without intermediate steps from the wall[105], or enclosed in a larger arch[106], or in a simple frame, is common.

One should remember here that these areas were integrated by the decorative frescoes (of which there were, and are, ample traces in Treviso, Asolo, Padova, etc.)[107] imitating tapestries; frescoes which could not have been lacking in Venice either on the more modest houses, like those we have mentioned, or on the houses on which the stonecutters were at work.

The inflected trefoiled arch flush with the wall is also found in that spread–out and depressed form which recalls the Islamic–like Venetian forms of which we have seen striking examples in the thirteenth century. But the perpetuation of this type of arch, which as far as I know is not found in windows and doors but only in arcades and loggias, can be seen in buildings of the fifteenth century. See the house in vicolo Rinaldi in Treviso (where this motif appears both in the porch and in the loggia); the arcade going up to Udine Castle (of 1487); and the loggia of the old Brescia Hospital, formerly the cloister of the Umiliati, erected by Ravanello da Orzinuovi in 1421 or 1436[108].

If the search for even the most modest manifestations of the two–centred pointed arch with terracotta archivolt may present some interest in Venice, it has no such interest, for our purposes, on the mainland, because it represents only one of the many manifestations of Lombard art. It is, however, more important to notice the presence again of the trefoiled inflected arch of lagunar derivation in sometimes quite charming and ornamented variants with terracotta decorations; as in Casa da Noal in Treviso, in via Canova 36–38, much damaged in the war, with the ornate two–light windows and a beautiful external staircase, entirely covered with frescoes, which should be of the first half of the fifteenth century[109]; or the floriated Casa Spessa dal Corno in the Piazza del Duomo in Treviso, where a three–light window with terracotta arches, placed in the middle, is flanked by two two–light windows, while in the wings there are two large single–light windows with balconies which display more openly a Lombard influence (not later than the middle of the fifteenth century)[110].

In Cividale, skilful terracotta workers, very probably Lombards, were the authors of very pointed single–light windows, with ample lights, in which the wide band of the archivolt is sometimes crowned by a flower finial and the arch of the window itself is cut out of the thickness of the wall, with an inflected simple or trefoiled tracing, a mixture of Lombard and Venetian which relates these surviving small fifteenth–century façades to each other[111].

*Between Gothic and Renaissance*

We shall now consider by themselves those buildings which show in part (and at times well combined with Gothic forms) Renaissance characteristics.

We have already seen some examples on the Lagoon, certainly earlier than the middle of the century and, in any case, earlier than the appearance of Pietro Lombardo. Such, for instance, as the portal of Palazzo Contarini degli Scrigni on rio di S. Trovaso. Consideration has also been given to certain remarkable structures where the Renaissance elements form part of the façade itself and condition it. An outstanding example is Palazzo Pisani Moretta.

Now, there are in Venice many other examples which provide the elements of a very complex problem. It is possible that some of these manifestations may even be earlier than that date of 1470 which marks the beginning of the 'Lombard' style (even leaving aside the gate of the Arsenale of Gambello, of 1460).

Indeed, we should not forget that in 1433 Michelozzo was erecting at S. Giorgio Maggiore that library which was to disappear in 1614, and that in 1458 Filarete was in Venice. A curious case of collusion between the Gothic and Renaissance architectures of Venice is documented by Bartolomeo Bon's refusal in 1461 to cede the project for a very large palace on the Grand Canal which he had drawn up for Francesco Sforza to the Florentine Benedetto Ferrini, to whom the Duke had subsequently entrusted the building of a house *a la moderna*, adding however that the 'façade towards the Grand Canal' was to be built 'in the Venetian manner'. It is not improbable that the drawing of a 'Palace on a marshy site' in Book XXI of his treatise on architecture reflects a compromise solution thought up by Filarete, entrusting to Bon the execution of the central seven–light window with marble parapet and wall[112]. This was a concession resulting in a hybrid devoid of any intention to merge the two opposed architectural conceptions. Filarete seems, indeed, in all the remainder of this project to draw from the Venetian style only the part characterized by the two lateral towers and the portico on the water side, taking their inspiration from the architecture of the thirteenth century[113]. Nor is it possible to attribute to Bon the still visible remains of the 'Ca' del Duca'.

An element which often appears in Venetian Gothic palaces and houses is a certain kind of colonnette with double shaft, employed in balustrades and not always, as one would suspect, due to later additions. It is an open problem and we do not intend to solve it here. We must, however, say at once that this type of small pilaster did not originate in Venice (as seems obvious) but certainly in Tuscany. The most ancient example known to me is the one offered by the base of Donatello's *Judith* (1457) and of those that can be traced in Tuscany it is the most ancient and the nearest, in the slenderness of its framework, to the Venetian examples. Indeed, the other examples which could be adduced show the motif (as used for balustrades) much more stocky (and without correspondence in Venice), as in the Villa Medici in Fiesole (about 1460)[114] and that of Poggio a Caiano (about 1480)[115].

The beautiful façade of Palazzo Erizzo–Nani–Mocenigo on the Grand Canal—very regular, with two four-light windows on the axis of symmetry and the corners marked by alternating quoins—recalls again the group we assembled around Palazzo Foscari. Not only do the balustrades of the *piano nobile* have colonnettes with double spindle but the architraved windows on the ground floor, not opened by breaching the wall[116], are already Renaissance; and as, on the basis of many other indications, the building is not later than 1480, the problem arises of the origin of these forms, which were certainly not born in Venice but imported. We must remember that they were made familiar in the second half of the fifteenth century by Laurana, by Michelozzo and by Fancelli. The problem of the architraved windows on the ground floor also arises in the case of other buildings dated to about 1470–80: Palazzo Nani Mocenigo at S. Trovaso, that of the Ambassador, Palazzo Giovanelli on the Grand Canal, and others still. A beautiful balcony, with colonnettes with double spindle, which is certainly of the same period as the beautiful Gothic façades—two three–light windows in the middle and two lateral axes on each side—can be seen in the centre of a building on rio di S. Giovanni in Laterano (Palazzo Gabrieli), with a simple door with two centres on the water, of the fifth order[117].

A quite singular case is that of the already mentioned Palazzo Mastelli (or del Cammello), where the balcony with spindle shaft colonnettes accompanies a 'Lombardic' floor, also worked out, like the Gothic one, with too much architectural licence. A large house on campo S. Stefano (2949–50) also presents a good instance of such coexistence. In fact, both the seven–light window on the first floor and the Lombard one on the floor above appear to be of the same period of time and are both provided with very long balustrades, equal to each other, which underline the remarkable width of the façade with an almost festive accent.

There is no lack of other types of 'balconies', architraved and of Tuscan origin, with true and proper colonnettes, carrying on the shaft a small capital in a classical–looking style. (It is sufficient to think of the most famous prototype, the balustrade of Palazzo Pitti by Brunelleschi.) The great Palazzo Molin on the rio dei Barcaroli shows, on the first floor, a typical example of these colonnettes, enclosed by strong pilasters at the corners. But an even better and older example is that offered by Palazzo Foscari, which would take us right to the sixth decade of the fifteenth century, unless we wish to see in these balconies a subsequent addition. Similar colonnettes exist also in other palaces of the second half of the fifteenth century, namely Palazzo Zacco, Palazzo Pesaro Papafava (which is among the oldest of this group) and Palazzo Duodo Balbi Valier.

Next, the most important element of all—the window—which contributes to place these buildings in time with greater certainty. Equally, the capitals and cornices attest the presence of Renaissance stonecutters working side by side with Gothic ones, whose activities extend well beyond the arrival of Lombardo, Coducci and of many others who, in Venice, on the Venetian mainland and on the lands by the Adriatic, erected hundreds of buildings whose critical history remains to be written.

These Renaissance manifestations merge with the Gothic in all sorts of ways, at times in an inorganic and almost casual manner, at times aligning themselves with the Gothic elements in a certain order, at times again, fusing with them and producing remarkable pages of architecture. And this happens over a considerable period of time, reaching the third decade of the sixteenth century.

Capitals, almost Bramantesque in style (and with classically inspired indentations in the impost stones of the arches), may be seen on the Gothic façade of the Morosini houses on rio del Fontego dei Tedeschi[118]. Windows of the fourth order in line with round–headed arches may be seen in calle Castagna (Castello 4762)[119]. Atop a house at the Giudecca (S. Biagio 788), with fourth order windows, there is a Renaissance cornice, perhaps of the same period as those[120].

One of the most picturesque examples of almost sublime incoherence in Venice is offered by the small Palazzo Morolin on rio di S. Polo. The Lombard four–light window (with balustrade with architraved colonnettes) is flanked by two single windows on each side, of the sixth order, each of which has on the upper side two free–standing, unframed paterae. The cornice is Gothic, but on the left side there is one of the most exquisite Lombardesque windows, with balcony[121].

Less whimsical and more harmonious is the façade of the beautiful small Palazzo Rossini at ponte dei Barcaroli at S. Fantin[122]. How should one interpret the Lombard three–light window on the first floor, with single Gothic windows with irregularly shaped trefoil arches (of the fourth, fifth and sixth order) close to it above and on the sides, making one think of an archaic foundation? Should we accept, quite hypothetically, that the 'Lombardesque' three–light window dates to about 1460, with the remainder considered on the basis of archaic–looking elements? We leave the question open. The façade of Palazzo Giovanelli–Dorigo on the Grand Canal near the Fondaco dei Turchi is more regular, with four architraved rectangular windows on the ground floor, in line with other Gothic ones of the sixth order, and a large four–light window with balustrade with architraved colonnettes, mentioned here because of its careful symmetry and rigorous alignment of Gothic and Renaissance elements (perhaps of 1480–90)[123].

Another example of 'co–existence' is revealed by the façade of Palazzo Sanudo in salizzada del Fondaco dei Turchi, with the axis of the two two–light windows displaced to the left, the upper one Lombardesque, the lower one Gothic sixth order (late fifteenth century, as seems to be confirmed by the upper cornice with modillions)[124].

The façade of a building, now Pasinetti property, on rio Pesaro (at the corner with rio S. Boldo) contains a fourth–order four–light window in line with another with round arches, Gothic windows on the first floor and Renaissance ones on the second, on the main façade as well as on the right side, the four–light window with round arches supported by Gothic capitals[125]. Another beautiful, homogeneous complex, with the Renaissance door almost certainly of the same time, is that of Palazzo Soranzo on rio S. Stin, with a four–light window and four single windows on the first floor (of the sixth order), rosette capitals and Gothic balcony with cherubim carved in relief in entirely Renaissance style; on the second floor a three–light window and single windows of the fourth order; the whole must be considered as conceived at the same time[126]. A very particular case is represented by Palazzo Da Mula in Murano, whose façade is better understood by isolating the central floriated Gothic four–light window with pseudo–Ionic, almost Renaissance capitals, together with the two large lateral windows, one on each side (two–light windows with small pendant capital in the middle and, above, a quatrefoil), framed (the four–light and the two windows) by the same Byzantine dentil ornament and by three balustrades with small architraved pilasters which align all these elements together with the four traceried oculi which are also aligned at the height of the upper horizontal cornices.

All these elements point to a time round about 1480 and to the hands of one or more stonemason–architects, rather than one architect, certainly one of the strangest cases that Venice can offer[127]. The examples probably go from around 1470 to around 1500, with Gothic stonecutters working side by side with those of the 'Renaissance'. Dates are lacking, but the elements which may be derived from the manifestations of taste of the two currents, which here cross and superimpose each other, concur in determining at least some approximate datings. Furthermore, it is clear that work in the 'German' manner was being done in Venice also after 1500.

The appearance of Ionic capitals, a more relaxed ordering of the façades, a general flattening of the projections, of the profiles and of the framework elements, make one think of the early years of the sixteenth century; as in Palazzo Maffetti on the fondamenta di S. Biagio at the Giudecca[128]; or, a little farther, Palazzo Foscari, also with two four–light windows (of the sixth and fifth order) and Ionic capitals on the *piano nobile* and a balcony of around 1520. More interesting is the rear façade which opens on the ground floor with surbased arches on columns recalling similar manifestations of the Palermitan architecture of the late fifteenth century (Palazzo Abatellis, Palazzo Aiutamicristo), a motif unparalleled in Venice[129]. Another example at the Giudecca may be found in the palace of the former Accademia dei Nobili, with a Renaissance façade which could be considered of the middle of the sixteenth century, in which, however, four Gothic windows of the fifth order are perfectly aligned on the first floor[130]. The rear façade, on rio della Pergola, of the already mentioned Palazzo Viaro–Zane at S. Maria Mater Domini is also a very special case: two five–light windows are greatly displaced to the left, the lower of the fourth order with Ionic capitals, the upper with round arches also with Ionic capitals; the four windows on the right are entirely Renaissance[131]. Another case is represented by Palazzo Bernardi on rio delle Beccarie. The water portal is Gothic, the first floor Renaissance; on the second floor a Renaissance three–light window is supported by Gothic columns while the edges of the ground and first floors are marked by two tall Gothic colonnettes, and the upper cornice is also Gothic (the right side, on rio dei Meloni, is entirely Lombard and very beautiful). Successive phases or 'co–existence' of various teams of workers?[132]

A last example, more balanced than the previous, is Palazzo Zen at S. Stin, with the usual arrangement (two four–light windows and the two lateral axes on each side), where there is a beautiful Renaissance balcony with spindle shafts on the first floor and, on the second, a Gothic loggia on Ionic columns. Here the last displays of the floriated Gothic find a refuge *in extremis*[133].

**1.** *House in calle delle Botteghe.* Elenco, 1905, p. 167, no. 330 (Dorsoduro 3287). A three-light window and two windows underneath a Gothic cornice.

**2.** *House in calle del Cristo.* Elenco, 1905, p. 9, no. 127 (S. Marco 2061). Three-light window with rosette capital and pilaster.

**3.** *House in calle della Madonna at S. Zanipolo.* Elenco, 1905, p. 61, no. 544 (Castello 6302); Maretto, 1959, p. 64 (belonging to a complex building block, patrician and popular). A four-light window with rosette capitals and two windows on each side; door of fourteenth-century type, above which there is the usual opening with segmental arch; of the other façade on calle Venier we have already spoken in connection with the fourth order.

**4.** *House in campo Bandiera e Moro, 3626.* Elenco, 1905, p. 47, no. 234.

**5.** *House in Marzarie San Salvador or del capitello.* Elenco, 1905, p. 25, no. 427 (San Marco 5023; to the fifteenth century). Gothic elements also on the side in calle dei Stagneri. Two axes of single windows on the side; pilaster with cable ornament on the corner.

**6.** *Salvadori Tiepolo House, at ponte della Piscina.* Tassini, 1879, p. 259 (says it was erected by the Salvadori in the fifteenth century). The access is from calle del Caffetier 1997 (S. Marco). Cf. Elenco, 1905, p. 9, no. 122.

**7.** *House in fondamenta Minotto at S. Croce* 151 and 152. Maretto, 1960, p. 50 (to the fifteenth century; with plans).

**8.** *House in fondamenta Misericordia.* Elenco, 1905, p. 79, no. 22 (Cann. 2504). Tall, narrow building, with the shield of the Scuola della Misericordia.

**9.** *The gratings.* These were very common [in Venice (Paoletti, 1920, p. 94; Molmenti, 1925, I, p. 296 et seq.). One can still see them in ramo del Cavalletto at S. Cancian (Cann. 5551 and 5552; in corte del Bianchi at no. 1508 of S. Aponal (S. Polo), in a two-light window of Palazzo Goldoni, in ramo di Ca' Bernardo at no. 2179a; and elsewhere.

**10.** *House of Caterina Cornaro.* Elenco, 1905, p. 142, no. 219 (S. Croce 2265); Chiminelli, 1912, p. 231; Lorenzetti, 1956, p. 466; Maretto, 1960, p. 58 (of the type in U). Inside, an external staircase, disintegrating but, in parts, still good; a two-light window and a three-light window with rosette capitals.

**11.** *House of Aldo Manuzio.* In rio Terrà Secondo di S. Agostino (S. Polo 2311). Elenco, 1905, p. 119, no. 187; Lorenzetti, 1956, p. 602.

**12.** *Palazzo Sanudo.* On corte del Carro; S. Marco 1626. Elenco, 1905, p. 7, no. 93.

**13.** *Palazzo Contarini Seriman.* Tassini, 1879, p. 95 (says it was founded in the fourteenth century by the Dolce family, on the strength of a statement of Sansovino); Paoletti, 1893, I, p. 34 (transmits the document concerning Pietro da Como); Elenco, 1905, p. 92, no. 469 (Cann. 4851) and p. 185 (the two corner pilasters with spiral are the remains of a Venier palace demolished after 1821); Lorenzetti, 1956, p. 393; Bassi, 1957, no. 19, p. 15 et seq. (on the baroque transformation inside). The building preserves Gothic parts outside, also on the sides (on the rio and on calle Venier).

**14.** *Palazzo Bragadin Carabba.* Mothes, 1859, pp. 211 and 212 (gets the name wrong; assigns it to about 1310); Tassini, 1863, 1915 ed., p. 105; Paoletti, 1893, I, p. 34 (to the fifteenth century); Elenco, 1905, p. 59, no. 514 (Castello 6048); Lorenzetti, 1956, pp. 355 and 356.

**15.** *Ca' Bernardo at San Polo.* Zanotto, 1847, p. 433 (sees it in very bad condition); Selvatico, 1852, pp. 170 and 171 (illustrates one of its capitals with 'coiled' foliage); Zanotto, 1856, p. 481; Ruskin, 1886, III, p. 279 (ascribed to 1380–1400; *a glorious palace... of the finest kind, superb in its effect of colour when seen from the side.* Gives it first place after the Ducal Palace); Mothes, 1859, p. 212 (to 1300–1400); Paoletti, 1893, I, p. 29 (sees 'the cyma recta profiles of the cornices' in which he recognizes 'already some classical influences'; deems it coeval with Palazzo Pesaro Orfei; Marini, 1905, p. 82 (to the fourteenth century); Elenco, 1905, p. 118, no. 177 (on rio di Ca' Bernardo; S. Polo 2195; to the fifteenth century); Lorenzetti, 1956, p. 602 (to the fifteenth century); Miozzi, 1957, I, pp. 439 and 443; Maretto, 1959, p. 21 and Plates XIII and XIII bis (typical one block house).

**16.** *Palazzo Caotorta.* Mothes, 1859, p. 212 (called Palazzo Spuerarolli: to 1300–40); Elenco, 1905, p. 12, no. 171 (S. Marco 3563); Venturi, 1924, fig. 291; Lorenzetti, 1956, p. 503.

**17.** *Palazzo Pesaro Orfei.* Fontana, 1845, Plate 42; Zanotto, 1847, pp. 430 and 431; Ruskin, 1886, III, p. 279 (*very late Gothic, just passing into Renaissance; unique in Venice, in masculine character, united with the delicacy of the incipient style*); Mothes, 1859, pp. 212 and 213 (to 1300–40); Tassini, 1879, p. 194 (to the fourteenth century); Paoletti, 1893, I, pp. 29 and 34 (says it is coeval with, and akin to, Palazzo Bernardo at S. Polo; notes the 'imposing and rich modillions' of the balconies, similar to those of Palazzo Contarini Fasan; dates it to 1480–1500); Marini, 1905, pp. 81 and 82 (to the fourteenth century); Elenco, 1905, p. 20, no. 327 and 328, p. 19, no. 311 (S. Marco 3780); Chiminelli, 1912, pp. 228 and 229; Lorenzetti, 1956, p. 488 ('the largest Gothic house in Venice'; gives its plan, which is very interesting).

**18.** *Lion heads.* We shall mention only a few, less well-known examples: in corte di Ca' Barzizza 1172, at S. Silvestro; on the fondamenta rio Marin at S. Croce 799–801; in calle del Spizier 1669, at S. Croce; in a house on rio e calle dei Scudi, at Castello; in a house on Zattere 1384 (Palazzo Moro; Elenco, 1905, p. 157, no. 167: with the Moro coat of arms; to the fifteenth century); another on fondamenta De Biasio at S. Croce 1299a (a sixteenth-century interpretation).

**19.** You may see it, in 1262–4, in St. Urbain at Troyes; and it seems superfluous to mention later instances, on the Continent and in England (a typical example, very similar to the Venetian one, is reproduced by Bond, 1905, p. 480, fig. 4, at Hunstanton); another, very typical example is in Carlisle Cathedral (Bond, 1913, II, p. 675).

**20.** *Palazzo Contarini Fasan; known as the House of Desdemona.* Clearly visible in the *View* of Jacopo de' Barbari; Zanotto, 1847, p. 431; Selvatico, 1847, p. 117; Idem, 1852, p. 229; Ruskin, 1886, III, pp. 283 and 284 (finds it notable more for riches than excellence of design; in spite of its diminutiveness, it is one of the principal ornaments of the very noblest reach of the Grand Canal, and that it would be nearly as great a loss, if it were destroyed, as the Church of La Salute itself); Burckhardt, 1925, p. 149; Zanotto, 1856, p. 581 (to the fourteenth century; 'easily excels other palaces... in the elegance of the mouldings and the wealth of the carvings'; 'the exquisiteness of the balconies and cornices is beyond compare'); Paoletti, 1893, I, p. 34; Raschdorff, 1903, Plate VII (to the fourteenth century); Marini, 1905, p. 81 (to the fourteenth century); Elenco, 1905, p. 10, no. 137 (S. Marco 2307; to the fifteenth century); Venturi, 1924, p. 311; Molmenti, 1925, p. 286; Lorenzetti, 1956, p. 613 (to c. 1475); Hubala, 1966; p. 780 (to c. 1475).

**21.** *Palazzo Bernardo Baglioni at S. Salvatore.* Tassini, 1879, p. 261; Elenco, 1905, p. 24, no. 412 (to the fifteenth century); Lorenzetti, 1956, p. 324 (to the fifteenth century); Forlati, 1926-7, p. 50 (speaks of the restoration of the five-floors façade on Marzaria del Capitello (S. Marco 4858); there remains, on the second floor, the beautiful three-light window already mentioned, between two sixth order windows, with remains of fifteenth-century frescoes and a fifteenth-century coat of arms in stone; two other windows on the third floor, a smoke-stack and the Gothic cornice. The façade of this building which gives on calle delle Ballotte (S. Marco 4866) also has a smoke-stack, two fourth order windows and a fifth order two-light window.

**22.** *Palazzo Contarini dal Bovolo.* Clochar, 1809, Plate 11 (façade and plan) and Plate 13 (internal vertical section showing clear Renaissance elements); Tassini, 1863, 1915 ed., p. 415; Idem, 1879, p. 260; Elenco, 1905, p. 22, no. 362 (S. Marco 4299); Lorenzetti, 1956, pp. 506 and 508 (to the fifteenth century); Bassi, 1965, p. 193 (to the early fifteenth century).

**23.** *Palazzo Molin in rio dei Barcaroli.* Fontana, 1845, p. 36; Zanotto, 1847, p. 429; Elenco, 1905, p. 8, no. 99 (S. Marco 1812 and 1827); Douglas, 1925, p. 140; Lorenzetti, 1956, p. 458 (to the fifteenth century). This great palace gives on rio dei Barcaroli and, on the left side, on rio dei Fuseri. A low wing, added later, extends it on the right. Was occupied by Hotel Vittoria.

**24.** *Palazzo Balbi-Michiel Malpaga.* According to Tassini (*Curiosità*, 1863, p. 400) it was erected by Fantino Michiel, who was Captain-General against the Turks in 1425; but he gives no indications of the erection year, difficult to establish from our data. Bertarelli Album, c. 1750, Plate 19; Mostra di Guardi, Catalogue, Venice, 1965, p. 313, fig. 26 (the drawing is in the British Museum).

**25.** *Palazzo Dolfin at S. Lorenzo.* Tassini, 1879, p. 250; Elenco, 1905, p. 54, no. 406 and p. 184 (calle Larga S. Lorenzo; Castello 5123); Lorenzetti, 1956, p. 363. Of 1450-80.

**26.** *Palazzo Donà at S. Maria Formosa.* Tassini, 1863, 1915 ed., p. 434; Idem, 1879, p. 247; Paoletti, 1893, I, p. 30 (notes the affinity of the relief of the portal with that of the land-side portal of Ca' Foscari); Elenco, 1905, p. 60, no. 531 (Castello 6126); Marini, 1905, p. 82 (to the fourteenth century); Venturi, 1924, fig. 292; Lorenzetti, 1956, p. 381.

**27.** *Palazzo Gritti Morosini at S. Angelo.* Visible in the *View* of Jacopo de' Barbari; Elenco, 1905, p. 18, no. 297 (S. Marco 3832); Lorenzetti, 1956,

(called, hesitatingly, palazzo Gritti). Central axis with three three-light windows one above the other, two lateral axes with single windows. Second mezzanine (below) and *piano nobile* of the sixth order; top floor of fourth order. Rosette capitals, except on the *piano nobile*, where they have thick leaves. Portal displaced to the left. Maretto, 1959, pp. 17 and 21 and Plate XXXII (reproduces the plan, a typical example of the C arrangement).

**28.** *Palazzo at S. Maria Formosa, Castello* 6123. Elenco, 1905, p. 60, no. 530; Maretto, 1959, Plate XXXI (with illustrations and plans). Beautiful courtyard with well-curb.

**29.** *Palazzo Duodo in campo S. Angelo.* Visible in the *View* of Jacopo de' Barbari. Tassini, 1863, 1915 ed., p. 25 (mentions a document from which it appears that a certain Giacomello Duodo, who lived in the fourteenth century, 'erected the palace at S. Angelo': but this can certainly not be identified with the present structure); Idem, 1879, p. 173 (to c. 1350); Elenco, 1905, p. 12, nos. 176 and 178 (to the fifteenth century) and p. 183 (to the fourteenth century; S. Marco 3584); Marini, 1905, p. 82 (to the fourteenth century); Lorenzetti, 1956, p. 502 (to the fifteenth century); Maretto, 1959, p. 21 and Plate XXXII (with the plan).
The rear façade, giving on a garden, has, in its details, an archaic looking character almost certainly due to its secondary importance.

**30.** *Palazzo Marcello ai Tolentini.* Tassini, 1863, 1915 ed., p. 422 (to the fourteenth century); Idem, 1879, p. 286; Elenco, 1905, p. 129, no. 15 (fondamenta Minotto, S. Croce 134).

**31.** *Palazzo Bembo.* Carlevarijs, 1703, Plate XCIV; Fontana, 1845, Plate 28; Zanotto, 1847, p. 426; Selvatico, 1852, p. 233 (to the fourteenth century); Burckhardt, 1925, p. 150; Ruskin, 1886, III, pp. 278-9 (to 1350-80); Zanotto, 1856, p. 599 (to the fourteenth century; is reminded of the Bons); Mothes, 1859, p. 231; Tassini, 1863, 1915 ed., p. 77 (in 'Calendario's school'); Elenco, 1905, p. 24, no. 402 (S. Marco 4793); Marini, 1905, p. 82 (to the fourteenth century); Lorenzetti, 1956, p. 459 and p. 627 (to the fifteenth century). Remarkable the great string-course cornice at the level of the *piano nobile*, of the thirteenth century and re-used here; remarkable also the edges with alternating quoins and cable ornament; on the rear façade two three-light windows (re-used and spoiled; the top floor and cornice remade in the late sixteenth century).

**32.** *Palazzo Pesaro Papafava.* Tassini, 1863, 1915 ed., p. 537 (a palace of this name is mentioned in 1732); Idem, 1879, p. 274; Elenco, 1905, p. 84, no. 327 (calle della Racchetta, Cann. 3764); Lorenzetti, 1956, p. 399 (to the fifteenth century); Trincanato, 1948, p. 94. The rear façade on calle della Racchetta has a second floor entirely of the fourth order, with five-light window in the middle (and isolated pilasters at the ends), six windows with segmental arches on the ground floor. Of more archaic quality because secondary—or really more ancient than the canal façade? This last has a very regular rhythm, recalling that of Ca' Foscari.

**33.** *Palazzo Loredan Gheltoff.* Tassini, 1879, p. 271; Elenco, 1905, p. 74, no. 148 (calle dell'Aseo, Cann. 1864); Lorenzetti, 1956, p. 406 (to the fifteenth century); Maretto, 1959, pp. 16 and 36 (the traversing hall reminds him of those of the thirteenth century and the plan seems to him also

archaic; puts it at the end of the fourteenth century). On the façade there are examples of windows of the fourth, fifth and sixth orders and the right wing is extended by two more axes. If it is difficult to place the façade earlier than the fifteenth century, the internal plan may well refer to a more ancient structure.

**34.** *Palazzetto Foscari at S. Sofia.* Zanotto, 1866, p. 603; Tassini, 1863, 1915 ed., p. 681 (on the façade there is the emblem of the family); Idem, 1879, p. 264; Elenco, 1905, p. 88; no. 387; Lorenzetti, 1956, p. 633 (to the fifteenth century). Next to these six-light windows, so typical, must be placed also that of Palazzo Barbaro at S. Vio; (Fontana, 1845, Plate 50; Ruskin, 1886, III, p. 278: mentioned as a good example of the early fourteenth century; Zanotto, 1856, p. 580: to the fourteenth century; Lorenzetti, 1956, p. 517: to the fifteenth century; Maretto p. 614: to the fifteenth century; Hubala, 1966, p. 763: to the fifteenth century).

**35.** *Palazzo Molin at S. Maurizio.* Tassini, 1879, p. 256; Elenco, 1905, p. 13, no. 2759 and nos. 196-7 (to the fifteenth century; Maretto, 1959, pp. 20 and) 68. The rear, on rio del Santissimo, has a large four-light window on the second floor and three portals with flower finials.

**36.** *Palazzo Longo.* Tassini, 1863, 1915 ed., p. 389 (says that it was erected by Niccolò Longo when, in 1381, the family was admitted to the Maggior Consiglio); Idem, 1879, p. 271 (put under seal in 1310 following the well-known plot); Elenco, 1905, p. 79, no. 231 (fond. della Misericordia, Cann. 2591; beginning of the fifteenth century); Lorenzetti, 1956, p. 406 (to the fifteenth century). It is evident that the dates 1310 and 1381 cannot refer to the present structure.

**37.** *Palazzo Soranzo - van Axel.* Fontana, 1845, Plate 48 (the façade on rio di S. Canciano has two four-light windows); Zanotto, 1847, p. 429; Ruskin, 1886, III, p. 347; Zanotto, 1856, p. 303 (to the fourteenth century); Mothes, 1859, pp. 209-10 (to 1300-40); Tassini, 1863, 1915 ed., p. 243, note 1; Idem, 1879, p. 277; Marini, 1905, p. 82 (to the fourteenth century); Elenco, 1905, p. 103, no. 637 (Cann. 6099; to the fifteenth century); Marzemin, 1912, p. 331; Chiminelli, 1912, p. 226; Paoletti, 1920, p. 92; Tursi, 1923 (mentions the age of the building, erected between 1473 and 1479 by Niccolò Soranzo, who had acquired from the Gradenigo an older structure; the remains of which—certainly thirteenth-century—were re-used in the fifteenth-century building: cornices—visible on the two façades—paterae; sold in 1652 by the Soranzo to the van Axel; acquired at the beginning of this century by Count Dino Barozzi, who undertook its restoration); Forlati, 1926-7, pp. 49, 52, 54, 61 and 64 (on the restorations); Toesca, 1950, p. 150 (transfers it from the fourteenth to the fifteenth century); Decker, 1952, Plates 107-9; Lorenzetti, 1956, p. 329; Maretto, 1959, p. 53 and Plate XIII (points out the singularity of the room distribution), typical example of the large 'two-families' house with two courtyards, two staircases and two *piani nobili*.

**38.** *Palazzo Zorzi Liassidi.* Zanotto, 1847, pp. 432 and 433; Idem, 1856, p. 211 ('most beautiful the profiles, the ornaments and the capitals; and noble, more than in any others, are the forms of the pointed arches'; to the fifteenth century); Mothes, 1859, pp. 201 and 205 (to the beginning of the fourteenth); Tassini, 1863, 1915 ed., p. 359;

Paoletti, 1893, I, p. 34 ('transitional'); Elenco, 1905, p. 45, no. 249 (calle della Madonna, Castello 3405); Lorenzetti, 1956, p. 318; Maretto, 1959, p. 42 (plans and illustrations; the plan is in C). Inside, on the courtyard, there remains a portico with wooden architrave and rosette capitals.

**39.** *Palazzo Contin.* Elenco, 1905, p. 77, no. 192: Cann. 2346–7; there are capitals with thick leaves on the *piano nobile*; with rosettes on the one above. The rear façade gives on rio di S. Fosca; it has a large six-light window above which there is another six-light window of the fourth order. This beautiful building has been severely tampered with.

**40.** *Palazzo Molin sulle Zattere.* Elenco, 1905, p. 157, no. 173 (Dorsoduro 1411); Lorenzetti, 1956, p. 541.

**41.** *Palazzo Corner della Frescada.* Tassini, 1863, 1915 ed., p. 294; Idem, 1879, p. 198 (the need for a 'rapid and efficacious restoration'); Elenco, 1905, p. 170, no. 386 (Dorsoduro 3911; fond. Frescada 3894; crosera S. Pantalon); Lorenzetti, 1956, p. 573 (middle of the fifteenth century); Maretto, 1959, p. 58 ('vigorous and rich axis of symmetry in the water-land direction—access from the canal—*portego* (hall)—courtyard—land access—according to a distributive plan which we could call in "U"', ascribes it to the beginning of the fifteenth century; two plans).

**42.** *Palazzo Zen at S. Stin.* Tassini, 1863, 1915 ed., p. 793; Idem, 1879, p. 282; Elenco, 1905, p. 121, no. 217 (S. Polo 2580; campiello Zen).

**43.** *Palazzo Pisani at S. Marina.* Visible in De' Barbari's *View*, left of SS. Giovanni e Paolo; Coronelli, II, 1709, Plate 67; Tassini, 1879, p. 245; Elenco, 1905, p. 67, no. 1 (Cann. 6104); Lorenzetti, 1956, pp. 327 and 329; Miozzi, 1957, I, p. 438; Maretto, 1959, pp. 17 and 51 (with plans and observations on the distributive characters).

**44.** *Palazzo Correr.* Zanotto, 1847, p. 433; Tassini, 1863, 1915 ed., p. 211; Marini, 1905, p. 82 (to the fourteenth century; points out the out-jutting of the roof); Elenco, 1905, p. 76, no. 180 (Cann. 2217; to the fifteenth century); Lorenzetti, 1956, p. 436 (to the fifteenth century). The human heads in the capitals suggest those of the Doge's Palace capitals made in the Bon workshop. A dating around 1460 is perhaps not improbable.

**45.** *Palazzo Cappello at S. Lorenzo.* Elenco, 1905, p. 61, no. 547 (fond. di S. Giovanni Laterano; Castello 6391). The floor and the rear, with original elements, give on to ponte and ramo Cappello. Pending a restoration, one may perhaps assume it to be of about 1450 or just a little earlier.

**46.** *Palazzo Nani Mocenigo.* Fontana, 1845, Plate 23; Zanotto, 1847, p. 426 (to the beginning of the fourteenth century); Idem, 1856, p. 497 (to the fourteenth century); Mothes, 1859, p. 216 (to 1300–40); Tassini, 1863, 1915 ed., p. 499 (first half of the fourteenth century); Elenco, 1905, p. 154, nos. 115 and 116 (fond. Nani, Dorsoduro 960 and 961; to the fifteenth century); Chiminelli, 1912, p. 234; Lorenzetti, 1956, p. 538 (to the fifteenth century). The side on calle Larga de Ca' Nani much tampered with.

**47.** *Palazzo Garzoni.* Coronelli, II, 1709, Plate 50; Zanotto, 1856, p. 563 (to the fifteenth century); Tassini, 1863, 1915 ed., p. 311 (property of the Garzoni only since the seventeenth century); Elenco, 1905, p. 17, nos. 265–6 (S. Marco

3417); Lorenzetti, 1956, p. 623 (to the fifteenth century). Of about 1470?.

**48.** *Palazzo Giustiniani at S. Moisè.* Visible in Jacopo de' Barbari's *View.* Coronelli, 1709, II, Plate 45; Fontana, 1845, Plate 54 (the balustrade on the cornice was already in existence then and, in addition, the 'Gothic' balcony on the third floor); Zanotto, 1847, p. 428 (the landing appears there already altered); Selvatico, 1852, p. 229 (to the fifteenth century); Zanotto, 1856, p. 579 (to the fifteenth century); Burckhardt, 1925, p. 149; Ruskin, 1886, III, pp. 289 and 300 (good late fourteenth-century Gothic, but much altered); Mothes, 1859, p. 230; Kugler, 1858–9, III, p. 577; Tassini, 1863, 1915 ed., p. 645; Schnaase, 1876, p. 234; Tassini, 1879, p. 206 (the Giustinian are known to have been at S. Moisè in 1310 and 1357; therefore he thinks it of, perhaps, the fourteenth century; 'it was rebuilt, or radically restored, towards the beginning of the sixteenth century', according to a document of 1506); Paoletti, 1893, p. 44 and note 9 (work is in progress on the palace also from 1477 to 1482 and various stonecutters are mentioned by name: a Piero, an Agostino da Bergamo, a Lorenzo di Alzano, a Martino Verzo (di Lorenzo), an Antonio, a Marino di Giovanni, a Bartolomeo da Bergamo, an Antonio Muratore—Bergamesque—a Matteo, an Andrea, a Bartolomeo Gobo; Elenco, 1905, p. 7, no. 84 (S. Marco 1364; to the fifteenth century); Lorenzetti, 1956, p. 611 (to about 1474); Hubala, 1966, p. 781 (to about 1474). The 'radical restoration' of 1506 may have concerned the part added on the left. For a good part of the nineteenth century it was the Albergo Europa.

**49.** *Palazzo Salamon.* Tassini, 1879, p. 266 (Salamon coats of arms on the façade); Elenco, 1905, p. 309, no. 3611 (Cann. 3609–11).

**50.** *House in campo S. Maria Formosa, Castello 6129.* Elenco, 1905, p. 60, no. 532; Maretto, 1960, Plate XXXI, with plan. The rear façade (with windows, without any distributive rule, in tufa and Istrian stone) gives on corte del Pestrin 6128–9. Worth noting, the cable ornament along the jambs and the astragals along the arches.

**51.** *Palazzo Bollani Dolfin.* Fontana, 1845, Plate 6; Zanotto, 1847, p. 432 ('recently' restored; to 1310); Elenco, 1905, p. 59, no. 517 (Castello 6073); Lorenzetti, 1956, p. 327. We have already spoken of the façade on campo di S. Marina, perhaps older.

**52.** *Palazzo Malipiero alla Feltrina.* Tassini, 1879, p. 255; Elenco, 1905, p. 11, no. 163 (S. Marco 2513); Lorenzetti, 1956, p. 517. Altered. Has a façade also on the canal.

**53.** *Palazzo Maravegia.* Elenco, 1905, p. 155, no. 128 (fond. Bollani, Dorsoduro 1071); Lorenzetti, 1956, p. 562. I owe to M. Muraro the observation that, to the view from the corner, if the viewer moves to the left, there is added the view of an axis (on calle della Toletta) which produces in this façade the illusion of a symmetrical integration.

**54.** *Palazzo Testa.* Tassini, 1879, p. 269; Elenco, 1905, p. 70, no. 57 (fond. S. Giobbe; Cann. 468); Lorenzetti, 1956, p. 444; Maretto, 1959, p. 51 (with plan). Interesting the door in red limestone, with somewhat Romanesque mouldings, framed by a Byzantine dentil ornament. The external staircase may have been remade in the last century.

**55.** *Palazzo Venier Contarini on the Grand Canal.*

Elenco, 1905, p. 11, no. 157 (between calle del Campaniel and rio di S. Maria in Zobenigo; S. Marco 2488); Lorenzetti, 1956, p. 615.

**56.** *Palazzo Zorzi alle Zattere.* Elenco, 1905, p. 158, no. 175 (Dorsoduro 1416–17). The setting of the two-light windows on the second floor is peculiar; they are placed exactly between the axes of the *piano nobile.*

**57.** We should mention *Palazzetto Duodo Balbi Valier* on the Grand Canal, with a graceful Lombardesque balcony, of which only the *piano nobile* remains (of the second half of the fifteenth century) (Zanotto, 1856, p. 606; Lorenzetti, 1956, p. 634); *Palazzo Pesaro Ravà at S. Sofia,* characterized by the too slender columns of the upper four-light window (Quadri, 1834, p. 27, says that the top floor was altered in his time; Zanotto, 1856, p. 603, knows that 'it got now an extensive and expensive restoration' and believes it to be of the fourteenth century; Lorenzetti, 1956, p. 633, puts it in the fifteenth); *Palazzo Tiepolo Passi* at S. Tomà, of which the *piano nobile,* much restored, remains, with a five-light window and rosette capitals (Tassini, 1863, 1915 ed., p. 733; Elenco, 1905, p. 122, no. 237: S. Polo 2774; Lorenzetti, 1956, p. 622); *Palazzo Trevisan dai Olivi* with the more beautiful façade on the Zattere and the other on campo di S. Agnese, with two four-light windows and rosette capitals (visible in J. de' Barbari's *View*) (Tassini, 1863, 1915 ed., p. 748, says it has been much reconstructed; Elenco, 1905, p. 152, no. 85: Dorsoduro 789–809 and 810); the two three-light windows, one above the other, with flower finials and rosette capitals, in campiello del Magazen, in the centre of a reconstructed façade, with ancient cornice and door (Elenco, 1905, p. 157, no. 166; Dorsoduro 1372); a façade with two dwarf two-light windows in line on the left and two other axes on the right, with an old door and corner colonnettes in calle del Pistor (Castello 5992); a façade with two three-light windows in line on the right and two other axes on the left in fond. dei Preti at S. Maria Formosa, with an ancient door (Castello 5849); the two *Palazzi Benzi-Zecchini* (fond. Madonna dell'Orto, Cann. 3458 and 3459, with rosette capitals, clumsily restored; Tassini, 1873, pp. 327 and 328 says they were erected in the fourteenth century by the Lioncini and passed in the seventeenth century to the Benzi; Idem, 1879, p. 66; Elenco, 1905, p. 82, nos. 283 and 284; Lorenzetti, 1956, p. 404) difficult to read, believed to be of the fourteenth century (Tassini, 1879, p. 66).

**58.** Abnormal forms are found now and then and are mentioned here for the sake of completeness and certainly not because of alteration in quality. Deformed trefoils may be seen in *Palazzo Bragadin-Bigaglia* (in Jacopo de' Barbari's *View* it appears as the first of a series of Gothic buildings, no longer in existence, to the left of the now vanished church of S. Giustina; Fontana, 1845, Plate 52; Zanotto, 1847, p. 432 (to the beginning of the fifteenth century—says it was altered by the restorations); Elenco, 1905, p. 61, no. 556: Cann. 6480; Lorenzetti, 1956, p. 374 (first half of the fifteenth century). Façade on rio di S. Giovanni Laterano with two three-light windows, two wings and two doors.

**59.** We mention the more interesting 'fragments', ignoring the minor or insignificant manifestations: Cann. 170, Lista di Spagna: a four-light window (sixth order) between two windows (Elenco, 1905,

p. 68, no. 30); the *palazzo* on fondamenta Crotta (Cann. 142-4) rio Terrà dei Sabioni; with two multi-light windows of the sixth order, single windows and rosette capitals, on the Grand Canal (Elenco, 1905, p. 68, nos. 27 and 28, now turned into a hotel); *Palazzetto Minotto on the Grand Canal:* a three-light window and two windows of the sixth order remain—Carlevarijs, Plate LXXII: there was then a five-light window, later partly arched (Elenco, 1905, p. 183: Sest. S. Marco; Lorenzetti, 1956, p. 615: to the fifteenth century); *Palazzo Corner Reali* on rio della Fava, at ponte della Fava, late fifteenth century, of which only the Gothic first floor remains, with a central four-light window and five single windows, of the sixth order (Elenco, 1905, p. 56, no. 458; Castello 5527); calle del Forno, Cann. 6391: sundry windows of the fifth and sixth orders belonging to a palazzo Cappello; an external staircase was demolished in 1939-40 (Elenco, 1905, p. 67, no. 13); Borgoloco, Cast. 6112: beautiful three-light window (of the sixth order) and door with segmental arch (Elenco, 1905, p. 60, no. 524); fond. rimpetto Mocenigo, at ponte della Rioda, S. Croce 2052: four-light window of the fifth order with rosette capitals (Elenco, 1905, p. 139, no. 185 bis); fond. S. Giacomo at Giudecca: four windows of the fifth type and upper cornice, remains of a large building; campo S. Stefano, S. Marco 2591: square door and beautiful seven-light window of the fifth order and capitals with thick leaves (Elenco, 1905, p. 15, no. 225); rear façade of *Palazzo Dario,* a beautiful three-light window with flower finials and other Gothic elements; Dorsoduro 351-3 (Torres, 1937, p. 19: considers genuine the upper loggia: Trincanato, 1948, p. 273); calle del Mandolin, at Castello: four windows of the fifth order symmetrically arranged, four remaining window-sills of the floor below, and upper cornice; fond. rio Marin, S. Croce 782: on the first floor four windows of the fourth order, on the second floor, on the same axis, four windows of the fifth order, symmetrical distribution (Elenco, 1905, p. 134, no. 86: beginning of the fifteenth century); fond. rio Marin, S. Croce 800: three-light window of the fifth order, with pilasters, joined on the left to a shorter window, two single windows on the right, a rather late complex (Elenco, 1905, p. 134, no. 88); Marzaria 2 aprile, S. Marco 5036: six scattered single windows of the fifth order and upper cornice, remains of a large Gothic house; Murano, casa Seguso, beautiful three-light window with flower finials and framing and four single windows in fond. Vereri 14 and 15 (Lorenzetti, 1956, p. 788). One may well think that palazzo Seguso has been altered.

**60.** *Portal of Palazzo Magno.* Elenco, 1905, p. 75, no. 168 (campo della Maddalena, Cann. 2143; Lorenzetti, 1956, p. 439).

**61.** A great portal of this type is found at ponte della Malvasia Vecchia (S. Marco 2597; Elenco, 1905, p. 12, no. 170).

**62.** Gabelentz, 1903, p. 230.

**63.** The tombstone of Abbot Hugues d'Arc formerly in St. Bénin in Dijon is of the year 1300 (*Bulletin Monumental*, 1945, p. 233); the motif appears again in the choir of Evron, with inflected extrados, dated to the fourteenth century (Lasteyrie, 1926-7, I, p. 151).

**64.** *Crowning over calle del Paradiso.* Selvatico, 1847, pp. 104-5; Idem, 1852, p. 114 (to the fourteenth

century); Mothes, 1859, p. 229 (a pupil of Andriolo); Tassini, 1863, 1915 ed., p. 538 (to the end of the fifteenth century); Idem, 1879, p. 94 ('commonly' ascribed to the fourteenth century; but the Foscari and Mocenigo coats of arms were carved after 1491); Elenco, 1905, p. 57, no. 476 (to the middle of the fifteenth century); Lorenzetti, 1956, p. 356 (beginning of the fifteenth century); Planiscig, 1916, p. 167 (to 1350-1400); Toesca, 1950, p. 418 (to the advanced fifteenth century). As one can see, a remarkable divergence of opinions. We put forward the suspicion that the slab with the images of the Virgin, the same on both sides and of the early fifteenth century, had been added in a second phase. The architecture is perhaps earlier (in harmony with the more ancient part of the house which supports this complex, and which is of 1300-50).

**65.** Gabelentz, 1903, p. 230.

**66.** In corte Petriana at S. Polo (Elenco, 1905, p. 114, no. 104); fond. Madonna dell'Orto, Cann. 3506 (Elenco, 1905, p. 82, no. 287); calle Larga XXII Marzo; the portal formerly of palazzo Morosini della Trezza in Lista di Spagna (Cann. 233) with two beautiful putti supporting a coat of arms (Elenco, 1905, p. 68, no. 33; Lorenzetti, 1956, p. 449); the one in campo della Maddalena (Cann. 2143; Elenco, 1905, p. 75, no. 168); the one at Ca' Bernardo at S. Polo (ramo de Ca' Bernardo, 2184; Elenco, 1905, p. 118, no. 176); that in fond. Duodo Barbarigo at S. Maria Zobenigo (S. Marco 2506; Elenco, 1905, p. 11, no. 162); the remarkable one in callesella Rota (Dorsoduro 877a); that in calle delle Rasse, in Palazzo Dandolo-Danieli (Castello 4581); the portal in calle Maggioni, Cann. 6007-8; (Elenco, 1905, p. 101, no. 621); the portal of Palazzo Loredan Gheltoff (Cann. 1864) and very many others.
A dated portal of this type is that of S. Andrea della Zirada, of 1475 (Paoletti, 1893, I, p. 49; Lorenzetti, 1956, p. 479). Of 1479 is that of the scuola dei Calegheri in campo S. Tomà with a relief in the lunette of St. Mark curing Anian (Lorenzetti, 1956, p. 572); Elenco, 1905, p. 123, no. 250. Less common, the ogee portal without architrave (in calle dei Mori, Cann. 3381; Elenco, 1905, p. 81, no. 277) and calle del Cafetier, S. Marco 3587 (almost an enlarged window).

**67.** *Portal in campo dei Mori.* (Cann. 3381).

**68.** Mutinelli, 1965, p. 251.

**69.** *Fermo, portal of the Monte di Pietà.* Venturi, 1924, pp. 337 and 338 (attributed to the direction of Giorgio da Sebenico); Serra, 1929, I, p. 220. The well-known portals of Pesaro also clearly show Venetian influences (Serra, 1929, I, p. 207).

**70.** *Ca' d'Oro well-curb.* Paoletti, 1893, I, pp. 22 and 23; Idem, 1920, p. 102.

**71.** Planiscig, 1930, pp. 87, 91 et seq.

**72.** Fogolari, 1932, pp. 28 and 43, 44.

**73.** On the *Ca' d'Oro well-curb* see also: Seguso, 1866, p. 7 (to Calendario's school); Ongania, 1889, Plates 181 and 182; Paoletti, 1893, I, pp. 22 and 23; Venturi, 1908, p. 986; Folnesics, 1914, pp. 48 et seq.; Paoletti, 1920, p. 102; Planiscig, 1921, p. 7 et seq.; F. Schottmüller in *Kunstchronik,* N. F. XXIII, Leipzig 1922, p. 322 (connects the *Charity* with the group of Madonnas in stucco and terracotta attributed by Bode to Ghiberti); Lorenzetti, 1956, p. 420; Fogolari, Nebbia, Mo-

schini, 1929, pp. 69 and 70; Planiscig, 1930, pp. 87 and 91 et seq. (asserts the collaboration of Nanni di Bartolo); Fiocco, in *Rivista d'Arte,* 1930, p. 155; Fogolari, 1932, pp. 28, 43 and 44. The beautiful well-curb, which had been sold, was recovered by Giorgio Franchetti and put back in Ca' d'Oro.

**74.** The *Contarini dalla Zogia well-curb.* Grevembroch, *Saggi di familiari ecc.*; Selvatico, 1852, pp. 129-30 (to the Bon school); Tassini, 1863, 1915 ed., p. 107; Idem, 1879, p. 292; Ongania, 1889, Plate 211; Paoletti, 1893, I, p. 23, n. 1; Douglas, 1925, p. 129; Pope-Hennessy, 1964, pp. 345-6, figs. 365-8 (no. 370). Even nearer to the Ca' d'Oro well-curb is that of Ca' Tiepolo at S. Fantin (see the allegorical figures seated on lions and the corner heads); Ongania, 1889, Plate 210; Planiscig, 1921, p. 8.

**75.** Tassini, 1863, 1915 ed., p. 107; Seguso, 1866, pp. 6 and 7; Ongania, 1889 and 1911, Plate III.

**76.** *Well-curb of Palazzo Morosini at S. Giovanni Laterano.* Seguso, 1866, pp. 6 and 7; Ongania, 1899, pp. 204 and 206; Paoletti, 1893, I, p. 23, n. 1; Planiscig, 1921, p. 8.

**77.** On the well-curbs in the two courtyards of *Palazzo Soranzo van Axel* see: Seguso, 1866, p. 7; Ongania, 1889 and 1911, Plate 11; Paoletti, 1893, I, n. 1; Idem, 1920, p. 102; Lorenzetti, 1956, p. 329.

**78.** *Well-curb of Palazzo Tiepolo Papadopoli.* Ongania, 1889 and 1911, Plate 27; Paoletti, 1893, I, p. 23, note 1.

**79.** On the *Menor della Gatta well-curb,* on fond. dei Pignoli at S. Zulian (S. Marco 4890): Tassini, 1863, 1915 ed., pp. 565-6; Idem, 1879, p. 126; Ongania, 1889, Plates 169 and 170; Paoletti, 1893, I, p. 23, n. 1; Elenco, 1905, p. 25, no. 418. Of octagonal type, more advanced in time, with some affinity in the treatment of animals (a feline, also here, forms the crest of a coat of arms) there is the well-curb, now at the Victoria and Albert Museum, originating from palazzo Saladini Moreschi of Verona, with the emblem of the Cornareggio family, considered of the middle of the fifteenth century (but this should certainly be moved forward). There are three old photographs of it, probably made in Venice (Naya, 2385-7).

**80.** Now no longer accessible *in situ.* Tassini, 1879, p. 30; Photo Naya, 2481.

**81.** Ongania, 1889 and 1911, Plate 69; Paoletti, 1893, I, p. 23, note 1 (fond. S. Biagio at S. Simeon Grande).

**82.** Ongania, 1889 and 1911, Plate 65.

**83.** Seguso, 1866, p. 7; Ongania, 1889 and 1911, Plate 87.

**84.** R. Brenzoni, *Il puteale dei Giusti in San Quirico,* in 'Studi Storici Veronesi', Verona, 1954.

**85.** Ongania, 1889, Plate 180 (to the fourteenth century).

**86.** Ongania, 1889 and 1911, Plate 132.

**87.** Ongania, 1889 and 1911, Plate 13; Tassini, 1863, 1915 ed., p. 303.

**88.** Tassini, 1863, 1915 ed., pp. 555-6; Ongania, 1889 and 1911, Plate 95 (to the fourteenth century). Note the presence of the cable ornament in the cornice.

**89.** Arslan, 1927, p. 12 et seq.

**90.** Ongania, 1911, Plate 72.

**91.** Ongania, 1889, Plate 174 (to the fourteenth century).

**92.** Ongania, 1889, Plate 224. Of Cristoforo Moro's time, with a Bernardinian monogram.

**93.** Ongania, 1889, Plate 227. Venetian Gothic well-curbs are found everywhere in the dominions of the Serenissima. See, for Istria: Ferrari-Antomazza, 1955, p. 87. See also Frey, 1913, fig. 56 and Cecchelli, 1932, p. 185 (Zara). Bettini has made known those of Scutari, of the type just discussed (*Rivista di Venezia* XII, 1933, pp. 543–4).

**94.** See J. Balogh, 1966, p. 246.

**95.** See J. Balogh, p. 244 et seq.

**96.** See: Thode, 1895, p. 85. Was built in 1428. The Gothic bridges of S. Rocco and campo S. Ternita are simpler. The ponte della Pietà on riva degli Schiavoni was entirely reconstructed in the last century.

**97.** *House in calle del Forno.* Elenco, 1905, p. 62, no. 564 (to the fifteenth century).

**98.** *Four-light window in campiello San Rocco.* Ruskin, 1886, II, pp. 258–9.

**99.** *Crosera S. Pantalon.* Trincanato, 1948, p. 264 et seq. (to the fourteenth century).

**100.** *Calle Zotti, two-light windows in brick.* Elenco, 1905, p. 86, nos. 349, 351 (to the fourteenth century); Maretto, 1959, p. 62 (to the fourteenth century).

**101.** *Calle del Forner, Castello.* Elenco, 1905, p. 59, no. 509 (to the fifteenth century).

**102.** *Fondamenta della Tana, windows.* Ruskin, 1886, II, p. 260, note and ill. in Plate XVII, 1 and 2; Elenco, 1905, p. 36, no. 94 (to the first half of the fifteenth century).

**103.** *Salizzada del Pistor* (Cann. 4555–9). Elenco, 1905, p. 90, no. 427 (to the thirteenth century); Lorenzetti, 1956, p. 393 (to the thirteenth century).

**104.** A beautiful example is the *house in via Soncin in Padova* with two two-light windows, one three-light and one four-light window (Forlati, 1926–7, pp. 50, 53 and 65; Gallimberti, 1934–9, p. 30; Idem, 1965, p. 19 et seq. to the fourteenth century). Examples are found also at Arquà (Giovannoni, 1928, p. 88); Semenzato, 1965, p. 230; in Treviso (in piazza della Vittoria 15–19: cf. Coletti, 1935, pp. 126 and 127; in Calmaggiore, 5–7: cf. Coletti, 1935, p. 58; in via Riccati 15*a*); in Asolo (the beautiful house, formerly Marcello, with Islamic-like cadences in the arches: cf. Semenzato, 1965, p. 209; Hubala, 1966, p. 70; cadences repeated in the openings of a beautiful house in Cittadella, Padova (three-light window, four lateral axes and a porch with three great arches). In Pordenone (corso Vittorio Emanuele nos. 10 and 49); Hubala (1966, p. 368) at Portogruaro (Palazzetto Muschietti in via Martiri della Libertà 19, on which see Brusin Zovatto, 1960, p. 205; in Belluno, the house formerly of the Capitano di Giustizia in via Santacroce 26; in the imposing rustic Palazzo Assessorile of Cles in Val di Non, of *c.* 1490 (suggested by N. Rasmo).

**105.** In Treviso (in via Tolpada 3: Coletti, 1935, p. 122; and in via Rialto); in Asolo, in the already mentioned casa Marcello and in other houses; at Conegliano (the Carpanè house, via della Madonna 51, with decorations attributed to Dario da Treviso: Semenzato, 1962, p. 299); at Zera Branco; at Serravalle (the Casoni house in via Casoni 24–6:

Semenzato, 1962, p. 299); at Pordenone (via Vittorio Emanuele 21).

**106.** At Pordenone (a two-light window in corso Vittorio Emanuele 45).

**107.** See, for Treviso: Botter, 1956.

**108.** See: A. Peroni in *Storia di Brescia*, II, 1963, p. 683, note 2. In the Brescian region this type of arch is found in the cloister of Gargnano, where an epigraph of 1424 may well refer to its building (cf. Panazza, *Storia di Brescia*, I, 1961: to the first half of the fourteenth century); in the Bornati house at Caionvico (Peroni, op. cit. p. 892), in the Carmine and S. Eufemia convents in Brescia, in the (formerly) Malvezzi house at Mompiano (Peroni, op. cit. pp. 686–7), in the Federici house at Erbanno (p. 704), etc.; not all anterior, I think, to the middle of the fifteenth century.

The inflected trefoiled arch, in poor forms, appears also in the Bergamo region (the Bottani house in via Gombito 28, Bergamo: cf. Angelini, 1942, p. 9; Carlo Nigra, *Il rifacimento delle facciate di Casa Centoris in Vercelli*, Turin, 1934, p. 8); while the mixtilinear arch appears at Alzano Lombardo (Angelini, op. cit.).

**109.** *Treviso, casa da Noal.* Coletti, 1935, p. 61 (to the first half of the fifteenth century; a chronology, in our opinion, not entirely improbable).

**110.** *Treviso, casa Spessa.* Coletti, 1935, pp. 70 and 77.

**111.** *Cividale houses.* See: Mutinelli, 1958, pp. 554, 561, 565, 566. We would mention the so-called house of Paolo Diacono (the third floor reconstructed in the nineteenth century), the beautiful Fontana house (corner of via Mazzini and via Cavour), another house in via Mazzini; the house in via Roma 3. Two two-light windows, in via Cavour 19 (the lower one connected with interlacing arches, in masonry, almost identical with that in corso Vittorio Emanuele 15 in Pordenone).

**112.** See on the subject: Beltrami, 1900; Franco, 1939, p. 267; Bassi, 1965, p. 193.

**113.** Bassi (1965, p. 193) sees the repetition of a similar decision in the 'unusual' plan of palazzo Contarini dal Bovolo with central courtyard and lower gallery on the rear façade.

**114.** Brought to my knowledge by Dr. Christoff Frommel, whom I warmly thank.

**115.** Those which one sees in the Venetian paintings of the late fifteenth century (e. g. in the *Donation of the relics of the Cross*, of Bastiani, at the Accademia) clearly do not have, for the purposes of this modest research, any indicative value, either chronological or stylistic.

**116.** *Palazzo Erizzo Nani Mocenigo.* Ruskin, 1886, p. 289; Zanotto, 1856, p. 587 (to the fourteenth century); Lorenzetti, 1956, p. 621 (to the fifteenth century); Maretto, 1959, p. 21. The ground floor windows are largely modern (cf. Quadri, 1834, p. 32).

**117.** *Palazzo Gabrieli at S. Giovanni Laterano.* Elenco, 1905, p. 54, no. 413 (Ramo II della Madonnetta, 5152).

**118.** *Morosini houses.* Tassini (1863, 1915 ed., p. 486) mentions an inscription in the interior (corte Morosina, 5826) saying that the palace foundations were laid in 1369 by Marino Morosini; an inscription still in existence. This inscription can-

not, however, refer to the façade on the rio, which is later by at least a century; see also: Tassini, 1879, p. 262; Elenco, 1905, p. 100, no. 590 (corte Morosina 5820–7); Lorenzetti, 1956, p. 392.

**119.** *Calle Castagna.* Elenco, 1905, p. 52, no. 376.

**120.** *Fondamenta S. Biagio* 788. Elenco, 1905, p. 176, no. 46 (Moro coat of arms of the beginning of the sixteenth century).

**121.** *Palazzetto Morolin-Michiel-Olivo.* Elenco, 1905, p. 121, no. 228 (S. Polo 2672); Lorenzetti, 1956, p. 571 (to the beginning of the sixteenth century). On the rear façade, in calle Morolin, a large and beautiful three-light window of the sixth order, surmounted by the cornice. Capitals with rosettes.

**122.** *Palazzo Rossini.* S. Marco 1828. The double water-gate also has 'Lombardesque' characters.

**123.** *Palazzo Giovanelli-Dorigo.* Zanotto, 1856, p. 610; Lorenzetti, 1956, p. 638 (the building has been restored).

**124.** *Palazzo Sanudo at the Fontaco dei Turchi.* Elenco, 1905, p. 138, no. 159 (S. Croce 1740); Lorenzetti, 1956, p. 471. The portal also, displaced towards the right of the façade, is of the later Gothic type already considered.

**125.** *House on rio Pesaro.* Visible in J. de Barbari's *View;* Elenco, 1905, p. 118 (mentions only the beautiful land door, of the fifteenth century, with the shield chiselled away; San Polo, fond. Bernardo 2196).

**126.** *Palazzo Soranzo at S. Stin.* Elenco, 1905, p. 120, no. 211 (S. Polo 2521, but it can be reached also from fond. Contarini 2542): attributes it to the first half of the fifteenth century.

**127.** *Palazzo Da Mula in Murano;* on fond. Vereri. Paoletti, 1893, I, p. 33: the windows with pensile capitals strongly bring to mind the Ca' d'Oro; Lorenzetti, 1956, p. 789 et seq.; Hubala, 1966, p. 282. The trefoiled aedicule inserted into the four-light window is certainly a later addition.

**128.** *Palazzo Maffetti.* Elenco, 1905, p. 176, no. 45. One can see by now the decidedly proto-sixteenth century character of the mezzanines.

**129.** *Palazzo Foscari at the Giudecca.* Elenco, 1905, p. 176, no. 48 (fond. S. Biagio 795; to the fifteenth century). Recently restored.

**130.** *Palazzo of the former Accademia dei Nobili at the Giudecca.* Elenco, 1905, p. 175, no. 35; fond. S. Eufemia 607–8. Two four-light windows with four windows on each side and a mezzanine above: a rather rare occurrence.

**131.** *Palazzo Viaro-Zane*, façade on the canal. S. Croce 3123. Elenco, 1905, p. 140, no. 197. The façade on the campo has been discussed.

**132.** *Palazzo Bernardi at S. Aponal.* Sest. S. Polo alle Beccarie 1319.

**133.** *Palazzo Zen Labia at S. Stin.* Tassini, 1863, 1915 ed., p. 793; Idem, 1879, p. 282; Elenco, 1905, p. 121, no. 217 (Sest. S. Polo; Campiello Zen 2580). Notice the leonine brackets of the first floor, transformed and adapted to the Lombard style. We mention in addition: a three-light window of the fourth order on rio della Madonnetta with Ionic capitals (Elenco, 1905, p. 114, no. 109, S. Polo 1953); a floor in calle della

Madonna near campo S. Angelo (S. Marco 3610) with an almost certainly coeval alignment of Gothic (fourth order and rosette capitals) and Lombard forms; a curious four-light window with interlaced arches on Ionic capitals in Barbaria de le Tole (Castello 6471); two-light window (fourth order) in corte del Sabion with Renaissance capital (Elenco, 1905, p. 150, no. 46: Dorsoduro 373); *Palazzo Tron Pisani* in Lista di Spagna, Cann. 125 (Elenco, 1905, p. 68, no. 25: one Gothic and one Renaissance floor, perhaps coeval (with reservations); the two Reggiani houses on fond. della Sensa 3335–6 (in the *piano nobile* three-light window and windows of the fifth order and a beautiful balustrade with double-spindle colonnettes; cf.

Elenco, 1905, p. 81, no. 268, where these houses are called *Palazzo Arrigoni*; and Maretto, 1959, p. 49: with useful remarks on the unusual plan); a five-light window, with Ionic capitals, in rio della Pergola.

*Palazzo Dolfin* in campo S. Marina (the first floor of the fourth order and the second round-headed: perhaps coeval) mentioned by Lorenzetti (1956, p. 327); the large house, in bad condition, in piscina S. Martino with apertures of the fifth and sixth order displaying Renaissance columns and capitals (Elenco, 1905, p. 40, no. 160; Castello 2516 and 2517A).

An example, really at the limit, of the use of the Venetian Gothic arch is presented by the three Zen palaces (fond. Ca' Zen, Cann. 4925) with a mixture, really rather bastard, of Gothic and Renaissance elements: the work of the patrician Francesco Zen († 1538). Zanotto speaks of the assistance of Sebastiano Serlio; and Selvatico reports a date of 1531 (Bertarelli Album, *c.* 1750, Plates 2–3; Coronelli, 112; Fontana, 1845, Plate 55; Zanotto, 1847, II, 2, p. 436; Selvatico, 1847, p. 366; Idem, 1852, p. 147; Zanotto, 1856, II, p. 313; Lorenzetti, 1956, p. 397; Venturi in *Storia dell'Arte*, XI/3, 1940; Thieme-Becker, XXXVI, 1947, pp. 455–6; Hubala, 1966, p. 874).

N.B. — *Edoardo Arslan's exposition of the Venetian Gothic contains also a part relating to Dalmatia which is being published elsewhere.*

234. *House at S. Marina. The balcony.*

235. *Palazzo Seriman at the Gesuiti.*

237-238. *Palazzo Bernardo at S. Polo. Details of the façade.*

239-240. *Palazzo Pesaro degli Orfei.*

241. *Palazzo Pesaro degli Orfei. Small balcony.*
242. *Palazzo Pesaro degli Orfei. Detail of the multi-light window.*
243-244. *Palazzo Pesaro degli Orfei. Details of the ornamentation.*

*245. Palazzo Contarini-Fasan on the Grand Canal.*
*246-247. Palazzo Contarini-Fasan on the Grand Canal. Details of the façade.*
*248. Palazzo Contarini-Fasan. Detail of the first-floor balcony.*

249-250. *Houses at S. Maria Formosa.*
251. *Detail of a portal at S. Maria Formosa.*

6126

256. Palazzo Papafava at the Misericordia.

257. *Palazzo Papafava at the Misericordia. Detail of the façade.*

258. *Palazzo Van Axel. Detail of the rear façade.*
259. *Palazzo Van Axel. Perspective view of the façade.*

*260-261. Palazzo Van Axel. The internal courtyard.*

*262. Palazzo Van Axel. Detail of the staircase of the smaller courtyard.*

263. *Palazzo Pisani in Campo S. Marina. Detail of the five-light window.*
264. *Palazzo Pisani in Campo S. Marina. Façade on rio di Panada.*
265. *Palazzo Pisani in Campo S. Marina. Façade on rio di S. Marina.*
266. *Palazzo Nani, formerly Barbarigo, in rio di S. Trovaso.*

*268. Well-curb of Bartolomeo Bon at Ca' d'Oro.*

269. *Well-curb in the courtyard of Palazzo Van Axel.*
270. *Well-curb in a palazzo at S. Maurizio.*
271. *Well-curb in the Museo Civico Correr.*
272. *Well-curb from Palazzo Contarini-Grimaldi. London, Victoria & Albert Museum.*

273. *Well-curb. Location unknown.*
274. *Goldoni well-curb in the Museo Civico Correr.*
275. *Well-curb in the courtyard of Palazzo Van Axel. Detail.*
276. *Goldoni well-curb. Museo Civico Correr. Detail.*
277. *Well-curb of S. Pietro in Volta. Museo Civico Correr. Detail.*

278. *Well-curb in Corte Petriana.*
279. *Well-curb of S. Pietro in Volta. Museo Civico Correr.*
280. *Well-curb in Campo S. Gregorio.*
281. *Well-curb in Campo S. Giovanni Crisostomo.*

*284-285. Palazzo Morolin.*

286. *Palazzo Erizzo.*

287. *Palazzo Da Mula in Murano.*

288. *Palazzo Da Mula in Murano. Detail of the façade.*

# BIBLIOGRAPHY

1486

B. VON BREYDENBACH, *Peregrinationes in Terram Sanctam*, Magonza.

1554

G.B. EGNAZIO, *De exemplis illustri virorum Venetae...*, Venice.

1579

F. SANSOVINO, *Lettera intorno al Palazzo Ducale e descrizione...*, Venice 1829.

1673

G. LUCIO, *Memorie istoriche di Tragurio...*, Venice.

1703

L. CARLEVARIJS, *Le fabbriche e vedute di Venezia...*, Venice.

1709

V.M. CORONELLI, *Singolarità di Venezia*, II, Palazzi.

1742

A. VISENTINI, *Urbis Venetiarum prospectus celebriores, Tabulis XXXVIII ab A.V. in tres partes distributi*, Venice.

M. ENGELBRECHT, 92 *vedute di Venezia* (Engravings).

c. 1750

*Trentun tavole e sessantun vedute di Venezia* (Engravings), Milano, Raccolta di Stampe Bertarelli, (Vol. M. 93).

1751–1819

D. FARLATI, *Illyricum sacrum*, Venice.

1754

*Monumenta Veneta... collecta, studio e cura Petri Gradonici... anno* 1754, Venice. Museo Correr.

c. 1760

*Teatro delle fabbriche più cospicue in prospettiva... della città di Venezia*, Venice, Alberizzi.

1760

G. GREVEMBROCH, *Saggi di familiari magnificenze preservate tra le moderne nelli chiostri e palaggi di Venezia*, Venice, Museo Correr.

G. GREVEMBROCH, *Pozzi e cisterne*, Cod. Gradenigo Dolfin n. 607, Venice, Museo Correr.

1778

T. TEMANZA, *Vite dei più celebri architetti...*, Venice.

c. 1782

GIAMPICCOLI, *Raccolta delle principali prospettive della città di Venezia*, Bassano.

1785

T. A. ZUCCHINI, *Nuova cronaca veneta ossia descrizione di tutte le pubbliche architetture...*, Venice.

1807

G. A. MOSCHINI, *Guida per l'isola di Murano*, Venice.

1809

P. CLOCHAR, *Palais, maisons et vues d'Italie*, Paris.

1815

G.A. MOSCHINI, *Guida per la città di Venezia...*, Venice.

1820

L. CICOGNARA, A. DIEDO, *Le fabbriche più cospicue di Venezia...*, Vol. II, Venice.

1821

DEZAN, *Iconografia delle trenta parrocchie di Venezia*, Venice.

1824–53

E.A. CICOGNA, *Delle iscrizioni veneziane, raccolte e illustrate*, Venice.

1827

STIEGLITZ, *Geschichte der Baukunst*, Nürnberg.

1828

G.A. MOSCHINI, *Nuova Guida di Venezia*, Venice.

1834

A. QUADRI, *Il Canal Grande di Venezia con 48 tavole*, Venice.

1837

G. CADORIN, *Notizie storiche della fabbrica del Palazzo Ducale e de' suoi architetti nei sec. XIV e XV*, Venice.

P. BETTIO, *Del Palazzo Ducale in Venezia, Lettera discorsiva*, Venice.

G. CADORIN, *Pareri di sedici architetti intorno al Palazzo Ducale di Venezia dopo l'incendio del* 1577, Venice.

1837–40

E. PAOLETTI, *Il fiore di Venezia*, Venice.

1838

L. CICOGNARA, A. DIEDO, G. SELVA, *Le fabbriche e i monumenti cospicui di Venezia*, Venice.

1845

G.J. FONTANA, *Venezia monumentale pittoresca. Sessanta fra i palazzi più distinti...*, Venice.

SMITH, *Architettura dei monumenti religiosi*, Paris.

G. CADORIN, *Memorie originali italiane riguardanti le Belle Arti*, Serie VI, pp. 105 et seq., N. 189–190, Bologna.

1846

J. POPPEL, M. KURZ, *Venedig, 24 Ansichten*, Munich.

1847

F. ZANOTTO, *Venezia e le sue lagune*, Venice, Vol. II, p. 2 and p. 418 et seq.

M. SANUDO, *Itinerario per la terraferma veneziana nell'anno* 1483, Padova.

P. SELVATICO, *Sulla architettura e sulla scultura in Venezia*, Venice.

1851–53

J. RUSKIN, *The Stones of Venice*, London (fourth edition, 1886).

**1852**

P. SELVATICO, LAZARI, *Guida artistica e storica di Venezia*, Venice.

**1853–61**

F. ZANOTTO, *Il Palazzo Ducale di Venezia*, Venice, (Vol. I, 1853; Vol. II, 1858; Vol. III, 1858; Vol. IV, 1861).

**1854–68**

E. VIOLLET-LE-DUC, *Dictionnaire raisonné de l'architecture française du XI au XVI siècles*, Paris.

**1856**

P. SELVATICO, *Storia estetico-critica delle arti del disegno...*, Lez. VIII del II Vol. Venice.
*Eine Ansicht des Dogenpalastes zu Venedig aus dem XIV. Jahrhundert*. In 'Mitteilungen der K.K. Zentralkommission zur Erhaltung der Baudenkmale', Vienna, I, pp. 183 et seq.
A. SAGREDO, *Sulle Consorterie delle arti edificative in Venezia*, Venice.
F. ZANOTTO, *Nuovissima Guida di Venezia e delle isole della sua laguna*, Venice.

**1857**

PIDROVI-BURGES, In *'Annales archéologiques'*, XVII, Paris, pp. 68 et seq. & p. 192 et seq.

**1858**

KUKULJEVIC, SAKCINSKI, In *'Slovnik Umjetn'*; Jugoslavia.
A. RICCI, *Storia dell'Architettura in Italia*, Modena.
W. LUBKE, *Geschichte der Architektur*, Berlin, Vol. I.

**1858–59**

F. KUGLER, *Geschichte der Baukunst*, Stuttgart.

**1859**

O. MOTHES, *Geschichte der Baukunst und Bildhauerei Venedigs*, Leipzig, I, pp. 179 et seq.
A. & L. SEGUSO, *Delle sponde marmoree e degli antichi edifici di Venezia*, Venice.
ESSENWEIN, *Die Loggia in Castello Vecchio zu Trient*, in 'Mitteilungen der K.K. Zentralkommission'; Vienna, IV.

**1860**

A. SAGREDO & F. BERCHET, *Il Fondaco dei Turchi in Venezia*. Addendum in 'Archivio storico italiano', p. 11, 1862, Venice.

**1861**

*Venise, Guide historique-topographique*, Trieste, pp. 125 et seq.

**1863**

G. TASSINI, *Curiosità veneziane ovvero origini delle denominazioni stradali di Venezia*, Venice (Fifth edition amended by E. Zorzi, Venice, 1915).

**1864**

A. DALL'ACQUA GIUSTI, *Il Palazzo Ducale di Venezia*, Venice.

**1865**

G.J. FONTANA, *Cento palazzi fra i più celebri di Venezia sul Canal Grande*, Venice.

**1866**

V. ZANETTI, *Guida di Murano...*, Venice.
F. ZANOTTO, *Nuovissima Guida di Venezia e delle isole della sua laguna*, Venice.
L. SEGUSO, *Dell'importanza delle vere dei pozzi per la Storia dell'Arte veneziana*, Venice.

**1868**

G. LORENZI, *Monumenti per servire alla storia del Palazzo Ducale di Venezia*, Venice.
SAKCINSKI, *Leben südslawischen Künstler*, Agram.

**1870**

G. TASSINI, *Sette Palazzi di Venezia, nuovamente illustrati*, Venice.

**1873**

G. TASSINI, *Quattro palazzi di Venezia*. In 'Archivio Veneto', 5, pp. 326 et seq.
G. TASSINI, *Alcuni appunti storici sopra il palazzo dei duchi di Ferrara in Venezia poscia Fondaco dei Turchi*. In 'Archivio Veneto', 6, p. 285.
G. TASSINI, *Cinque palazzi di Venezia*. In 'Archivio Veneto', 5, pp. 100 et seq.

**1876**

C. SCHNAASE, *Geschichte der bildenden Künste im Mittelalter*, Düsseldorf, Vol. V, pp. 225–236.

**1877**

V. JOPPI & G. OCCIONI-BONAFFONS, *Cenni Storici sulla Loggia Comunale di Udine*, Udine.
R. CATTANEO, *La Basilica di S. Marco*, Venice.

**1879**

G. GELCICH, *Le lettere e le arti alle bocche di Cattaro: memorie storiche*, Venice.
G. TASSINI, *Alcuni palazzi ed antichi edifici di Venezia*, Venice.

**c. 1880**

A. DELLA ROVERE, *Il Palazzo Ducale di Venezia*, Mestre.

**1881**

FULIN-MOLMENTI, *Guida artistica e storica di Venezia...*, Venice.
E.A. FREEMAN, *Sketches from the Subject and Neighbourlands of Venice*, London.

**1884**

A.J. HARE, *Venice*, London.
B. CECCHETTI, *Vita dei Veneziani nel '300*. In 'Archivio Veneto', 1884. N.S. XIV, T. XXVII, pp. 5 et seq., vol. XXVIII, pp. 267 et seq.

**1885**

G. TASSINI, *Edifici di Venezia distrutti*, Venice.

**1886**

B. CECCHETTI, *La facciata della Ca' d'Oro dello scalpello di Giovanni e Bartolomeo Buono*. In 'Archivio Veneto', vol. XXXI, p. 1 & pp. 201 et seq.
A. FORCELLINI, *Della riapertura degli archi ciechi del Palazzo Ducale di Venezia*. In 'Arte e Storia', V, pp. 225 et seq.

**1887**

G. GRUYER, *Le palais des princes d'Este à Venise*. 'Gazette des Beaux Arts', 36.

G. BONI, *La Ca' d'Oro e le sue decorazioni policrome*. In 'Archivio Veneto', Vol. 34, p. 1 and pp. 115 et seq.
B. CECCHETTI, *Nomi di pittori e lapicidi antichi*. In 'Archivio Veneto', Vol. XXXIII, pp. 43 et seq.

**1888**

*Il palazzo Giovanelli in Venezia*, Venice, Visentini.

**1889**

R. CATTANEO, *L'architettura in Italia dal secolo VI al Mille circa*, Venice (the French edition dates from 1891).
TIMARCHI, *I restauri del Palazzo Ducale di Venezia*. In 'Archivio storico dell'Arte', II, pp. 428 et seq.
F. ONGANIA, *Raccolta delle vere da pozzo (marmi puteali) in Venezia*, Venice.
A.G. MEYER, *Das venetianische Grabdenkmal der Frührenaissance*. In 'Jahrbuch der preussischen Kunstsammlungen', 1889, pp. 79 et seq. & pp. 187 et seq.

**1890**

R. CATTANEO, *Storia architettonica della Basilica*. In C. BOITO, *La Basilica di S. Marco*, pp. II, Vol. VIII, Venice, pp. 101–197.
C.A. LEVI, *I campanili di Venezia*, Venice.

**1891**

F. ONGANIA, *Raccolta delle vere da pozzo in Venezia*, Venice.

**1893**

P. PAOLETTI, *L'architettura e la scultura del Rinascimento in Venezia*, Venice.
P. MOLMENTI E D. MANTOVANI, *Calli e canali in Venezia*, Venice.

**1894**

P. GIANNUZZI, *Giorgio da Sebenico, architetto e scultore*. In 'Archivio Storico dell'arte', VII, pp. 397 et seq.
V. JOPPI, *Contributo quarto ed ultimo alla storia dell'arte nel Friuli* (R. Dep. Veneto di Storia Patria), Venice, p. 150.
V. LAZZARINI, *Filippo Calendario, l'architetto della tradizione del Palazzo Ducale*. In 'Nuovo Archivio Veneto', IV, pp. 429 et seq.
C. ENLART, *Origines françaises de l'architecture gothique en Italie*, Paris.

**1895**

H. THODE, *Uber die Entstehungszeit einiger venezianischen Kirchen*, in 'Repertorium für Kunstwissenschaft', pp. 81 et seq.
URBANI DE GHELTOF, *Guida artistico-storica della scuola di S. Giovanni Evangelista*, Venice.

**1896**

A. VUCETICH, *I Palazzi, le case storiche e gli avanzi storici di Venezia, Sestiere di Dorsoduro, Parrocchia dell'Angelo Raffaele*, Mestre.

**1898**

G. PAULI, *Venedig*, Leipzig.

**1900**

L. BELTRAMI, *La "Ca' del Duca" sul Canal Grande*, Milan.
A. POGATSCHNIG, *Guida di Parenzo*, Trieste.

**1902**

L. De Beylie, *L'habitation byzantine*, Grenoble.

C. De Fabriczy, *Niccolò di Pietro Lamberti di Arezzo*. 'Archivio Storico Italiano', pp. 308 et seq.

**1903**

H. von der Gabelentz, *Mittelalterliche Plastik in Venedig*, Leipzig, pp. 308 et seq.

O. Raschdorff, *Palastarchitektur in Oberitalien und Toskana vom XIII bis zum XVIII. Jahrhundert*, Berlin.

**1904**

H. Thode, *Franz von Assisi*, II, Berlin, pp. 368 et seq.

**1905**

Comune di Venezia, *Elenco degli Edifici monumentali e dei frammenti storici e artistici della città di Venezia*, Venice.

G. Gerola, *Monumenti veneti nell'isola di Creta*, Venice.

E. Marini, *Venezia antica e moderna*, Venice.

F. Bond, *Gothic architecture in England*, London.

E. Musatti, *Guida storica di Venezia*, Milan.

**1906**

C. Enlart, *Origine anglaise du style flamboyant*, in 'Bulletin Monumental'.

**1907**

Hare & Baddeley, *Venice*, London.

**1908**

A. Venturi, in 'Storia dell'Arte'. VI, Milan.

**1909**

L. Simeoni, *Verona, Guida...*, Verona.

P. Molmenti, *Ca' d'Oro o Ca' Doro?* In 'Arte e Storia', 28, pp. 33 et seq.

**1910**

C. Enlart, *Origine anglaise du style flamboyant. Réponse à M Anthyme Saint Paul*. In 'Bulletin Monumental', pp. 125 et seq.

P. Molmenti, *Il Palazzo Ducale di Venezia*. In 'Nuova Antologia', 16 August 1916, Rome.

A. Tamaro, *Pirano*, Trieste.

**1911**

F. Apollonio, *La Chiesa e il Convento di S. Stefano in Venezia*, Venice.

**1912**

C. Chiminelli, *Le Scale scoperte nei palazzi veneziani*. In 'Ateneo Veneto', XXXV, Vol. I, fasc. 3, pp. 209 et seq.

G. Marzemin, *Le abbazie veneziane di S. Ilario e Benedetto e di S. Gregorio*, Venice.

**1913**

F. Bond, *An Introduction to English Church Architecture...*, Oxford.

G. Bragato, *Da Gemona a Venzone*, Bergamo.

A. Moschetti, *Un quadriennio di Pietro Lombardi a Padova*. In 'Bollettino del Museo Civico di Padova', (XVI, 1913, pp. 99 et seq.; XVII, 1914, pp. 43 et seq.).

G. Orlandini, *Origine del teatro Malibran, la casa dei Polo e la corte del Milion*, Venice.

P.L. Rambaldi, *La chiesa dei Santi Giovanni e Paolo* Venice.

**1914**

P. Ubertalli, *Il Palazzo Ducale di Venezia*, Milan.

H. Folnesics, *Studien zur Entwicklungsgeschichte der Architektur und Plastik des 15 Jahrhunderts in Dalmatien*. In 'Jahrbuch des kunsthistorischen Instituts der K.K. Zentral Kommission', VIII, Vienna.

A. Moschetti, (see: 1913-Moschetti).

**1915**

L. Planiscig, *Denkmale in den südlichen Kriegsgebieten*, Vienna.

**1916**

D. Frey, *Renaissances Einfluss bei Giorgio da Sebenico*. In 'Monatshefte für Kunstwissenschaft', IX, pp. 39 et seq.

P. Molmenti, *La Ca' d'Oro*, Rome.

L. Planiscig, *Geschichte der venezianischen Skulptur im XIV Jahrhundert*. In 'Jahrbuch der Kunsthistorischen Sammlungen...', XXXIII, Vienna.

**1919**

B. Rumor, *Guida di Vicenza*, Vicenza.

**1920**

P. Paoletti, *La Ca' d'Oro*. In 'Venezia - Raccolta di studi d'arte e di storia, pubblicati a cura del Museo Correr', Vol. I, Milan-Rome.

A. Scolari, *La chiesa di S. Maria dei Frari e il suo restauro in Venezia...*

**1921**

L. Planiscig, *Venezianische Bildhauer der Renaissance*, Vienna.

Polák, in Thieme-Becker, *Allgemeines Lexikon der bildender Künstler...*, XIV, p. 335, (on Gojkovic).

**1923**

A. Tursi, *Un palazzo veneziano del Quattrocento*, Bergamo.

A. Venturi, *L'Architettura del Quattrocento*, Milan, Vol. I.

M. Ongaro, *Il Palazzo Ducale di Venezia*, Venice.

**1923–24**

A. Foratti, *La loggia del Comune in Udine*. In 'Bollettino d'Arte', pp. 291 et seq., Rome.

**1924**

G. Fogolari, *La Chiesa di S. Maria della Carità di Venezia*. In 'Archivio Veneto-Tridentino', V, pp. 57 et seq.

K.M. Swoboda, *Römische und romanische Paläste*, Vienna.

A. Venturi, *Storia dell'arte italiana*, VIII, II, pp. 277 et seq. & pp. 322 et seq., Milan.

**1924–25**

G. Boni, *Ca' d'Oro*. In 'Architettura e arti decorative', 4, p. 481.

**1925**

J. Burckhardt, *Der Cicerone*, Leipzig.

H.A. Douglas, *Venice on foot*, London.

G. Franceschini, *Case gotiche e edifici palladiani*, Vicenza.

P. Molmenti, *Storia di Venezia nella vita privata*, Part I, Chapter IX, pp. 266 et seq.

**1926**

R.M. Lossar, *Guida di Parenzo*, Parenzo.

G. Lorenzetti, *Venezia e il suo Estuario*, Milan.

I. Tiozzo, *Chioggia*, Chioggia.

R. Gallo, *La Chiesa di S. Elena*. In 'Rivista mensile della città di Venezia', November, Venice.

G.G. Zorzi, *Contributo alla storia dell'arte vicentina nei secoli XV e XVI*. In 'Miscellanea di storia veneto-tridentina', Venice, Vol. II.

**1926–27**

F. Forlati, *Restauri di architettura minore nel Veneto*. In 'Architettura e AA. DD.', IV, p. 6, pp. 49 et seq.

R. De Lasteyrie, *L'architecture religieuse en France à l'époque gothique*, Paris, Vol. 2.

**1927**

W. Arslan, *Una vera da pozzo della bottega di Bartolomeo Bon*. In 'Cronache d'Arte', Bologna, fasc. I, pp. 12 et seq.

P. Toesca, *Storia dell'Arte Italiana*, (Il Medioevo), I, Turin.

**1927–28**

G. Fogolari, *Il Palazzo Ducale di Venezia*, Milan.

G. Fogolari, *La Ca' d'Oro*. In 'Le Tre Venezie', III, pp. 16 et seq.

G. Fiocco, *Il pittore della Ca' d'Oro*. In 'Rivista mensile della città di Venezia', VI, Venice.

G. Fiocco, *I Lamberti a Venezia*. In 'Dedalo', pp. 287 et seq., pp. 343 et seq., pp. 432 et seq.

A. Moschetti, *Pietro e altri lapicidi lombardi a Belluno*. In 'Atti del R. Istituto Veneto di S.L. e A.', Vol. 87, pp. 1481 et seq.

**1928**

C. Budinis, *Dal Carnaro al Friuli*, Trieste.

G. Fiocco, *La lunetta nel portale della Scuola Grande di S. Marco*. In 'Rivista di Venezia', pp. 177 et seq.

G. Giovannoni, *Arquà Petrarca, restauro di vecchie case*. In 'Architettura e Arti decorative', October, pp. 68 et seq.

**1929**

K. Escher, *Englische Kathedralen*, Munich-Berlin.

L. Serra, *L'arte nelle Marche*, I, pp. 215 et seq., Pesaro.

S. G. Wiener, *Venetian Houses and Details*, New York.

**1929–30**

G. Fogolari, *L'urna del Beato Pacifico ai Frari*. In 'Atti del R. Istituto Veneto di S.L. ed A.', p. II, pp. 937 et seq.

E. Rigoni, *Notizie di scultori toscani a Padova nella prima metà del Quattrocento*. In 'Archivio Veneto', VI, pp. 118 et seq.

G. Fogolari, Nebbia, Moschini, *La R. Galleria Giorgio Franchetti alla Ca' d'Oro*, Venice.

A. Moschetti, *Pietro Lombardo*. In Thieme-

Becker, *Allgemeines Lexikon der bildenden Künstler*, Leipzig, Vol. XXIII, p. 343.

*Un restauro a Venezia. Casa Monico in campo S. Lio*. In 'Architettura e arti decorative', 9, pp. 527 et seq.

1930

K.H. Clasen, *Die gotische Baukunst*, Wildpark, Potsdam.

G. Fiocco, veview of: E. Rigoni, *Notizie di scultori toscani a Padova nella prima metà del Quattrocento*. In 'Rivista d'Arte', January-March, pp. 151 et seq.

G. Fiocco, *Bisanzio, Ravenna, Venezia*. In 'Rivista del Comune di Venezia', Venice, February, pp. 57 et seq.

G. Fogolari, *Gli scultori toscani a Venezia nel Quattrocento e Bartolomeo Bon veneziano*. In 'L'Arte'.

C. Gamba, *L'opera di Pietro Lamberti*. In 'Il Marzocco', XXXV, Number 22, Florence.

J. Meurgey, *Les principaux manuscrits à peintures du Musée Condé à Chantilly*, Paris, p. 176, (*Description ou Traictè du gouvernement et régyme de la cyté et seigneurie de Venise*) (fin du XVe siècle).

L. Planiscig, *Die Bildhauer Venedigs in der ersten Haelfte des Quattrocento*. In 'Jahrbuch der kunsthistorischen Sammlungen in Wien', N.S. IV, Vienna.

1930-31

G. Fiocco, *La segnatura del capitello della Giustizia*. In 'Atti del R. Istituto di S.L., ed A.' T. XC, p. II, pp. 1041 et seq.

1932

*La nuova sistemazione dell'Istituto Esposti nei restaurati palazzi Cappello e Gritti*. In 'Rivista di Venezia', II, pp. 335 et seq., Venice.

G. Fogolari, *Ancora di Bartolomeo Bon, scultore veneziano*. In 'L'Arte', pp. 27 et seq.

G. Fogolari, *I Frari e i Santi Giovanni e Paolo* Milan.

1933

M. Abramic, *Ivan Pribislavic*. In Thieme-Becker, *Allgemeines Lexikon der bildenden Künstler*, XXVII, p. 396.

G. Boschieri, *Le vicende storiche della Ca' d'Oro*. In 'Rivista di Venezia', XII, pp. 415 et seq.

C. Enlart, *Manuel d'archéologie française*, Paris.

R. Gallo, *Il portico della Carta del Palazzo Ducale*. In 'Rivista di Venezia', XII, pp. 283 et seq.

G. Lorenzetti, *Un prototipo veneto-bizantino del Palazzo Ducale di Venezia*. In 'Miscellanea Supino', pp. 123 et seq. Florence.

1934-39

N. Gallimberti, *Architettura civile minore del Medioevo a Padova*. In 'Bollettino del Museo Civico di Padova', X-XI, p. 5, Padova.

1935

M. Ongaro, *Il Palazzo Ducale di Venezia*, Venice.

M. Botter, *Le facciate dipinte di Treviso e le loro decorazioni a finte tappezzerie*. In 'Treviso, Rassegna del Comune', II, p. 39.

L. Coletti, *Treviso*, Rome.

A. Venturi, *Giorgio Orsini*. In 'Enciclopedia Treccani', XXV, p. 619.

1936

E. Lavagnino, *Storia dell'arte medioevale italiana*, Turin.

M. Salmi, *L'Abbazia di Pomposa*, Rome.

S. Bettini, *Padova e l'arte cristiana d'Oriente*. In 'Atti dell'Istituto Veneto di S.L. ed A.', Vol. CXCI/2, Venice.

c. 1937

D. Torres, *La casa veneta*, Venice.

1937-38

G. Mariacher, *Premesse storiche alla venuta dei lombardi a Venezia nel '400*. In 'Atti del R. Istituto Veneto di S.L. ed A.', Venice, XCVII, p. II, pp. 577 et seq.

1938

A. Barbacci, *Il ritrovamento di una porta gotica a Verona*. In 'Bollettino d'arte', October, Rome.

1939

F. Franco, *L'"interpolazione" del Filarete trattatista fra gli artefici del Rinascimento architettonico a Venezia*. In 'Atti del IV Convegno nazionale di storia dell'architettura', Milan.

G. Mariacher, *Matteo Raverti nell'arte veneziana del primo Quattrocento*. In 'Rivista d'arte', XXI, p. 23 et seq., Rome.

1940

Peronato, *Vicenza, la città dei palazzi*, Vicenza.
S. Bettini, *Venezia*, Novara.

1942

L. Angelini, *Arte minore bergamasca*. In 'Rivista di Bergamo', Bergamo, October, November.

D. Valeri, *Guida sentimentale di Venezia*, Venice.

1943

Rusconi, *Pezzi erratici trentini*. In 'Trento'.

1944

L. Behling, *Gestalt und Geschichte des Masswerks*, Halle.

1948

E.R. Trincanato, *Venezia minore*, Milan.

M. Hürlimann, *Englische Kathedralen*, Zürich.

1949

A. Mantelli, G. Zaffrani, *Choix de textes sur Venise*, Turin.

L. Serra, *Il Palazzo Ducale di Venezia*, Rome.

G. Fiocco, *La casa veneziana antica*. In 'Rend. dell'Accademia Nazionale dei Lincei', Rome, Vol. IV, fasc. 1-2, pp. 38 et seq.

G. Fogolari, *Il Palazzo Ducale di Venezia*, Milan (re-issue of 1927 edition).

1950

G. Mariacher, *Il Palazzo Ducale di Venezia*, Florence.

G. Mariacher, *New Light on Antonio Bregno*. In

'The Burlington Magazine', London, XCII, May, pp. 123 et seq.

P. Toesca, *Il Trecento*, Turin.

1950-51

G. Mariacher, *Appunti per un profilo storico della scultura veneziana*. In 'Atti dell'Istituto Veneto di S.L. ed A.', Volume CIX, pp. 225 et seq.

1951

G. Mariacher, *Il continuatore del Longhena a Palazzo Pesaro...* In 'Ateneo Veneto', CXLII, Vol. 135, n. I, pp. 1 et seq.

1952

H. Decker, *Venedig, Antlitz und Kunst der Stadt*, Vienna.

G. Rossi, G. Salerni, *I capitelli del Palazzo Ducale di Venezia*, Venice.

L. Torres Balbas, *Arquitectura gotica*, (Ars Hispaniae), Madrid.

1953

S. Bettini, *Venezia*, Novara, (re-issue of 1940 edition).

Barbieri, Cevese, Magagnato, *Guida di Vicenza*, Vicenza.

M. Muraro, *Nuova guida di Venezia e delle sue isole*, Florence.

G.G. Zorzi, *Nuova rivelazione sulla ricostruzione delle sale del piano nobile del Palazzo Ducale di Venezia dopo l'incendio dell'11 Maggio 1574*. In 'Arte Veneta', Venice, 7, pp. 123 et seq.

1954

G. Mazzotti, *Le ville venete*, Treviso.

M. Muraro, *Les villas de la Vénétie*, Venice.

G. Mariacher, *Capitelli veneziani del XII e XIII secolo*. In 'Arte Veneta', Venice, pp. 43 et seq.

1955

J. Pope-Hennessy, *Italian Gothic Sculpture*, London.

L. Stone, *Sculpture in Britain, The Middle Ages*, London.

1956

C. Zangerolami, *Indicatore anagrafico di Venezia*, Venice.

A. Sartori, *Santa Maria Gloriosa dei Frari*, Padova.

C. Webb, *Architecture in Britain, The Middle Ages*, London.

M. Botter, *Ornati a fresco di case trivigiane*, Treviso.

F. Harvey, *The English Cathedrals*, London.

T. Pignatti, *Piazza S. Marco*, Novara.

G. Lorenzetti, *Venezia e il suo estuario*, Venice.

1957

E. Miozzi, *Venezia nei secoli. La città*, Vol. I, Venice.

E. Bassi, *L'edilizia veneziana nei secoli XVII e XVIII*. In 'Critica d'Arte', n. 19, pp. 2 et seq.

1958

C. Mutinelli, *Cividale. Guida storico-artistica*, Udine.

F. Forlati, in 'Storia di Venezia', Venice, vol. II.

1959
H.E. FRIEDRICH, *Venedig*, Münich.

1960
E. BELVEDERE, *Il Palazzo Ducale di Venezia*, Milan.

E. BASSI, E. TRINCANATO, *Il Palazzo Ducale nella storia e nell'arte di Venezia*, Milan.

BRUSIN-ZOVATTO, *Monumenti romani e cristiani di Julia Concordia*, Pordenone.

O. DEMUS, *The Church of San Marco in Venice*, Washington.

P. MARETTO, *L'edilizia gotica veneziana*, Rome.

S. MURATORI, *Il problema critico dell'età gotica*. In P. Maretto, *L'edilizia gotica veneziana*.

S. MURATORI, *Studi per una operante storia urbana di Venezia*, Rome.

1961
CHECCHI, GAUDENZIO, GROSSATO, *Padova*, Padova.

G. SCATTOLIN, *Le Case Fondaco sul Canal Grande*, Venice.

1962
E. BASSI, *Appunti per la storia del Palazzo Ducale di Venezia*. In 'Critica d'Arte', pp. 25 et seq. and pp. 41 et seq.

M. D'ELIA, *Ricerche sull'attività di Giorgio Sebenico a Venezia*. In 'Commentari', XIII, p. 2.

E.R. TRINCANATO, *Il museo dell'Opera di Palazzo Ducale*. In 'Bollettino dei Musei Civici Veneziani', Venice, 7, 3, 4, pp. 10 et seq.

1963
J.S. ACKERMAN, *Sources of the Renaissance Villa*. In 'The Renaissance and Mannerism', Princeton, Vol. II of the Report on Twentieth International Congress of Art Historians, pp. 6 et seq.

M. MURANO, A. GRABAR, *Les Trésors de Venise*, Geneva.

J. POPE-HENNESSY, *La Scultura Italiana - Il gotico*, Milan.

1964
E. BASSI, *Il Palazzo Ducale nel '300*. In 'Bollettino del Centro Internazionale di Studi di Architettura A. Palladio', Vicenza, VI, II, pp. 181 et seq.

M. MURARO, *Civiltà delle ville venete*. Conferenza tenuta il 23 ottobre 1964 alla Biblioteca Hertziana di Roma, Venice.

T. PIGNATTI, *Palazzo Ducale - Venezia*, Novara.

J. POPE-HENNESSY, *Catalogue of Italian Sculpture in the Victoria & Albert Museum*, London.

A.M. ROMANINI, *L'architettura gotica in Lombardia*, Milan.

R. SALVADORI, *Venezia, 'paradiso' di Ruskin*. In 'Emporium', Bergamo.

1965
P. MARETTO, *L'Urbanistica veneziana del Trecento*. In 'Bollettino del Centro Internazionale di Studi di Architettura', Vicenza, VII, II, pp. 232 et seq.

C. MUTINELLI, *Il gotico in Friuli*. In 'Bollettino del Centro Internazionale di Studi d'Architettura A. Palladio', Vicenza, VII, Part II, pp. 343 et seq.

N. RASMO, *L'architettura Gotica a Trento*. In 'Bollettino del Centro Internazionale di Architettura', Vicenza, VII, II, pp. 256 et seq.

P.L. ZOVATTO, *Guida del Museo e della città di Portogruaro*, Portogruaro.

F.Z. BOCCAZZI, *La basilica dei Santi Giovanni e Paolo*, Venice.

W. WOLTERS, *Uber zwei Figuren des Jacobello delle Masegne in S. Stefano zu Venedig*. In 'Zeitschrift für Kunstgeschichte', pp. 113 et seq.

C. SEMENZATO, *L'architettura gotica a Treviso e nel suo territorio*. In 'Bollettino del Centro Internazionale di Studi di Architettura A. Palladio', Vicenza, II, pp. 293 et seq.

C. SEMENZATO, *L'architettura gotica a Padova e nel suo territorio*. In 'Bollettino del Centro Internazionale di Studi di Architettura A. Palladio', Vicenza, II, pp. 280 et seq.

S. BETTINI, *L'architettura gotica veneziana*. In 'Bollettino del Centro Internazionale di Studi di Architettura A. Palladio', Vicenza, VII, II, pp. 165 et seq.

E. BASSI, *L'architettura gotica a Venezia*. In 'Bollettino del Centro Internazionale di Studi di Architettura A. Palladio', Vicenza, VII, II, pp. 185 et seq.

F. BARBIERI, *L'architettura gotica civile a Vicenza*. In 'Bollettino del Centro Internazionale di Studi di Architettura A. Palladio', Vicenza, VII, II, pp. 167 et seq.

N. GALLIMBERTI, *Il tessuto urbanistico di Padova medioevale*, Padova, February.

1966
J. WHITE, *Art and Architecture in Italy*, 1250 to 1400, London.

J. BALOGH, *Studi sulla collezione di sculture del Museo di Belle Arti di Budapest: I Pozzi Veneziani*. In 'Acta Historiae Artium', Budapest, XII.

E. ARSLAN, *Qualche appunto sul Palazzo Ducale di Venezia*. In 'Bollettino d'arte';, Roma, pp. 58 et seq.

E. HUBALA, P. TIGLER, W. TIMOFIEWITSCH, M. WUNDRAM, *Oberitalien*, II, Stuttgart.

1967
A. ALPAGO NOVELLO, *Il Palazzo dei vescovi di Feltre*, Feltre,

E.R. TRINCANATO, G. MARIACHER, *Il Palazzo Ducale di Venezia*, Florence.

*I should now like to thank those who have helped me and I would mention first of all Count Vittorio Cini; then Carla Barbantini, Alessandro Bettagno, Antonio Caracciolo, Lina Padoan Urban. Immediately after, I should name Silvano De Tuoni and Giannina Piamonte.*

*Among Venetian scholars I thank my colleagues Elena Bassi and Renata Trincanato, Lucia Bellodi Casanova, Mario Guiotto, Giovanni Mariacher, Pietro Marigonda, Terisio Pignatti, Angelo Tursi, Francesco Valcanover, Pietro Zampetti; and remember sadly Rodolfo Gallo. Nor could I forget the names of the students of architecture Brunella Brunello, Paolo Cacciari, Maria Grazia Fugagnollo and Tiziano Inguanotto.*

*Among foreigners, I remember gratefully: the late Marcel Aubert, Christoff Frommel, Klàra Garas, Pierre Heliot, Peter and Linda Murray, John Pope-Hennessy.*

*Among Venetian scholars, or residents in the Tre Venezie, I remember also: Franco Barbieri, Gino Barioli, Gian Pietro Bordignon Favero, Benedetto Civiletti, Decio Gioseffi, Lucio Grossato, Nicola Jvanoff, Luigi Menegazzi, Nicolò Rasmo, Aldo Rizzi, Antonio Rusconi, Fr. Antonio Sartori, Antonia Veronese, Maria Walcher Casotti.*

*In Lombardy I owe warm thanks to: Clelia Alberici, Giulia Bologna, Giuseppe Fermeglia, Mercedes Garberi Precerutti, Liliana Grassi, Giuseppe Lorenzi, Elisa Mariani Travi Franco, Augusto Merati, the late Gilda Rosa, to Vettore Pisani, Felice Valsecchi; and, naturally, to my pupils: Rossana Bossaglia, Luisa Cogliati Arano, Lelia De Longhi Fraccaro, Fernanda De Maffei, Franco Renzo Pesenti, Angiola M. Romanini, Luigina Rossi Bortolatto, Chiara Tellini Perina and Gian Luigi Verzellesi.*

# LIST OF ILLUSTRATIONS